INTERNATIONAL COURTS AND TRIBUNALS SERIES

General Editors

RUTH MACKENZIE

CESARE P.R. ROMANO

MIKAEL RASK MADSEN

Transplanting International Courts

INTERNATIONAL COURTS AND TRIBUNALS SERIES

A distinctive feature of modern international society is the increase in the number of international judicial bodies and dispute settlement and implementation control bodies; in their case-loads; and in the range and importance of the issues they are called upon to address. These factors reflect a new stage in the delivery of international justice. The International Courts and Tribunals series has been established to encourage the publication of independent and scholarly works which address, in critical and analytical fashion, the legal and policy aspects of the functioning of international courts and tribunals, including their institutional, substantive, and procedural aspects.

Transplanting International Courts

The Law and Politics of the Andean Tribunal of Justice

KAREN J. ALTER

Northwestern University and iCourts: Center of Excellence for International Courts, University of Copenhagen

LAURENCE R. HELFER

Duke University and iCourts: Center of Excellence for International Courts, University of Copenhagen

OXFORD
UNIVERSITY PRESS

OXFORD
UNIVERSITY PRESS

Great Clarendon Street, Oxford, OX2 6DP,
United Kingdom

Oxford University Press is a department of the University of Oxford.
It furthers the University's objective of excellence in research, scholarship,
and education by publishing worldwide. Oxford is a registered trade mark of
Oxford University Press in the UK and in certain other countries

First published 2017
First published in paperback 2019

Published in the United States of America by Oxford University Press
198 Madison Avenue, New York, NY 10016, United States of America

British Library Cataloguing in Publication Data
Data available

Library of Congress Cataloging in Publication Data
Data available

ISBN 978–0–19–968078–8 (Hbk.)
ISBN 978–0–19–883880–7 (Pbk.)

To Brian and David, for making this book possible

Series Editors' Preface

Scholarship on regional international courts was until recently almost entirely focused on two courts in Europe: the Court of Justice of the European Union and the European Court of Human Rights. With few exceptions, there was little actual knowledge of how international courts in Africa, Latin America, and elsewhere operate in practice. This book, alongside other publications by its authors Karen J. Alter and Laurence R. Helfer, significantly closes that gap.

The book pulls together ten years of research to provide the first in-depth empirical analysis of the origins, evolution, successes, and failures of the Andean Tribunal of Justice. It shows how the Tribunal has developed from a little-known institution established by a small group of developing states in the Andean region to become the world's third most active international court.

Alter and Helfer also explore the connections between the European Court of Justice, set up in the 1950s, and the Andean Tribunal of Justice. The book's guiding research question is precisely the extent to which the Tribunal can be understood as a transplant—or clone—of the European Court of Justice. The Andean Tribunal borrows a set of institutional design features from the Court of Justice. Most significantly, it allows for preliminary references from national courts and administrative agencies and also provides other avenues for private litigants and supranational bodies to access the Tribunal to enforce Andean law.

Notwithstanding these institutional commonalities, the authors also clearly demonstrate that law and politics operate in a significantly different way in the Andean region than in Europe. A major finding of the book is that the Andean Tribunal has managed to emulate the success of its European counterpart only in a single issue area—intellectual property. The Tribunal has become a major institution in the development of intellectual property rules in the Andean region, but in practically all other areas of Andean integration law its activity and influence is limited. This identification of what Alter and Helfer aptly name an "island of effective international adjudication" is helpful for rethinking the differentiated pathways of other regional courts currently evolving in many corners of the world.

Alter and Helfer also analyze how the Tribunal navigates the moment when member states are deeply divided with respect to the goals and future of the Andean integration project. The book provides timely insights that apply to other regions, and that may provide fresh ideas for Europeans struggling with a similar set of concerns.

Professor Mikael Rask Madsen
Director, iCourts
University of Copenhagen
October 2016

Prologue

I first met Karen Alter when I was Secretary of the Court of Justice of the Andean Community (Andean Tribunal) in 2005 when she first visited me, guided by that inquisitive spirit that characterizes good scholars. A couple of years later I met Larry Helfer too when he and Karen decided to visit the General Secretariat of the Andean Community in Lima, Peru. At that time they were barely acquainted with the rather unknown field of Andean Community law. As someone who has been linked to this body of law for a long time, I found their academic curiosity very striking. Ever since, I have kept abreast of their research. It turns out that writing seriously about a topic that is foreign to one's own legal tradition and about which little has been written is not only complicated but also a quite audacious task.

Transplanting International Courts: The Law and Politics of the Andean Tribunal of Justice expresses the adventurous spirit of these two researchers. The book aims to introduce the reader to the intricacies of the practice of Andean Community law from the perspective of comparative law, to discover the similarities and differences between that system and European law, and to explain the successes and failures of the Andean Tribunal.

The book rightly states that the Andean Tribunal was designed and established to resemble the Court of Justice of the European Union. The authors refer to the most notable characteristics that the two tribunals share in terms of their powers, competences, and procedures. In this way, both courts must solve cases in which a Member State or a body or institution of the Community fails to perform a legal obligation, where the applicant seeks the annulment of a measure alleged to be contrary to Community law, where the Community body or institution fails to act when it is legally obliged to do so, and where litigants request a preliminary ruling interpreting Community law.

However, it must be borne in mind that the creation of the Andean Tribunal is not the result of a mere intention to mimic the European model, nor is it the outcome of an academic exercise for the sake of consistency with national models. The reasons that lead a group of countries to opt for a judicial mechanism to solve disputes between them at the regional level, having other alternatives available at their disposal, are the result of complex economic, legal, and political factors.

Among those reasons, I must highlight the conviction, shared by many in the Andean Community and certainly by its founders, that it is through a profound integration between our countries that we will be able to increase opportunities for commercial growth and economic development. Both multilateralism and bilateralism have proven that they can sometimes resolve favorably some of our needs but they usually tend to meet the interests of some rather than others. Learning from our history, it was equally clear, both in the initial design of the Andean Community and at present, that profound integration requires a guarantor who shares similar characteristics. If the legal correlate of this ideal of profound integration is supranationality (the term being understood as a system of legal rules with direct application and direct effect in Member Countries), the legal guarantor of supranationality could only be a supranational Tribunal.

I must also emphasize the role played by democratic ideals—of the founders of the Cartagena Agreement, the Presidential Council, the Council of Ministers of Foreign Affairs, some national bureaucrats in charge of integration issues, and several officials of Andean Community institutions—in the design and functioning of the institutional model that the Tribunal reflects. In this way, the constitutional design of the Andean Community took into account that if a powerful Commission of Plenipotentiaries was to be established and charged with issuing legislation that would automatically be imposed in all Member Countries and supersede their own national legislation, it was also necessary to create other bodies responsible for balancing and supervising such power, ensuring the maintenance of a system of the rule of law. Since the executive branch of integration—that is, the General Secretariat—was partially subordinated to the Commission, the body created to strike such balance was the Andean Tribunal. It is necessary to bear in mind that for this reason, and to ensure compliance, membership in the Treaty Creating the Andean Tribunal and membership in the Cartagena Agreement are legally intertwined.

Subsequently, in the second half of the 1990s, these democratic ideals would become even more peremptory and present with the adoption of a political instrument of the first order: The Andean Democratic Charter, signed by the Presidents of all the Member Countries.

In sum, the creation and functioning of the Andean Tribunal is primarily the product of a political conviction of its own that legitimized a type of governance at the Community level for a given integrated territory. This conviction was not only reiterated but also amplified with the adoption of the Cochabamba Protocol in the second half of the 1990s, and I think it still remains today in the minds and bodies of many in the Andean Community.

Turning to the more concrete terrain of the Andean Tribunal's performance in the years since its creation, I must first of all concur with the authors in praising the authority that the Tribunal has succeeded in establishing in the field of intellectual property. According to the authors, this success can be attributed principally to the fact that the Tribunal has built key alliances with national administrative bodies responsible for granting this form of legal protection. The authors also explain this success by reference to the level of involvement of the Andean citizens in the matter and the degree of legal advocacy achieved.

That being so, let me emphasize, however, the decisive role played in this outcome by the General Secretariat of the Andean Community and before it, by the *Junta* of the Cartagena Agreement. These bodies developed a very detailed and in-depth common regime that internalized the characteristics of the region, created genuine cooperative links to national authorities, and responded to their needs in ways that in substance—except for the protection of pharmaceutical test data, which was modified due to the influence of free trade agreements—have remained stable for decades until today. In addition, the General Secretariat and the *Junta* developed important legal concepts and doctrines in reasoned opinions issued prior to actions for alleged infringement before the Andean Tribunal. These concepts and doctrines were often taken up by the Tribunal in its judgments. Of course, I must also add, as do the authors, the important influence of the self-interest of citizens and lawyers to act in favor of development and dissemination of regional integration. This is something that in this field of law can be appreciated with much clarity.

Unfortunately, I also have to agree with the authors that, after thirty-six years of existence, the Andean Tribunal has not been able to assert its authority in other fields of integration law to the same degree as in intellectual property matters. According to the authors, the Tribunal's lack of performance in these areas may be explained by the difficulties of judicial action in environments characterized by political and economic instability, a culture of disrespect for the law, and the lack of independence of the judiciary from political power, among other reasons.

In my experience, however, it is true that some judges may feel the need to adjust their decisions to the circumstances of the moment, not necessarily as a result of corruption but simply because of the influence of a pragmatic necessity to survive in a hostile political environment in which prevalence of the rule of law is not yet common ground. Yet it is also true that similar challenges are faced by most national and international courts today, as the authors recognize, including those working in more politically and economically stable environments.

Besides, the Andean region has advanced a great deal in terms of democracy, macroeconomic stability, respect for institutions, and law enforcement, and so has the Andean Community. In fact, it must be recognized that Community law in intellectual property as well as in other areas has very often acted as a real retaining wall against external pressures of all sorts seeking to change or distort it to impose interests alien to those represented by the law, and that the Andean Tribunal's judges very often have well served the ideals of Andean integration. The degree of respect for law may be influenced by external conditions, but ultimately depends on the degree to which it has been internalized by the individual as a moral imperative and social value.

From a less philosophical but more functional perspective, a partial explanation of the sometimes variable performance of the Andean Tribunal can be found in the relative lack of specialized legal knowledge among national judges and most lawyers. Integration law is not normally included in the curricula of most faculties of law in the Andes, unlike European Community law in Europe. Likewise, there is insufficient dissemination of information about Andean integration among citizens and social actors, who are focused instead on other integration schemes and free trade agreements which, in turn, silently utilize and benefit from the ideas of Andean integration.

To conclude my remarks on the Andean Tribunal's performance, I must point out that I found refreshing the authors' demystification of certain conceptual premises and methodological generalizations that are the result of a Eurocentric and Westernized analysis of the law but that do not even apply in vast areas of the Western Hemisphere. One of these generalizations is that international judges are usually assumed to be creatures eager to expand their influence and authority through lengthy and complicated judgments. In this vein, the authors point out that their comparative study leads them to conclude that this is not necessarily the case.

Experience shows that international judges are not towering sages imparting wisdom that all will respect, as many people imagine, but rather they are often cautious, conservative creatures who prefer to move within the safe limits of written law. This rather less glamorous description of the image of international judges that can be inferred from the findings of Karen and Larry's work is certainly much more human. This allows us to approach the study of judicial action with more realism, and to be surprised, from time to time, with pieces of jurisprudence that transcend the limits of written rules to actually create law. Along those lines, it is necessary to recognize that although the Tribunal's actions in areas of Andean Community law other than intellectual property have been much more discreet, its jurisprudence has nevertheless generated real progress in the conceptualization and practice of certain fundamental legal principles of the regional integration process. The overarching concept of "unjustified restriction to trade" to preserve the "free movement of goods" (known as the Trade Liberalization Programme in Andean jargon) or the very notion of "non-discriminatory treatment" as a general concept of Andean law where regulation has been very deficient, come to my mind as examples.

Even though the Andean integration process seems at times doomed to repeat the myth of Sisyphus, and even when local leaders, guiding or following their local bureaucracies, remain bitterly divided over continuing Andean integration or ending it, the Community has proven to be a necessary bridge that maintains the life of international political and commercial relations between the neighbors, particularly where bilateral relationships have been insufficient or unsuccessful. In terms of legal design and political modeling, the Community has also proven to be permeable to the needs of Member States to carry out legislative changes in their territories and to channel the implementation of projects that otherwise would be lost. Finally, exceptions aside, the Community has proven to be, both for Member Countries and for their citizens, an accessible forum in terms of availability, time, and money to resolve their controversies, representing, particularly for the private sector, the only direct conduit they have to seek legal remedies against the resistance of their own national authorities or those of the other Member Countries to comply with Andean-level commitments.

Based on what has been said, the reader will understand why Karen and Larry finish their work by concluding that the Andean Tribunal is the oldest, most active and in some respects the most successful regional court operating outside of Europe. For my part, I could not be more satisfied with their work. I wish you, dear Reader, a pleasant and challenging journey with the hope that this book will encourage you to further the work of the authors and perhaps to visit us.

Mónica Rosell*

* Mónica Rosell is Chief of the Legal Advising Service of the General Secretariat of the Andean Community. This Prologue is written in her personal capacity and does not necessarily express the views or opinions of the institution she serves.

Acknowledgments

This book—the product of nearly a decade of collaboration—is a deep case study of the most successful transplant of the European Court of Justice (ECJ). Our examination of the Andean Tribunal of Justice (ATJ or Tribunal) began in 2004, twenty years after the Quito-based Tribunal began to hear cases. We had certain presumptions when we began this project. We knew that the ECJ had served as the engine of legal integration in the European Community, and that the ECJ's legal and political authority was built upon its relationship with national judges. The same appeared to be true in the Andean Community, in that the vast majority of ATJ cases were preliminary rulings responding to references from national courts in the four Andean member states.

Karen Alter began to research the Andean legal system by asking Elena Herrera-Beaumont, her Spanish research assistant, to code the subject matter and origin of the cases available on the Tribunal's website. This coding revealed that most ATJ cases involve intellectual property (IP) law and originate in a handful of national courts. Unable to find literature on the cases or on the ATJ, Karen and Elena traveled to Quito to visit the Tribunal and its judges. She also spoke with Venezuela's ambassador to Ecuador, a founding ATJ judge, IP lawyers, and national judges responsible for most Ecuadorian court references to the Tribunal, and she met Mónica Rosell, then serving as the Legal Secretary to the ATJ, who generously agreed to write a preface to this book.

Karen's interviews generated some preliminary findings, but the reasons for the overwhelming predominance of IP cases on the ATJ's docket remained a mystery. This led Karen to contact Larry Helfer, an expert on international courts and international intellectual property law. Larry still recalls, from his first telephone conversation with Karen, the exciting prospect of studying an international tribunal whose rulings interpret a little-known body of regional IP law that seeks to strike a balance between the protection of patents and trademarks and other societal values, in particular public health and consumer protection.

This book, published nearly ten years later, is comprised of significantly revised, updated, and expanded versions of several journal articles that Karen and Larry published as their research on the Andean legal system unfolded. The publications were sequenced to first provide little-known empirical and historical information about the origins, evolution, and activities of the Andean Community and the Tribunal, followed by more focused explorations of particular theories and topics, and finally the drawing of general conclusions. The journal articles were structured to be cumulative, in that each article built upon the foundations laid by the prior publications.

Throughout our investigation, the ECJ was our primary reference point. This explains the book's empirical focus on preliminary rulings. In the European context, preliminary rulings are the predominant mechanism by which the ECJ has developed its innovative legal doctrines. We thus can and have learned a lot about the Andean legal system by studying ATJ preliminary rulings, both individually and over time.

It turns out, however, that the noncompliance procedure (the Andean label for what in Europe is called the infringement process) is also quite important. As we explain in Part I of the book, in 1996 member states restructured the Andean legal system to give private litigants access to the ATJ (via complaints to the Andean General Secretariat) to challenge national laws and policies as contrary to Andean Community law. This access provides litigants with a way to avoid relying on national judges to refer cases to the Tribunal.

For this book, we asked research assistants to update our coding of ATJ preliminary rulings through 2014, and to code all ATJ noncompliance judgments. We have significantly revised our earlier research in light of this new material. Yet our analysis remains incomplete. The noncompliance procedure requires the General Secretariat to issue reasoned opinions in response to noncompliance complaints. Especially in the first fifteen years of the Tribunal's operation, these reasoned opinions were a key source of guidance on the content and political impact of Andean law—a source to which we have given insufficient attention, as Mónica Rosell rightly observes in her preface.

Our collaborative research has also expanded to include international courts in Africa that are based on the ECJ model, and we have benefitted tremendously from the wonderful research community at iCourts: The Danish National Research Foundation's Centre of Excellence for International Courts at the University of Copenhagen. Having studied other judicial transplants, we can say without hesitation that the ATJ is the most successful ECJ copy. The more we investigate the ATJ, the more we are impressed by what Andean judges and officials have accomplished—even as we acknowledge the limitations of the larger Andean integration project and of its legal system.

Comparing the Andean Tribunal to the ECJ provided a logical theoretical starting point for our research. But it also implicitly imported a number of assumptions and expectations about how the Andean legal system would operate. Exploring these assumptions, and revisiting their implications for our prior writings, proved to be as fruitful as our exploration of the Andean Tribunal itself. Karen went back to some of her unpublished European research, and began a dialogue with a group of young historians investigating previously unavailable archives on the ECJ's early years. Larry drew upon the Andean studies to reconsider his influential 1997 *Yale Law Journal* article, coauthored with Anne-Marie Slaughter, on what makes international courts effective. We feature our updated understanding of supranational adjudication in Europe in Part III of this book.

Any errors in this book are our own. We had invaluable assistance with coding and summarizing ATJ cases, which are available only in Spanish, from Isabella Bellera, Maria Borges, Daniel Echeverri, Flo Guerzovich, Gilda Anahi Gutierrez, Elena Herrera-Beaumont, Dominic Lerario, Juan Mayoral, Catalina Milos Sotomayor, Karla Quintana-Osuna, Rebecca Stubbs, Ryan Mellske, Osvaldo Saldías (also a coauthor of Chapter 2), Alvaro Sanmartin Baez, and James Waters. Flo Guerzovich (also a coauthor of Chapter 5), Rachel Moscowitz, and Ioannis Panagis provided crucial technical help with our database of ATJ cases.

For financial and institutional support, we acknowledge and thank the Danish National Research Foundation Grant no. DNRF105, iCourts, the Buffett Institute of Global Affairs at Northwestern University, the Center for International and Comparative Law at Duke University, the Northwestern Dispute Resolution Research Center, and the Center for the Americas at Vanderbilt University.

Our works in progress benefited from comments and suggestions made at numerous workshops, conferences, and lectures, including at iCourts, Duke University Law School, the Fordham International Law–International Relations Colloquium, the Harvard Law School Faculty Workshop, the Harvard International Law–International Relations Workshop, the Oñati International Institute for the Sociology of the Law, the Texas Law School faculty workshop, the Tufts International Law–International Relations Seminar, the University of Illinois Urbana-Champaign's European Union Center, the U.S. Patent and Trademark Office Seminar on Specialized Intellectual Property Courts, and the Vanderbilt Roundtable on the Law and Politics of International Cooperation.

We also benefitted tremendously from the feedback of many colleagues, including David Art, Graeme Austin, Arnulf Becker Lorca, Gabriella Blum, David Boyd, Jamie Boyle, Anu Bradford, Curt Bradley, Rachel Brewster, Dan Brinks, Daniel Drezner, Martin Flaherty, José Augusto Fontoura Costa, Tom Ginsburg, Flo Guerzovich, James Hallock, Darren Hawkins, Leslie Johns, Alexander Krasteve Panayotov, Thomas Lee, Katerina Linos, Mikael Rask Madsen, Juan Mayoral, Ralf Michaels, Gerald Neuman, Sol Picciotto, Kal Raustiala, Morten Rasmussen, Diana Rodríguez Franco, Cesare Romano, Osvaldo Saldías, Antoine Vauchez, Christopher Whytock, and Ingrid Wuerth.

Every chapter in this book is either new or substantially revised and updated. Our thinking and writing has benefitted from the peer review, editorial feedback, and careful copy editing of earlier versions of the following chapters: Chapter 2, published in the *American Journal of Comparative Law* (60 (6): 709–744, 2012); Chapter 3, published in the *New York University Journal of International Law and Politics* (41: 871–930, 2009); Chapter 4, published in the *European Law Journal* (17 (5): 701–715, 2011); Chapter 5, published in the *American Journal of International Law* (109 (1): 1–47, 2009); Chapter 8, published in *International Organization* (64 (4): 563–592, 2010); and Chapter 9, published in Karen J. Alter, *The European Court's Political Power* (Oxford University Press, 2009). We have also benefited from the editorial support of Oxford University Press, especially Merel Alstein, Eve Ryle-Hodges, John Louth, Nancy Rebecca, and Janet Walker.

* * * * * * *

Looking at the ATJ through the lens of the ECJ, and the ECJ through the lens of the ATJ, has taught us much. Perhaps most significantly for our future research, it has taught us that the ATJ's experience in adapting ECJ structures and doctrines to the more politically, legally, and economically fraught contexts in the Andes provides fruitful guidance for other international courts around the world.

We employ multiple research methods in our empirical investigation of the law and politics of the ATJ. By definition, this means that ours is a rear-view mirror analysis. We finished this book during a moment of great uncertainty: the economic and political collapse in Brazil and Venezuela, the Brexit vote, the decision of several African countries to withdraw from the ICC, the election of US President Trump with a populist anti-globalization political agenda, and signs that nationalism and populism are on the rise in Europe. This global uncertainty makes this book even more important, because the ATJ has survived multiple rounds of legal, political, and economic turbulence. We draw many lessons from the ATJ's experience, but leave for future writings any investigation of the future of international courts in this brave new world we are now entering.

Karen J. Alter, Evanston, IL
Laurence R. Helfer, Durham, NC
December 7, 2016

Contents

III. RECONSIDERING INTERNATIONAL ADJUDICATION IN EUROPE IN LIGHT OF THE ANDEAN EXPERIENCE

List of Tables and Figures

List of Abbreviations

AFIDRO	*Asociación de Laboratorios Farmacéuticos de Investigación y Desarrollo* (Association of Pharmaceutical Research Laboratories of Colombia)
AIDIFAN	*Asociación de Industrias Farmacéuticas Nacionales* (Association of Pharmaceutical Industries of National Origin of Peru)
AJE	*Association Française des Juristes Européens*
ALAFAR	*Asociación de Laboratorios Farmacéuticos* (Association of Pharmaceutical Laboratories of Colombia)
ALBA	*Alianza Bolivariana para los Pueblos de Nuestra América*
ASINFAR	*Asociación de Industrias Farmacéuticas de Colombia* (Association of Pharmaceutical Industries of Colombia)
ATJ	Andean Tribunal of Justice
BAT	British American Tobacco
CACJ	Central American Court of Justice
CCJ	Caribbean Court of Justice
CET	Common External Tariff
COMEX	Ecuador Board of Foreign Trade and Investment
EACJ	East African Court of Justice
ECJ	European Court of Justice (Court of Justice of the European Union)
ECtHR	European Court of Human Rights
ECOWAS	Economic Community of West African States
EIIP	*Instituto Ecuatoriano de la Propiedad Intelectual* (Ecuadorian Institute of Intellectual Property)
FIDE	*Fédération Internationale de Droit Européen*
FTAA	Free Trade Area of the Americas
GATT	General Agreement on Tariffs and Trade
IACtHR	Inter-American Court of Human Rights
ICC	International Criminal Court
ICJ	International Court of Justice
IMF	International Monetary Fund
INDECOPI	*Instituto Nacional de Defensa de la Competencia y de la Protección de la Propiedad Intelectual* (National Institute for the Defense of Competition and the Protection of Intellectual Property of Peru)
INTAL	Institute for the Integration of Latin America and the Caribbean
IP	intellectual property
MERCOSUR	Southern Common Market
NAFTA	North American Free Trade Agreement
OHADA	Organization for the Harmonization of Corporate Law in Africa
PM	Phillip Morris
SADC	Southern African Development Community
SAPI	*Servicio Autónomo de la Propiedad Intelectual* (Autonomous Intellectual Property Service of Venezuela)
SENAPI	*Servicio Nacional de Propiedad Intelectual* (National Intellectual Property Service of Bolivia)

SIC	*Superintendencia de Industria y Comercio* (Superintendent of Industry and Commerce of Colombia)
TPP	Trans-Pacific Partnership
TRIPS	Agreement on Trade-Related Aspects of Intellectual Property Rights
UN	United Nations
UNASUR	*Unión des Naciones Suramericanas* (Union of South American Nations)
US	United States
WGE	*Wissentschaftliche Gesellschaft für Europarecht*
WIPO	World Intellectual Property Organization
WTO	World Trade Organization

PART I

SUPRANATIONAL LEGAL TRANSPLANTS

1

Lessons from the Andean Tribunal of Justice

Thirty Years as a Legal Transplant

Most international courts today are regional courts, responsible for adjudicating treaties that bind states within a defined geographic area. The first generation of regional courts was established in Europe—the European Court of Justice (ECJ) and the European Court of Human Rights (ECtHR).[1] Later regional courts copied key design features of one of these two courts, in effect transplanting a European model of international adjudication to other area of the world—mostly comprising developing countries—where law and politics operate very differently.

This book provides the most in-depth analysis to date of a transplanted regional court. In particular, we investigate the origins, evolution, successes, and failures of the Andean Tribunal of Justice (ATJ or Tribunal), an international court with jurisdiction over a small group of developing states in South America. In addition to analyzing one of the oldest transplanted international courts (now in operation for more than three decades), our study of the ATJ seeks to shed light on the challenges facing regional courts in developing country contexts and the strategies their judges use to address those challenges.

In 1979, Andean political leaders added a court to their struggling regional integration project to help improve respect for Andean legal rules. For inspiration, they turned to the highly successful ECJ, copying its design features and legal doctrines. The ATJ has since become the world's third most active international court, with over 2,800 legally binding rulings to date.[2]

The Tribunal's impact, however, has been uneven. The ATJ has been strikingly successful in one domain of Andean law—intellectual property (IP)—a subject

[1] K.J. Alter, *The New Terrain of International Law: Courts, Politics, Rights*. Princeton, NJ: Princeton University Press, 2014, 87–94. We use the original titles of the European Court of Justice (ECJ) and European Community (EC) rather than the present-day Court of Justice of the European Union (CJEU) and European Union (EU) because our comparison between the Andes and Europe focuses on an earlier period of European integration.

[2] The ATJ issued 2,853 rulings from its founding through 2014. In comparison, as of that same date the ICJ had issued 85 judgments in contentious cases and 26 advisory opinions and had denied jurisdiction or admissibility in 26 cases; the WTO dispute settlement system had adopted 201 panel reports and 134 AB rulings; the ITLOS court had issued 18 decisions and 2 advisory opinions. In 2015, the ICC had at different stages of investigation and prosecution 22 cases involving 26 individuals and 9 "situations."

Transplanting International Courts: The Law and Politics of the Andean Tribunal of Justice. First Edition. Karen J. Alter and Laurence R. Helfer. Published 2017 by Oxford University Press.

that accounts for the overwhelming majority of its rulings. In areas traditionally associated with regional integration—such as trade restrictions, non-tariff barriers, and other barriers to the free movement of goods and people—the Tribunal, unlike its European cousin, has been much less active and influential. Yet Andean judges have continued to receive complaints and issue rulings even during periods when ideological schisms sapped political support for Andean integration as a whole.

Our interest in the ATJ began as a sort of natural experiment. The Andean Tribunal and Andean Pact's founding charter, the Cartagena Agreement, are very similar to the ECJ and the European Community's Treaty of Rome. Both tribunals also have very active dockets. Comparing the two courts side-by-side allows us to explore judicial institutions with similar structures and doctrines that operate in very different legal and political contexts.

As we learned more about the ATJ we became interested in a second issue—how the Tribunal has survived and even prospered in a relatively inhospitable climate. The Andean Community has endured numerous travails—years of economic and political instability, armed insurgencies and transborder military skirmishes, and deep ideological differences among its member states. In addition, all Andean countries share the reality that their relationships with non-Andean countries, such as the United States, China, and countries in Europe, are more politically and economically consequential than relations with their South American neighbors. The ATJ's resilience in the face of this ongoing turbulence makes it an important topic for understanding whether and when international judges can shape international law and politics, especially when the going gets tough.

In terms of theory, our study of the Andean Tribunal engages with three strands of legal and political science literature on international courts. First, we consider how the ATJ's thirty-year trajectory has been shaped by its origins as a legal transplant. The Andean officials who created the ATJ hoped to emulate the ECJ's contributions to European integration.[3] Yet they also feared that a bold international court, one that fully embraced the European model of expansive judicial lawmaking, might exacerbate political tensions in the region and strengthen the hand of integration opponents.

A key contribution of this book is to investigate the extent to which the ATJ has achieved the aspirations of its founders who transplanted an ECJ-style court to the Andes. Chapter 2 analyzes the decision to copy and adapt the ECJ model, and then to revise the ATJ's initial design to emulate the ECJ more directly. Chapter 3 compares the subject-matter caseload of the two courts and their differing relationships with national judges. Chapter 4 explains where Andean judges have followed

[3] On the ECJ's contributions to European integration, see J. Weiler, The Transformation of Europe. *Yale Law Journal* 1991, 100 (8): 2403–83; A. Stone Sweet, *The Judicial Construction of Europe*. Oxford: Oxford University Press, 2004; A.-M. Burley and W. Mattli, Europe before the Court. *International Organization* 1993, 47 (1): 41–76; R. Dehousse, *The European Court of Justice: The Politics of Judicial Integration*. New York, NY: St. Martin's Press, 1998; J. Tallberg, *European Governance and Supranational Institutions: Making States Comply*. London: Routledge, 2003; M. Pollack, Delegation, Agency and Agenda Setting in the EC. *International Organization* 2003, 51 (1): 99–134.

the ECJ's doctrinal lead and where they have diverged and developed distinctive doctrines tailored to the political realities of the Andean legal system. Chapter 8 investigates the two courts' different penchants for expansive judicial lawmaking, and Chapter 9 examines the role of jurist advocacy movements in the two regions. The lessons we draw can help advance studies of the eleven other regional courts that adopt the ECJ's design features and legal doctrines,[4] and about the politics of supranational international legal transplants more generally.[5] We argue that the ATJ's experience may well be more informative for these courts than that of its progenitor—the ECJ.

The book's second theoretical contribution is the use of detailed coding and analysis of ATJ rulings to revisit debates about the effectiveness of international courts. Early scholarship on this topic asked a simple question—do states comply with judgments against them?[6] For the ATJ, compliance with its preliminary rulings is the norm. Yet states have mostly ignored the Tribunal's judgments finding them in breach of Andean law. But these simple statistics mask a more complex and multifaceted reality, one that aligns with recent scholarship that distinguishes compliance from effectiveness and evaluates the latter by reference to a court's mandate and goals[7] and the extent to which its rulings lead to "observable, desired changes in behavior."[8]

When we launched our study of the Andean legal system more than a decade ago we had contrasting expectations about the ATJ's effectiveness. Because the Tribunal is modeled on its European cousin, we were not surprised that its docket is dominated by preliminary rulings. Our intuition was that private litigants would not file complaints and national judges would not send references to the Tribunal unless there were economic or other benefits from doing so. The large number of preliminary rulings thus suggested that the ATJ was having an impact on Andean law and politics. On the other hand, considering the region's history of economic and political turbulence, strong presidents, weak judiciaries, and fragile rule of law, we thought it highly unlikely that the ATJ could change state behavior to the same extent as had its European counterpart.

The reality revealed by our study lies between these two extremes. The ATJ is effective by any plausible definition of that term, but only within a single issue area—intellectual property—an island that remains isolated from other areas of

[4] See K.J. Alter, The Global Spread of European Style International Courts. *West European Politics* 2012, 35 (1): 135–54.

[5] M.R. Madsen and A. Huneeus, Between Global Scripts and Regional Politics: A Comparative History of the American, European and African Human Rights Systems. *International Journal of Constitutional Law* (forthcoming).

[6] L.R. Helfer and A.-M. Slaughter, Toward a Theory of Effective Supranational Adjudication. *Yale Law Journal* 1997, 107 (2): 282–4.

[7] Y. Shany, *Assessing the Effectiveness of International Courts*. Oxford: Oxford University Press, 2014; L.R. Helfer, The Effectiveness of International Adjudicators. In: *Oxford Handbook on International Adjudication*. C. Romano, K.J. Alter, and Y. Shany (eds), 464–82. Oxford: Oxford University Press, 2014.

[8] K. Raustiala, Compliance and Effectiveness in International Regulatory Cooperation. *Case Western Reserve Journal of International Law* 2000, 32(3): 387–440, 393–4.

Andean law, where the Tribunal is under-utilized and mostly ignored. Equally as surprising, although national courts send many preliminary references to the ATJ, the predominant domestic support for the Tribunal has come not from national judges but from the IP administrative agency officials who actively seek out the ATJ's guidance on unsettled issues of Andean IP law. This finding is revealed in our analysis of the ATJ's interlocutors (Chapters 3 and 5), in our analysis of how the Tribunal has navigated four politically fraught cases (Chapter 6), and in our exploration of the lack of an Andean jurist advocacy movement (Chapter 9).

Our book also contributes a new dimension to the study of international court effectiveness by analyzing the ATJ's resilience during times of political turmoil. Since Venezuela's exit from the Andean Community in 2006, the member states have been divided between two neoliberal-leaning governments (Colombia and Peru) and two leftist-populist regimes (Bolivia and Ecuador).[9] This ideological schism has blocked meaningful advances in regional integration and diminished support for Andean institutions. In some respects, in fact, the Community has moved backwards over the last decade, as reflected in the abrogation of the Common External Tariff in 2015, discussed in Chapter 7. Yet the deep relationship between the Andean judges and domestic IP administrators has sustained and protected the ATJ during this period of crisis. Moreover, the Tribunal has remained a viable judicial forum even for high-stakes noncompliance suits, although one such suit—a challenge to Ecuadorian President Rafael Correa's deviations from Andean free trade rules—risks exacerbating the current crisis and may call into question the survival of the Andean Community, and thus the ATJ (Chapter 7).

These findings have important implications for the effectiveness of international adjudication more generally. Regional courts in the developing world operate in challenging environments that more closely resemble those in the Andes than those in Europe. The judges on these fledgling courts are struggling to overcome major legal and political hurdles to removing regional trade barriers, creating a common market, and protecting human rights. As discussed in Chapters 8 and 10, the ATJ's experience suggests that even if international courts cannot fully overcome these challenges, cultivating and maintaining the support of a core domestic constituency may be necessary both for their effectiveness and for survival in tough political times.

A third theoretical contribution of our Andean research relates to a recently developed framework for analyzing the variable authority of international courts. Our revisions to this book coincided with a project we co-directed that explores variations in the creation, expansion, and dissipation of an international court's de facto

[9] The term "leftist-populist" is controversial in Latin America. See, e.g., R.S. Jansen, Populist Mobilization: A New Theoretical Approach to Populism. *Sociological Theory* 2011, 29 (2): 75–96. We nevertheless believe that the label applies to the governments led by Presidents Chavez, Correa, and Morales in Venezuela, Ecuador, and Bolivia, respectively. Each regime, albeit to different degrees, has made anti-establishment public appeals, organized referenda to circumvent constitutional limits, employed extra-legal tactics to thwart opponents, and dismantled institutional checks and balances within each national legal system.

authority. This framework enables comparative assessments of judicial authority along multiple dimensions—between tribunals, over time, across issue areas, and in different countries—and evaluates how different institutional, political, social, and other contextual factors shape the authority of international courts.[10] In this book, we apply the authority framework to analyze how the wider geopolitical context in which the Andean Community is situated helps to explain the changes to the ATJ's authority during the last decade of political turbulence. The authority framework also helps us to conceptualize the difference between an international court's legal authority and its political power, an issue we explore in Chapters 7 and 10.

In addition to considering the ATJ's contributions to these three theoretical debates, this book provides an opportunity to revisit our own scholarship. Our previous work, written individually, focused on the ECJ and the ECtHR, two international courts that have issued thousands of judgments, many of which have developed the law boldly and expansively, changed the behavior of governments significantly, and reshaped the law and politics of European integration and human rights profoundly. Emphasizing the importance of compulsory jurisdiction, private access provisions, and direct effect to explain the relative success of the two European courts, our earlier publications implicitly suggested that replicating these key design features could lead to similar outcomes by other international tribunals.

Karen Alter launched her career by studying how the ECJ convinced national judges to accept its authority. Her first two books, *Establishing the Supremacy of European Law* (2001) and the *European Court's Political Power* (2009), explore variation in the ECJ's political influence over time, within member states, and across issue areas. Our co-authored comparison of the Andean and European experiences led us to reassess Alter's earlier understanding of EC legal integration. In particular, superficial similarities between the two institutions—the predominance of national court references on both courts' dockets, the common assertion of the direct effect and supremacy of Community law, and the ATJ's frequent citations to ECJ rulings—are belied by a more complex reality. Whereas in Europe private actors have invoked a broad range of European laws to challenge national policies and practices, in the Andes private litigants primarily invoke Andean IP law. In addition, the ATJ's mostly timid and formalist interpretations of Community rules diverge from the ECJ's bolder, purposive approach.[11] These surprising findings led us to

[10] The project was spearheaded by iCourts, the Danish National Research Foundation's Center of Excellence for International Courts, based at the University of Copenhagen Faculty of Law. It is published as: K.J. Alter, L.R. Helfer, and M.R. Madsen, The Variable Authority of International Courts. *Law and Contemporary Problems* 2016, 79 (1): 1–36; K.J. Alter, L.R. Helfer, and M.R. Madsen, *International Court Authority*. Oxford: Oxford University Press, 2017.

[11] We recognize that judges can use formalist or textualist interpretive techniques to expand the meaning and scope of law in ways that constrain national sovereignty and government discretion. Our essential point is that the ATJ uses formalist interpretations as a judicial strategy to build support for its rulings, and, in addition, that the Tribunal avoids expansionist lawmaking, for example by refusing to constitutionalize the Cartagena Agreement and by eschewing references to the goals and aspirations of integration as a teleological guidepost for interpreting Andean law. By strictly adhering to the letter of Andean legal texts, and by allowing member states to define the pace and scope of regional integration, the ATJ faithfully enforces Community rules while putting the onus on states to modify those rules by following accepted legal procedures.

reconsider whether mobilization in favor of ECJ litigation was as spontaneous as prevailing theories had suggested, and whether all international judges are expansionist lawmakers. This questioning is reflected in the conclusion of Chapter 3 on the ATJ's interlocutors, in Chapter 8's comparison of the two court's lawmaking across time, and in Chapter 9's discussion of the importance of jurist advocacy movements.

Laurence Helfer, writing with Anne-Marie Slaughter in 1997, published *Toward a Theory of Effective Supranational Adjudication*, a pioneering study of the ECtHR and ECJ.[12] Helfer and Slaughter examined the success of both European tribunals, explained the importance of private litigant access to that success, identified a checklist of factors associated with effective adjudication in Europe, and considered the prospects for building a broader community of law to support such adjudication elsewhere. In the ensuing years, states have created new global and regional courts and quasi-judicial review bodies in human rights, criminal law, international economic law, and the law of the sea. The dockets of many of these institutions are growing, mainly in response to suits by private litigants and other non-state actors. A deep study of the ATJ—the third most active international court by number of rulings and one of the oldest regional judicial body outside of Europe—provides an opportunity to revisit Helfer and Slaughter's theory of effective international adjudication in the context of developing countries characterized by weak domestic judiciaries, limited protection of individual rights, and less deeply embedded commitments to the rule of law. This reassessment is the subject of Chapter 10.

The remainder of this chapter considers the Andean Tribunal as an international legal transplant. The next section provides an overview of Andean and European integration and the role of the ATJ and ECJ in the two regional integration processes. We also explain the decision to compare the ATJ's first twenty-five years of operation (1984–2007) to the ECJ's first quarter of a century (1958–83), supplemented by an analysis of seven additional years of litigation and legal and political developments in the Andean Community. We then identify five key findings that have general relevance to the comparative study of international courts. We conclude with a roadmap of the book that explains the issues analyzed in each chapter and previews the chapter's major findings.

Comparing Staggered Twenty-Five-Year Periods of International Adjudication: The ECJ (1958–83) and the ATJ (1984–2007)

Throughout this book, we compare and contrast the experiences of the Andean Tribunal to the ECJ, the judicial body on which it was modeled. Our comparative analysis encompasses several dimensions, including institutional design, legal doctrine, judicial lawmaking, and the impact on regional and national law and politics.

[12] Helfer and Slaughter, 1997. Chapter 10 updates this analysis and explains the shift from "supranational" to "international" courts.

Our decision to examine the two courts side by side raises a methodological challenge. The ECJ is an older institution than the ATJ, one that operates in a far more favorable legal and political environment than its junior cousin in the South America. It would thus be misleading to evaluate the two courts over their entire lifespans, or to investigate each court's activities in the same calendar years.

To address these concerns, we focus our comparison on roughly the first quarter century of each tribunal, two staggered twenty-five-year time periods—1958–83 for the ECJ, and 1984–2007 for the ATJ—during which the two courts faced a number of similar challenges.[13] We also include data and analysis of the next seven years of ATJ activities to highlight the two courts' divergent trajectories during a period of political crisis within the Andean Community.

To situate this comparative analysis, we first provide an overview of the early years of the Andean and European integration projects. We then explain how we selected the beginning and end points of each staggered time period. We conclude by briefly contrasting the marked divergence of the two Communities and their respective courts after these periods of comparison.[14]

The Andean integration project was launched in 1969 when the small and underdeveloped nations on the mountainous western edge of South America formed a regional pact to promote economic growth, regulate foreign investment, and harmonize national laws. The fundamental drivers of Andean integration have remained the same over time. Andean states have relatively small economies and are deeply dependent on trade with richer and bigger countries in Latin America, the United States, and elsewhere. Political leaders in the region believed that integration would make Andean markets more attractive to investment and trade. They also sought to benefit from adopting collective solutions to shared problems, as well as from the added leverage of presenting a united front when negotiating with larger trading partners. Although governments have often disagreed about the substance of Andean policies and the strategies to achieve them, they continue to assert that integration is desirable for these reasons.[15]

For its first sixteen years of existence (1969–83), the Andean Pact did not include an international court. Although political leaders expressed a long-term desire to build a common market for which a judicial body might have been helpful, their

[13] We recognize, of course, that there are many significant differences between the two regional integration projects. The Andean Community today has four small member states that together hold less than one-fifth of the population of the EU. Their economies are less developed and tiny by comparison. In addition, terrain in the Andes is rugged and regional infrastructure is underdeveloped, creating significant logistical barriers that hinder intra-Community trade and industrial growth.

[14] The European Community grew from six members in 1958 (France, Germany, Italy, Luxembourg, The Netherlands, and Belgium) to nine in 1973 (when the United Kingdom, Ireland, and Denmark joined), to ten members in 1981 (when Greece joined). Spain and Portugal joined the EC in 1985. During most of the period studied here, the Andean integration project had five member states. The original Andean Pact included Bolivia, Chile, Colombia, Ecuador, and Peru. Chile withdrew in 1976. Venezuela joined in 1973 and withdrew in 2006.

[15] For more on the origins of the Andean Pact and the ATJ, see O. Saldías, *The Judicial Politics of Economic Integration: The Andean Court as an Engine of Development*. New York, NY: Routledge, 2013, 84–97.

more pressing goal was to speed the region's economic and industrial development. The principal policy instrument they adopted—import substitution—sought to replace expensive imported goods with local substitutes whose production would generate jobs across the region. The Pact also heavily regulated foreign investment with the goal of transferring technology from foreign firms to local producers and retaining profits within the region. As we later explain, these policies soon floundered, and the resulting flouting of Andean rules was one of the motivations for creating the Tribunal. We do not dwell on this early period, however, since our focus is on the origins and evolution of the ATJ.

European integration began with the Schuman Plan of 1950, a proposal to put Germany's coal and steel industries under collective supranational management. The European Coal and Steel Community, formally constituted in 1952, included a Court of Justice. The ECJ's role in this Community was to review actions and omissions of the supranational High Authority and to facilitate uniform interpretation its rules and regulations.[16] The six original member states enlarged the ECJ's jurisdiction in 1958 with the founding of the European Economic Community.[17]

We thus begin our staggered comparison of the two courts at the point in each regional integration project when international judges acquired the authority to interpret their respective Community's founding charters—the Treaty of Rome and the Cartagena Agreement. For the ECJ, this date is 1958; for the ATJ it is 1984.

As originally drafted, the Treaty of Rome and the Cartagena Agreement were similar in content and goals. Both instruments created supranational governance structures and set out a framework for building a common market. In Europe, these structures included the European Council of Ministers, a legislative body comprised of national executives that adopted legally binding regulations and directives, and the European Commission, a supranational institution tasked with proposing and overseeing the implementation of Community rules.

The Andean Pact emulated these European institutions using different names for analogous bodies. The Andean *Comisión*, comprised of national executives from each of the member states, adopted Andean secondary legislation (known as *Decisiones*) that were directly applicable in national legal orders. A regional executive body, the *Junta* (later the restructured and renamed the General Secretariat), supervised the implementation of those *Decisiones*. The Treaty of Rome also contained a chapter defining the ECJ's jurisdiction, subject-matter competences, and access rules. These provisions were absent from the Cartagena Agreement. However, the 1979 Treaty establishing the ATJ, which was closely modeled on the Treaty of Rome's articles pertaining to the ECJ, completed the suite of Andean governance institutions.

In terms of substantive obligations, the two Communities' founding charters prohibited governments from imposing new barriers to intra-regional trade and

[16] A. Boerger-De Smedt, La Court de Justice dans les Négociationis du Traite de Paris Instituant la CECA. *Journal of European History* 2008, 14 (2): 7–34.

[17] For more on how the ECJ's jurisdiction and mandate changed in this shift, see K.J. Alter, *Establishing the Supremacy of European Law: The Making of an International Rule of Law in Europe*. Oxford: Oxford University Press, 2001, 5–11.

required national treatment of goods from other member states. The treaties also provided for the phased removal of tariff and nontariff barriers via secondary legislation—regulations and directives in the EC; *Decisiones* in the Andean Pact. In both regions, these timetables proved to be overly optimistic and states later extended them.

In addition to formal similarities in institutional architecture and substantive rules, the European legal system of the early 1960s and the Andean legal system of the mid-1980s faced comparable practical challenges. Although sometimes forgotten today, the European integration project was, in its early years, widely viewed as precarious and unlikely to succeed.[18] Reviews of Andean integration in the 1980s expressed similar skepticism. Governments continued to exempt many economically important industries from the Andean Free Trade Programme,[19] and the Latin American debt crisis late in the decade created pervasive economic instability that brought the Andean integration project to the brink of failure.[20]

For ECJ and ATJ judges, the tenuous political foundations of the two integration schemes raised daunting a question—how to attract the cases needed to establish their legal authority. In their early years, both courts faced wide variations in the willingness of national judges in different member states and at different levels of the judicial hierarchy to refer cases involving issues of Community law. Both tribunals capitalized on the opportunities of the early cases that did arrive, adopting rulings that were doctrinally important but whose political significance was not immediately apparent.

Both the ECJ and ATJ were similarly active during their first twenty-five years. The ECJ issued 305 noncompliance judgments and 1,808 preliminary rulings (an average of 86.1 cases per year). The ATJ, part of a much smaller geographic, demographic, and economic region, issued 85 noncompliance judgments and 1,338 preliminary rulings between 1984 and 2007 (an average of 71.5 per year).[21]

As the legal and political significance of these rulings became apparent, both courts attracted repeat players—legal entrepreneurs who sought out cases to promote regional integration.[22] Many of these private litigants urged both courts to overcome the political impediments to integration with teleological interpretations

[18] France's President De Gaulle refused to accept a shift to qualified majority voting, using his "empty chair policy" to block all community decision-making until his terms were met. In the 1960s and 1970s, European governments showed little appetite for European integration. See D. Dinan, *Europe Recast: A History of the European Union*. Boulder, CO: Lynn Rienner, 2004, 104–64. S. Hoffmann, Obstinate or Obsolete? France, European Integration, and the Fate of the Nation-State. *Daedalus* 1966, 95 (3): 863–4.

[19] W.P. Avery and J.D. Cochraine, Innovation in Latin American Regionalism: The Andean Common Market. *International Organization* 1973, 27 (2): 181–223; R. Vargas-Hidalgo, The Crisis of the Andean Pact: Lessons for Integration among Developing Countries. *Journal of Common Market Studies* 1979, 27 (3): 213–26.

[20] T.A. O'Keefe, How the Andean Pact Transformed Itself into a Friend of Foreign Enterprise. *International Lawyer* 1996, 30 (4): 811–24.

[21] ECJ data from Stone Sweet, 2004, 72–9. Stone Sweet's data covers 1960–85. The Andean data are from Chapter 4 in this book, which provides a more complete comparison of litigation patterns.

[22] On the role of repeat players in ECJ litigation, see W. Mattli and A.-M. Slaughter, Revisiting the European Court of Justice. *International Organization* 1998, 52 (1): 186–9; R. Rawlings, The Eurolaw

of Community legal rules. The ECJ responded with a series of bold and expansive decisions that were influential in advancing the EC's goals. The ATJ was more modest, declaring violations of Andean rules when the judges discerned a political commitment to common policies but otherwise giving broad deference to national governments.

Our period of comparison ends in Europe in the mid-1980s when a crisis in the European Monetary System led France to commit to deeper regional integration.[23] France's move paved the way for national political leaders to adopt the Single European Act of 1985, an overhaul of the EC that established a fully functioning common market and a long-delayed shift to qualified majority voting.[24] The Single European Act also increased the pace and scope of regional integration, triggering an expansion of EC secondary legislation, the vigorous pursuit of noncompliance actions by the Commission to push states to implement that legislation, and a marked rise in ECJ litigation by private actors.

In the Andes, the twenty-five year period ends in 2007, the effective date of Venezuela's departure from the Andean Community. By this time, the regional consensus in favor of economic liberalization and free trade had fractured badly. Two states—Colombia and Peru—remained largely committed to these policies and pursued free trade deals with the United States and Europe. The election of three populist presidents—Hugo Chavez in Venezuela in 1999, Evo Morales in Bolivia 2005, and Raphael Correa in Ecuador in 2006—created a tense political climate that hampered further advances in integration. The final break came in 2006 when Venezuela withdrew from the Community after Colombia and Peru announced that they would enter into bilateral free trade agreements with the United States.

These two dates—1985 in Europe and 2007 in the Andes—mark the point when the two regional integration projects diverged sharply. The EC continued to take bold steps toward building a single market and closer economic union. In South America, the political and ideological schisms among the four remaining member states and a focus on other regional cooperation schemes—most notably MERCOSUR (the *Mercado Común del Sur*) and UNASUR (the *Unión de Naciones Suramericanas*)—sapped political support for the Andean integration project and Community institutions.

The trajectories of two regional courts also diverged after these dates. In Europe, the creation of the Tribunal of First Instance in 1988 doubled the capacity of European judges to adjudicate cases. Additional reforms followed in response to the shift from the EC to the European Union and the expansion into Eastern

Game: Some Deductions from a Saga. *Journal of Law and Society* 1993, 20: 309–40. ATJ repeat players include firms in the aluminum and alcohol sectors, pharmaceutical companies, businesses with lucrative trademarks, and importers and exporters subject to Andean taxes.

[23] C. Parsons, *A Certain Idea of Europe*. Ithaca, NY: Cornell University Press, 2003, 149; K. McNamara, *The Currency of Ideas: Monetary Politics in the European Union*. Ithaca, NY: Cornell University Press, 1998 at chapter 6; A. Moravcsik, *The Choice for Europe*. Ithaca, NY: Cornell University Press, 1998, chapter 4.

[24] Moravcsik, 1998, chapter 5.

Europe—events that added fresh complaints and new subject-matter competences to the ECJ's docket.[25]

For the ATJ, the decade following Venezuela's departure is best described as a struggle to maintain the status quo in the face of growing political turbulence. Preliminary references involving IP registrations remained the bread and butter of the Tribunal's work, but referrals involving other areas of Andean law increased modestly, and ATJ judges cultivated relationships with new domestic partners, including the Peruvian and Bolivian IP agencies and a new specialized IP court in Peru. Suits alleging noncompliance with Andean law, however, all but vanished from the Tribunal's docket. Given the wider political turmoil in the Community, the survival of the rule-of-law island for IP disputes that the ATJ helped to build is remarkable.

Lessons Learned from Studying the Andean Tribunal

Our study of the ATJ adds to a flourishing literature on comparative international courts. Scholars have analyzed a small number of these judicial bodies comprehensively, most notably the ECJ, the ECtHR, the WTO dispute settlement system, and the Inter-American Court of Human Rights. We know far less, however, about the other twenty international tribunals operating in the world today, even as their dockets are growing.

Our contribution to this body of knowledge draws upon a rich variety of sources. Working over a decade with the help of research assistants, we coded and analyzed most of the ATJ's more than 2,800 decisions through 2014. We made four trips to the region and conducted more than fifty interviews in Spanish and English with government officials, lawyers, national and Andean judges, and Community officials. Our investigations in the Andes were also shaped by our research and fieldwork on the two European tribunals, as well as other ECJ-style transplants in west, east, and southern Africa, and the differently structured integration systems in MERCOSUR and the Association of South-East Asian Nations (ASEAN).

We highlight below five broad lessons from our research and findings that contribute to the comparative study of international courts.

Adapting transplanted international legal institutions to local contexts

Our book provides new evidence for evaluating theories about transplanted legal institutions. The literature on legal transplants, discussed in Chapter 2, indicates that slavish copies of existing legal institutions are likely to be ignored or resisted by local actors. This is especially true of transplants in developing countries, whose officials often adopt formal institutions and laws in response to pressure from

[25] These reforms are summarized in Alter, 2014, 86.

multilateral organizations, foreign donors, and trading partners. This institutional mimicry may appear significant on paper but it often occurs without any meaningful change in actual practices.

In contrast, scholars find that efforts to adapt legal institutions to local contexts helps transplants take root. Modifications of a pre-existing template often reflect efforts by proponents of importation to respond to local actors' needs. The decision to add an ECJ-style court to the Andean integration project supports this finding. National political leaders added elements protective of national sovereignty to the ECJ model, limiting which noncompliance suits the Andean *Junta* could investigate as well as the guidance that the ATJ could provide in preliminary rulings. However, they discovered later that these modifications undermined the ability of the Andean legal system to induce compliance with Community rules.

Most studies of legal transplants take a single snapshot of an imported institution, usually at or close to the moment of transplantation. Our analysis of the ATJ reveals this focus to be incomplete. The willingness of political leaders to revisit initial transplant decisions—often years later—provides an opportunity to assess how well a transplant has grafted onto the local context and to revise the original model in light of experience.

The first cohort of Andean judges adhered to the original ATJ Treaty faithfully. They rejected invitations from litigants to adopt ECJ-style purposive interpretations of the Cartagena Agreement to overturn political compromises that impeded the broader goals of Andean integration. The ATJ's circumspection helped to build trust with national governments, and with that trust came a greater willingness to expand the Tribunal's mandate. When governments overhauled the Andean legal system in the mid-1990s, they also restructured the ATJ, granting private litigants the ability to file noncompliance suits with the Tribunal and authorizing judges to examine the facts of preliminary rulings. These changes contributed to the increasing activity and influence of the Andean Tribunal over the next decade.

Not all international courts seek to expand their influence and authority

All international courts are called upon to adjudicate cases in which the applicable legal rules do not, on their own, clearly dictate the outcome of the dispute. In this limited sense, all international judges are lawmakers, and such lawmaking is generally uncontroversial and even welcomed. The ATJ is no exception.

Yet some international courts do more, identifying new obligations or imposing constraints on states that have little if any basis in legal texts or the intentions of their drafters. Both the ECJ and the ECtHR regularly engage in such expansive judicial lawmaking. Because much of the early literature on international courts focused on these two long-standing tribunals, many commentators assumed that all international judges are predisposed to expand their influence and authority.

This assumption has been called into question as our knowledge of other international courts has expanded. For example, the WTO Appellate Body and panels adhere closely to treaty texts, often favoring dictionary definitions of key terms over contextual or purpose-driven interpretations. In addition, recent studies of courts in east and west Africa reveal that international judges rarely expand the law or demand that governments adopt major policy change. Instead, the judges on these courts are generally circumspect in their interpretive approaches and in the remedies they award to successful litigants.[26]

Our study reveals that the Andean Tribunal is situated closer to the latter group of more restrained international courts. This finding is theoretically interesting not only because the ATJ is modeled on the bolder and more audacious ECJ, but also because we identify specific instances when Andean judges had clear opportunities to emulate their European colleagues but chose not to do so.

We do not suggest that the ATJ has never engaged in lawmaking. For example, the Tribunal's earliest rulings unequivocally asserted the direct effect and supremacy of Andean secondary legislation in national legal orders. But these assertions were part of the bargain that national political leaders agreed to when they created the Tribunal. When later cases provided an opening to take the next steps in building legal integration, Andean judges pulled back. As we explain in Chapter 4, they either copied ECJ doctrines in form but not in substance or eschewed those doctrines altogether in favor of local alternatives—such as the *complemento indispensable* principle—that give greater deference to national decision-makers.

We also analyze the ATJ's default preference for legal circumspection, explaining in Chapter 8 why that formalist approach may well be appropriate for the politically fraught context in which the Tribunal operates. Circumspection implies a strict textual adherence to legal rules, even if judges dislike the normative or political implications of such interpretations. Since this approach reflects a similarly cautious conception of adjudication held by national judges in the Andes, this legal formalism increases the palatability of ATJ rulings to local legal audiences.

The predominance of formalism in the region also means that, unlike their counterparts in Europe, national courts in the Andes rarely refer bold or provocative questions to the ATJ even when pressed to do so by private litigants. Instead, they often pose the same questions in case after case, knowing in advance what the ATJ's answer will be. To outsiders, this repetition may appear pointless and inefficient. It also sometimes frustrates attorneys who participate in Andean litigation. Yet, as we explain in Chapter 5, formalism and repetition served an important purpose. They habituated respect for legal rules so that when politically contentious cases later arose, legal actors could defend their decisions by invoking long-standing and deeply entrenched rules and procedures.

[26] K.J. Alter, L.R. Helfer, and J. McAllister, A New International Human Rights Court for West Africa: The Court of Justice for the Economic Community of West African States. *American Journal of International Law* 2013, 107 (4): 737–79; J. Gathii, The Variation in the Use of Sub-Regional Integration Courts between Business and Human Rights Actors: The Case of the East African Court of Justice. *Law and Contemporary Problems* 2016, 79 (1): 37–62.

The larger theoretical point is that circumspection may be more prevalent than early scholarship on international courts assumed. In particular, formalist reasoning may be a prudent strategy for tribunals that face legally and politically inhospitable environments. By scrupulously adhering to their delegated powers, international judges may survive long enough to gain a toehold of support among litigants who challenge unequivocal legal violations that fall within the courts' jurisdiction. If the Andean experience is any guide, future studies should thus not assume that international judges either seek out or inevitably capitalize on opportunities to expand their authority and influence.

Expanding the interlocutors and compliance partners of international courts

The first generation of scholarship on international courts—including our own early writings—emphasized the links between national and international judges in activating international litigation and providing a mechanism for compliance with international court rulings. To be sure, not all such relationships have been mutually supportive or beneficial. Karen Alter analyzed the resistance of some national courts in Europe to referring cases to the ECJ and to accepting foundational EC legal doctrines.[27] In a different part of the world, Laurence Helfer attributed the backlash against human rights treaties in several Caribbean countries to negative interactions between national and international judges over challenges to the death penalty.[28] Yet most scholars have long presumed the centrality of court-to-court relationships to the success or failure of international adjudication.[29]

Our extensive study of the ATJ reveals that this view is inaccurate in at least two respects. First, the Andean Tribunal's primary interlocutors and compliance partners are not national courts but are instead domestic administrative agencies that review applications for IP protection and regulate other market subjects. The agencies' trademark and patent registration decisions account for the overwhelming majority of ATJ preliminary rulings. Agency officials actively consult and apply the Tribunal's interpretation of Andean IP *Decisiones*, offer advice on revising them, and seek out the ATJ's guidance by encouraging national courts to refer cases. This close relationship has also helped the ATJ survive skepticism by national judges and structural reforms of national legal systems in Venezuela and Ecuador.

The Tribunal, attuned to the interests of its principal audience, recently overturned its past practice and now hears cases referred directly from administrative agencies. Direct references bypass appeals to national courts. They also reduce the

[27] K.J. Alter, The European Legal System and Domestic Policy: Spillover or Backlash. *International Organization* 2000, 54 (3): 489–518.

[28] L.R. Helfer, Overlegalizing Human Rights: International Relations Theory and the Commonwealth Caribbean Backlash against Human Rights Regimes. *Columbia Law Review* 2002, 102 (7): 1832–911.

[29] E.g., see K.J. Alter, Who Are the Masters of the Treaty?: European Governments and the European Court of Justice. *International Organization* 1998, 52 (1): 125–52; A. Nollkaemper, *National Courts and the International Rule of Law*. Oxford: Oxford University Press, 2011.

time and expense of ATJ litigation for private businesses, and enable Andean judges to be more responsive to requests for interpretive guidance from the IP agencies.

Meanwhile, as we explain Chapter 3, most national judges in the Andean Community at first resisted sending preliminary references to the Tribunal. Their opposition stemmed in part from a belief that their "independence and exclusive judicial function," to quote a decision of the Supreme Court of Peru, would be infringed by surrendering interpretive power to a tribunal outside the national judicial hierarchy.[30] However, the courts' resistance can also be attributed to the absence of jurist advocacy movements—groups of pro-integration attorneys, self-interested litigants, legal academics, and government officials who banded together to educate national judges about the Andean legal system and actively promote references to the ATJ in order to build integration through law.

The importance of jurist advocacy movements to the effectiveness of international adjudication is the second corrective insight offered by our study of the Andean Tribunal. As discussed in Chapter 9, the conventional explanation for the ECJ's success in building integration through law is the pursuit of self-interest by private litigants and judges. This explanation overlooks the crucial support that national Euro-law associations provided to the fledgling ECJ by providing test cases, serving as the ECJ's kitchen cabinet, building support for the ECJ's bold doctrinal moves, and creating an impression that integration was gaining acceptance in national legal orders.

The absence of similar jurist advocacy networks in the Andes helps to explain why sporadic efforts by pro-integration legal entrepreneurs to increase the ATJ's profile and influence never gained traction. The broader lesson is that future studies of why international adjudication succeeds or fails should look beyond the formal connections between national and international judges and the atomistic pursuit of self-interest by attorneys and litigants. Equally, if not more important, may be other public and private bodies—such as administrative agencies, national human rights institutions, bar associations, and social movement organizations—whose members mobilize, whether openly, behind the scenes, or both, to support or oppose international courts.

Judicial strategies for building the international rule of law in fraught environments

The ATJ created an island of effective international adjudication for intellectual property disputes in an environment that is fraught in at least three respects. First, Andean countries have experienced multiple waves of economic, political, and social instability since the Andean Pact's founding in 1969. The resulting turbulence has whipsawed Andean-level policies and led to a major overhaul of regional institutions in the 1990s. Second, Andean countries lack strong domestic rules of

[30] The Peruvian Supreme Court's decision is discussed in *Resolución* 771, General Secretariat Noncompliance *Decreto* No. 173-2003.

law or long-standing commitments to judicial independence. Laws and institutions on the books have often been ignored in practice, and executives in several states maintain tight control over judicial appointments and promotions. Third, progress in the Andean Community has faltered over the past decade. National political leaders remain bitterly divided over whether to continue Andean integration or dismantle it and pursue other regional cooperation projects.

Most observers would expect an international court faced with these unfavorable conditions to have little if any impact. Where political connections and corruption are endemic, individuals and firms are often dubious about invoking domestic legal rules and institutions, let alone placing their trust in a distant tribunal that oversees an unfamiliar legal system to which governments are only sporadically or half-heartedly committed. Yet these difficult conditions more closely resemble those confronting most international courts today—especially courts in developing countries that are modeled on the ECJ and ECtHR—than the far more supportive legal and political contexts in Europe on which many theories of international adjudication are based.

How do international judges operate in such challenging environments? The ATJ's experience suggests several plausible answers. First, the ATJ has developed interpretive techniques to avoid direct confrontation with political actors. For example, Chapter 4 discusses the *complemento indispensable* doctrine which the ATJ has applied to allow governments to set the pace and scope of Andean integration. When Andean law is unequivocal, the Tribunal will enforce it in full, but the ATJ allows the member states to legislate in areas not governed by Andean law as long as national legislation does not directly conflict with Andean *Decisiones.*

Second, the ATJ has built alliances with the IP legal community. Non-specialists generally view intellectual property as a complex and technical subject. Chapter 5 explains how intellectual property came to be regulated by Andean law, and why local IP stakeholders preferred to have Andean bodies interpret this law. Because national administrators and litigants repeatedly requested preliminary references of IP cases, the ATJ was able to elicit the support of national judges for such referrals. The Tribunal has maintained this support despite changes in national judicial systems and even as government enthusiasm for Andean integration has waned.

Third, the ATJ has occasionally benefitted from the efforts of judicial entrepreneurs. These rare individuals stepped out of a judge's traditional role to promote the Tribunal and cultivate a wider network of supporters. Chapter 7 discusses a number of judicial entrepreneurs who at different times generated cases for the ATJ or helped overcome judicial and political resistance to the Tribunal's rulings.

Our in-depth investigation of the ATJ's thirty-year history suggests that scholars who study other international courts should investigate other examples of facilitating or impeding circumstances and judicial entrepreneurship—combinations that can enhance or reduce a court's visibility, catalyze or impede the flow of cases, and augment or diminish the impact of its decisions. We return to this subject in Chapter 10, the book's conclusion, where we discuss the broader lessons of our study of the ATJ for the effectiveness of international courts more generally.

Defending regional IP laws that protect local values and interests

Intellectual property laws are usually adopted at the national level, influenced by the requirements of multilateral IP treaties and by pressure from countries with powerful IP industries, especially the United States and Europe. In the Andes, however, IP rules are collectively negotiated and adopted at the supranational level.[31] These Andean *Decisiones* have direct domestic effect, so that Andean IP law *is* national law. Chapter 5 explains how the ATJ and national IP agencies built an island of effective supranational adjudication. Of interest to scholars of intellectual property is how the ATJ–agency relationship has helped to develop and retain a distinct set of IP rules in the region.

As we explain in Chapter 5, Andean governments restructured national IP agencies as part of the neoliberal reforms of the "Washington Consensus." This restructuring also added consumer protection, competition, bankruptcy, and other market regulation subjects to the agencies' purview. In applying this wider mandate, the agencies sought to balance IP protection against other public values and policy goals. For example, Andean IP agencies worried that consumers may be confused by similar trademarks. They have thus adopted legal doctrines to avoid such confusion, including carefully scrutinizing coexistence agreements and claims that a mark is famous and thus protectable across the Community, and permitting the owner of a trademark registered in one Andean country to oppose an application by a third party to register a confusingly similar mark in another.[32] The agencies also assist indigenous communities and small and medium-size enterprises—actors often left out of the IP system—to protect their intellectual know-how using collective trademarks and distinctive signs.[33]

The IP rule-of-law island has also created an institutional space to resist powerful foreign interests that have put pressure on individual Andean governments to defect from regional IP legislation and adopt stronger IP protection standards. International IP treaties such as the WTO Agreement on Trade-Related Aspects of Intellectual Property Rights (TRIPS) permit ratifying states (especially developing countries) to tailor IP protection to other important societal objectives. The Andean countries have capitalized on the flexibility provisions in TRIPS by making a collective decision to limit IP protection—especially drug patents, pharmaceutical test data, and certain trademark rights—to promote public health, reduce local drug prices, and protect consumers.

When the United States, pharmaceutical firms, and some trademark owners put pressure on Andean officials to provide stronger IP protection than Andean law allows, the ATJ provided a hospitable forum for generic drug companies

[31] Governments can supplement Andean IP legislation with complementary national laws and regulations pursuant to the *complemento indispensable* doctrine, a topic explored in Chapter 4.

[32] B. Moller, Advantages of Andean trademark system from a Peruvian perspective, *Lexology* (October 28, 2014), available at <http://www.lexology.com/library/detail.aspx?g=46778d51-d30e-4739-aee1-ae6c6203cb69>.

[33] INDECOPI (Peru): The Promotion of Marks and Other Distinctive Signs to Compete in the Market, available at <http://www.wipo.int/sme/en/best_practices/peru.htm>.

and other opponents of such protection to challenge these efforts as contrary to regional rules. The backing of the ATJ also provided cover for domestic IP agencies and some national courts to reject arguments for expansive protection made by foreign IP rights holders. As a result of these developments, Andean law today retains limitations on patents and trademarks that many other developing countries have abandoned in the face of pressure from the United States and foreign IP industries. Our findings in Chapter 5 should thus be of particular interest to policy-makers and scholars interested in the ongoing contestations over international and domestic IP law.

A Roadmap of the Book

We began our collaboration ten years ago with a shared interest in understanding the ATJ's surprisingly high litigation rates and the predominance of intellectual property cases on the Tribunal's docket. This book consolidates, deepens, and augments our previously published studies with updated research, case coding, and interviews.

The Andean legal system continues to surprise us. Although the Community is undergoing a major crisis, the IP island of effective international adjudication has remained remarkably resilient—the total output of ATJ decisions has doubled, and the number of non-IP rulings has also increased. Our updated and expanded analysis thus raises an important new question: can an international court survive or even flourish when the states subject to its jurisdiction are questioning the very foundations of the legal integration enterprise that is the court's *raison d'être*?

Most of the chapters in this book began as freestanding articles, each of which explores a different aspect of the ATJ's origins, evolution, and survival. We edited our earlier publications, cross-referencing to material covered elsewhere in the book to avoid repetition. Where relevant, we updated the analysis to reflect developments occurring in the last seven years. Each chapter engages the legal and political science literature relevant to the questions posed in that chapter. We also added four new chapters, including this introduction. The roadmap below guides readers through the chapters, highlighting our updated and revised findings, and identifying areas for future research.

Chapter 2, Transplanting the European Court of Justice to the Andes, explains why national political leaders decided to add a court to the South American integration project. After considering a variety of options, governments chose to model the Andean Tribunal on the ECJ. However, they did not slavishly copy the ECJ's design features and legal doctrines. Instead, they selectively adapted those that were appropriate to the more sovereignty-protective Andean context, preserving greater state control over the Tribunal and its role in interpreting regional legislation. Chapter 2 explains why the member states came to see these original adaptations as undermining the effectiveness of the Andean legal system and why, in a 1996 Protocol to the Cartagena Agreement, they revised the

Tribunal to bring the ATJ's jurisdiction and access rules closer to those of its European predecessor.

Our theoretical objective in Chapter 2 is to explore systematically how the decision to copy and adapt the ECJ model affected the ATJ's subsequent trajectory. To achieve this goal, we engage with the literatures on legal transplants, neofunctionalism, and the global diffusion of ideas about European integration. We find the legal transplant literature to be the most useful, but we also explain how the politics of international judicial transplants differs from imports and exports of domestic legal institutions.

Chapter 3, The Andean Tribunal of Justice and its Interlocutors: Understanding Litigation Patterns in the Andean Community, presents data on national court interactions with the Andean Tribunal. We analyze case referral patterns from each of the five member states and discuss cross-country variations. We also explain the resistance of some national courts to referring cases and how that resistance was eventually overcome. Chapter 3 also highlights the fundamentally different nature of the ATJ's relationships with national judges as compared to the analogous relationships in the EC. In Europe, the symbiosis between the ECJ and national courts helped to build integration through law. In the Andes, effective international adjudication is mostly an island confined to intellectual property disputes. Domestic administrative agencies that review IP applications are the ATJ's primary interlocutors and compliance partners; national judges have remained largely passive intermediaries.

We significantly revised our previously published research to take account of developments after our analysis ended in 2007. The changes in the ensuing years are substantial: a doubling of national court references, a tripling of cases concerning legal issues other than intellectual property, and ATJ rulings that encourage references from new judicial and administrative interlocutors. We also expanded the scope of our investigation. Our original research focused on preliminary references. For this book we investigated whether private litigants challenged national laws via the Andean noncompliance procedure. We find considerable evidence to support this claim from our analysis of noncompliance cases. Chapter 6 further explores the interplay of preliminary ruling and noncompliance suits in politically fraught cases challenging national laws and policies that arguably violate Andean rules.

Chapter 4, The Divergent Jurisprudential Paths of the Andean Tribunal of Justice and the European Court of Justice, explains how the ATJ has significantly diverged from several foundational integration law doctrines developed by the ECJ. Our updated analysis discusses how the ATJ refined the *complemento indispensable* principle—a doctrine that permits national laws and regulations to implement and fill gaps in Andean *Decisiones*—to delineate the boundary between Community and national legal authority and to uphold the primacy of clear Andean rules. The ATJ has also asserted the supremacy of Andean law over conflicting bilateral and multilateral treaties, and has accepted preliminary references from administrative agencies and arbitral panels. In addition, the Tribunal has for the first time addressed human rights, stating, albeit in dictum, that governments must prioritize the socio-economic rights of Community citizens over free trade and integration rules.

Chapter 5, Islands of Effective International Adjudication: Constructing an Intellectual Property Rule of Law in the Andean Community, explains how the ATJ became both active and effective with respect to IP disputes, and why intellectual property remains an island of effective adjudication that has not expanded to other areas of Andean law. We describe the ATJ's interactions with the domestic administrative agencies responsible for intellectual property and explore how the Tribunal's rulings shaped agency decisions and procedures to bolster adherence to the rule of law.

Chapter 5 also documents how the relationship between Andean judges and agency officials enabled the Tribunal to confront national governments under pressure from the United States and multinational drug companies to violate Andean law. We demonstrate that Andean IP rules, especially those relating to pharmaceutical patents, differ from those elsewhere in Latin America due largely to the Tribunal's defense of public health and consumer protection and to political leaders' reluctance to interfere with the enforcement of ATJ judgments by the IP agencies. A new coda to this chapter explains how the legal and institutional contexts within which Andean IP rules are embedded help to bolster the island's stability and protect it from significant meddling by governments.

Chapter 6, The Judicialization of Andean Politics: Cigarettes, Alcohol, and Economic Hard Times, published here for the first time, offers a different lens through which to examine the law and politics of the ATJ. Whereas other chapters in the book systematically study different categories of Tribunal decisions or preliminary reference patterns, Chapter 6 follows the twists and turns of four politically and legally fraught disputes. These disputes were contentious in that they were linked to wider political fights among national leaders and Community officials, were carefully monitored by influential foreign actors, and had the potential to establish precedents with far reaching consequences for Andean integration.

As a group, the four cases show governments, interest groups, and litigants mixing adjudicatory and policy-making strategies in order to affect policy outcomes. We find that the ATJ protects itself by being faithful to laws on the books while policing good governance practices. However, the four disputes also reveal the ease with which member states respond to ATJ rulings by changing Andean secondary legislation. The Tribunal's preference, it seems, is to apply Andean rules as written and put the onus on member states to act collectively to change the law.

Chapter 7, The Authority of the Andean Tribunal of Justice in a Time of Regional Political Crisis, also new to this book, considers the geopolitical factors now threatening the Andean Community and how the ATJ has responded to this crisis. We also explain why the ATJ's IP island continues to thrive even as threats to the larger integration project loom larger. We then return to the Ecuador noncompliance dispute, introduced in Chapter 6, and consider how developments in the Andean integration process may affect the influence and power of the ATJ in the future.

Chapter 8, Nature or Nurture? Judicial Lawmaking in the European Court of Justice and the Andean Tribunal of Justice, explores a different issue raised by the ATJ's origins as a legal transplant: when do international judges engage in expansive judicial lawmaking? Although many scholars assert that international courts are hard-wired for self-aggrandizement, our comparative study of the ATJ and the ECJ reveals that the political contexts in which courts are embedded are critical to how expansively they interpret their authority. Chapter 8 develops the Andean Community analogue to Joseph Weiler's famous account of the ECJ's transformation of Europe.[34] We explore how variations in political support for integration over time have influenced lawmaking by international judges in the Andes and in Europe. We focus in particular on the ATJ's refusal to follow the ECJ in transforming the Andean Community's founding treaty, the Cartagena Agreement, into a constitutional blueprint for regional integration.

When first published as a journal article, this chapter ended with a conjecture about the ATJ's future as the political consensus supporting Andean integration had begun to unravel. Seven years of additional data allow us to explore how the ATJ has fared during the decade following Venezuela's withdrawal from the Community and the ensuing schism between the remaining four member states. We explore examples of lawmaking in the crisis period that could develop into or come to be seen as expansionist lawmaking. We find that over the last decade of crisis, the Tribunal has mostly stayed the course it charted during the heyday of regional integration. It has continued to enforce regional rules that reveal member states' intent to create common Andean policies and eliminate or restrict national regulations. And it has confined its bolder pronouncements to non-binding dicta that plant a seed for potential doctrinal growth in the future without imposing contemporary restrictions on governments.

Chapter 9, Jurist Advocacy Movements in Europe and the Andes, builds upon Chapter 8's insight that not all international courts are expansionist by nature. We use a socio-legal method of analysis, examining the actions and behavior of legal entrepreneurs and Euro-law associations to document the nurturing that lay behind the ECJ's legal revolution. Our analysis finds that lawyers in both Europe and the Andes migrate across legal roles, helping to draft legislation as members of supranational institutions, litigating cases as cause lawyers or when representing private litigants, serving as sympathetic national judges, and acting as academic commentators to help to amplify the impact of judicial rulings.

While legal entrepreneurs existed in both regions, we contrast the combined efforts of an extensive jurist advocacy movement Europe to the isolated and limited impact of legal entrepreneurs in the Andes, who are not part of a larger advocacy network. We argue that expansive judicial lawmaking requires careful nurturing by jurist advocacy movements—groups of sympathetic judges, attorneys, academics, and government officials united by a political objective that is greater than any one actor. Jurist advocacy movements encourage and facilitate lawmaking that promotes legal integration by vetting test cases, publicizing a court's doctrinal achievements, and contributing to the formation of a new legal field. Originally written by Karen Alter in order to reconsider her prior understanding of the ECJ's legal revolution,

[34] Weiler, 1991.

this chapter's revised analysis offers a more general treatment of the role and functions of jurist advocacy movements for effective international adjudication.

Chapter 10, Reconsidering What Makes International Courts Effective, revisits the arguments and predictions in Toward a Theory of Effective Supranational Adjudication, Helfer's groundbreaking 1997 study, with Anne-Marie Slaughter, of the ECtHR and ECJ.[35] Many scholars continue to assert that the large caseloads and generally high compliance rates of the two European tribunals are a product of values shared by Europe's liberal democracies, including their commitment to the rule of law, the protection of individual rights, and a history of addressing common problems through international institutions.[36]

The nearly two decades of international adjudication that followed the publication of Helfer and Slaughter's article reveal that this claim is incomplete in at least two respects. First, the ECtHR and ECJ are facing new challenges to their authority by national executives and national judges. This is true not only in countries, such as Russia and Hungary, where the rule of law and judicial independence are fragile and increasingly under threat, but also in long-standing democracies such as the United Kingdom. Second, and more relevant for this book, international courts are beginning to function in developing countries and in regions of the world where Helfer and Slaughter expected they would have difficulty doing so.

The Andean Tribunal is the oldest, most active, and in some respects the most successful regional court operating outside of Europe. Yet as this book reveals, the ATJ's ability to induce member states to respect Andean law has significant limits. We find the Tribunal to be bold, legally innovative, influential, and effective within an island of IP law where the ATJ enjoys the active support of lawyers and administrative agencies and the tacit support of national judges. The flourishing of this island reveals that establishing an international court in a developing country context does not per se hinder the efficacy of international adjudication. Beyond the domain of IP law, however, the ATJ is limited by its lack of compliance partners and by significant economic and political turbulence. Yet Andean judges still demand that states respect clear Community law, even where there are no compliance partners to ensure respect for its rulings, and even if member states then respond by changing Andean law or withdrawing from the regional integration project.

The balance among these competing forces involves letting member states set the scope and pace of Andean integration, including by revising and retrenching Andean rules to fit political realities. The ATJ also allows states to suspend core legal commitments in response to economic crises, so long as governments follow proper legal procedures and convince either the Andean General Secretariat or the other member states to sanction a temporary derogation from regional free trade rules.

[35] Helfer and Slaughter, 1997.

[36] E.A. Posner and J.C. Yoo, A Theory of International Adjudication. *California Law Review* 2005, 93 (1): 1–72.

This give-and-take between political and legal actors breaks down, however, when member states are deeply divided and thus unable to act collectively. In Europe, the ECJ used these moments to promote integration through law. In the Andes, however, the ATJ's involvement may actually exacerbate conflicts by reducing the possibility for quiet noncompliance as a political safety valve. This is the situation that the ATJ currently faces, a reality that potentially threatens the future of the Tribunal and of the Andean integration project more generally.

2

Transplanting the European Court of Justice to the Andes

with Osvaldo Saldías[†]

This chapter contextualizes the decision to create a court for the Andean Pact modeled on the European Court of Justice (ECJ) by exploring what governments expected a regional court to add to the Andean integration process. The European Community (EC) invented the model of a regional integration court, breaking from the tradition of international tribunals as arbiters of solely interstate disputes. The policy-makers involved in creating the Andean Pact did not, however, see a need for an ECJ-style court. This chapter explains the reasons underpinning their later decision to add a such court to the Andean integration project, and why the EC model was seen as especially attractive. We situate this analysis within a discussion of the literature on legal transplants, constructing a dialogue between this literature, neofunctionalist theory, which considers how functional interests generated a political demand for European legal institutions, and scholarship on the emulation and diffusion of European ideas.

In the 1950s, in the wake of a devastating world war, European countries began a process of pooling sovereignty collectively to rebuild their societies. This process—which involved the creation of supranational institutions to promote economic, legal, and political integration—soon attracted new adherents. Beginning in the 1960s, other governments around the world emulated Europe's model of regional integration, proposing common markets and copying EC institutions.

From its inception, the EC included a court of justice, but early replications of European integration did not.[1] Although these regional integration projects did not live up to the aspirations of their proponents, few attributed their failure to the lack

† Senior Research Fellow, Humboldt University of Berlin. Author of *The Judicial Politics of Economic Integration: The Andean Court as an Engine of Development*. New York, NY: Routledge, 2013.

[1] The Benelux system is a partial exception. Belgium, The Netherlands, and Luxembourg created a customs union in 1947, without a court. When all three countries joined the EC, they continued their union to coordinate regulations in areas not covered by the EC. In 1965, the member states adopted the treaty establishing a Benelux Court of Justice, although the court was not created until 1975. K.J. Alter, *Establishing the Supremacy of European Law: The Making of an International Rule of Law in Europe*. Oxford: Oxford University Press, 2001, 11–27.

Transplanting International Courts: The Law and Politics of the Andean Tribunal of Justice. First Edition. Karen J. Alter and Laurence R. Helfer. © Karen J. Alter and Laurence R. Helfer 2017. Published 2017 by Oxford University Press.

of a supranational judicial body. Rather, scholars stressed the absence of economic and political preconditions required for regional integration to succeed.[2]

The inattention given to supranational judicial systems in the 1960s and early 1970s reflected the limited role that the ECJ played in advancing European integration. The ECJ made doctrinally important rulings during these years, but it refrained from applying those rulings in ways that provoked controversy. As a result, ECJ case law was of greater legal than political significance.

Politicians, practitioners, and scholars began to pay more attention to the ECJ in the late 1970s, when the court's rulings began to dismantle national barriers to the free movement of goods, capital, labor, and services. These actors came to view the ECJ as an engine to help overcome political blockages and to build integration through law.[3] Observers also credited the ECJ's alliance with national courts as the reason for member states' increasing respect for EC rules and for coordinated interpretations of common EC rules across borders. When critics began to question the EC's political accountability and democratic legitimacy, proponents of integration responded by citing the ECJ's key role in upholding the rule of law. The court ensured that Europe's supranational administrative institutions faced legal checks, just as did domestic administrative bodies, and its review of the validity of EC legislation further bolstered the accountability of European institutions, even if some claimed that the ECJ was biased in favor of Community over state interests.

The ECJ's increasingly important role in promoting European integration eventually led other regional integration systems to establish their own supranational courts. The Andean Pact was one of the first regional integration systems to add a court, a move which has been subsequently followed by a number of other systems.[4] The original Andean Pact provided for the adoption of regional legislation that was directly applicable within member states, but it lacked a judicial body to interpret or help enforce those rules. By the late 1970s, member states began to draft a treaty to create a supranational court. In 1984 they created the Andean Tribunal of Justice (ATJ or Tribunal), explicitly modeling its design on the ECJ. Initially the Tribunal received few cases. Chapter 3 documents how the ATJ's docket has grown over time to the point that the ATJ is the third most active international court today based on number of decisions issued (after the ECJ and the European Court of Human Rights).[5]

[2] J.S. Nye, Comparing Common Markets: A Revised Neofunctionalist Model. *International Organization* 1971, 24 (4): 796–835; W. Mattli, *The Logic of Regional Integration*. Cambridge: Cambridge University Press, 1999; P. Schmitter, A Revised Theory of European Integration. *International Organization* 1970, 24 (4): 836–68.

[3] J. Weiler, The Transformation of Europe. *Yale Law Journal* 1991, 100 (8): 2403–83; A. Stone Sweet, *The Judicial Construction of Europe*. Oxford: Oxford University Press, 2004; R. Cichowski, *The European Court and Civil Society: Litigation, Mobilization and Governance*. Cambridge: Cambridge University Press, 2007; M.P. Maduro, *We the Court: The European Court of Justice and the European Economic Constitution*. Oxford: Hart Publishers, 1998.

[4] For more on ECJ copies, see K.J. Alter, The Global Spread of European Style International Courts. *West European Politics* 2012, 35 (1): 135–54.

[5] K.J. Alter, *The New Terrain of International Law: Courts, Politics, Rights*. Princeton, NJ: Princeton University Press, 2014, 72–5.

In the 1990s, the end of the Cold War, the rise of the Washington Consensus,[6] and the creation of the World Trade Organization spawned a new wave of regional integration. This wave incorporated supranational judicial institutions that had proved to be so important to advancing integration in Europe.[7] There are now eleven operational international courts closely modeled on the ECJ. Eight of these courts replicate the ECJ's noncompliance procedure that authorizes the Secretariat, member states, and sometimes private litigants to challenge national policies that conflict with Community rules, and eight replicate the preliminary reference mechanism that allows, and sometimes requires, national courts to suspend legal proceedings and send questions of interpretation of Community law to the supranational court.[8]

Transplanting European laws and legal institutions to other areas around the world is hardly a new phenomenon. Many legal systems incorporate transplants from France, Britain, Germany, Spain, and the Scandinavian countries.[9] This chapter explores a different and under-studied issue: the consequences of copying a European supranational judicial institution. Specifically, we ask two related questions: how did the existence of the ECJ influence the ATJ's founding, and how, if at all, has the ECJ's experience—its doctrinal innovations and the responses of litigants and governments to watershed rulings—shaped the ATJ's trajectory?

We first summarize and synthesize the literature on legal transplants, regional integration, and the diffusion of ideas in order to provide a framework for examining how transplanting supranational judicial institutions shapes the trajectory of the transplanted copies. We then explain why Andean Community member states decided to emulate the ECJ, and investigate adaptations that Andean leaders made as they considered the ECJ's track record.

Subsequent chapters analyze the ATJ's operation as a legal transplant. Chapter 3 examines the activation of the Andean preliminary ruling system. Chapter 4 identifies a number of areas where the ATJ chose to diverge from the ECJ's jurisprudential path. Chapters 8 and 9 explain why the ATJ has not followed the ECJ's strategy of becoming an engine for European legal integration, first examining how the ATJ responded to shifting support from political leaders, and then investigating why

[6] The "Washington Consensus" was the term coined by John Williamson to encompass a package of reforms advocated by a set of Washington-based institutions, including the World Bank and the International Monetary Fund. Originally the term applied to a specific set of policies, but now it is used to denote the neoliberal economic reform agenda of pro-market economists and policy-makers. J. Williamson, What Washington Means by Policy Reform. In: *Latin American Adjustment: How Much Has Happened.* J. Williamson (ed.), 5–20. Washington, DC: Institute for International Economics, 1990.

[7] Alter, 2014 at Chapter 3.

[8] Ibid., 92. The copies are discussed in more detail in Alter, 2012. The numbers here are slightly different to reflect the transformation of the SADC Tribunal from an ECJ-style international court to an interstate tribunal.

[9] D. Berkowitz, K. Pistor, and J-F. Richard, The Transplant Effect. *American Journal of Comparative Law* 2003, 51: 163–203; W. Jacoby, *Imitation and Politics: Redesigning Modern Germany*. Ithaca, NY: Cornell University Press, 2000; W. Jacoby, Inspiration, Coalition and Substitution: External Influences on Postcommunist Transformations. *World Politics* 2006, 58 (4): 623–51.

legal communities failed to coalesce in support of the Tribunal as a promoter of Andean integration.

Our analysis reveals several key findings. First, mimicry is the principal mode through which the ECJ model was diffused. Second, court copying is selective rather than wholesale. Considering the slow political embrace of the ATJ after its founding—and its eventual success relative to that of other Community courts—we argue that adapting a regional court to local legal and political contexts is likely to be necessary for a successful transplantation. Third, we find that copying brings many benefits in the form of expertise and material assistance from exporting countries. A fourth conclusion follows from our overall comparison of the two institutions: importing a supranational court does not necessarily copy the institution's politics and the evolution of its legal doctrines. Specifically, we find that states can import an ECJ-style court without replicating its penchant for judicial lawmaking, an issue we explore further in Chapter 8.

Transplanting, Emulating, or Appropriating: The Diffusion of Supranational Legal Institutions

How do institutions diffuse around the world? When do borrowed institutions thrive in new contexts? These questions have long interested practitioners and scholars.[10] This section summarizes and synthesizes three distinct lines of scholarship that focus on the legal dimensions of the diffusion question—literatures on legal transplants, neofunctionalist theory, and the spread of European ideas and institutions. These bodies of scholarship generate distinct expectations about how regional integration institutions, transplanted or otherwise, become intrinsic parts of a local integration project. Putting these fields into conversation with one another generates new expectations that our study of the Andean experience confirms.

Insights from the literature on legal transplants

Legal transplants have a long lineage dating back at least as far as the Roman Empire. The concept of a "legal transplant" is primarily a metaphor.[11] In medicine, transplants replace damaged body parts, with the hope that the body will be fooled into thinking the transplant is original. For legal transplants, in contrast, the foreign nature of the transplant is precisely the attraction. Legal transplants often seek to emulate best practices or to import "foreignness" into a context where actors who favor importation have lost confidence in existing laws and institutions.

[10] The literature is vast. For an overview see E.R. Graham, C.R. Shipan, and C. Volden, The Diffusion of Policy Diffusion Research in Political Science. *British Journal of Political Science* 2013, 43 (3): 673–701; Jacoby, 2006.

[11] D. Nelken and J. Feest, *Adapting Legal Cultures*. Portland, OR: Hart Publishing, 2001.

Scholars who study transplants recognize that the transplant analogy is imprecise in another way. Nearly all contemporary legal systems consist of some amalgam of indigenously generated laws, imported legal traditions, and laws and institutions that emulate global practices or practices in other countries. As a result, it is increasingly difficult to distinguish transplanted from homegrown laws and legal systems.[12]

Commentators are also troubled by the claim that transplanting foreign institutions improves local practices, an idea sometimes associated with colonialism and imperialism. In the nineteenth century, European governments transplanted their institutions to help "civilize" the populations they colonized. Following the Second World War, the United States transplanted its own institutions around the world, including constitutional review, elections, and business associations. The end of the Cold War ushered in a period of economic liberalism and a renewed enthusiasm for legal transplants by international institutions such as the International Monetary Fund and World Bank. This recent penchant for exporting model laws and institutions has been especially controversial where its proponents asserted the superiority of the Western industrial model of market regulation and common law national legal systems.[13]

Notwithstanding these persistent critiques, scholars and policy-makers have continued to explore when and how transplanting laws and legal institutions changes the behavior and politics of the actors at the site of the transplant. Their studies suggest a number of conclusions. First, transplants are more likely to succeed when law is transplanted within the same legal family because, as Alan Watson explains, the success of a transplant will depend on its ability to graft onto existing legal norms and practices.[14]

Second, transplants not adapted to local contexts are unlikely to be effective. Daniel Berkowitz, Katharnia Pistor, and Jean-Francois Richard argue that legal transplants succeed only where they respond to local demand and where they are adapted to local needs. In the absence of these conditions, the authors observe a "transplant effect"—a formal copying of rules that creates a "mismatch between preexisting conditions and institutions and the transplanted law, which weakens the effectiveness of the imported legal order."[15] Their key insight is that, in the absence of local demand and adaptation, transplanted legal rules and institutions that look the same on paper are often ignored in practice.

Third, the act of creating and diffusing laws or legal institutions may itself shape understanding of the transplant such that what is actually transplanted is not a true copy but instead reflects the normative preferences of transplant advocates. Original laws and institutions are revised through conversations about the rationales for and

[12] P. Legrand, What Legal Transplants? In: Nelken and Feest, 2001, 55–69.
[13] E.g., R. La Porta, F. Lopez-de-Silanes, A. Shleifer, and R.W. Vishny, Law and Finance. *Journal of Political Economy* 1998, 106 (6): 1113–55.
[14] A. Watson, Legal Transplants and Law Reform. *Law Quarterly Review* 1976, 97: 79–84.
[15] Berkowitz, Pistor, and Richard, 2003 at 171.

objectives of the transplant. This recasts imported legal rules through selected invocations and stylized interpretations of the prototype.[16]

These insights apply to supranational transplants in distinctive ways. For example, the finding about legal families helps to explain why common market legal systems are especially likely to emulate the ECJ. Architects of these systems select from a menu of existing laws and institutions. For international economic law, there are two dominant models: the dispute resolution system of the General Agreement on Tariffs and Trade (GATT), later subsumed by the World Trade Organization (WTO), and the EC's supranational judicial system.

The WTO model relies on states to file complaints, which are reviewed by ad hoc panels whose decisions can be appealed to a standing Appellate Body. The WTO also uses a system of reciprocal sanctions to enforce these decisions. Complaining states that prove violations of WTO obligations can raise tariffs on imports from violating countries in order to induce compliance.

In contrast, the EC model has four distinctive features not found in the WTO system:

1. *Directly applicable Community legal rules.* Supranational legislative bodies adopt legal rules that are directly applicable in domestic legal orders.
2. *A preliminary ruling mechanism.* National judges can refer to the supranational court questions of interpretation regarding Community rules.
3. *Challenges to the validity of decisions and actions of supranational institutions.* Both private actors and states can challenge the validity of supranational legal rules, and private actors can challenge administrative decisions that directly affect them.
4. *Noncompliance procedures allow nonstate actors to challenge state actions that violate Community rules.* A supranational body investigates allegations of noncompliance and files complaints with the supranational court.

ECJ transplants need not copy all four of these design features. They can also choose features from both the ECJ and WTO models selectively. Most ECJ emulators in fact copy at least three of these features, albeit with some variations.[17] As we next explain, the ATJ includes all four features, adds a WTO-like system of reciprocal sanctions, and includes other adaptations of the ECJ's design.

From this literature we take the following lines of inquiry. First, we investigate the channels, agents, and mechanisms involved in diffusing the ECJ model. Second, we explain how the ECJ's experience shaped adaptations of the model in the Andean context. Third, we explore the limitations and challenges of supranational legal transplants in general. Before turning to this analysis, we first review how the literature on transplants of legal institutions intersects with theoretical debates about the dynamics of legal integration and the literature on the diffusion of European ideas.

[16] M. Graziadei, Legal Transplants and the Frontiers of Legal Knowledge. *Theoretical Inquiries in Law* 2009, 10 (2): 723–43.

[17] Alter, 2012.

Insights from the literature on neofunctionalist theory and supranational integration

The success of European integration led early supporters to develop neofunctionalism, an institution-based theory of political process, to predict the evolution of all regional integration projects. Proponents believed that supranational institutions would forge alliances with substate actors to address common functional problems whose solution would propel integration forward. In the 1960s, adherents of neofunctionalism predicted that regional integration would become a global phenomenon. Ernst Haas, the theory's most prominent advocate, recognized that the success of European integration was unusual, in that EC member countries were economically advanced and ideologically similar. But he and other neofunctionalist scholars nonetheless expected regional integration processes to develop elsewhere in the world and yield similar economic and political outcomes.[18]

By the 1970s, however, neofunctionalists had thoroughly repudiated the theory and candidly acknowledged its many shortcomings. First, the theory failed to predict the trajectory of regional integration in other locales. Second, even in Europe the theory did not apply as expected. The dynamism of the integration process proved to be fragile and subject to political turbulences that slowed forward momentum. The sharp discrepancies between theoretical predictions and empirical reality led Haas to declare neofunctionalism to be "obsolescent."[19] Ever since, most political scientists have shied away from invoking the theory.[20]

Neofunctionalism is, however, very much alive as a theory of legal integration. The theory was resurrected by Anne-Marie Slaughter (then Burley) and Walter Mattli, who argued that Haas had accurately predicted how legal (rather than political) integration evolves.[21] Slaughter and Mattli observed that the structure of the European system allowed legal integration to proceed via alliances between supranational and subnational actors who worked together to promote their mutual self-interest. The authors predicted that EC law would inevitably spill into new legal domains as litigants realized that ECJ precedents could apply to a broad range of issues. Slaughter and Mattli also argued that law could more easily be shielded from political opposition, and they observed that the ECJ frequently sought to "upgrade the common interest" by linking individual cases to larger Community objectives.

[18] E.B. Haas, International Integration: The European and the Universal Process. *International Organization* 1961, 15 (3): 366–92; E.B. Haas, The Study of Regional Integration: Reflections on the Joy and Anguish of Pretheorizing. *International Organization* 1970, 24 (4): 607–46.

[19] E.B. Haas, *The Obsolescence of Regional Integration Theory*. Berkeley, CA: University of California Press, 1975.

[20] For a discussion of the rise and fall of neofunctionalist theory, see J. Caporaso and J. Keeler, The European Union and Regional Integration Theory. In: *The State of the European Union*. C. Rhodes and S. Mazey (eds), 29–62. Boulder, CO: Lynne Rienner/Longmann, 1995. A new introduction added to Haas' rereleased classic, *Beyond the Nation State*, explores how Haas' neofunctionlism inspired contemporary political science theories. E.B. Haas, *Beyond the Nation State Functionalism and International Organization*. Colchester: ECPR Press, 2008.

[21] A.-M. Burley and W. Mattli, Europe before the Court. *International Organization* 1993, 47 (1): 41–76.

In short, the expansion and penetration of supranational law into national legal orders followed the political dynamics Haas expected: alliances between supranational and subnational actors, spillovers, and the enhancement of common interests.

Alec Stone Sweet later extended these insights, linking neofunctionalism to a theory of how international courts contribute to the creation of law. Stone Sweet argued that a general dynamic emerges in the presence of both economic rules that promote intra-Community trade and of a legal system open to self-interested actors. Where these conditions exist, economic self-interest leads litigants to invoke international economic law before supranational judicial bodies. Since law is inevitably incomplete, courts will be drawn into developing it. The result is the construction of new legal rules, which lead to new cases, which create additional opportunities for litigation and expansion of the law. Stone Sweet's theory does not require embracing the teleology advanced by Haas; it accepts that politicians can revise legal rules and thereby redirect the integration trajectory. But the theory suggests that such interventions will be rare and that courts will, over time, expand the scope and reach of the law.[22]

Stone Sweet views law, trade, and litigation as creating virtuous circles of law generation. However, the relationship among these three elements is under-specified. In particular, it is unclear whether bottom-up economic interests generate demand for international legal rules—so that both governments and courts primarily respond to the self-interest of firms—or, conversely, whether a top-down political commitment to integration drives firms to invest in cross-border production and trade and to litigate when rules are ambiguous. The issue of whether bottom-up demand or top-down policy choices drive legal integration goes to the heart of the debates about legal transplants. The transplant literature suggests that importing foreign laws and institutions is insufficient to stimulate local demand, to signal a credible commitment by governments, or to give domestic actors a stake in implementing or enforcing legal rules. To the contrary, the transplanted nature of foreign laws and institutions—especially those seen as externally imposed—may signal that national political commitment is lacking.

The legal transplants literature thus homes in on a key challenge that derailed Haas' neofunctionalist theory: how to create local demand for transplanted institutions and laws. Neofunctionalism cannot answer this question because it is based on the same contested assumptions that guided policy-oriented enthusiasts of legal transplants during the period of the Washington Consensus. Even shedding the teleology of early neofunctionalism, the theory retains an expectation that transplanted free market rules and institutions will trigger economic actors to trade, invest, and litigate. Mattli, Slaughter, and Stone Sweet added a legal dimension to this equation, drawing attention to the importance of litigation as a tool for spurring market-integrating lawmaking and judicial precedent as a mechanism of policy spillover. Yet self-interest remains the under-specified engine of this theoretical

[22] A. Stone Sweet, Judicialization and the Construction of Governance. *Comparative Political Studies* 1999, 32 (2): 147–84.

apparatus. It is far from clear, however, why local litigants, scholars, and judges would embrace transplanted rules, let alone view their respective self-interests as aligning with regional integration initiatives. We return to this issue in Chapter 9, which discusses the ideological motivations of jurist advocacy movements.

Insights from the literature on the diffusion of European ideas

Supranational transplants also provide evidence to assess theories of how ideas, policies, and institutions diffuse across borders. Scholars who advance such theories are interested in the mechanisms of diffusion and the resulting transformation of politics and identities. Tanja Börzel and Thomas Risse identify five such mechanisms: (1) exporters of ideas and institutions can use legal, economic, or physical coercion; (2) exporters can manipulate the utility calculations of political elites, for example by conferring or withholding inducements; (3) exporters can socialize importers, dispersing their ideas and institutions using normative pressure such that local actors internalize a foreign model; (4) supporters of external ideas and institutions can use persuasion, providing reasoned arguments that convince local actors to accept exported models; and (5) adopters may emulate, either by drawing lessons for themselves or by mimicking foreign models to reap benefits or send signals to external and internal actors.[23]

Risse and Börzel are primarily interested in the mechanisms of diffusing ideas about the European Union. They also suggest, however, that each mechanism shapes the extent to which a foreign import becomes domestically entrenched.[24] For example, the authors expect persuasion and socialization to have the greatest potential to transform the identities and interests of recipients. They see mimicry as reflecting an indirect influence by the ideational exporter, and they assert that political scientists know very little about how emulation works in practice.

The literature on legal transplants offers insights that help to refine these expectations. Berkowitz, Pistor, and Richard argue that the way in which local recipients receive the law will determine the success of the legal transplant. They expect that

> a voluntary transplant increases its own receptivity when it makes a significant adaptation of the foreign [model] to initial conditions, in particular to the preexisting formal and informal legal order. Changes in the transplanted rules or legal institutions indicate that the appropriateness of these rules has been considered and modifications were made to take into account domestic legal practice or other initial conditions.[25]

In other words, blind mimicry, or copying inspired by coercion and inducement, is likely to generate a "transplant effect" in which local actors resist transplanted ideas

[23] T.A. Börzel and T. Risse, *The Transformative Power of Europe: The European Union and the Diffusion of Ideas, Working Paper of the Kfg Nr. 1.* Berlin: Frei Universität Berlin, 2009.

[24] The mechanisms are also relevant to testing the claims of neofunctionalist theory. For example, if mimicry were the dominant mode of transplantation, it would cast doubt on whether there is an inherent logic of integration that arises when other regions copy the European model.

[25] Berkowitz, Pistor, and Richard, 2003 at 179.

and institutions. By contrast, the existence of local adaptations may indicate that importers are considering local needs and making adjustments that increase the likelihood of the transplant's success. We return to this debate in the conclusion to this chapter.

Copying the ECJ: Creating the Andean Tribunal of Justice

This section describes the transplantation of the European Community model to the Andes, including the eventual adoption of an ECJ-style court. In 1969, Chile, Bolivia, Colombia, Ecuador, and Peru agreed to create a common market to spur regional economic growth.[26] The five Andean member countries did not trade extensively with each other, but they hoped that a regional market would attract foreign capital, increase each state's negotiating leverage with other nations, and induce investors to keep profits in the region.[27] Andean leaders adopted the European integration model but used it to achieve different substantive goals. Whereas Europe initially focused on market liberalization and support for the coal, steel, and agriculture industries, Andean governments promoted a policy of import substitution that sought to lesson dependency on foreign markets, build manufacturing sectors to take advantage of local capabilities, and diminish economic disparities across the region.[28]

The Andean Pact's policies never had much impact, however. National governments assumed that an influx of foreign capital would provide the funds needed for economic development. Few businesses, however, wanted to build factories in remote areas lacking in infrastructure and political stability. These systemic impediments to investment were compounded by heavy-handed legal regulation. For example, the first Andean investment code, *Decisión* 24, permitted foreign firms to repatriate only 14% of their profits, required investors to issue licenses to domestic firms, and mandated the transfer of technologies protected by intellectual property into the region.[29]

The controversies surrounding import substitution defined the Andean Pact, shaping its political structure, its policies, and ultimately its early failure. Regulations such as *Decisión* 24 were nominally binding but were honored mostly in the breach. Frequent changes of government and a dearth of foreign investment also sapped the political will for integration.[30]

[26] F.-V. García Amador, *The Andean Legal Order: A New Community of Law.* Dobbs Ferry, NY: Oceana Publications, 1978, 105.

[27] W.P. Avery and J.D. Cochraine, Innovation in Latin American Regionalism: The Andean Common Market. *International Organization* 1973, 27 (2): 198–9.

[28] S. Horton, Peru and Ancom: A Study in the Disintegration of a Common Market. *Texas International Law Journal* 1982, 17, 40–1.

[29] Ibid., at 44–50. For an analysis of the controversies that *Decisión* 24 engendered, see D.E. Hojman, The Andean Pact: Failure of a Model of Integration? *Journal of Common Market Studies* 1981, 20 (2): 139–60, 151–6.

[30] J.E. Adams, A New Andean Agreement: Rules of Origin Replace the Investment Code. *Arizona Journal of International and Comparative Law* 1994, 11: 389–427, 401–5.

In terms of institutions, the Andean Pact's founding treaty, the Cartagena Agreement, largely copied those of the EC. It established a supranational governance structure that included a *Comisión* of national executives to adopt Andean secondary legislation (referred to in Spanish as "*Decisiones*") and a regional administrative body (the "*Junta*") that supervised their implementation. The original Andean Pact did not include a court, and *Decisiones* did not have direct domestic effect. According to David Padilla, most Latin American trade agreements in the 1970s lacked legalized dispute resolution bodies, an omission he attributes to the fact that economists—the chief negotiators of these treaties—were wary of "legalism" and feared that formal adjudication mechanisms would engender litigation by politically conservative lawyers.[31] Why, then, did Andean governments eventually decide to create the ATJ?

The decision to create the Andean Tribunal of Justice

From the Andean Pact's inception, governments believed that they possessed the authority to implement the Cartagena Agreement via presidential decrees, and they used such decrees to bring the treaty into force.[32] This route had the advantage of avoiding national parliaments, in which fractious political parties might attempt to block or revise implementing legislation.[33] However, the approach engendered opposition from business elites, who disliked the Andean Pact's import substitution policies and invoked the failure to submit the treaty to national parliaments to challenge its validity. These efforts to derail the integration process through litigation ultimately failed. The manner in which governments responded to these challenges, however, suggested that Andean law would not be given domestic effect—a prospect that acted as a catalyst for national political leaders to create a supranational court.

Business elites filed a key lawsuit in Colombia in 1971. The country's Supreme Court dismissed the suit, invoking a long-standing doctrine that disallows invalidation on procedural grounds of treaties adopted in good faith.[34] But the ruling applied only to the Cartagena Agreement itself, implicitly suggesting that Andean *Decisiones* needed parliamentary approval to be valid in Colombia.[35] The court's ruling also included an integration-friendly dissenting opinion, which intimated that the concerns about Andean secondary legislation would be alleviated if there were an Andean tribunal to hear challenges to that legislation.

[31] D. Padilla, The Judicial Resolution of Legal Disputes in the Integration Movements of the Hemisphere. *Lawyers of the Americas* 1979, 11 (1): 75–95.

[32] In Colombia, *Decreto* No. 1245 of August 8, 1969; in Chile, *Decreto* No. 428 of July 30, 1969; in Peru, *Decreto* No. 17.851 of October 14, 1969; in Ecuador, *Decreto* No. 1932, October 24, 1969; and Bolivia, *Decreto* No. 08985, November 6, 1969.

[33] Avery and Cochraine, 1973, 198.

[34] Colombian Supreme Court, ruling of July 26, 1971, published in *Derecho de la Integración* No. 10, 160–80.

[35] F. Orrego Vicuña, La Incorporación del Ordenamiento Jurídico Subregional al Derecho Interno: Análisis de la Práctica y Jurisprudencia de Colombia. *Derecho de la Integración* 1972, 52: 52.

One year later, businesses opposed to the Andean Pact filed a second suit in the Colombian Supreme Court. This time they challenged the Andean investment code, whose strict limits on repatriation of profits galled pro-free market businesses and politicians in the region.[36] The lawsuit argued that the Colombian Constitution prohibited implementing the investment code by presidential decree. Applying the logic of its earlier ruling, the Supreme Court agreed, holding that the code could only be implemented by the parliament.

The Colombian rulings made clear the cost of not having a supranational court. If national courts could invalidate Presidential decrees implementing *Decisiones*, Andean rules and the Andean integration process could be undermined by rear-guard domestic litigation. The solution that the leaders later adopted—making Andean rules supreme and directly applicable, but also reviewable by an Andean tribunal—was intended to avoid this problem by providing a designated judicial venue for challenging Andean laws, thereby helping national executives to achieve their collective goals despite political opposition at home.

Proponents of an Andean court regularly invoked the two Colombian rulings when advocating for the creation of a supranational judicial review mechanism.[37] The *Junta* itself also referred to the Colombian rulings when discussing the benefits of revising the Andean legal system. In 1972, six months after the second Colombian ruling, the *Comisión* announced its support for a tribunal. The *Comisión* directed the *Junta* to produce a report on the "necessity to create a court" for the region.[38] The question of what type of court remained open, however.

The choice of the ECJ model

When Andean officials discussed creating a supranational court, several potential models were available for their consideration. The officials could have emulated an early regional tribunal, the Central American Court of Justice, which heard ten cases between 1907 and 1917 before its founding treaty expired, or they could have embraced the GATT dispute settlement system (which at the time allowed member states to block cases from proceeding). In addition, emulating the GATT would not have established the direct effect of Andean *Decisiones* nor created a mechanism for supranational judicial review of Andean institutions and their actions. Without such review, national courts might continue to challenge the authority of Community law or interpret Andean rules in inconsistent ways. A third alternative—the ECJ—was the most obvious fit given the pre-existing similarities between other Andean and European institutions. The selection of the ECJ was all but assured when the *Junta* asked the Institute for the Integration of Latin America and the Caribbean (INTAL) to evaluate the best model for the Andean Pact.

[36] L.W. Thomas, The Colombian Supreme Court Decision on the Andean Foreign Investment Code and Its Implications for the Law of Treaties. *Journal of International Law and Economics* 1973, 113–28.

[37] O. Saldías, *The Judicial Politics of Economic Integration: The Andean Court as an Engine of Development*. New York, NY: Routledge, 2013, 75–6.

[38] *Sexto Período de Sesiones Extraordinarias, Acta Final*, December 9–18, 1971, Lima, Peru.

INTAL is a research center established by the Inter-American Development Bank in 1965 with the mission of promoting and consolidating regional integration.[39] Its network of consultants—many of whom are part-time scholars—provides technical assistance to implement and enforce integration policies. INTAL served as a conveyer belt for the transmission of European ideas into conversations about integration in Latin America. At the time, many INTAL consultants had been educated and trained in European universities, and they continued to attend pro-integration academic events in Europe. A few had even worked with major European integration scholars such as Ernst Haas. Through these connections, INTAL members were socialized to support integration initiatives. They distributed pro-integration ideas in Latin American through three publications: *Revista Integración Latinoamericana, Derecho de la Integración*, and *Serie Publicaciones INTAL*.

The INTAL network recommended bundling the creation of an ECJ-style tribunal together with foundational ECJ doctrines establishing the direct effect and supremacy of Community law in national legal orders. By incorporating these legal doctrines into its recommendation for an ECJ-style court, INTAL also implicitly endorsed the ECJ's view that the Treaty of Rome is a constitutional document that private actors can draw upon to promote regional integration. The unstated inference was that the Cartagena Agreement should be imbued with a similar constitutional status.

INTAL's recommendations were an important influence on the creation of the ATJ. In June 1972, the *Junta* convened a Meeting of Experts that included INTAL consultants, Professor Gerard Olivier (the Assistant Director General of EC Legal Services), and ECJ Judge Pierre Pescatore. Following this meeting, the *Junta* prepared a draft of a treaty establishing the ATJ. Member state representatives discussed the draft in November 1972, and in December a joint *Junta*–INTAL working group presented a proposal to the *Comisión*.[40] The proposal focused on two key requirements—the doctrines of supremacy and direct effect, and a supranational mechanism to review the legality of Community acts. Copying the ECJ's preliminary reference procedure achieved both of these goals. It created a regional judicial body to review Andean rules, to ensure their uniform interpretation by national judges, and to "reduce unnecessary and sometimes disproportionate political tensions" with those judges—an implicit reference to the Colombian Supreme Court rulings.[41]

Applying the literature on transplants reviewed earlier in this chapter, one can say that the *Junta* and INTAL chose the ECJ model based on a combination of persuasion and socialization. The individuals involved genuinely favored creating a supranational tribunal to address the widely recognized problem of noncompliance with

[39] For more on INTAL and its influence on the ATJ's creation, see Saldías, 2013, 66–72.

[40] García Amador, 1978.

[41] The report explicitly referenced the Colombian Supreme Court's decisions, and the minority opinion in the 1971 ruling. See Junta Del Acuerdo De Cartagena JUNAC, *Informe De La Junta Sobre El Establecimiento De Órgano Jursidiccional Del Acuerdo De Cartagena* (Grupo Andino ed., 1972), 142 (hereafter JUNAC Recommendation).

Andean *Decisiones* and to further regional integration.[42] However, they reached this conclusion after repeated interactions with European officials and judges who may have wanted to spread the ECJ model to other regions.

Emulating Europe: Implementing the *Junta*'s recommendation for an Andean Tribunal

Enthusiasm for creating an Andean judicial body seems to have been strongest among the members of the *Junta* and the INTAL network. Political and business leaders were less convinced. In 1975, Elizabeth Ferris interviewed seventy-five policymakers, technocrats, and private sector representatives in six Andean countries, asking their opinions about various initiatives including the *Junta*'s proposal to create an Andean court. Those whom Ferris interviewed saw little need for a supranational court.[43]

The *Junta* first presented the proposal for a court in December 1972. In 1974 and again in 1975, it presented statements about the proposal to the heads of the member states, arguing for the drafting of a treaty to establish a court. Andean political leaders do not appear to have been overtly hostile to the proposal. On the contrary, they authorized the *Junta* to proceed with drafting a treaty. Still, no definitive action was taken for five-and-a-half years until a treaty creating the ATJ was presented for adoption in August 1978.[44]

We found no conclusive explanation for this lengthy period of inaction. Perhaps the member states were distracted by the Andean Pact's larger political difficulties, such as Venezuela's accession to the Andean Pact in 1973 and the Pinochet coup in the same year, which ultimately led to Chile's withdrawal from the Pact in 1976. In addition, the Andean investment code continued to be extremely controversial, and one could reasonably ask whether a supranational legal body would have helped defuse that issue.

The Andean Pact's difficulties in the 1970s underscored that something fundamental needed to change if the member states were to move the integration process forward. Yet even during this troubled period, the EC continued to serve as a model.

Europe also faced significant challenges to integration in the 1970s. In response, it adopted several institutional innovations. In 1970 the EC launched the European Political Cooperation initiative to coordinate member states' foreign policies, and in 1974 it formalized the system of councils of heads of states to adopt major decisions related to integration. In 1979 the EC replaced a regional legislative body comprising national parliamentarians with direct elections to a new European Parliament.

[42] R. Vargas-Hidalgo, The Crisis of the Andean Pact: Lessons for Integration among Developing Countries. *Journal of Common Market Studies* 1979, 27 (3): 224.

[43] E.G. Ferris, National Political Support for Regional Integration: The Andean Pact. *International Organization* 1979, 33 (1): 99–100.

[44] García Amador, 1978, 105–7.

When integration advocates later revived the Andean integration project, they tracked these developments. The Pact's relaunch also provided the impetus for creating the ATJ. In 1979, the member states agreed to create an Andean Parliament and a Council of Foreign Ministers. In the same year, they finally adopted the Treaty Establishing the Tribunal of Justice of the Cartagena Agreement,[45] accepting the 1972 text drafted by INTAL almost in toto, which the *Junta* had incorporated into its 1975 recommendation.[46]

Andean officials were clearly aware that the ECJ had served as an engine to promote regional integration, but they may not have fully appreciated how the different elements of the ECJ model collectively contribute to the judicialization of integration politics. Chapter 6 considers the importance of the ECJ's multiple access points, revealing how savvy litigants sometimes use the preliminary ruling, noncompliance, nullification, and ommission procedures sequentially or in tandem to surmount hurdles to the review or enforcement of Community law.

Adapting the ECJ Model

The Original ATJ Treaty replicated the ECJ's main design features: a noncompliance procedure that authorized the *Junta* to challenge member state violations of Andean law; a preliminary reference mechanism for national courts to send questions involving the interpretation of Andean law to the Tribunal; and a nullification procedure that allowed states and private litigants to challenge the legality of Andean acts.[47] Although the treaty does not refer to the supremacy of Community law, supremacy was a key component of the *Junta*'s proposal, together with the doctrine of direct effect, which the treaty expressly mentions.[48]

Members of INTAL appear to have been persuaded of the benefits of the ECJ model, but the group's proposal also made a number of adaptations that reflected their learning lessons from the ECJ's experience. For example, the ATJ Treaty explicitly directed national courts to implement the Tribunal's preliminary rulings interpreting Andean law, a requirement absent from the Treaty of Rome but that had become part of ECJ doctrine.[49] The Treaty also included more detail about the timing of judicial proceedings and the length of the judges' terms of office.[50]

45 Original ATJ Treaty.

46 The only difference concerned the nullification procedure. The *Junta*'s draft allowed individuals to file nullification suits as long as the infringing act was applicable to them. The final version required that the suing individuals show that the infringement caused them direct injury. Compare Original ATJ Treaty, Article 19 with Article 14, in JUNAC Recommendation (see note 41), 148. Andean *Comisión* 1972: *Décimo Período de Sesiones Extraordinarias de la Comisión*, COM/XE-acta final.

47 The treaty authorized states to challenge Andean *Decisiones* they had not voted for, and it allowed private litigants to challenge acts that caused them injury. Original ATJ Treaty, Articles 17–19.

48 JUNAC Recommendation (see note 41), 139 and 148.

49 Original ATJ Treaty, Article 31.

50 E.B. Keener, The Andean Common Market Court of Justice: Its Purpose, Structure, and Future. *Emory Journal of International Dispute Resolution* 1987, 2 (1): 37–72.

Other alterations of the ECJ model appear to protect national sovereignty. As noted earlier, the ATJ noncompliance procedure empowered the *Junta* to challenge member state violations of Andean law. Unlike in Europe, however, only states, not private actors, could complain to the *Junta* about such violations.[51] In addition, the absence of a supranational procedure to challenge omissions by Andean officials meant that private actors could not contest the *Junta*'s refusal to pursue a noncompliance suit. An observer at the time suggested that there was a tacit "gentlemen's agreement" among member states to avoid lawsuits against each other. An omissions procedure could potentially circumvent this agreement by forcing the *Junta*'s hand.[52] The concerns about a zealous use of the noncompliance procedure may have been informed by the experiences of the ECJ, which had adjudicated complaints raised by private parties that member states would have preferred to ignore.[53]

Although barred from pursuing noncompliance complaints at the supranational level, private actors were free to file such suits in national courts. In principle, national judges could then refer questions of Andean law to the Tribunal. However, the ATJ Treaty suggested that the Tribunal should exercise restraint in responding to these references. Article 30 directed the ATJ to "restrict its interpretation to defining the content and scope of the norms of the juridical structure of the Cartagena Agreement. The [Tribunal] may neither interpret the contents and scope of national law, nor judge the facts in dispute."[54] This language plausibly reflects an awareness of the ECJ's well-known practice of broadly interpreting questions posed by national courts, analyzing the facts of the case (a task nominally reserved to national judges), and suggesting pro-integration applications of domestic rules.[55]

The ATJ faithfully adhered to these limitations when it began to hear cases. The first noncompliance proceeding involved a private litigant who attempted to file suit directly with the Tribunal rather than with a national court. The ATJ dismissed the suit, citing the treaty provision barring private actors from raising noncompliance cases.[56] When the same legal issue later arose in preliminary references involving challenges to a Colombian tariff on aluminum imports from Venezuela, the ATJ adhered to its limited role of interpreting Andean law in the abstract and not addressing the facts of the case.[57]

[51] Article 23 of the Original ATJ Treaty authorized the *Junta* to pursue noncompliance suits, but Article 24 specified that only member states could bring noncompliance cases to the *Junta*.

[52] Eduardo Hurtado Larrea, Los Incumplimientos y La Acción Asignada a La Competencia Del Tribunal, in *El Tribunal de Justicia Del Acuerdo de Cartagena* (BID-INTAL ed., 1985) (quoting columnist Manuél José Cárdenas of the Colombian newspaper *El Tiempo*).

[53] Alter, 2001, 80–5, 151–3.

[54] Original ATJ Treaty, Article 30.

[55] F. Mancini, The Making of a Constitution for Europe. *Common Market Law Review* 1989, 26 (4): 595–614, 606.

[56] ATJ Noncompliance Judgment 1-AI-87.

[57] See Chapter 4 for an analysis of these doctrinal developments.

One should not, however, overstate these adaptations of the ECJ model. The architects of the Andean legal system expected that private actors would challenge noncompliance with Community rules in national courts.[58] Moreover, the drafters adopted an innovation intended to enhance state adherence to Andean rules. Unlike the EC, which did not then include a procedure for penalizing noncompliance with ECJ rulings, the ATJ Treaty adopted a GATT-like system that authorized retaliatory trade sanctions if a state refused to follow an ATJ judgment against it.[59]

When the Tribunal began operations in 1984, it faced a slew of practical challenges that the ECJ had not experienced. Most notably, the funds that member states had pledged to the ATJ were delayed, the Tribunal lacked a permanent building to house its operations, and the *Junta*, member states, and national courts filed only a handful of cases.[60] The paucity of cases was partly an artifact of the political stalemate that impeded the creation of a common market. In the 1980s, the Andean investment code remained controversial, member countries clung to rules that exempted most products traded within the region, and governments were preoccupied by economic and political crises related to high levels of foreign debt.[61]

By the early 1990s, however, the member states once again reinvigorated the Andean integration project. They began in 1991 by laying the groundwork for a Common External Tariff. Over the next five years, they amended the Cartagena Agreement, replaced the import-substitution policy with a free trade model, and rechristened the new integration project as the Andean Community.[62] In 1997, the member states also replaced the largely ineffectual *Junta* with a General Secretariat, increased the size of its budget, and appointed a cadre of young lawyers eager to use the Secretariat's enhanced resources to promote regional integration.[63]

Reforming the Andean legal system was part of this wider institutional overhaul. The reforms reflected what political leaders had learned about that system over the previous decade. Notwithstanding the ATJ Treaty's unambiguous text, member states often opposed the *Junta*'s attempts to file noncompliance suits with the Tribunal. In addition, private litigants rarely used the preliminary reference mechanism to challenge national policies contrary to Community rules.

The Cochabamba Protocol of 1996, which amended the Original ATJ Treaty, was intended to address these shortcomings, and its adoption brought the Tribunal

[58] In rejecting the private litigant's noncompliance suit in ATJ Noncompliance Judgment 1-AI-87, the ATJ suggested that private litigants should instead raise such challenges in national courts.

[59] W. Phelan, Enforcement and Escape in the Andean Community: Why the Andean Community Is Not a Replica of the European Union. *Journal of Common Market Studies*, 2015, 53 (4): 840–56.

[60] Interview with former ATJ judge (B).

[61] Hojman, 1981; *The Andean Community and the United States: Trade and Investment Relations in the 1990s*. M. Rodríguez Mendoza, P. Correa, and B. Kotschwar (eds). Organization of American States, 1998.

[62] T.A. O'Keefe, How the Andean Pact Transformed Itself into a Friend of Foreign Enterprise. *International Lawyer* 1996, 30 (4): 811–24.

[63] Interviews with former official (B) of the General Secretariat Legal Advisor's Office.

even closer to the ECJ model.[64] Member states augmented the nullification procedure by eliminating a requirement that private litigants show direct injury from Community acts.[65] The Revised ATJ Treaty also added an omissions procedure to enable litigants to challenge an Andean institution's failure to act, and it relaxed restrictions on preliminary references by indicating that ATJ judges could now address how Andean rules applied to the facts of cases when doing so was necessary for their rulings.[66]

The most profound changes, however, involved the noncompliance procedure. Member states recognized that private litigants were not raising noncompliance challenges in national courts and that national judges were not referring those challenges to the ATJ. To remedy the dearth of cases, the Protocol went beyond the ECJ's noncompliance procedure. It repealed the ban on private actors filing complaints with the General Secretariat alleging violations of Andean law, it authorized private actors to raise noncompliance cases directly with the ATJ if the General Secretariat refused to act on or rejected the complaint,[67] and it directed those actors to enforce ATJ noncompliance judgments by seeking compensation from national judges for damages caused by the violations.[68] These provisions gave the Secretariat leverage as it negotiated noncompliance issues with member states; the Secretariat could now say that one way or another, the suit would reach the ATJ and, perhaps, national courts. The result of these reforms was an Andean legal system that, much like the EC, provided private parties with multiple avenues to challenge state noncompliance. We explore the political and legal consequences of these multiple avenues in Chapter 6.

The Cochabamba Protocol reforms also reflected learning by Andean actors. The drafters of the Original ATJ Treaty incorporated ECJ doctrines on the direct effect and supremacy of Community law and required national judges to follow the Tribunal's rulings. However, they also adapted the ECJ model to protect national sovereignty, for example by authorizing private actors to bring noncompliance suits in national courts but not at the Community level. The next generation of Andean leaders recognized that this adaptation had in fact undermined the system's ability to induce adherence to Andean rules. Their solution was to incorporate the institutional features of the EC legal system that the founders had originally rejected, and to enhance those features by allowing private actors to bring noncompliance cases directly to the ATJ.

[64] Protocol of Cochabamba Amending the Treaty Creating the Court of Justice, May 28, 1996 (Revised ATJ Treaty). The General Secretariat advocated these reforms so that it could credibly argue that its own failure to initiate noncompliance suits would trigger such suits by private actors. Interview with retired official (C) of the General Secretariat Legal Advisor's Office and a negotiator of early Andean *Decisiones* regulating intellectual property.

[65] Ibid., Article 19. The provision instead provided that the challenged act should affect the individual's "legitimate interests."

[66] The Revised ATJ Treaty also authorizes the ATJ to hear arbitrations; and Community labor disputes. Ibid., Articles 37–40. The ATJ has only rarely exercised these functions.

[67] Ibid., Article 25.

[68] Ibid., Article 30.

Conclusion: Supranational Transplants—Lessons from the Andean Tribunal of Justice

The next few chapters explain how the ATJ's trajectory has been quite different than that of the ECJ. Chapter 3 discusses the Tribunal's relationship with national judges. Chapter 4 analyzes four important legal issues where the ATJ intentionally diverged from ECJ doctrines. Chapter 5 explains how the ATJ forged alliances with domestic intellectual property agencies. Foreshadowing these discussions, we reflect here on what the copying of the ECJ model into the Andean legal system tells us about the processes of supranational transplantation.

A common issue that emerges from the three literatures discussed in this chapter is the existence and extent of local demand for transplanted laws and institutions. Neofunctionalist theory assumes that private litigants who stand to benefit from regional integration will raise claims before supranational courts and thereby help to develop Community rules. Studies of the export of ideas offer other reasons why local actors may either embrace or reject transplants. The scholarship on legal transplants suggests that laws and institutions copied in response to coercive external pressure or unreflective mimicry are likely to be resisted or remain unused. In contrast, transplants that local actors embrace voluntarily, and transplants that are adapted to local needs, are more likely to be effective.

How, then, did the existence of the ECJ shape the ATJ's founding and its subsequent trajectory? Andean leaders, aware of the ECJ's well-known activism, included safeguards in the original ATJ Treaty to limit the ability of private actors to challenge national laws. Perhaps most importantly, private actors were barred from filing noncompliance suits with the *Junta* or the Tribunal. Instead, they were limited to requesting national judges—most of whom were unaware of, or unsympathetic to, Andean law—to refer cases to the ATJ. Only a handful of such referrals were ever made outside the exceptional area of intellectual property (discussed in Chapter 5; the content of other referrals are analyzed in Chapter 3). In those cases that reached the Tribunal, the Original ATJ Treaty deterred the judges from applying Andean laws to the facts, thus limiting the guidance that the Tribunal could give to national courts.

The Revised ATJ Treaty, adopted in 1996, relaxed these structural constraints. The member states adopted a package of institutional reforms to increase the effectiveness of the Andean legal system and expand the Tribunal's docket. These adaptations suggest lessons drawn both from the ATJ's first twelve years and from the EC legal system. Notwithstanding these changes, which we discuss in greater detail in Chapter 4, the ATJ has continued to issue mostly narrow, technical rulings and to avoid the expansionist judicial lawmaking of its European cousin.

One reason for the Tribunal's circumspect approach is that the ATJ has confronted the same basic challenge that all supranational transplants face: how to enlist the support of key domestic interlocutors and compliance constituencies. In Europe, the ECJ cultivated national judges as key allies in promoting legal integration. In copying the ECJ's preliminary ruling system, and in authorizing private litigants to bring suit invoking Andean rules in domestic courts, Andean officials opened the door for the ATJ to forge its own alliances with domestic judges. As we explain in Chapter 3, however, these judges declined to become the Tribunal's active partners. Once the initial barriers to referrals were surmounted, national judges refer cases only when Andean rules unambiguously require them to do so, but they do not work in tandem with the ATJ to develop Community law. They do not send expansive questions to the Tribunal, and they generally display little appetite for defying governments by setting aside domestic laws or decrees that conflict with Andean law.

The ATJ has, however, forged a different set of alliances, with domestic administrative agencies responsible for protecting intellectual property. Chapter 5 explains how these agencies apply Andean *Decisiones* to determine whether to register applications for trademarks and patents. The agencies were thus logical interlocutors for ATJ judges. Agency officials repeatedly sought the Tribunal's guidance to clarify ambiguities and lacunae in Andean law, and they have habitually applied those rulings even when doing so challenges national executive or legislative decisions. The ATJ and the agencies have developed a symbiotic relationship that has helped to establish intellectual property as a distinctive "island of effective international adjudication" in the Andean Community legal system.

These findings have important implications for neofunctionalism, including its revival as a theory of legal integration. Neofunctionalism predicts that an alignment between the demands of private litigants and the interests of supranational judges will promote regional integration. Our study indicates, however, that it is insufficient for litigants to challenge domestic rules. A supranational court must also provide a hospitable venue for invoking Community law to dismantle conflicting national policies. The ATJ's refusal to interpret Andean law purposively to help litigants further their economic interests created a vicious circle that—with the exception of intellectual property disputes—has inhibited the filing of additional cases and diminished the domestic influence of Andean law.[69]

In sum, the ATJ's experience suggests—contrary to the expectations of neofunctionalist theory—that transplanting supranational laws and legal institutions is insufficient in itself to stimulate local demand for those laws and institutions. This is so even when a handful of entrepreneurial litigants present a supranational court with opportunities to embed the foreign transplant locally, and even when at least some supranational actors are interested in promoting integration. In Chapter 9, we return to the issue of the differential support for international courts from jurist advocacy movements in Europe and in the Andes.

At the level of legal doctrine, the ATJ's selective emulation of ECJ jurisprudence offers insights for ideational diffusion theory. The ECJ is widely viewed as

[69] See Chapter 8 for more on this point. This is also true for ECJ preliminary rulings, which can either increase or decrease litigation on specific issues. See K.J. Alter, The European Legal System and Domestic Policy: Spillover or Backlash. *International Organization* 2000, 54 (3): 489–518, 512–15.

authoritative by judicial and legal communities around the world. This exalted stature offered a ready blueprint for Andean judges: slavishly follow the ECJ's doctrinal innovations and defend that decision by referencing the many design similarities that the two courts share. However, the ATJ chose not to chart this course, suggesting that socialization is not the mechanism through which the ECJ model has diffused. Instead, the Tribunal's *à la carte* approach suggests lesson-drawing—a type of emulation in which the judges recognized that legal doctrines that served salutary functions in Europe might not work well in the Andes, where the pace and scope of integration was more modest and shaped by significant turmoil in domestic politics. This process, as opposed to blind mimicry, gave Andean judges the discretion to pick and choose which EC legal doctrines were germane to the Andean context and consonant with local political realities.

Some legal scholars have argued that the European experience is *sui generis* in ways that preclude the ECJ from serving as a template for other international courts.[70] The extent to which the ATJ has selectively copied from the ECJ reveals, however, that a supranational court can be a model in some respects but not in others. In particular, the ATJ's refusal to emulate the ECJ's penchant for expansionist lawmaking (discussed further in Chapter 8) suggests that transplanting key design features and legal doctrines does not necessarily result in transplanting judicial activism in the interpretation of key legal texts.

Looking to the future, there are several reasons to expect that the ECJ will continue to be an influential model for other similarly designed international courts. The ECJ has developed extensive and well-reasoned legal doctrines that have benefitted from a large and stable secretariat (the European Commission), a cadre of professional clerks (known as *référéndaires*), and an active and ongoing dialogue with critics including law faculty and national high court judges. ECJ rulings are also translated into multiple languages and posted online, making it easy for judges around the world to access and review them.

The ECJ will also continue to serve as a model because the European Union is interested in spreading supranational courts to other regions and helping them to flourish. European officials provide free consultations, encourage judicial networks, and give in-kind and financial support to resource-poor governments and supranational judges.[71] European universities also invite students from around the world to study European integration, generating pro-integration scholarship by local actors.

[70] J. Alvarez, The New Dispute Settlers: (Half) Truths and Consequences. *Texas International Law Journal* 2003, 38: 25–7; E.A. Posner and J.C. Yoo, A Theory of International Adjudication. *California Law Review* 2005, 93 (1): 55–7.

[71] In the Andean context, this support took a variety of forms. As previously noted, INTAL consulted with ECJ judges during conversations about creating an Andean Tribunal. The EC later negotiated an associate agreement with the Andean Community to bolster Andean integration efforts. The EC and its member states also provided financial support for the work of the *Comisión Andina de Juristas*, which undertook initiatives to promote Andean legal integration, including disseminating rulings on the ATJ's website and facilitating the Tribunal's outreach to national judges. Interviews with official (C) of the *Comisión Andina de Juristas*.

Officials provide these forms of aid with no overt strings attached because they believe the European model is worth emulating.[72]

Given these developments, it is hardly surprising that the judges who serve on international tribunals, and the scholars who write about these tribunals, continue to invoke ECJ rulings. This should not, however, mislead observers to conclude that judicial practices around the world are more alike than they actually are. In this respect, the ATJ's significant deviations from the ECJ model, discussed in Chapters 4 and 8, are noteworthy. While we expect supranational courts to consider how the ECJ has handled analogous legal issues, ECJ transplants may ultimately find that they have more in common with each other than with their common parent. Seen from this perspective, the ATJ—which has more than thirty years of experience—may in fact be a better guide for other ECJ transplants to consult and possibly emulate.

72 T. Lenz, Spurred Emulation: The EU and Regional Integration in Mercosur and SADC. *West European Politics* 2012, 35 (1): 155–73; Alter, 2012.

PART II

LAW AND POLITICS IN THE ANDEAN TRIBUNAL OF JUSTICE

3

The Andean Tribunal of Justice and its Interlocutors

Understanding Litigation Patterns in the Andean Community

This chapter explains how and why national courts in the Andean Community began to send preliminary references to the Andean Tribunal of Justice (ATJ or Tribunal). We identify the source of the vast majority of ATJ preliminary rulings as disputes over the registration of trademarks and patents by national intellectual property (IP) agencies, a category of cases that we analyze in depth. To complete the discussion of national court activation patterns, the chapter also considers the small number of ATJ preliminary references that do not involve IP.

Many scholars consider domestic judicial enforcement of international court rulings as key to ensuring to international law's efficacy.[1] This presumption derives from studies of Europe's two international tribunals—the European Court of Justice (ECJ) and European Court of Human Rights (ECtHR)—which are effective in large part because of their dialogue with national courts about the meaning and application of European Community (EC) law and European human rights law.[2] In the EC, this dialogue is facilitated by a preliminary ruling system that both authorizes and requires national judges to refer unsettled questions of EC law to the ECJ as they arise during domestic litigation. After the ECJ answers the questions, the case returns to the national court where the judge applies that interpretation to the facts.

The preliminary ruling mechanism provides a unique conduit for trans-judicial dialogue. Spurred by requests from private litigants who benefitted from favorable EC rules, national judges in Europe became the ECJ's primary interlocutors

[1] The literature is vast. For an overview, see A. Nollkaemper, *National Courts and the International Rule of Law*. Oxford: Oxford University Press, 2011; Y. Shany, *Assessing the Effectiveness of International Courts*. Oxford: Oxford University Press, 2007.

[2] L.R. Helfer and A.-M. Slaughter, Toward a Theory of Effective Supranational Adjudication. *Yale Law Journal* 1997, 107 (2): 273–391; K.J. Alter, Who Are the Masters of the Treaty?: European Governments and the European Court of Justice. *International Organization* 1998, 52 (1): 125–52. Chapter 10 of this book reconsiders, in light of two decades of experience, the claim that the effectiveness of the ECJ and ECtHR is due primarily to their relationships with national judges.

Transplanting International Courts: The Law and Politics of the Andean Tribunal of Justice. First Edition. Karen J. Alter and Laurence R. Helfer. Published 2017 by Oxford University Press.

and compliance partners. The foundational doctrines of European integration—supremacy, direct effect, pre-emption, and implied powers—were all products of early preliminary references.[3] Over time, as national judges referred a growing number of cases, they became habituated to following ECJ decisions and to adjudicating the treaty-compatibility of domestic laws.[4] With international rules woven into the fabric of domestic legal systems, governments could not defy the ECJ without also calling into question the independence and authority of their own courts.

The Andean Community preliminary reference mechanism is a close copy of its EC cousin,[5] but it functions very differently than its counterpart in Europe. Although recent studies have analyzed other modes of interaction between national and international judges, this chapter focuses on preliminary rulings to explain how the most active preliminary reference system outside Europe was activated and operates in practice. We document national, temporal, and subject-matter variation in ATJ preliminary rulings during the Tribunal's thirty years of operation. Our analysis, based on a detailed coding of Andean case law through 2014,[6] reveals several important findings.

First, the number of preliminary references, barely a trickle in the Tribunal's first decade, increased dramatically beginning in 1995. Another uptick began in 2013, and it is likely to continue for the foreseeable future. Second, there is significant cross-country variation regarding which courts make references, and just a handful of national courts in three countries are responsible for nearly all ATJ preliminary rulings. Third, the overwhelming majority of references (more than 90%) address intellectual property issues. Fourth, although the number of non-IP references has

[3] E. Stein, Lawyers, Judges and the Making of a Transnational Constitution. *American Journal of International Law* 1981, 75 (1): 1–27; J. Weiler, The Community System: The Dual Character of Supranationalism. *Yearbook of European Law* 1991 (1): 257–306.

[4] J. Weiler, A Quiet Revolution—The European Court of Justice and Its Interlocutors. *Comparative Political Studies* 1994, 26 (4): 510–34; A.-M. Burley and W. Mattli, Europe before the Court. *International Organization* 1993, 47 (1): 41–76.

[5] As in Europe, the Andean preliminary ruling system requires national courts of last resort to refer questions involving Community law. E.B. Keener, The Andean Common Market Court of Justice: Its Purpose, Structure, and Future. *Emory Journal of International Dispute Resolution* 1987, 2 (1): 50; R.V. Toledo, Dispute Settlement in Andean Community Law. In: *Inter-Governmental Trade Dispute Settlement: Multilateral and Regional Approaches.* Julio Lacarte and Jaime Granados (eds), 245–64. London: Cameron May, 2004, 246–7; O. Saldías, Supranational Courts as Engines of Disintegration: The Case of the Andean Community (Free Univ. of Berlin Working Paper on European Integration No. 5, 2007, available at <http://citeseerx.ist.psu.edu/viewdoc/download?doi=10.1.1.588.9948&rep=rep1&type=pdf>. Other copies of the preliminary reference mechanism authorize but do not require references. See K.J. Alter, The Global Spread of European Style International Courts. *West European Politics* 2012, 35 (1): 135–54.

[6] Our detailed coding includes publicly available ATJ preliminary rulings that can be downloaded from *Comunidad Andina—Documentos Oficiales*, available at <http://www.comunidadandina.org/Documentos.aspx?GruDoc=11>. Summary statistics on the Tribunal's own website shows a slightly larger number of references. *Tribunal de Justicia de la Comunidad Andina—Informe Estadístico*, available at <http://www.tribunalandino.org.ec/sitetjca/index.php>. Information we obtained from various Andean officials lists numbers of cases that differ from both websites. We have been unable to reconcile these inconsistencies, which account for the modest discrepancies in the number of preliminary references discussed at various places in this book. We emphasize, however, that patterns and trends we identify are unaffected by these discrepancies.

expanded in the last several years, the content of ATJ rulings remains remarkably similar, and remarkably limited. Even when given opportunities to opine on a wider array of issues or to develop legal doctrines to advance Andean integration through law, the ATJ has remained highly deferential to national decision-makers. This pattern reflects a broader political reality that sharply differs from the EC—national judges are mostly reluctant participants in the Andean legal system.

This chapter also highlights several broader implications of the structure and operation of the Andean legal system. Even when national courts are given explicit instructions to work with their regional counterparts to enforce international law, domestic judicial support cannot be taken for granted. Our detailed analysis of why most national judges reluctantly embraced the treaty-mandated obligation to refer cases to the ATJ highlights the barriers that litigants face when they seek to invoke international legal rights in domestic courts. At the same time, our findings also reveal that there is more than one way for an international tribunal to influence the domestic legal order and the behavior of governments. Other domestic actors—such as administrative agencies—can serve as reliable interlocutors and compliance partners for international tribunals even where national judges are indifferent or resistant.

The remainder of this chapter proceeds as follows. We first provide an overview of the Andean preliminary reference system, explaining patterns of referrals and identifying factors that favored or hindered the system's activation in each member state. Next we demonstrate that the Andean preliminary reference mechanism is primarily driven by the relationship between the ATJ and domestic IP agencies, with national courts acting as relatively passive intermediaries. We then discuss an important 2014 ruling in which the ATJ authorized and encouraged administrative agencies to bypass national courts and send references directly to the Tribunal.

The next section of the chapter analyzes ATJ decisions that do not pertain to intellectual property. Our principal finding is that although the subject matter of Andean adjudication has expanded somewhat in recent years, this has not altered the relationship between the Tribunal and national judges. However, a wider comparison reveals a striking and little-known fact: the ATJ's non-IP decisions—which we refer to as "outlier" rulings—are more numerous than the entire dockets of several other international courts modeled on the ECJ, including courts that have preliminary ruling mechanisms.

The final section of the chapter compares the Andean and European experiences, contrasting the relationship between national judges and the respective tribunals in each region. In the EC, the judges on lower and specialized courts used ECJ references strategically to expand their power.[7] In the Andean Community, by contrast, national judges have a narrow conception of their relationship with the ATJ and have refrained from using the Andean legal system as a tool of judicial empowerment. This reticence limits the incentives of private litigants to use national court

[7] K.J. Alter, *Establishing the Supremacy of European Law: The Making of an International Rule of Law in Europe*. Oxford: Oxford University Press, 2001.

cases to challenge government policies that violate Andean free trade and integration rules, and it discourages the ATJ from issuing more purposive interpretations of Andean law.

We return to the usage of these Andean legal procedures in Chapter 6, which discusses how litigants invoke the different legal procedures sequentially or in tandem to influence the interpretation of Andean law and to promote their interests.

The Legal and Institutional Framework of the Andean Preliminary Ruling Mechanism

As Chapter 2 explains, the Andean legal system initially did not include a tribunal. When member states later decided to create the ATJ, they modeled its jurisdiction directly on that of the ECJ, including the preliminary reference mechanism. As in the EC, lower courts were permitted to make references to the Tribunal and courts of last instance were required to do so.

The ATJ's mandate for reviewing references was narrower than its European counterpart. Article 30 of the Original ATJ Treaty directed the Tribunal to "restrict its interpretation to defining the content and scope of the norms of the juridical structure of the Cartagena Agreement. The [Tribunal] may neither interpret the contents and scope of national law, nor judge the facts in dispute."[8] This language appears to reflect Andean governments' awareness of the ECJ's well-known practice of broadly interpreting questions posed by national courts, suggesting how to analyze the facts of the case (a task nominally reserved to national judges), and adopting pro-integration interpretations of Community legal rules.

Chapter 2 describes the political and institutional problems that plagued the Andean Pact and that quickly engulfed the new Tribunal. Chapter 5 explains why, in the 1990s, the member states adopted a broad array of free market and deregulatory reforms that they incorporated into a relaunched Andean integration effort. These institutional reforms also extended to the ATJ. Previously only states could ask the *Junta* to investigate another state's violation of Andean law; the 1996 Cochabamba Protocol, codified as the Revised ATJ Treaty, authorized private actors to file noncompliance complaints with the General Secretariat, subject to a right of appeal to the Tribunal.[9] The Protocol also modestly expanded the ATJ's authority in preliminary rulings by providing that its judges could address how Andean law applies to the facts of the cases referred by national courts.[10]

These institutional changes were prerequisites for activating the Andean legal system. We analyze these changes in detail in Chapter 5. Here we focus on how these developments laid the groundwork for the activation of the Andean preliminary reference mechanism.

[8] Original ATJ Treaty, Article 30. [9] Revised ATJ Treaty, Articles 23–31.

[10] Ibid., Article 34 (authorizing the ATJ to "refer to th[e] facts when essential for the requested interpretation").

Intellectual property has long occupied a central place in Andean integration. In the early 1990s, the member states adopted three *Decisiones* that required progressively higher levels of IP protection.[11] These revisions were consistent with the period's economic liberalization policies. The same economic forces also led to the creation of new domestic IP agencies. In 1992, Peru established the National Institute for the Defense of Competition and the Protection of Intellectual Property (INDECOPI), an agency that cobbled together subjects including intellectual property, antitrust, consumer protection, and bankruptcy. In that same year, the Colombian government established a Superintendent of Industry and Commerce and entrusted it with a similar array of competencies. Other Andean countries also created or restructured domestic IP agencies over the next several years.

Among the functions that the new agencies performed was the review of applications to register trademarks and patents. Inasmuch as the IP protection rules in the five member states were codified in Andean law, agency officials applied regional rules to resolve registration disputes. Inevitably, some of the private firms involved in these disputes were dissatisfied with the agencies' registration decisions and challenged them in court. Since the outcome of such challenges turned on the interpretation of Andean IP rules, these businesses and their attorneys asked national judges—who had little experience in applying the new IP rules—to refer the cases to the ATJ. As we now explain, these challenges to IP administrative agency decisions comprise the overwhelming majority of the Tribunal's docket.

An Overview of Preliminary Reference Patterns in the Andes

Our analysis of ATJ case law up to and including 2014 reveals several interesting findings. First, preliminary rulings dominate the ATJ's docket, a dominance that has existed since references increased dramatically beginning in the mid-1990s. Second, although there is wide variation in when national courts began to refer cases to the ATJ and in the number of cases referred, most referrals are concentrated in a small number of courts. Third, the subject-matter of references overwhelmingly concerns intellectual property, notwithstanding the fact that Andean law spans a wide array of other issues relating to regional integration. Fourth, national courts repeatedly pose very similar questions about Andean IP law, and the Tribunal provides the same answers to those questions in case after case. Even in cases that do not involve intellectual property, the questions that national judges ask are generally narrow and technical. As we will explain, taken together, these patterns reveal that the Andean and European legal systems, although similar in design, operate very differently in practice.

[11] Andean *Decisión* 311; Andean *Decisión* 313; and Andean *Decisión* 344.

Preliminary references from national courts dominate the ATJ's docket

The ATJ's jurisdiction includes four major types of cases: (1) preliminary rulings (*interpretaciones prejudicial*) referred by national courts, primarily in suits initiated by private parties; (2) noncompliance actions (*acciones de incumpliemento*), initiated by the General Secretariat or private litigants; (3) nullification actions (*acciones de nulidad*) filed by member states or by private actors;[12] and (4) failure to act complaints (*recursos por omisión*), usually raised by private actors against Andean officials. Figure 3.1 shows that preliminary references have dominated the ATJ's docket. Between its first ruling in 1987 and the end of 2014, the ATJ issued a total of 2,679 rulings in response to references from national courts, far outstripping the number of cases initiated by other mechanisms. We provide a detailed examination of these references before analyzing trends and patterns in noncompliance, nullification, and omissions cases that the large number of preliminary rulings obscures.

Figure 3.1 reveals that the number of preliminary ruling requests increased beginning in 1993, and grew steadily after 1995. Indeed, the ATJ issued only thirty-two preliminary rulings from 1984 to 1994, its first decade of operation. The rise in references coincided with the change in Andean IP rules and the restructuring of the IP

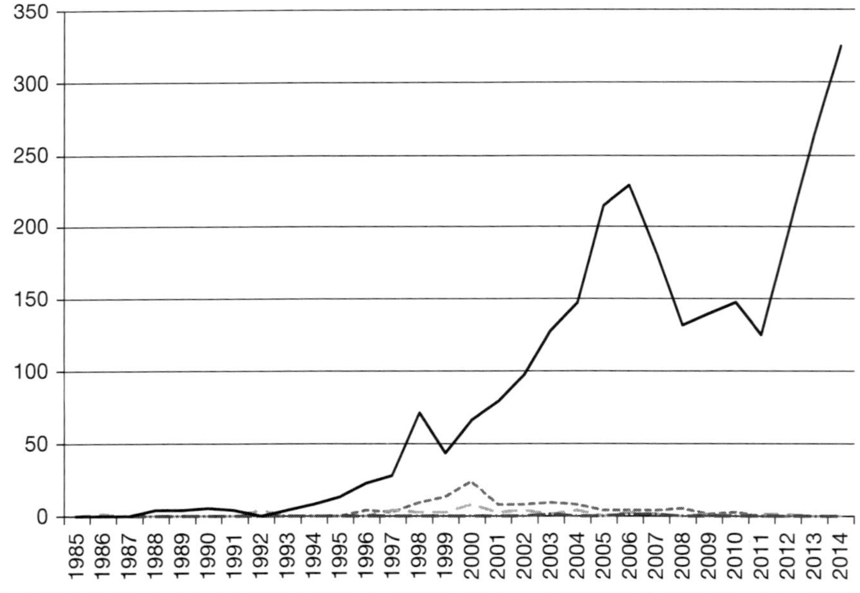

Figure 3.1 Andean Tribunal litigation by type of action (1985–2014) ($N = 2{,}853$)

[12] Data on the initiators of noncompliance and nullification suits, 2012–14, provided by the ATJ Registrar.

administrative agencies, a shift we explore in detail in Chapter 5. The steadily increasing demand for Andean litigation initially peaked in 2006, when the ATJ issued 224 rulings. The next several years saw a modest decline in the number of preliminary rulings, followed by sharp increases in 2013 (265 rulings) and 2014 (325 rulings). The ATJ website indicates that 691 reference requests were filed in 2015, surpassing all previous levels. These increases are due primarily to a growing number of references from a new specialized court in Peru that reviews all decisions by INDECOPI, the Peruvian IP agency, as well as direct references from IP administrative agencies in all four member states. We discuss these developments later in this chapter.

Cross-national and cross-court variations in references to the ATJ

Our coding reveals significant cross-national variation in references to the ATJ. Colombian courts are responsible for 1,674 of all 2,679 preliminary references, or 62.4%, with the second and third largest number and percentage of referrals from Ecuador (523, or 19.5%) and Peru (469, or 17.5%), respectively. In striking contrast, Venezuelan courts referred only two cases before withdrawing from the Andean Community in 2006, and Bolivian courts had referred eleven cases by the end of 2014 (0.4%).

Mapping this variation over time reveals pivot points when referrals began to rise sharply in each member state. Colombia was the first country to send a case to the ATJ in 1987. No other state's courts submitted a request for nearly a decade. Only in the mid-1990s did courts in Ecuador start to refer cases, beginning with three cases decided in 1994. The ATJ received only two requests from Peru through 2004, after which date the number of referrals rose sharply, fell, and rose again. Figure 3.2 charts the cross-national variation, excluding Venezuela.

Our interviews corroborated this pattern. Lawyers and judges attested that, after a particular date, national courts in Colombia, Ecuador, and Peru habitually referred appeals from IP agencies to the Tribunal.[13] The pattern resembles uncorking a tap, with each uncorking producing a sharp increase in the ATJ's docket.

A finer grained analysis, provided in Table 3.1, discloses that relatively few courts refer cases to the ATJ. Of the 1,674 references from Colombia, for example, the overwhelming majority of cases emanated from a single court—the First Chamber of the Council of State (*Consejo de Estado*)—a first- and last-instance judicial body. A similar pattern exists in Peru, where the Permanent Chamber of Constitutional and Social Rights of the Supreme Court was initially the source of all but a handful of references from that country. In 2012, however, after the government created a new specialized IP tribunal to review challenges to INDECOPI registration decisions, this judicial body became the primary source of Peruvian references. In Ecuador, there is significantly more variation, with five different administrative courts providing most of the references to the ATJ.

[13] Interview with five national judges (A) from the *Sala Primera del Consejo de Estado de Colombia*; Interview with national judge (A) of the *Sala de Derecho Constitucional y Social Permanente de la Corte Suprema de Justicia de Peru*; Interview with three national judges (A) of the *Tribunal Distrital No. 1 de lo Contencioso Administrativo de Ecuador*.

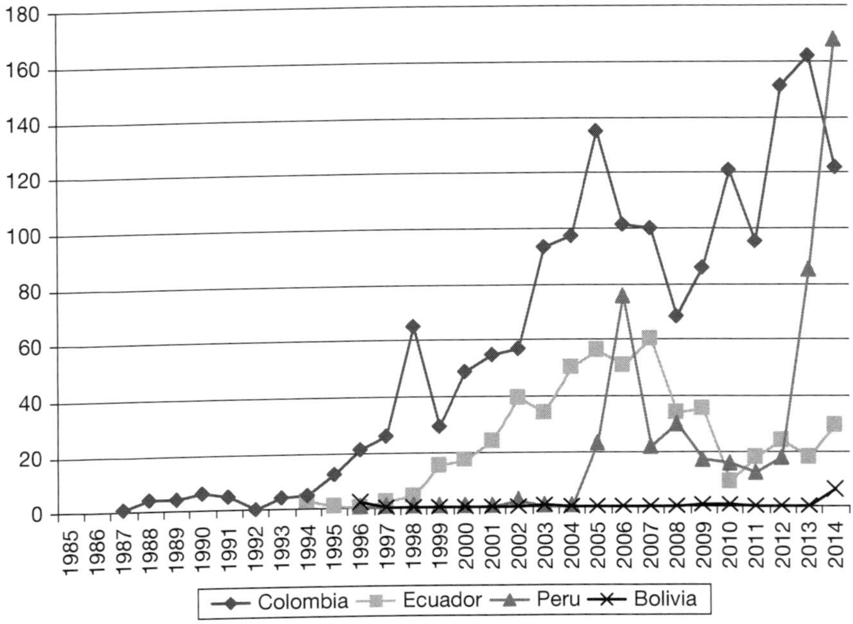

Figure 3.2 ATJ preliminary rulings, 1984–2014. By country and year (N = 2,679)

This clumping of cases in specific courts underscores the reality that the overwhelming majority of preliminary references pertain to a single subject: intellectual property. Where only one or a few courts have jurisdiction over this subject, surmounting barriers to referrals could readily generate a flood of cases in a short period of time and produce the sharp uptick in referrals shown in Figure 3.2. Conversely, when jurisdiction over IP disputes is dispersed or transferred to new judicial bodies, the resulting shift in reference patterns may simply reflect a change in which bodies refer what are essentially the same disputes.

Table 3.1 also reveals that other national courts refer questions to the ATJ far less frequently. Several features of these cases are nonetheless noteworthy. First, the Colombian Constitutional Court has made four references, a fact worth underscoring given the few constitutional courts in Europe that have referred cases to the ECJ. Second, a handful of arbitral bodies have made references following a 2011 ATJ noncompliance judgment interpreting Andean law to require such references. Third, rulings in 2014 authorized the Peruvian and Bolivian IP agencies to send questions directly to the Tribunal, further expanding the number of bodies that refer cases.[14] Finally, national courts that infrequently refer cases are the source of most of the "outlier" decisions unrelated to IP that we discuss in greater detail later in this chapter.

[14] One ruling (ATJ Preliminary Ruling 121-IP-2014) concerns the Peruvian IP agency, INDECOPI; the other (ATJ Preliminary Ruling 105-IP-2014) is from the Bolivian IP agency, SENAPI. A report on

Table 3.1 Preliminary references from national courts in the Andean Community, 1984–2014 ($N = 2{,}679$)

	Total references	Percentage
Bolivian courts (from four different courts; plus three recent references from the IP administrative agency)	11	0.4%
Colombian courts	**1674**	**62.4%**
Consejo de Estado de la República de Colombia (multiple Salas, but predominantly the Primera Sala which reviews IP registration issues)	1615	61.6%
Fourteen other Colombian courts, arbitral bodies, and the IP administrative agency	59	2.2%
Ecuadorian courts	**523**	**19.5%**
Primera Sala del Tribunal de lo Contencioso Administrativo de la República del Ecuador, Distrito de Quito	195	7.4%
Segunda Sala del Tribunal de lo Contencioso Administrativo de la República del Ecuador, Distrito de Quito	177	6.7%
Tribunal Contencioso Administrativo N° 2 del Distrito de Guayaquil	36	1.4%
Tribunal Distrital de lo Contencioso Administrativo Con Sede en Quito	45	1.7%
Tribunal Distrital de lo Contencioso Administrativo N° 3, Con Sede en la Ciudad De Cuenca	20	0.76%
Twelve other Ecuadorian courts	50	1.9%
Peruvian courts	**469**	**17.5%**
Sala de Derecho Constitucional y Social Permanente de la Corte Suprema de Justicia	277	13.6%
Octava Sala Especializada en lo Contencioso Administrativo, Corte Superior de Justicia de Lima	148	5.6%
Eleven other Peruvian courts and the IP administrative agency	44	1.7%
Venezuelan courts	**2**	**< 0.1%**
Total	**2679**	**100%**

The differences in referral patterns in the European and Andean Communities are significant. In the EC, certain national courts also account for a large percentage of ECJ preliminary rulings. Overall, however, a much wider variety of courts refer cases, both because European litigation involves a broader array of legal issues

the ATJ's activities in 2015 notes that twenty-five preliminary references were received from Colombia's Unfair Competition and Industrial Property Working Group, two references from the Directorate of Distinctive Signs of the Superintendency of Industry and Trade of Colombia, and six references each from SENAPI and INDECOPI. *Tribunal de Justicia de la Comunidad Andina, Informe de Labores Gestión*, 2015 at 9.

(see Figure 3.6) and because courts at all levels of the national judicial hierarchy make references. Lower courts have been especially active in referring cases to the ECJ, although only courts of last instance are obliged to do so.[15] There is less frequent lower court involvement with the ATJ. This partly reflects the fact that Andean countries have smaller economies and populations than many European nations, and the structure of their judicial systems are flatter. However, lower courts of general jurisdiction have also been reluctant to refer cases to the ATJ. In contrast, when Peru recently created a specialized tribunal to hear challenges to IP agency registrations decisions, the judges have referred nearly every case to the ATJ following a Peruvian Supreme Court ruling indicating that such references were legally required. We explore the implications of these differences between the two Community legal systems at the end of this chapter.

The limited subject-matter variation of ATJ preliminary rulings

Figures 3.3 and 3.4 reveal the dominance of IP in references from national courts in the Andean Community. We divide the data into two time periods that reflect our initial coding of references between 1984 and 2007, and a subsequent study of references between 2008 and 2014.

Of the 1,338 ATJ preliminary rulings issued up to and including 2007, 1,303 (97%) concerned intellectual property: 1,165 (87%) interpreted Andean trademark legislation; 103 (8%) involve Andean patent rules; 11 (less than 1%) dealt with copyrights; and 24 (less than 2%) concern other types of IP, such as industrial designs and utility models. All but a handful of these cases began as challenges to an administrative agency's decision to grant or deny an application to register a trademark, patent, or other IP right. Only thirty-five of the 1,352 preliminary rulings through 2007 (3%) are "outlier" cases unrelated to IP.[16]

An overview of the following seven years of data reveals only modest changes. Of the 1,341 preliminary rulings issued between 2008 and 2014, 1,262, or 94.1%, relate to intellectual property, although the distribution among subjects within IP has shifted somewhat as compared to the earlier period (see Figure 3.4). The most noteworthy development is a modest increase in outlier decisions. Whereas the ATJ issued only thirty-five such rulings in its first two decades, it received seventy-nine preliminary reference requests (or 5.9%) concerning Andean law issues other than IP during the next seven years. We discuss the most significant outlier decisions later in this chapter and in Chapter 4.

The substantive homogeneity of Andean references is strikingly different from the EC, where preliminary rulings canvass a broad range of issue areas regulated by EC law. In Europe, litigation initially focused on subjects governed

[15] For a breakdown of national court referrals to the ECJ, see A. Stone Sweet and T. Brunell, The European Court and the National Courts: A Statistical Analysis of Preliminary References, 1961–95. *Journal of European Public Policy* 1998, 5 (1): 66–97.

[16] Due to rounding, these figures do not add up to exactly 100%.

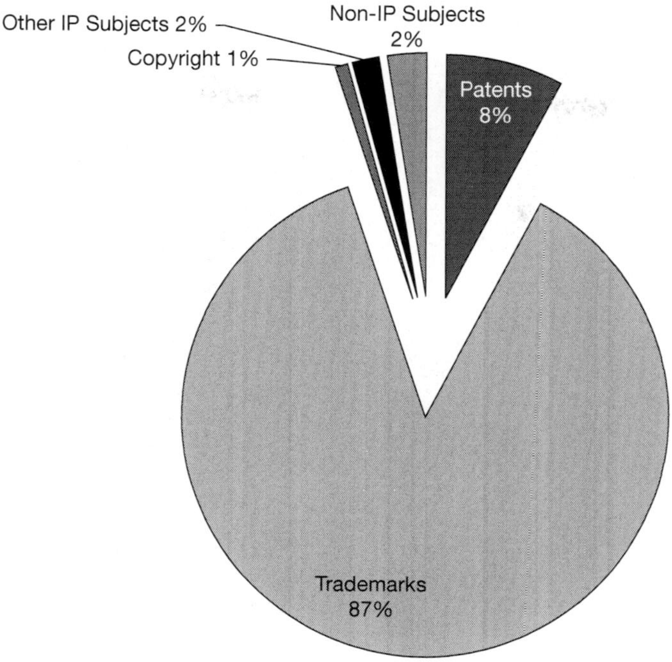

Figure 3.3 ATJ preliminary rulings, 1984–2007. Distribution by subject matter (*N* = 1,338)

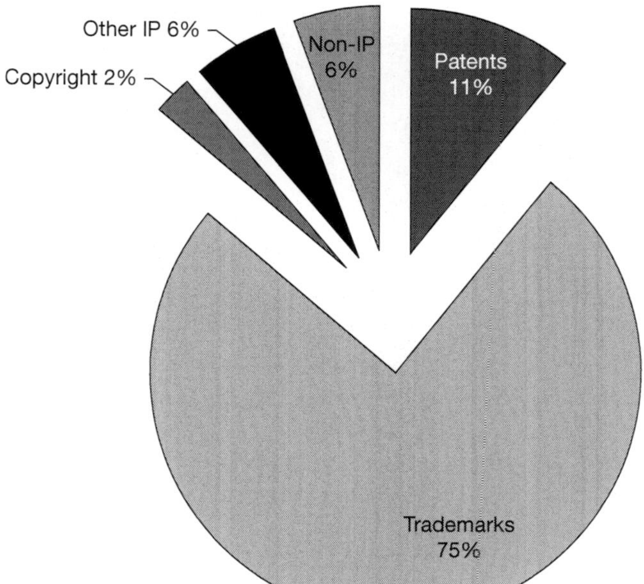

Figure 3.4 ATJ preliminary rulings, 2008–2014. Distribution by subject matter (*N* = 1,341)

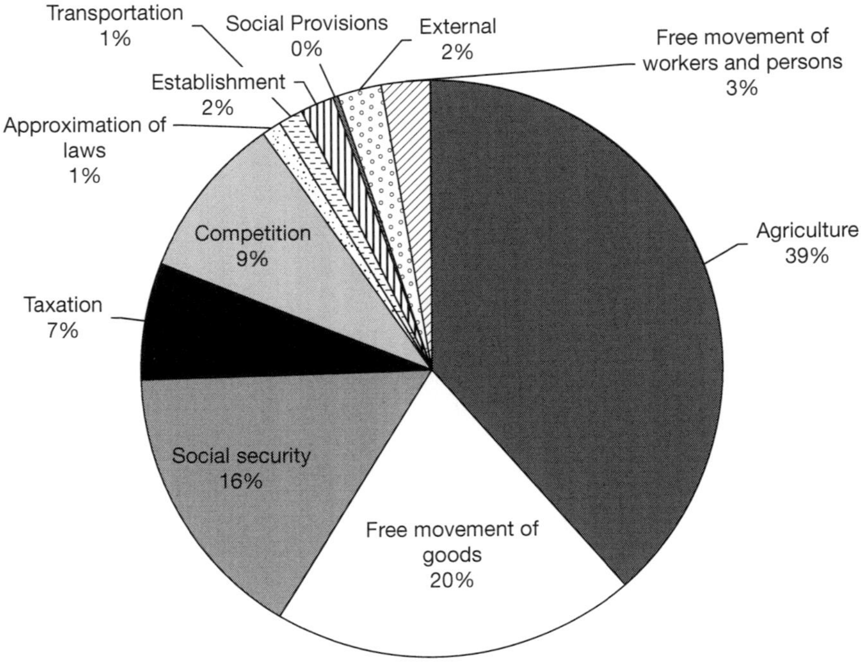

Figure 3.5 ECJ preliminary rulings, 1958–1974. Distribution by subject matter ($N = 369$)

Stone Sweet documents that between 1959 and 1975, the European Community adopted few regulations and directives. The number of regulations and directives adopted per year peaked at 100 in 1972, but for most of this period the number of secondary rules agreed to tended to be significantly lower. This trend changed in 1975 (A. Stone Sweet, Judicialization and the Construction of Governance. *Comparative Political Studies* 1999, 32 (2): 59).

by secondary legislation. Figure 3.5 depicts litigation from the European Community's founding until 1975, a period when the European officials had adopted few harmonized policies. The subject matter of ECJ decisions during these years was wider than the ATJ's, although over 90% of disputes involved just five issue areas.

The EC has always been significantly larger economically than the Andean Community, and hence has generated more preliminary references. The greater diversity of subjects adjudicated by the ECJ also reflects the EC's expanding legislative agenda, which increased significantly beginning in 1975.[17] The scope of Andean secondary legislation has also expanded over time, but harmonized secondary laws exist in fewer subject areas, most notably taxes, insurance, transportation, and some agricultural issues. Figure 3.6 depicts the subject-matter variation of ECJ preliminary rulings up to and including 1994, a thirty-six year period comparable

[17] A. Stone Sweet, Judicialization and the Construction of Governance. *Comparative Political Studies* 1999, 32 (2): 72–3.

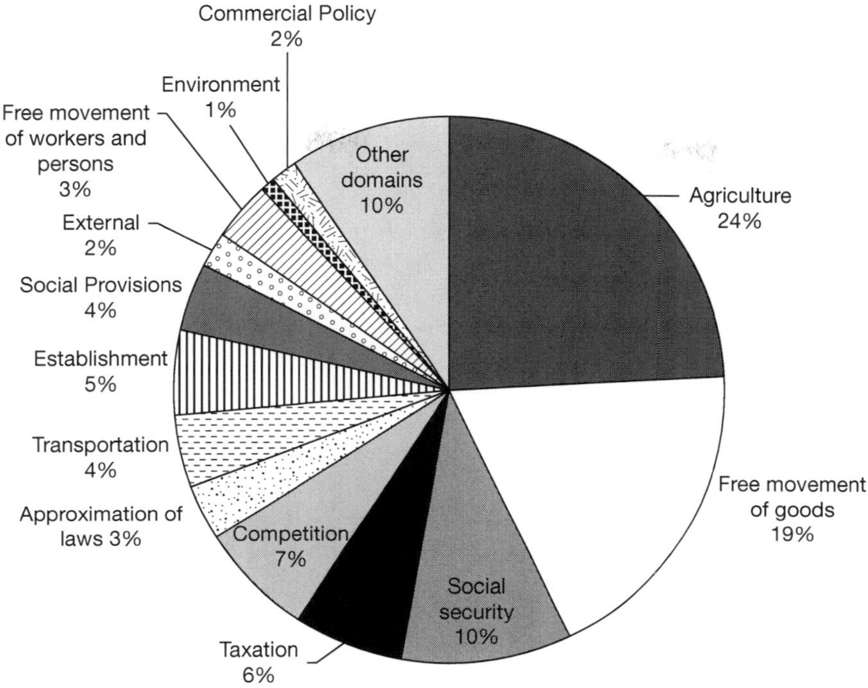

Figure 3.6 ECJ preliminary rulings, 1958–1994. Distribution by subject matter ($N = 3{,}767$) (A. Stone Sweet, Judicialization and the Construction of Governance. *Comparative Political Studies* 1999, 32 (2): 72–3)

to the first three decades of the ATJ. Comparing this longer time period shows the much greater diversity of litigation in Europe.

National judges pose narrow, repetitive questions of Andean IP law and the ATJ responds in kind

Given the uniform nature of Andean preliminary references, our finding that ATJ decisions are highly repetitive should not be surprising. National court appeals from IP agencies often raise the same legal issues, such as whether two trademarks are likely to cause confusion, whether a trademark is famous, and whether an invention satisfies the requirements for patentability.[18] National judges, in turn, repeatedly ask the ATJ to interpret the same provisions of Andean law even where the Tribunal has already made plain its interpretation of those provisions. The ATJ responds to these requests in kind, regurgitating its analysis and often literally cutting and

[18] ATJ Preliminary Ruling 90-IP-2004, 3, 5–8 (likelihood of confusion); ATJ Preliminary Ruling 162-IP-2004, 7–8, 11 (famous trademarks); ATJ Preliminary Ruling 49-IP-2005, 5–6 (patentability).

pasting paragraphs from its earlier rulings. While this repetition is a source of frustration for many IP lawyers in the region, we explain in Chapter 5 that repetition has helped to build national judicial and administrative support for the ATJ.

Some observers may claim that the ATJ's duplicative jurisprudence is an artifact of the civil law tradition, where judicial rulings apply only to the case at hand. But most national courts in Europe are part of the same tradition. The key distinction between the European and Andean Communities is found not in national legal systems but rather in a doctrine known as *acte clair*, a judge-made rule that the ECJ created to dissuade national courts from referring cases that raise settled legal issues.[19] The ECJ discouraged such references to enable it to focus on more important disputes and to develop the scope and reach of EC law.[20]

In our interviews, we asked whether the ATJ should also adopt *acte clair*, as some scholars in the region have suggested.[21] Some attorneys mused that the Tribunal's docket would be much smaller if it did so. A few national judges candidly admitted that the ATJ's copycat jurisprudence limited the Tribunal's interference with their discretion to decide cases. For their part, ATJ judges are uncertain whether to adopt *acte clair*. Former ATJ President Ricardo Vigil Toledo asserts that the doctrine has not taken hold because the Tribunal can respond to preliminary ruling requests in less than two months (as compared to an average of two years for the ECJ), and because the uniform legal systems and language of the Andean countries have resulted in fewer challenges than in Europe to ensuring the uniform application of Community law.[22] For now, the cost of continuing with the status quo is fairly low. If the ATJ's docket continues to expand, however, the Tribunal may one day revisit the issue.

Activating and Sustaining the Links Between National Courts and the ATJ

This section considers why some national courts began to refer preliminary references to the ATJ far more quickly than others. In particular, we investigate why Colombia was first to refer cases and why it has continued to be the largest source of ATJ rulings. We also explore why Ecuadorian and Peruvian courts did not refer cases for many years, and why Bolivia and Venezuelan courts have made so few

[19] Case 283/81, *Srl CILFIT v. Ministry of Health*, 1982 E.C.R. 3415.

[20] M. Rasmussen, The European Court's Acte Clair Strategy in C.I.L.I.T. Or Acte Clair, of Course! But What Does It Mean? *European Law Review*, 1984, 9 (4): 242–59.

[21] P. Bueno Martinez and A. Daniel Perotti, La Teoria del Acto Reclamado: Resulta Necesaria su Aplicación en el Marco de la Interpretación Judicial Andina. *Dikaion, Universidad de la Sabana* 2005, 19 (14): 146–52; A. Daniel Perotti, Algunas Consideraciones sobre la Interpretación Prejudicial Obligatoria en el Derecho Andino. *Gaceta Juridica de la Comunidad Europea*. D-213, 2001, 46.

[22] R.V. Toledo, *La Estructura Juridica y el Futuro de la Comunidad Andina*. Madrid: Thompson Reuters Aranzadi, 2011, 130.

references. Our coding, supplemented by interviews, helps to explain these variations in judicial activation patterns.

Colombia

Four factors help to explain the initial preliminary references from Colombia in 1987 and the increase in referrals beginning in the mid-1990s. First, Colombia has played a leading role in drafting regional laws since the Andean Pact's founding. This is particularly true with regard to intellectual property, because Colombian IP laws were older and more developed than those of other member states.[23] In fact, the first Andean IP legislation, *Decisión* 85, adopted in 1974, "followed almost to the letter" the patent and trademark provisions of the 1971 Colombian Code of Commerce.[24] This old lineage meant that there was a basic familiarity with the content of Andean IP legislation among lawyers in Colombia.

A second factor reinforced this concordance of domestic and regional law. Colombia was the only Andean member state to give direct effect to *Decisión* 85 without adopting implementing legislation.[25] Since the only relevant law was Andean law, it was easier for national courts to accept that the ATJ should be involved in its interpretation.

A third explanation concerns informal advocacy by self-interested attorneys. The first Colombian reference to the ATJ in 1987 was made by Germán Cavelier, the respected head of a Bogotá law firm and a professor of international law at the prestigious Universidad de Nuestra Señora de Rosario. Before the *Consejo de Estado*, Cavelier challenged the refusal of the Colombian IP agency to register the trademark of the Swedish car manufacturer Volvo. He argued that the *Consejo* was required to refer the case to the ATJ and implied that its failure to do so could subject Colombia to a noncompliance suit. Cavelier also spoke with former judges on the Colombian court who successfully lobbied their successors to refer the case to the Tribunal.[26]

The structure of the Colombian judicial system reveals a fourth factor that facilitated ATJ referrals. In all Andean states, as in many Latin American countries, judges receive special training and make their careers in the judiciary.[27] According to the judges, attorneys, and government officials whom we interviewed, many members of this professional judicial class feared that references to the ATJ would undermine their autonomy. In Colombia, however, governmental and administrative decisions,

[23] G. Cavalier, *Complición Histórica de las Leyes Colombianas Sobre Propriedad Industrial*. Bogota: Cavelier Abogados, 2002.

[24] Saldías, 2007, 15.

[25] R.-S. Manrique, The Andean Community's Intellectual Property Regime. In: *The Andean Community and the United States: Trade and Investment Relations in the 1990s*. M. Rodríguez Mendoza, Patricia Correa, and Barbara Kotschwar (eds), 212–19. Organization of American States, 1998, 214–19.

[26] Interview with four attorneys (H) at Colombian branch of a multinational law firm.

[27] L.A. Hammergren, *Envisioning Reform: Improving Judicial Performance in Latin America*. University Park, PA: Pennsylvania State University Press, 2007.

including IP registrations, are typically reviewed by the *Consejo de Estado*, a first- and last-instance administrative court that is separate from the rest of the judicial system.[28] Members of the Council come from many backgrounds, including the judiciary, politics, academia, the private bar, and public administration. After passing a qualifying examination, they are appointed to non-renewable eight-year terms and then return to their former careers. The Council's distinctive structure and appointment process suggest that its members would be less concerned that ATJ referrals would undermine the prestige, influence, or autonomy of their office—a fact confirmed by our interviews.[29]

After the first reference in the 1987 Volvo case, the First Chamber of the *Consejo de Estado*—the section that reviews involving intellectual property issues—continued to refer IP cases to the ATJ. As shown in Figure 3.2, there were only a small number of such cases until the mid-1990s, at which point referrals rose dramatically. This increase followed the creation of the Superintendent of Industry and Commerce in 1992 and the overhaul of Andean IP rules summarized earlier and discussed in more detail in Chapter 5. According to one Colombian attorney, as a result of these changes more businesses began to request trademark and patent registrations or to oppose the registrations of their competitors, and the *Consejo* "started to use the Andean system" more frequently to help it resolve these disputes.[30]

Ecuador

In contrast to Colombia, courts in Ecuador did not refer any cases to the ATJ until 1994, and regular referrals did not begin until 1999. One reason for this pattern was uncertainty as to whether intermediate appellate courts were required to send cases to the Tribunal. In Europe, lower courts readily refer cases to the ECJ. In the Andean Community, by contrast, until very recently most referrals have been made by last-instance courts. This pattern is well developed in Ecuador. Formally, the Supreme Court of Ecuador is that country's highest judicial body, but the *Ley de Casación* makes its review an extraordinary remedy (*el recurso extraordinario de Casación*) to be granted only in extremely limited circumstances. Thus, for all practical purposes, lower appellate courts are the last-instance level of review for issues of Andean law.

Litigation was required to resolve whether lower appellate courts were required to refer cases. The key case involved a dispute between Proctor & Gamble ("P&G") and an Ecuadorian company, New Yorker Guayaquil S.A. ("New Yorker"). New Yorker challenged P&G's termination of a contract to manufacture and distribute products bearing P&G trademarks. P&G appealed a trial court ruling to the Superior Court of Guayaquil and requested a reference to the ATJ. The Superior Court refused on the ground that it was not a court of last instance. P&G then

28 This system borrows from the French model where a separate quasi-judicial administrative branch oversees review of government actions.

29 Interview with five judges (A) of the *Sala Primera del Consejo de Estado de Colombia*.

30 Interview with attorney (A) from a commercial and administrative law firm in Bogotá, Colombia.

appealed to the Supreme Court and also filed a complaint with the Andean General Secretariat. Both petitions included allegations that Ecuador violated Andean law when the Superior Court refused to send a reference to the ATJ.

In 1998, the General Secretariat upheld P&G's complaint. It interpreted the ATJ Treaty as requiring references from appellate courts where the only further appeal is an extraordinary remedy.[31] Six months later, the Supreme Court of Ecuador reversed the Superior Court's decision. The high court agreed with the General Secretariat that P&G's "request for a preliminary interpretation was mandatory for the Superior Court and by not doing so the court violated [the ATJ Treaty] and the *Ley de Casacion*."[32] Shortly thereafter, the General Secretariat issued a new decree confirming that Ecuador was now in compliance with Andean law.[33]

As shown in Figure 3.2, Ecuadorian courts began to send a steady stream of cases to the ATJ in 1999. Our interviews with attorneys confirmed that the P&G dispute was the catalyst for these referrals.[34] The P&G litigation also helps to explain why referrals from Ecuador originate from multiple lower courts, as distinguished from Colombia, where nearly all referrals are made by a single first- and last-instance court.

If the P&G litigation was the turning point for referrals from Ecuador, what explains the first three cases referred by that country's courts in 1994? Meetings between Andean and national judges suggest a plausible answer. The President of the ATJ in the early 1990s was Gallo Pico Mantilla, a lawyer and former government minister from Ecuador. He met informally with some of the judges serving on Ecuador's administrative courts, explained the ATJ's relative lack of work, and urged them to refer cases.[35] The judges sent a few cases in the mid-1990s, but then stopped, in part because the country's IP law was itself in flux. Ecuador's legislature adopted a revised IP code in 1999. A draft of the legislation envisioned creating a specialized IP tribunal. The tribunal was never created, but the expectation that IP suits would one day be resolved by a specialized domestic tribunal provided a ready excuse for Ecuadorian judges to refrain from making regular references to the ATJ.[36]

In the late 1990s, Ecuador's Supreme Court was renowned for its independence and opposition to corruption.[37] Chapter 6 discusses two examples where Ecuador's Supreme Court and its Constitutional Court enforced rulings of the ATJ and General Secretariat by nullifying the government's retaliatory trade sanctions against Colombia, albeit without referring the cases to the ATJ. Between 1998

[31] *Resolución* 171, General Secretariat *Decreto* No. 51-98 (December 17, 1998).

[32] *Recurso de Casación*, Third Civil and Commercial Law Courtroom of the Supreme Court of Ecuador, October 5, 1999 (Claim No. 13-99; Res. No. 468-99).

[33] *Resolución* 356, General Secretariat *Decreto* No. 08-2000 (February 9, 2000).

[34] Interview with attorney (A) from commercial and administrative law firm in Colombia.

[35] Interview with former ATJ judge (A).

[36] Interview with three national judges (A) of the *Tribunal Distrital No. 1 de lo Contencioso Administrativo de Ecuador*.

[37] See Ecuador: the politics of justice, *The Economist* (July 31, 1997), available at <http://www.economist.com/node/152840>.

and the election of President Rafael Correa in 2007, Ecuador had four presidents, none of whom lasted more than three years in office. The political turmoil included purges of Ecuador's Supreme Court in 2004 and Constitutional Court in 2005. The executive intervention in the judiciary continued under President Correa, who implemented a series of "reforms" that further undermined the independence of national judges.[38]

How has this political upheaval affected preliminary references to the ATJ? A review of the last seven years of data shows a decline in referrals from Ecuador from 2008 through 2010, followed by a modest uptick, with cases holding steady at eighteen to twenty per year. The number of preliminary rulings remains below the pre-2007 peak of more than fifty cases per year. However, the ATJ's 2015 annual report indicates that Ecuadorian courts referred forty-two cases in 2015, all but one of which concerned Andean IP law.[39]

The relatively low number of references may reflect judicial timidity in the current domestic political climate, an issue we discuss in Chapter 7. That chapter also reviews Andean-level legal challenges to import certification rules and safeguards that Ecuador has imposed in response to its current economic crisis. Litigants from Peru and Colombia filed complaints directly with the General Secretariat. It is striking that these litigants did not even bother to raise these challenges with Ecuadorian judges, notwithstanding the rulings of the country's two high courts, discussed earlier and in Chapter 6, that overturned domestic import restrictions that violated Andean law.

Peru

Unlike in Colombia and Ecuador, the activation of ATJ referrals from Peru was protracted and involved open resistance by national judges. Once that opposition was overcome, however, a flood of references from the Peruvian Supreme Court followed. The flood quickly abated, however, and the number of references declined until the creation in 2013 of a specialized appellate court, and a 2014 ATJ ruling permitting references directly from a trademark bureau within Peru's IP agency, INDECOPI.

As previously described, all domestic IP agencies in the Andes apply Andean IP rules to decide whether to register applications for trademarks and patents. The agencies, and the attorneys who appear before them, were thus logical interlocutors for Andean judges. In 1999 or 2000, a partner in a well-known Peruvian law firm specializing in intellectual property asked INDECOPI's administrative tribunal to refer a question of Andean IP law to the ATJ in a pending case. The agency made

[38] See Otto Reich and Ezequiel Vázquez Ger, How to destroy a judicial system in three easy steps. *Foreign Policy Online* (June 13, 2012), available at <http://foreignpolicy.com/2012/06/13/how-to-destroy-a-judicial-system-in-three-easy-steps/>; Independence in Ecuador's Judicial Reform Process (2014), available at <http://www.dplf.org/sites/default/files/indjud_ecuador_executivereport_eng.pdf>.

[39] *Tribunal de Justicia de la Comunidad Andina, Informe de Labores Gestión* 2015, 69.

the request but the ATJ rejected it. We found no written record of this decision, but its existence was confirmed by several Peruvian attorneys, judges, and government officials. According to a Peruvian judge on the ATJ, Andean judges viewed the INDECOPI tribunal as an administrative rather than a judicial body and thus ineligible to request a preliminary reference under the ATJ Treaty.[40] As a formal matter, this distinction is correct, but it ignores the fact that the INDECOPI tribunal performs a quasi-judicial function—the review of registration decisions by the agency's patent and trademark offices—that in other member states is carried out by courts.

Lacking a direct link between the agency and the ATJ, IP attorneys seeking preliminary references were first required to appeal INDECOPI registration decisions to the Peruvian courts. Attorneys described the likelihood of pursuing such appeals as small because of the expense and time involved and because national judges were unfamiliar with IP law. The disincentive to appeal was compounded by the fact that in the few cases in which attorneys did appeal, Peruvian judges refused requests to refer the cases to the ATJ.[41]

In response to this situation, the same IP attorney filed a complaint with the Andean General Secretariat. The attorney argued that Andean law required the Supreme Court of Peru (which has wider appellate jurisdiction than its Ecuadorian counterpart) to request preliminary references. In a 2000 decree, the General Secretariat agreed, issuing a formal finding of noncompliance against Peru that echoed its earlier noncompliance decree against Ecuador.[42]

The parties to an unrelated trademark case then pending before the Supreme Court of Peru cited this decree in support of their request for a reference, but the Peruvian judges again refused to send the case to the ATJ. They reasoned that the "independence and exclusive judicial function" of the national judiciary would be threatened if they applied the Tribunal's interpretation of Andean law.[43] Following this decision, the IP attorney, now supported by the Peruvian government, filed a second complaint with the General Secretariat. In a 2003 decree finding a continuing breach of Peru's treaty obligations, the Secretariat reaffirmed its prior analysis. It reasoned that although national judges have discretion to decide in good faith whether a dispute raises issues of Andean law meriting a referral to the ATJ, in trademark disputes Andean law is the only applicable law and so the Supreme Court must ask for a preliminary reference.[44]

In the months following the 2003 decree, Andean and Peruvian officials made a concerted effort to persuade the Supreme Court to change its ways. The General Secretariat is located in Lima, the country's capital, which facilitated meetings at which Andean officials sought to convince Peruvian high court judges to begin

[40] Interview with former ATJ judge (B).

[41] Interview with attorney (C) from an IP law firm in Peru.

[42] *Resolución* 459, General Secretariat Noncompliance *Decreto* No. 38-2000 (December 5, 2000).

[43] The decision of the Supreme Court of Peru is discussed in *Resolución* 771, General Secretariat Noncompliance *Decreto* No. 173-2003 (authors' translation).

[44] See *Resolución* 771.

making references. The Secretariat also partnered with the Andean Committee of Jurists, which organized a conference in Lima with the members of the Supreme Court's Chamber of Constitutional and Social Rights. The conference participants explained the obligation to refer cases and provided specific instructions on how to do so.[45] According to a judge on the Supreme Court at the time, the conference and subsequent meetings convinced the judges to begin referring cases in 2005.[46]

The time was right for the Court to give up its exceptional position. In 1996 Peru had opted out of the newly created Andean Free Trade Area, but in the 1997 Sucre Protocol it agreed to participate fully by the end of 2005.[47] Peru was thus in the process of normalizing its relations with the Andean Community when its judges came under pressure. As the country became more active in the Andean system, the refusal of its courts to refer cases to the Tribunal appeared increasingly problematic, especially because a Peruvian administrative agency favored references in IP cases.

Why did Peruvian judges resist sending references far longer than their colleagues in Colombia and Ecuador? The structure of the Peruvian judicial system suggests one plausible explanation. Judges reach the Supreme Court after studying at the *Academia de la Magistratura*, a training that does not include Andean law. In addition, judges frequently change positions within the judiciary. When the judge whom we interviewed assumed the Presidency of the Chamber of Constitutional and Social Rights—the Supreme Court division responsible for IP appeals—her first inclination was to replicate past practice and not to refer cases to the ATJ. None of the judges "had experience consulting the Tribunal ... We thought the Tribunal was about relations for the Andean Community, and didn't see implications for Peruvian courts."[48] The judge also offered two suggestions as to why her predecessors did not refer cases: first, her colleagues did not have regular contact with their counterparts in other Andean countries, and second, although one of her predecessors later served on the ATJ, he did not, unlike the Ecuadorian ATJ judge described earlier, personally lobby his colleagues to refer cases.

As these events reveal, judicial misconceptions about Andean law and the Andean legal system were difficult to dislodge and were only overcome by cumulative pressure from the government, the private bar, and Andean officials. Once the barriers were surmounted, however, a sharp spike in Peruvian references followed in 2005 and 2006. Yet as Figure 3.2 shows, the number of references then declined and remained low until 2013 and 2014, when they increased sharply again.

[45] See *El Principio de Cooperación Judicial Entre el Tribunal Andino y los Tribunales Nacionales en el Marco de la Comunidad Andina*, November 28, 2003; telephone interviews with official (C) of the *Comisión Andina de Juristas*.

[46] Interview with national judge (A) of the *Sala de Derecho Constitucional y Social Permanente de la Corte Suprema de Justicia de Peru*.

[47] Chapter 6 discusses Peru's exceptional status within the Andean Community in the 1990s.

[48] Interview with judge (A) of the *Sala de Derecho Constitucional y Social Permanente de la Corte Suprema de Justicia de Peru*.

Our interviews in Peru help to explain this seesaw pattern. According to national judges and officials in INDECOPI, references dropped between 2007 and 2012 for several reasons. First, the vast majority of ATJ referrals were made by Peru's apex court rather than lower courts. Litigants seeking references thus had to appeal their cases through the levels of the country's judicial system—a time-consuming and costly process. Second, Peru's generalist judges (and some attorneys) had limited knowledge of specialized topics such as IP law and were often unaware of the Andean legal system or the ability to refer cases. Third, for those cases that judges did refer, the questions they posed were often repetitive, abstract, and unhelpful to the litigants. Fourth, many businesses and their attorneys preferred to target their arguments to INDECOPI's specialized bodies—such as the Directorate of Distinctive Signs—and its IP administrative tribunal, whose officials had training and extensive experience with IP matters.[49]

In 2013, after Peru had experienced several years of rapid economic growth, there was "a political decision to improve [the] legal system as it deals with market themes. As part of this reform, the government created a super-specialized judicial body ... to strengthen the market."[50] The new specialized administrative court was given jurisdiction over appeals from INDECOPI. The judges received training in IP law and were told that they had an obligation to refer cases involving Andean law.[51] They soon began doing so, sending more than 140 cases to the ATJ in 2013 and 2014. One judge attributed the rise in referrals to the strong economy, which made trademarks more valuable.[52] The administrative court has also informally sought the ATJ's guidance to draft more specific questions whose answers will presumably be more useful to the judges and the litigants.

A second event relevant to the increase in referrals from Peru is a November 2014 ATJ ruling accepting a reference from two INDECOPI bodies, the Directorate of Distinctive Signs and the Commission of Distinctive Signs.[53] Reversing its earlier position, the Tribunal concluded that both bodies are empowered to resolve contested proceedings that require the application of Andean law and thus meet a functional test for deciding which administrative entities can refer cases.[54] INDECOPI officials anticipate that reference requests from IP litigants and attorneys will increase now that the two bodies can send cases directly to Andean judges in Quito.[55]

[49] Interviews with officials (E) of INDECOPI.

[50] Interview with judges (B) of the *Octava Sala Especializada en lo Contencioso of the Sala Especializada de lo Contencioso Administrativo.*

[51] As part of the reforms, the Supreme Court of Peru was refashioned as a cassation-style court with limited jurisdiction. As with Ecuador's judicial system, discussed earlier this chapter, this change means that lower-level appellate judges are, in most suits, courts of last instance and are thus obligated to refer cases.

[52] Interview with judge (C) of the *Sala de Derecho Constitucional y Social Permanente de la Corte Suprema de Justicia de Peru.*

[53] ATJ Preliminary Ruling 121-IP-2014.

[54] Ibid., para. 48.

[55] Interview with officials (E) of INDECOPI.

Bolivia and Venezuela

In stark contrast to Colombia, Ecuador, and Peru, national courts in the two remaining Andean Community member states have referred a total of thirteen cases—eleven from Bolivia and two from Venezuela—during the first thirty years of the ATJ's existence.

The first Bolivian case involved a challenge by the foreign-owned TELECEL to a tax on long-distance telephone rates. In response to a reference from the Supreme Court of Bolivia, the ATJ refused to address the merits of the case because the Andean law in question applied only to transborder disputes.[56] Three Bolivian cases involve the Simón Bolívar Andean University, an Andean institution located in Bolivia over which the ATJ has exclusive competence.[57]

Bolivian references to the ATJ concerning IP issues began in 2009. Yet despite the ATJ's careful effort to explain to the *Sala Plena del Tribunal Supremo de Justicia* the preliminary reference procedure and its requirements, as well as the substance of Andean IP law, these rulings did not generate a stream of cases.[58] In 2014, the ATJ accepted three cases referred directly by the Bolivian IP agency SENAPI, and an additional two IP references from the *Sala Plena*. Although we are uncertain why this court—which appears to be the judicial body in charge of IP issues—has referred only four IP cases in the last five years, Andean judges have been working with their Bolivian counterparts and with SENAPI officials to overcome these blockages.[59] In 2015, Bolivian courts and adjudicatory agencies requested thirty-four preliminary rulings, all but one of which concerned IP.[60]

As for the two cases from Venezuela, in 1998 the Venezuelan Supreme Court referred a dispute in which the plaintiff had asked a national judge to nullify a Venezuelan ministry decision. The case raised the question of whether Andean law required Venezuela to implement a common Andean policy to improve the competitiveness of the regional shipping industry.[61] Later that year, a different court referred a case concerning Andean IP protection for computer software arising out of a copyright infringement action brought by the Microsoft corporation.[62]

We asked the individuals whom we interviewed to explain the dearth of referrals from these two countries. In the case of Bolivia, the respondents pointed to several factors.[63] Bolivia is the poorest country in the Andean Community and its judicial and administrative infrastructure is underdeveloped. The government frequently

[56] ATJ Preliminary Ruling 87-IP-2002.

[57] Two of the cases are labor disputes, ATJ Preliminary Rulings 179-IP-2011 and 180-IP-2011, and one concerns the tax status of the University, ATJ Preliminary Ruling 67-IP-2014.

[58] ATJ Preliminary Rulings 78-IP-2009 and 79-IP-2009.

[59] Interviews with ATJ judge (H).

[60] Data is from the *Tribunal de Justicia de la Comunidad Andina, Informe de Labores Gestión* 2015, 69.

[61] The plaintiff, an Andean maritime company, challenged a decision by the Venezuelan Ministry of Transportation and Communication, which had denied the plaintiff's request that a Brazilian competitor be barred from access to Venezuelan ports. ATJ Preliminary Ruling 19-IP-98.

[62] ATJ Preliminary Ruling 24-IP-98.

[63] Interviews with official (C) of the *Comisión Andina de Juristas*; Interview with official (A) of the *Asociación Nacional de Laboratorios Farmacéuticos de Peru* (ALAFARPE).

changes the composition of the Bolivian Supreme Court, and the high turnover rate makes it difficult to build relationships between the ATJ and Bolivian judges.[64] The Bolivian Constitution also lacks a provision authorizing the government to delegate lawmaking powers to the Andean Community.[65] Recognizing the supremacy of Andean law and making referrals to the ATJ thus poses a greater legal risk for Bolivian judges than it does for jurists in other member states. There has been little reason to incur this risk because, at least until recently, the domestic demand for IP protection has been weak. In the early 2000s, IP owners characterized the Bolivian IP agency as "seriously under-funded, lack[ing] a cadre of trained personnel, and lack[ing] any mechanism by which to enforce intellectual property rights."[66] The preliminary references sent by SENAPI and by the courts beginning in 2014 suggest that this situation is changing, perhaps reflecting a growing demand from firms to protect intellectual property in Bolivia.

Bolivia's political commitment to Andean integration has also waned over the previous decade. As will be discussed in Chapter 7, President Evo Morales reacted favorably to Venezuelan President Hugo Chavez's decision in 2006 to withdraw from the Community, and Bolivia has joined other alternative integration projects that Venezuela has promoted. In 2013, Bolivia joined MERCOSUR as an associate member, becoming a dual participant in two South American free trade pacts, a decision that may divert political and economic attention away from Andean integration.[67]

The explanation for the dearth of preliminary references from Venezuela is different. Venezuela did not lack the legal or administrative capacity to implement Andean rules, and the two referrals from the late 1990s suggested a potential opening for national judges to send other cases to the ATJ. The possibility of such requests diminished, however, following the election of President Chavez in 1998. In 2002, the Andean Commission of Jurists established a project to increase awareness of the Andean legal system in national judiciaries. The Commission's efforts made little headway in Venezuela due to the politicization of the country's Supreme Court.[68]

In addition, Chavez's appointment of numerous provisional judges made it exceptionally risky to refer cases to an international tribunal not controlled by the government. The possibility of additional ATJ references from Venezuela vanished entirely with the country's formal withdrawal from the Andean Community in 2006. Nevertheless, some national judges and the country's IP agency have continued to apply Andean IP *Decisiones* following the withdrawal, a topic we discuss in greater detail in Chapter 5.

[64] Interviews with official (C) of the *Comisión Andina de Juristas*.

[65] E. Tremolada, Application of the Andean Community Law in Bolivia, Ecuador, Peru, and Venezuela in Comparison with the European Union Experience. *Jean Monnet/Robert Schuman Paper Series* 2006, 6 (3).

[66] International Intellectual Property Alliance, 2002 Special 301 Report: Bolivia 310, 313.

[67] See "Bolivia will hold double membership of Mercosur and the Andean Community," *MercoPress*, June 24, 2013, available at <http://en.mercopress.com/2013/06/24/bolivia-will-hold-double-membership-of-mercosur-and-the-andean-community>.

[68] Interviews with official (C) of the *Comisión Andina de Juristas*.

Concluding observations

Once attorneys and Andean officials overcame national judicial resistance, the judges and lawyers we interviewed indicated that the relevant courts in three of the five member states habitually referred IP registration cases to the ATJ. Several distinctive features of the region's IP system contributed to this result. IP was regulated by Andean (rather than national) rules that were comprehensively revised in the early 1990s. As a result, there were no entrenched bureaucratic or judicial actors committed to the domestic resolution of disputes. Intellectual property cases also raised legal issues that many national judges did not fully understand. The regional, novel, and technical nature of Andean IP rules helps to explain why the domestic IP administrative agencies were eager to seek guidance from the ATJ. The next section describes the symbiotic relationship that developed between agency officials and Andean judges and analyzes its consequences.

Domestic Intellectual Property Agencies as the Engine of Andean Preliminary References

As discussed in the introduction to this chapter, scholars have identified national courts as key actors in giving effect to ECJ rulings in domestic law. In the Andean context too, national judges seek references from their Andean colleagues and apply the preliminary rulings once the ATJ has spoken. However, our analysis and coding of the case law and interviews with key stakeholders reveal that, unlike in Europe, national judges are mostly passive intermediaries who do not engage in an active dialogue with the ATJ. Instead, our research discloses that domestic IP agencies are the ATJ's principal interlocutors and compliance partners, repeatedly seeking the Tribunal's guidance and habitually applying ATJ rulings that address ambiguities and lacunae in Andean IP rules. The General Secretariat has reinforced this symbiotic relationship by consulting agency officials regarding revisions to Andean IP legislation as interpreted by the ATJ.[69]

The intellectual property agencies' influence on Andean jurisprudence

Chapter 5 analyzes the many ways in which ATJ jurisprudence has established intellectual property as an island of effective international adjudication in the Andean Community. In brief, the agencies are avid consumers of the Tribunal's case law, which has not only clarified Andean IP rules but also bolstered the agencies' commitment to the rule of law by augmenting the procedures that administrators follow when reviewing contested IP applications. Here we focus on two other developments that reveal the primacy of the ATJ's relationship with the IP agencies

69 Interviews with former official (B) of the General Secretariat Legal Advisor's Office.

rather than national courts: how agency officials frame the legal issues presented to the Tribunal and shape Andean IP jurisprudence in light of their substantive policy preferences, and a 2007 doctrinal shift that for the first time created a direct link between agency officials and ATJ judges.

The domestic IP agencies shape the questions that national courts present to the ATJ in several ways. First, the agencies have the initial opportunity to interpret and apply Andean IP rules when deciding whether to grant an application for a trademark or a patent. In so doing, they identify and analyze any unsettled legal issues that may later be the subject of a reference to the Tribunal. Second, the agencies participate as parties in litigation challenging their registration decisions. When private actors ask national courts to overturn agency rulings, they often name the agencies themselves as defendants. As parties to national court proceedings, the agencies can suggest to national judges which legal issues should be referred to Andean judges. Third, the IP agencies sometimes participate as defendants in litigation before the ATJ, providing information to the Tribunal in defense of their substantive policy preferences and registration decisions.

The agencies' influence on ATJ case law is especially apparent in the area of trademark coexistence agreements: contracts between two or more trademark owners that establish the rules by which the marks can be used in the same market for the same or similar goods or services. Coexistence agreements provide important benefits to business competitors, enabling them to "market ... their products to the public without the fear of defending a trademark infringement lawsuit."[70] Whether such agreements benefit consumers is less clear, however, since consumers may be misled by goods or services whose trademarks are confusingly similar.

In many countries, including the United States and Mexico, IP agencies and national courts give strong deference to coexistence agreements in deciding whether two similar trademarks are eligible for registration.[71] The judge-made law in the Andean Community is starkly different. In assessing the validity of coexistence agreements, the ATJ considers not only the private rights of trademark owners but also the interests of consumers who purchase their goods and services. For example, the Tribunal has held that coexistence agreements "do not create legal rights, do not ... exempt a trademark from a study of its eligibility for registration, and do not render inapplicable an analysis of consumer confusion by the [agency's trademark] examiner."[72] The ATJ has also stressed the critical role of Andean trademark law in protecting consumers.[73]

The ATJ's focus on the public interest originated with the IP agencies in Peru and Colombia, both of which, as explained earlier, have a mandate to protect consumers as well as intellectual property. In Peru, INDECOPI developed an internal

[70] M. Moss, Trademark "Coexistence" Agreements: Legitimate Contracts or Tools of Consumer Deception? *Loyola Consumer Law Review.* 2005, 18 (2): 199.

[71] See ibid., 210–13; J.M. Murphy, The Confusing Similarity Standard in Mexican Trademark Law. *Trademark Reporter*, 2006, 96 (6): 1190.

[72] ATJ Preliminary Ruling 79-IP-2003, 11 (quoting ATJ Preliminary Ruling 15-IP-2003).

[73] ATJ Preliminary Ruling 85-IP-2003, 11–12; ATJ Preliminary Ruling 41-IP-99, 5.

culture that holds consumer rights in high regard.[74] The agency has a division devoted to enforcing consumer protection laws and educating Peruvians about unlawful market practices. INDECOPI's pro-consumer orientation also influenced its interpretation of Andean IP rules.[75] In the 1990s, the agency's administrative tribunal invalidated trademark coexistence agreements that failed to take consumer interests into account adequately. The Colombian IP agency developed a similar approach, emphasizing the importance of "societal concerns" in evaluating trademark applications.[76]

When businesses challenged the agencies' refusal to register confusingly similar trademarks, the ATJ drew upon these practices and concluded that coexistence agreements must take consumer interests into account.[77] In a series of preliminary rulings, the ATJ extended this principle and required the parties to such agreements to adopt measures to prevent confusion among consumers concerning their products' origins; promote fair commercial practices and competition; record agreements with the domestic IP agencies; and subject agreements to the scrutiny of agency examiners, who may refuse registration on grounds of consumer confusion.[78]

Applying these pro-consumer standards, the IP agencies, the ATJ, and national courts have rejected or modified trademark coexistence agreements involving large multinational corporations such as Starbucks, Mars, Sony, General Motors, Deutsche Bank, Sun Microsystems, Novartis, L'Oréal, and Unilever. Some of these rulings had adverse economic consequences for the firms involved. For example, a 2004 decision of the Colombian *Consejo de Estado* rejecting a coexistence agreement between Starbucks and Mars had "a strong impact on the business world, as Starbucks ... has not been able to open markets in some of the Andean Community countries for this same reason."[79]

Establishing a direct link between the ATJ and the IP agencies

For the first two decades of the ATJ's operation, the private litigants who sought Andean-level review of IP agency registration decisions were required to appeal the decisions to national courts, since only courts were competent to refer questions of Andean law to the ATJ. The time and expense involved in litigating a case through several layers of judicial review—as well as the reluctance of many national judges to refer cases to the Tribunal—deterred businesses and their counsel from challenging the agencies' decisions. The same impediments

[74] D.G. Becker, Justice for Peruvian Consumers? INDECOPI and Consumer Protection. In: *Paper presented at the XXIII Int'l Congress of the Latin American Studies Association.* Washington DC, 2001.

[75] Interview with official (B) of INDECOPI.

[76] Interview with official (C) of the *Superintendencia de Industria y Comercio* (SIC).

[77] E.g., ATJ Preliminary Ruling 17-IP-2005, 13; ATJ Preliminary Ruling 177-IP-2004, 12.

[78] Annual Review, The Twelfth Annual International Review of Trademark Jurisprudence. *Trademark Reporter.* 2005, 95 (2): 267–581: 348.

[79] Ibid., 348; see also ATJ Preliminary Ruling 104-IP-2002.

to Andean-level review also blocked agency officials from seeking the ATJ's guidance on unsettled questions of Andean law. As described earlier, when the Peruvian agency INDECOPI attempted to refer a case directly to the Tribunal in 1999 or 2000, the ATJ rejected it.

In 2007, however, the ATJ accepted a direct referral from the Colombian IP agency. The Tribunal did not expressly overrule its past practice, but it devoted several paragraphs to explaining how the ruling squared with Article 33 of the Revised ATJ Treaty,[80] which authorizes "national judges" to make preliminary references.

> It is clear that today it is not sufficient to use organic or fundamental criteria (*criterio organico*) to analyze the nature of [judicial] acts, since judicial acts may not only come from judges. The State can ascribe judicial acts to organs different from those exercising judicial power. For this reason, the Tribunal considers it important to interpret article 33 … in a broad way. This broad interpretation will allow the identification of actors with standing to request preliminary interpretation that are empowered to issue judicial resolutions … [T]he term "national judge" shall be interpreted in such a way as to include organs that carry out judicial functions as long as they fulfill the requirements established in domestic law. These organs will have standing to request a preliminary interpretation when they resolve a controversy where Andean Law is at issue in the exercise of their powers.[81]

In late 2014 the ATJ further expanded this functional approach, accepting references from the INDECOPI Directorate of Distinctive Signs and the Commission of Distinctive Signs,[82] and from the Bolivian IP agency SENAPI.[83] These decisions give the ATJ a direct pipeline to the agency administrators who are most interested in receiving guidance regarding the proper interpretation of Andean IP rules.

INDECOPI officials identified a number of advantages of this new arrangement. Businesses and their attorneys can obtain the Tribunal's guidance quickly and inexpensively; the ATJ can resolve doctrinal disagreements between different units within the agency; and administrators with specialized knowledge and experience can pose more precise and helpful questions for the Tribunal to answer.[84] For Bolivia, the new referral procedure also bypasses a long-standing judicial blockage to references.[85] For Peru, however, the procedure raises unresolved questions regarding the relationship between the ATJ and the recently created specialized administrative court that reviews all appeals from INDECOPI.[86]

[80] Revised ATJ Treaty, Article 33 ("National judges hearing a case in which one of the provisions comprising the legal system of the Andean Community should be applied or is litigated, may directly request the [ATJ's] interpretation of such provisions, providing that the verdict is susceptible to appeal under national law.").

[81] ATJ Preliminary Ruling 14-IP-2007, 7–8 (authors' translation).

[82] ATJ Preliminary Ruling 121-IP-2014.

[83] E.g., ATJ Preliminary Ruling 104-IP-2014; ATJ Preliminary Ruling 105-IP-2014.

[84] Interview with officials (E) of INDECOPI.

[85] Interviews with ATJ judge (H).

[86] Interview with national judges (B) of the *Octava Sala Especializada en lo Contencioso Administrativo de Peru*.

Analyzing the Outlier Cases: A Review of Non-Intellectual Property Preliminary Rulings and Noncompliance Judgments

Our analysis thus far reveals that preliminary references relating to Andean IP law share many similar attributes. Are the relatively few references not involving IP issues significantly different? In particular, do these outlier cases raise important legal issues or provide opportunities for the ATJ to expand the scope and reach of Andean law?

Our initial analysis of these questions explored the thirty-five outlier preliminary rulings issued through 2007. We found that although the cases involved a variety of substantive issues, such as taxes, tariffs, and non-tariff barriers, the type of questions posed and the nature of the ATJ's answers were similar to the IP references. In particular, national judges asked fairly narrow and specific questions and the ATJ responded with narrow and specific answers that adhered closely to the letter of Andean law. Moreover, in all of these outlier cases the relationship of the dispute to Andean law was manifest, which helps to explain why even reticent national judges might recognize the need for a reference.

Our review of the next seven years of case law identified seventy-nine outlier preliminary rulings. We also investigated whether disputes over non-IP rules enter the Andean legal system by another route. The Revised ATJ Treaty authorizes private litigants to invoke the noncompliance procedure to challenge government policies as contrary to Community law. Our previously published work noted the existence of this procedure and discussed a few key noncompliance judgments but we did not analyze the procedure in depth. We have now obtained additional information on the Andean noncompliance process and include a selection of that data in our updated analysis of the outlier cases as a group.

Outlier preliminary rulings

Table 3.2 summarizes the subject-matter of outlier preliminary rulings, revealing the modest expansion of non-IP litigation in the Andean legal system. This change represents a marked increase in non-IP decisions in a short period of time, even if, as Figure 3.4 reveals, these cases remain a very small percentage (6%) of the ATJ's total docket.

Our analysis of the seventy-nine outlier rulings from 2008 up to and including 2014 suggests that litigant demand, rather than judicial curiosity, explains the increase in the number and subject matter variety of references. Many of the cases are highly technical, asking for ATJ guidance regarding specific provisions of Andean legislation on cross-border issues such as double taxation, customs valuations, and information required on official customs and tax related forms. These regional rules are not particularly new and the legal issues raised have limited significance beyond the immediate facts. We also see a number of repeat player cases in which the same firm—or firms that trade in similar products—files multiple suits challenging nearly identical individual decisions or actions of national

Table 3.2 Outlier preliminary rulings 1984–2014 ($N = 114$)

Subject-matter	Outliers 1985–2007	Outliers 2008–2014
Taxes (including in free trade zones, challenges to double taxation, requests for refunds of VAT)	18	21
Customs (including valuations, certificates of origin, and cargo manifests)	4	24
Questions about functioning of the Andean legal system	1	2
Tariffs	3	6
Free trade programme	0	7
Agrochemical pesticides	1	2
Insurance	1	1
Labor disputes involving Andean institutions	0	2
Social security	0	1
Safeguards	1	0
Transport	1	4
Telecommunication	1	5
Cosmetics	0	1
Common External Tariff	1	0
Investment	1	0
Regulation of slaughterhouses	0	1
Phytosanitary rules for imports	0	1
Technology transfer	1	0
Trade in services	1	0
Regulation of imported used engine parts and vehicle transmissions	0	1
Total	35	79

administrators.[87] Difficulties faced by firms in procuring documentation from Venezuelan officials after that country's withdrawal from the Community generated several legal disputes involving transactions initiated when Venezuela was still a member state. Taken together, these patterns suggest that private litigants—mainly commercial entities involved in intra-regional trade or transactions—are pressing national judges to make references in non-IP cases where the litigants

[87] E.g., the firm Discwafer filed multiple claims against Colombian officials demanding special taxation rates for goods exported within the free trade zone. E.g., ATJ Preliminary Ruling 190-194-IP-2007; ATJ Preliminary Ruling 12-15-IP-2008. Oil companies have also raised several cases involving the lack of adequate certificates of origin for imports. E.g., ATJ Preliminary Ruling 88-IP-2011; ATJ Preliminary Ruling 90-IP-2011; ATJ Preliminary Ruling 96-IP-2012; ATJ Preliminary Ruling 69-IP-2013; ATJ Preliminary Ruling 80-IP-2013.

perceive that Andean law provides more favorable treatment than a conflicting or ambiguous domestic regulation.

Although the ATJ in general remains a cautious interpreter of Andean law, we also discern a consistent theme in the recent outlier cases: the more detailed the legislation at issue, the less wiggle room the Tribunal allows for national discretion. For example, in one customs case the ATJ agreed that national administrators could verify the worth of imported goods using a variety of valuation methods, but the Tribunal was nonetheless clear that Andean law precluded the officials from giving the goods a "minimum valuation," a finding that cast doubt on the validity of a Colombian customs regulation.[88]

Also interesting are preliminary references that Andean judges have treated as opportunities to suggest hierarchies among the Community's human rights, health, and environmental protection objectives. In a 2008 ruling, the ATJ decided that the scope of regional regulations governing the health and hygiene of cattle trading and slaughterhouses "go beyond purely business purposes, efficiency and productivity" and should be interpreted in light of "first order" values "such as health, life and protection of the right to a healthy environment."[89] In a 2009 ruling involving Andean pesticides legislation, the Tribunal found that the "ultimate goal" of the law, "is the protection of life, health and the environment," and it stated that "the interpretations of any provision of this *Decisión* must be made in accordance with this essential purpose."[90] Two rulings in 2012 declared that "fundamental rights prevail over historical, political, social, cultural and economic situations,"[91] and that "[h]uman rights, among which are the rights to life, health, physical integrity and a healthy environment, are basic minimums without which it would be impossible to meet the objectives of the sub-regional integration process; they are thus general principles of Andean Community law."[92] So far, these bold proclamations do not appear to affect the outcome of the disputes. We provide further discussion of these jurisprudential innovations in Chapter 4.

Overall, the recent increase in outlier cases is noteworthy for a number of reasons. First, the cases raise a wider array of legal issues regulated by Andean law. Second, ATJ judges have used some of these rulings to refine existing Andean legal doctrines and suggest possibilities for expanding the Tribunal's legal and political salience to a wider array of government officials and private actors. Third, although national judges continue to frame mostly narrow and technical questions, the ATJ has sometimes been more prescriptive in answering those questions, especially where Andean law comprehensively regulates the subject. In particular, the Tribunal has used *obiter dictum* (non-binding statements not directly relevant to the outcome of the case) to explain the hierarchical relationship among Andean law, WTO law, and human rights.

88 ATJ Preliminary Ruling 44-IP-2009, 26–9.
89 ATJ Preliminary Ruling 90-IP-2008, 12.
90 ATJ Preliminary Ruling 114-IP-2009, 19.
91 ATJ Preliminary Ruling 100-IP-2011, 11.
92 ATJ Preliminary Ruling 116-IP-2012, 8.

Outlier noncompliance cases

As explained in Chapter 2, the original ATJ Treaty included a noncompliance procedure that only member states could activate. Following the reforms of 1996, private actors could ask the Andean General Secretariat to investigate a state's alleged noncompliance and issue a *Resolución* determining whether the challenged domestic policy or regulation was contrary to Andean law.[93] If the state remained in breach, the Secretariat could then ask the ATJ to hear the case and issue a legally binding judgment confirming the violation. If Andean officials decided not to pursue a complaint, the private plaintiff could itself bring the suit before the ATJ.

Data on the noncompliance procedure are incomplete. The number of cases per year is available on the Tribunal and Andean Community websites, as are most ATJ noncompliance judgments. These publically available materials do not, however, include systematic data on topics such as the subject matter of disputes, the number of complaints filed at each stage of the process, or the sanctions awarded, if any. Andean officials provided us with an unpublished study that reviews the noncompliance procedure from 1984 through 2007,[94] as well as a report that reviews all noncompliance judgments through 2014 in which the ATJ found a violation of Andean Law.[95] Although these materials do not allow for the kind of detailed analysis that we provide for preliminary references, they do enable us to make three overarching observations about the noncompliance process and its place in the Andean legal system as a whole.

First, the ratio of intellectual property to non-IP disputes in noncompliance cases is almost precisely the inverse of the ratio in preliminary rulings. The ATJ issued 113 noncompliance judgments between 1984 and 2014, finding violations in 69 cases.[96] Only eight of these violations concern Andean IP rules.[97] The remaining violations involve a range of regional integration topics, most notably free movement of agricultural products and other goods, the Common External Tariff, price supports, customs, and transportation issues.

[93] The data on *Resoluciones* and earlier administrative decisions known as *Dictámenes* have even more extensive gaps than the information on ATJ noncompliance suits. We thus do not address these administrative decisions in this book but flag them as an important area for future research.

[94] *Informe de la Secretaría General de la Comunidad Andina* 2006–2007 (report on file with authors).

[95] *Informe TJCA, 1984–2014, Acciones de Incumplimiento y Acciones de Nulidad*, available at <http://www.tribunalandino.org.ec/sitetjca1/Informe%20unificado%20final%2084-2014.pdf>. There is very little published scholarship on the noncompliance procedure. See W. Phelan, Enforcement and Escape in the Andean Community: Why the Andean Community Is Not a Replica of the European Union. *Journal of Common Market Studies* 2015, 53 (4): 840–56; M.A. Sasaki Otani, El Sistema de Sanciones por Incumpliemiento en el Ámbito de la Comunidad Andina. *Anuario Mexicano de Derecho Internacional* 2012, 15: 301–37.

[96] The majority of noncompliance suits brought to the ATJ during these three decades (82 out of the 113 cases) were referred by the Secretariat. Member states referred only four suits (three by Venezuela; one by Colombia). Private litigants filed the remaining twenty-seven suits. Whereas Secretariat-initiated cases almost always result in a Tribunal finding of noncompliance, private litigant cases can end with the ATJ dismissing the case or declaring that no violation has occurred. The ATJ Registrar reports twenty-six noncompliance decisions finding suits inadmissible, invalid, or untimely. This number closely corresponds to the twenty-seven suits initiated by private litigants.

[97] We discuss the IP noncompliance cases in detail in Chapter 5.

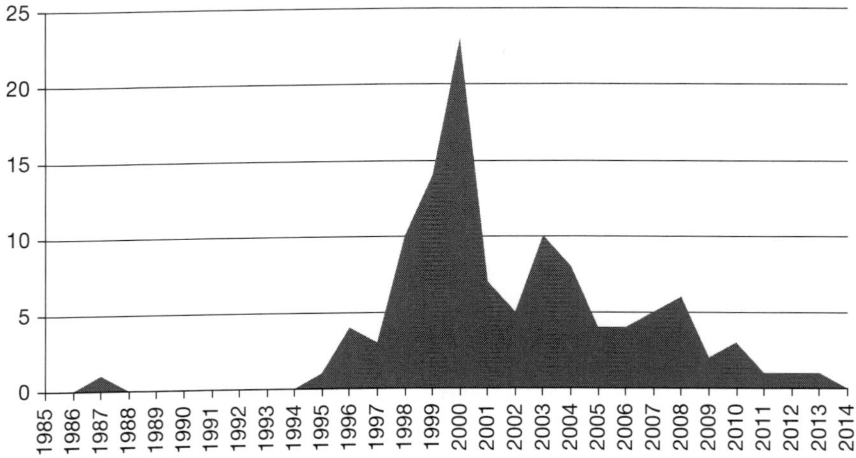

Figure 3.7 ATJ noncompliance judgments 1984–2014 (*N* = 113)

Second, the number of ATJ noncompliance judgments over time differs sharply from that of preliminary rulings. Both types of cases experienced a sharp uptick beginning in the mid-1990s. However, the noncompliance suits spike in 2000, followed by a decade of intermittent decline, after which the cases all but vanish from the ATJ's docket (Figure 3.7). Annual preliminary rulings, in contrast, have generally trended higher, with peaks in 2005 and 2014 (Figure 3.2).

The heyday of noncompliance suits coincides with the decade between 1996 and 2006 when political support for the Andean integration project was at its height. When national governments flouted Andean rules during this period—for example, as occurred during the administration of Peruvian President Alberto Fujimori—private litigants and the General Secretariat were not shy about challenging their actions. In 2006, Venezuela withdrew from the Community, removing its large economy from the region free trade pact and significantly reducing the financial support available for Andean institutions. Chapters 7 and 8 discuss the ideological schisms that then paralyzed Andean policymaking. The crisis period also affected the noncompliance procedure, reducing the number of suits to a trickle (Figure 3.7). A General Secretariat official offered an explanation for this decline, a sense that politics had overtaken law, leading to the self-censorship or shelving of private actor noncompliance suits.[98]

When we visited the General Secretariat in December 2014, we learned that officials were investigating a number of private actor noncompliance and nullification complaints. These investigations coincide with a high-profile November 2014 decision (discussed in Chapter 7), in which the Secretariat found that Ecuador violated Andean free trade rules. The ATJ's 2015 annual report notes that

98 Interview with official (D) of the Andean General Secretariat.

ten noncompliance suits, five nullification suits, and one omission suit were filed in that year.[99] The rise in investigations suggests that once private firms believed that Secretariat officials would resume robust enforcement of Community rules, noncompliance and nullification suits once again flowed into the Andean legal system.

A third noteworthy feature is the relationship between the noncompliance procedure and preliminary references. Private firms and their attorneys in a given industry sometimes file noncompliance suits and preliminary reference requests simultaneously or sequentially, seeking to ramp up pressure on government officials and increase the likelihood of an ATJ finding that a domestic regulation or policy is contrary to Andean law. According to one Colombian lawyer active in the Andean legal system, the choice between filing suit with the General Secretariat or in a national court depends on several factors: "First, the nature of the process; second, the familiarity of Colombian and Andean bodies with the subject matter; third, how long the process will take; fourth, whether firms are open to going to an international tribunal; and fifth, the political circumstances."[100]

The strategic use of Andean litigation appears in a variety of disputes, including challenges to pipeline and second-use patents (discussed in Chapter 5), suits involving the ownership of cigarette brands and municipal marketing rules for alcohol in Colombia (discussed in Chapter 6), and litigation involving an Andean *Decisión* regulating agricultural pesticides.[101] In the last set of cases, the ATJ twice condemned Peru for adopting domestic procedures that circumvent the environmental review required by Andean law. Litigants returned to court a third time, leading the Tribunal to "warn that the affected parties may claim damages pursuant to Article 30 of the [Revised ATJ Treaty], which codifies the principle of the monetary liability of the Member States for violations of Andean Law."[102] As we explain in Chapters 7 and 9, the member states then modified the contested Andean *Decisión*, making its requirements more in line with Peru's existing administrative procedures.[103]

In sum, a complete understanding of outlier cases in the Andean legal system must consider both the preliminary reference mechanism and the noncompliance procedure. Private litigants may have greater success in challenging domestic laws and policies as contrary to Andean legislation by avoiding national judges—who, as we have explained, are often reluctant to refer cases to the ATJ or to ask probing questions whose answers might cast doubt on those laws and policies—and turning instead to the General Secretariat. Future studies of the Andean noncompliance procedure based on more complete data may reveal other ways in which private actors strategically use Andean litigation to achieve their goals.

[99] *Tribunal de Justicia de la Comunidad Andina, Informe de Labores Gestión* 2015. On the date this book went to press, the ATJ had not issued any decisions in these cases.

[100] Interview with attorney (A) from a commercial and administrative law firm in Colombia.

[101] ATJ Preliminary Ruling 114-IP-2009, at 16. The finding is repeated in a similar case, ATJ Preliminary Ruling 115-IP-2009, 34.

[102] ATJ Noncompliance Judgment 1-AI-2012, 20.

[103] *Decisión* 804, adopted April 28, 2015; see also Interview with ATJ judge, November 17, 2015.

Broader Implications of the Differences Between the Andean and European Legal Systems

We now build on the foregoing analysis to compare the relationships that national courts in the European and Andean Communities have developed with their respective international tribunals. We focus on the willingness or reticence of national judges to engage in a dialogue with their regional colleagues, and on differences in how the two tribunals respond to referred questions.

In the European context, it is an article of faith widely shared by judges and scholars that national court references have been the engine driving legal integration, providing opportunities for the ECJ to promote negative integration—the removal of barriers to free trade—and to engage in gap-filling and expansionist law-making. The following statement by ECJ Judge Federico Mancini, which describes how the ECJ constructed a constitution for Europe, exemplifies this belief:

> The Court would have been far less successful had it not been assisted by two mighty allies: the national courts and the Commission. It is sufficient to mention here that by referring to Luxembourg sensitive questions of interpretation of Community law, the national courts have been indirectly responsible for the boldest judgments the Court has made. Moreover, by adhering to these judgments in deciding the cases before them, and therefore by lending them the credibility national judges usually enjoy in their own countries, they have rendered the case law of the Court both effective and respected throughout the Community.[104]

Note Mancini's use of the term "allies." This word choice reflects the reality that many national judges supported the ECJ's efforts to bolster and expand EC law. This support created opportunities for the ECJ to engage in a dialogue with national courts, which has left its stamp on the scope and substance of EC law (much as the ATJ's administrative partners have shaped Andean doctrines concerning regional IP rules).

A key factor facilitating these court-to-court communications in Europe was the wide variety of national judges willing to refer cases that asked legal questions with far-reaching import. For example, a low-level tariff commission requested the ruling that yielded the ECJ's historic doctrine of direct effect, and a small claims court referred the case that led the ECJ to announce the supremacy of EC law.[105] In some cases, references reflected the judge's openness to or enthusiasm for European integration. Our discussion of the role of jurist advocacy movements in Europe (Chapter 9) provides further evidence that some of the ECJ's most seminal judgments occurred in cases constructed by cause lawyers or provocatively framed by the court's internal lawyers (*commissaires du gouvernement*) who argued the cases. Sometimes, national judges on lower and specialized courts acted strategically,

[104] F. Mancini, The Making of a Constitution for Europe. *Common Market Law Review* 1989, 26 (4): 597.

[105] Case 26/62, *Van Gend en Loos v. Nederlandse Administratie der Belast ingen* [1963] ECR 1; Case 6/64, *Costa v. Ente Nazionale per L'Energia Elettrica (E.N.E.L.)* [1964] ECR 585.

sending questions to the ECJ to circumvent the constraints of national law or higher court doctrine.[106] In addition, because judges at different levels of national legal systems referred questions to the ECJ, private actors in Europe had access to multiple venues in which to pursue EC litigation strategies. None of these dynamics is present in the Andes, where the judicial hierarchy is flatter (because some first-instance courts are also last-instance courts) and where judges (who are often unfamiliar with Andean law) are less attuned to how strategic behavior can influence the development of legal doctrine.[107]

The willingness of national courts to serve as interlocutors also influenced the prescriptive nature of the ECJ's responses to referred questions. Judge Mancini openly acknowledged the extent to which the ECJ has guided national judicial decision-making:

> It bears repeating that … national judges can only request the Court of Justice to interpret a Community measure. The Court never told them they were entitled to overstep that bound: in fact, whenever they did so—for example, whenever they asked if national rule A is in violation of Community Regulation B or Directive C—the Court answered that its only power is to explain what B or C actually mean. But having paid this lip service to the language of the Treaty and having clarified the meaning of the relevant Community measure, the court usually went on to indicate to what extent a certain type of national legislation can be regarded as compatible with that measure. The national judge is thus led hand in hand as far as the door; crossing the threshold is his job, but now a job no harder than child's play.[108]

The practice in the Andean Community is quite different. As we have explained, the ATJ rarely issues purposive preliminary rulings with outcome-determinative consequences for domestic litigation. However, Chapter 4 discusses more recent decisions suggesting that where Andean legislation is very clear, the ATJ will direct national judges to invalidate conflicting domestic laws and policies. A number of other recent rulings include statements in *obiter dictum* invoking the Community's larger societal objectives. These statements, which are loftier than the ATJ's modest interpretive approach in most of its decisions, may plant seeds that the Tribunal may nurture in future decisions.

Why were European courts more willing to engage with the ECJ whereas Andean judges remain reticent? Joseph Weiler considered the first part of this question in an article entitled The European Court of Justice and its Interlocutors.[109] Weiler highlighted three factors to explain national judicial support for the ECJ. First, there was the formal legal obligation to refer questions. Second, there was growing peer pressure as courts in other countries accepted the ECJ's authority. Finally, and

[106] Alter, 2001, 48–52.

[107] Osvaldo Saldías explains how the status quo of a limited and formalist ATJ reflects the preferences of national judges in the Andes: "If higher courts can project an image of compliance with international law by repeatedly referring cases to the [ATJ], but maintain … the control of the scope and content of the referrals, it attains both goals; increased credibility as well as keeping high levels of judicial discretion." O. Saldías, *The Judicial Politics of Economic Integration: The Andean Court as an Engine of Development*. New York, NY: Routledge, 2013, 122.

[108] Mancini, 1989, 606.

[109] Weiler, 1994.

most significantly, Weiler argued that national judges were empowered by their relationship to the ECJ:

[N]ormative acceptance of the ECJ's constitutional construct and practical utilization [of the preliminary reference mechanism] by national courts may be rooted in plain and simple judicial empowerment. Whereas the higher courts acted diffidently at first, the lower courts made wide and enthusiastic use of the ... procedure in many member states. This is understandable both on a commonsense psychological level and on an institutional plane as well. Lower courts and their judges were given the facility to engage with the highest jurisdictions in the Community and, even more remarkable, to gain the power of judicial review over the executive and legislative branches, even in those jurisdictions where such power was weak or nonexistent ... The ingenious nature of [the preliminary reference mechanism] ensured that national courts did not feel that the empowerment of the ECJ was at their expense. After all, it is they who held the valve. Without the cooperation of the national judiciary, the ECJ's power was illusory.[110]

The first two factors Weiler identified also operate in the Andean Community, although, as we have shown, with somewhat lesser force. With respect to the judicial empowerment factor, Weiler's statement glosses over the fact that in the EC's early years many national judges were reluctant to engage with the ECJ. To the contrary, as Renaud Dehousse has noted, some lawyers and judges viewed EC law and ECJ rulings as disrupting deep structures in national legal systems.[111] The creation of a cooperative trans-judicial relationship thus took significant time. Writing on the recognition of ECJ authority in the 1970s, Stuart Scheingold observed:

The picture with respect to the recognition of the authority of the Court of Justice ... and the supremacy of Community law is a mixed one ... [I]n most matters there has been a real reluctance by national courts to [request preliminary rulings] ... [O]nly in Holland can the primacy of Community law be taken for granted. Elsewhere, the status of Community law and the willingness to use [the preliminary ruling mechanism] remain in doubt, although national judges seem increasingly receptive on both counts.[112]

The Andean Community also faced this initial reticence. Yet through personal diplomacy and persistence on the part of litigants, national judges on some courts—especially those charged with reviewing intellectual property matters—eventually accepted the obligation to refer cases to the ATJ. Yet those judges remain legal formalists; few ask provocative questions or explore the full scope and reach of Andean law. It is thus fair to say that few national judges view their ATJ colleagues as allies in a broader project of building regional integration through law.

We posit three plausible explanations for the divergent trajectories of the Andean and European legal systems. First, national judges in the Andes may not be as

[110] Ibid., 523.

[111] R. Dehousse, *The European Court of Justice: The Politics of Judicial Integration*. New York, NY: St. Martin's Press, 1998, 173.

[112] S. Scheingold, The Law in Political Integration: The Evolution and Integrative Implications of Regional Legal Processes in the European Community. Cambridge, MA: Harvard University Center for International Affairs, 1971, 34.

independent as their counterparts in Europe. Bolivia has always had a weak judiciary, and in both Venezuela and Ecuador populist leaders have repeatedly substituted sitting judges with more docile replacements. Yet, it is also true that democratization movements have increased the assertiveness of many courts in Latin America, especially in the area of human rights, with the result that judges in many countries operate with more independence and exert more influence over executive branch officials and legislatures.[113] These trends towards judicial assertiveness have not, however, spilled over to national court interactions with the ATJ.

Second, the support of administrative agencies may have been as important in Europe as it has been in the Andean countries. The more diverse range of references to the ECJ would reflect, in this view, the larger volume of EC secondary legislation[114] and the greater number of administrative agencies seeking to coordinate their domestic policies. Seen from this perspective, the ECJ's success would be attributable in part to the fact that its mission interacted synergistically with the efforts of national judges and agency officials to build national administrative states constrained by the rule of law.[115]

Such an account may explain many European preliminary references. But it does not explain the most provocative referrals that enabled the ECJ to constitutionalize EC law. Still, this account suggests that if we stripped away those references asking bold questions and developing foundational doctrines, we would be left with a European legal integration process that evolved much as it has in the Andean Community. If this explanation is correct, we would expect to find higher levels of supranational engagement in issue areas where detailed European secondary legislation existed and where administrative agencies were open to working with the ECJ to clarify ambiguities and close lacunae in this legislation.

A third explanation draws on broader political and social forces. Perhaps European judges were initially as reticent as their Andean counterparts, but a few were also part of or influenced by the networks of advocates who were striving to build European integration through law.[116] As the number of stakeholders in the

[113] D. Kapiszewski and M. Taylor, Doing Courts Justice? Studying Judicial Politics in Latin America. *Perspective on Politics* 2008, 6 (4): 749–50; E. Lutz and K. Sikkink, International Human Rights Law and Practice in Latin America. *International Organization* 2000, 54 (3): 633–59.

[114] A. Stone Sweet, *The Judicial Construction of Europe*. Oxford: Oxford University Press, 2004, 58.

[115] F. Bignami, Creating European Rights: National Values and Supranational Interests. *Columbia Journal of European Law* 2005, 11: 241–352; P. Lindseth, The Contradictions of Supranationalism: Administrative Governance and Constitutionalization in European Integration since the 1950s. *Loyola of Los Angeles Law Review* 2003, 37 (2): 363–406.

[116] K.J. Alter, Jurist Advocacy Movements in Europe: The Role of Euro-Law Associations in European Integration (1953–1975). In: *The European Court's Political Power.* K.J. Alter (ed.), 63–91. Oxford: Oxford University Press, 2009; M. Rasmussen, From Costa v. Enel to the Treaties of Rome: A Brief History of Legal Revolution. In: *The Past and Future of EU Law: The Classics of EU Law Revisited on the 50th Anniversary of the Rome Treaty*. M. Poiares Maduro and L. Azoulai (eds), 69–85. Portland: Hart Publishing, 2010; M. Rasmussen, Establishing a Constitutional Practice of European Law: The History of the Legal Service of the European Executive. *Contemporary European History* 2012, 21 (3): 375–98; A. Vauchez, Une élite d'intermédiaires? Genèse d'un Capital Juridique Européen. *Actes de la recherche en sciences sociales* 2007a, No. 166–7: 54–65; A. Vauchez, Judge-Made Law. Aux Origines Du Modèle Politique Communautaire (Retour Sur Van Gend en Loos et Costa C. Enel). In: *Une Europe*

EC has risen, so too has the ability of the ECJ to harness private litigants, judges, and popular support to build integration through law.[117] If this explanation is accurate, then the regional differences we observe would be attributable to the lack of jurist advocacy networks in the Andean Community that might have encouraged at least some national judges to become ATJ allies. We explore this idea further in Chapter 9.

These three explanations are not mutually exclusive. However, it matters which is correct because the broader implications of each explanation are different. If judicial independence is a prerequisite to national courts serving as interlocutors for international tribunals, then regional integration processes mediated by those tribunals—and perhaps international legal regimes more generally—will face absolute limits on their ability to penetrate national jurisdictions where the rule of law is weak or unstable. The second explanation suggests that, for economic regulation at least, a key factor determining the success of international legal regimes will be the existence of administrative actors that are committed to the correct enforcement of national and international legal rules. If, by contrast, the third explanation is correct, then bold efforts to constitutionalize international law may require the support of advocacy networks comprising lawyers, academics, and at least some judges. Absent such support, the evolution of international legal systems may more closely resemble the Andean than the European experience.

Conclusion: Energizing the ATJ's Interlocutors

We began our research into the Andean legal system expecting that preliminary rulings would function much as they do in the EC. A cursory view of the ATJ's docket supports this assumption. The vast majority of Tribunal rulings are the result of referrals by national courts, and we see national variation in reference rates not unlike that in Europe.

A deeper investigation of these trends, however, revealed two patterns that we did not anticipate: first, that nearly all disputes involve intellectual property issues, and second, that preliminary references are concentrated in only a few national courts. The two patterns are related—because so few non-IP disputes are referred to the ATJ, most referred cases originate in the small number of national courts that have jurisdiction over IP issues.

Equally unexpected is the finding that domestic IP administrative agencies are the ATJ's primary interlocutors and compliance constituencies. The ATJ has responded to the agencies' concerns by clarifying ambiguous provisions of Andean

Des Élites? Réflexions Sur La Fracture Démocratique De L'Union Européenne. Olivier Costa and Paul Magnette (eds), 139–66. Brussels: Presses de l'Université libre de Bruxelles, 2007b; A. Vauchez, The Transnational Politics of Judicialization: Van Gend en Loos and the Making of EU Polity. *European Law Journal* 2010, 16 (1): 1–28.

[117] R. Cichowski, *The European Court and Civil Society: Litigation, Mobilization and Governance*. Cambridge: Cambridge University Press, 2007.

IP law, and the agencies, in turn, have influenced ATJ doctrine to reflect the agencies' dual mandate to protect consumers as well as IP owners. In striking contrast to Europe, national courts in the Andes are mostly passive intermediaries. Many national judges are aware of their obligation to refer cases involving Andean law, a point that the ATJ continues to underscore in recent rulings. However, judges refer mostly narrow and technical questions, refraining from using the Andean litigation to expand their legal authority. At least during periods of political consensus in favor of integration, this domestic judicial reticence has led private firms and lawyers to approach the ATJ through an alternative route: noncompliance complaints initially filed with the Andean General Secretariat and later referred to the Tribunal.

Compared to Europe, where at least some national judges use preliminary references to promote doctrinal evolution and judicial empowerment, the practice of Andean judges may seem timid. The ATJ has issued 114 non-IP outlier preliminary rulings from its founding in 1984 through 2014, and 113 noncompliance judgments, many if not most of which arose from complaints initiated by private actors. However, when compared to other sub-regional courts in Africa and Latin America—which are far less active—the fact that the ATJ has ruled on a range of economic integration issues is noteworthy.

The findings in this chapter also raise broader questions about the conditions under which we should expect national courts to be in the vanguard of efforts to enforce international law. A comparison of the Andean and European experiences highlights the importance of identifying factors that convince national judges to embrace or reject their role as co-enforcers of international legal rules. In the Andean context, it took persistent and coordinated action by litigants, lawyers, ATJ judges, and Community officials to surmount national judicial barriers to preliminary references. These pressures succeeded in part because they were applied at a time when the broader political climate favored judicial engagement—in particular, when newly restructured domestic IP agencies clamored for guidance on Andean IP rules and national governments supported the application of those rules. Our findings thus underscore the close links between national legal practices and domestic political conditions. Rather than assuming national courts will act as either compliance constituencies or compliance opponents for international rulings, scholars should instead investigate the political conditions that shape where, when, and how national judges engage with international law and international courts. We explore these issues in Chapter 10.

4

The Divergent Jurisprudential Paths of the Andean Tribunal of Justice and the European Court of Justice

There are many reasons we might expect a convergence in the jurisprudence of the European Court of Justice (ECJ) and the Andean Tribunal of Justice (ATJ). Both courts are part of regional integration projects that seek to eliminate barriers to the free flow of goods and services. Both courts review challenges by private actors to national laws and practices that create barriers to integration and trade. The countries that comprise both projects are also members of the World Trade Organization (WTO), where they face potential challenges to Community and national laws that run afoul of WTO law, and risks that divergences in legal doctrine may contribute to the fragmentation of international economic law. The fact the ECJ was a model for the Andean Tribunal—together with the court's widely touted success as an engine of integration and the groundswell of legal support for many of its doctrinal innovations—provides additional reasons for the ATJ to emulate its European predecessor. In fact, given the ECJ's greater experience in adjudicating regional integration issues and its access to a deeper well of legal expertise, the path of least resistance for Andean judges might well have been to emulate, if not slavishly copy, European jurisprudence.

This chapter explores several areas for which, notwithstanding these forces that might be expected to push toward convergence, the ATJ has instead chosen to diverge from the ECJ and to chart its own jurisprudential course. We focus in particular on five instances where the Andean Tribunal was presented with opportunities to emulate the ECJ's doctrinal innovations but declined to do so.[1] Our analysis synthesizes thirty years of ATJ jurisprudence, focusing on the relationship between Community law, national law, and other international obligations, including human rights and WTO law.[2]

[1] In a recent working paper, Conway reaches a similar conclusion: G. Conway, The Legal Reasoning of the Andean Court of Justice in Comparative Context. *iCourts Working Paper Series* 2016 (56): 18.

[2] The ATJ has also developed a distinctive jurisprudence relating to Andean intellectual property law, an issue we explore in greater depth in Chapter 5. A separate publication, not included in this book, delves more deeply into the distinctive aspects of ATJ jurisprudence regarding access to medicines. L.R. Helfer and K.J. Alter, The Influence of the Andean Intellectual Property Regime on Access to Medicines in Latin America. In: *Balancing Wealth and Health: The Battle over Intellectual Property and*

Transplanting International Courts: The Law and Politics of the Andean Tribunal of Justice. First Edition. Karen J. Alter and Laurence R. Helfer. Published 2017 by Oxford University Press.

The ECJ is famous for its teleological interpretation of the founding EC treaties, which it deployed in its first twenty-five years of operation to develop the legal doctrines of direct effect, supremacy, implied powers, and the human rights authority of EC institutions, including itself. In its earliest rulings, the ATJ unequivocally endorsed the direct effect and supremacy of Community law, but it later developed a distinctive legal doctrine—the *complemento indispensable* principle—that gives governments significant leeway to fill gaps in and supplement Community rules. Much Andean litigation involves fleshing out the contours of this doctrine and its relationship to the supremacy of Andean law. The ATJ has also diverged from the ECJ in largely avoiding human rights issues, and in being more deferential to the application of Community law by national judges. In one area, however, Andean judges have arguably been bolder than their European counterparts: upholding the supremacy of Andean rules over bilateral and multilateral treaties.

An overarching finding of this chapter is that the ATJ has a consistent jurisprudential voice, one it has developed in response to a steady stream of preliminary references and the support of the politically attuned Andean General Secretariat, which investigates noncompliance suits before they are referred to the ATJ. Although the ATJ's case law is not well known beyond the region, it is not surprising that the Tribunal has developed a distinctive jurisprudence that responds to the often significant political, economic, and legal challenges to Andean integration. Whereas the ECJ developed legal doctrines that intentionally and sometimes aggressively promoted European integration, the ATJ has adopted a more modest stance. Its case law upholds and enforces Andean rules when governments have endorsed common Community policies. Alongside this recognition, however, the Tribunal has created legal space for overlapping domestic regulations, and it respects the member states' collective decision to restore legislative competence to the national level.

Integration enthusiasts, especially those who believe wholeheartedly in the ECJ's bolder doctrinal innovations, may dislike much of the ATJ's jurisprudence. Yet we identify an important virtue of the Tribunal's decision *not* to serve as an engine of integration. This choice has allowed the ATJ to weather the sometimes sharp swings in political support for the Andean Community. It is also an approach that offers an alternative model for international courts operating in other developing country contexts where political support for economic integration or international legal cooperation is weak or uneven across time and issue areas.

This chapter is organized as follows. We first discuss the ATJ's adoption of the ECJ doctrines of the supremacy and direct effect of Community law and explain how the Tribunal modified these doctrines in its subsequent jurisprudence. We then discuss three legal issues—the ATJ's decision to let member states define the pace and scope of integration, to allow governments to augment Community legislation via domestic laws and executive decrees, and to respect the factual and interpretive

Access to Medicines in Latin America. R. Cooper Dreyfuss and C.A. Rodríguez Garavito (eds), 247–62. Oxford: Oxford University Press, 2014.

discretion of national judges—that together reveal that the ATJ conceives of itself as playing a far more modest role in promoting regional integration than does its bolder European predecessor. We conclude by discussing the hierarchies that the ATJ has identified between Andean law and the protection of human rights, and between Andean law and other international agreements, including the WTO and bilateral treaties.

The ATJ Demands Less of Member States than Does the ECJ

The supremacy and direct effect of Community law

Early ATJ rulings embraced the direct effect and supremacy of Community law. These two ECJ-created doctrines are foundational pillars of the EC constitutional legal order.[3] Although now taken for granted, recent historiography reveals how the ECJ struggled to develop these doctrines.[4] Andean judges avoided the challenges that their predecessor faced, instead drawing on the ECJ's handiwork with relative ease.

The first ATJ preliminary ruling in 1987 provided an opportunity to explain how the Andean legal system worked. The case did not involve the supremacy of Andean law, but the ATJ nonetheless noted that member states had endorsed the "full validity" of the following principles:

> a) the legal system of the Cartagena Agreement has its own identity and autonomy, constitutes a common law and is part of the national legal systems, b) the legal system of the Agreement prevails within the framework of its competences, over the national norms, without unilateral acts or measures from the Member Countries being able to oppose this legal system, c) the *Decisiones* implying obligations for the Member Countries come into effect on the date indicated.[5]

The ATJ thus ratified the view that the Andean Pact's founders also intended to emulate the ECJ's foundational European law doctrines. The Tribunal also explicated its relationship to national courts, underscoring its exclusive competence to interpret Andean law and national judges' exclusive power to apply that law to the facts of the case. This division of authority mirrored the plain language of the Original ATJ Treaty.[6] By reiterating the Treaty's dictates, the ATJ may have sought

[3] F. Mancini and D. Keeling, From CILFIT to ERTA: The Constitutional Challenge Facing the European Court. *Yearbook of European Law* 1992, 11: 1–13; E. Stein, Lawyers, Judges and the Making of a Transnational Constitution. *American Journal of International Law* 1981, 75 (1): 1–27.

[4] M. Rasmussen, The Origins of a Legal Revolution: The Early History of the European Court of Justice. *Journal of European History* 2008, 14 (2): 77–98; M. Rasmussen, Establishing a Constitutional Practice of European Law: The History of the Legal Service of the European Executive. *Contemporary European History* 2012, 21 (3): 375–98; A. Vauchez, The Transnational Politics of Judicialization: Van Gend en Loos and the Making of EU Polity. *European Law Journal* 2010, 16 (1): 1–28.

[5] ATJ Preliminary Ruling 1-IP-87, 3.

[6] Original ATJ Treaty, Article 30 ("The [Tribunal] shall restrict its interpretation to defining the content and scope of the norms of the juridical structure of the Cartagena Agreement. The [Tribunal] may not interpret the content and scope of domestic law nor judge the substantive facts of the case.").

to reassure national courts that the Tribunal would not encroach on their exclusive domain—something that the ECJ had repeatedly done in practice.[7]

In its second preliminary ruling, the ATJ incorporated another ECJ doctrinal innovation. The case raised the question of the status of national laws that conflicted with Andean rules but that nevertheless remained on the statute books. The ATJ reasoned as follows:

> As far as the effect of the norms of integration on national norms, the doctrine and jurisprudence indicate that, in the case of conflict, the internal rule will be superseded by the community one, which will be applied preferentially, since the competence in such a case corresponds to the community. In other words, the internal norm becomes inapplicable, to the benefit of the community norm. The [ECJ] has repeatedly given this indication (see principally the *Costa/ENEL* decision of June 15, 1964, and the *Simmenthal* decision of March 9, 1978) in agreement on this point with the spirit of the norms of the Andean integration. This effect of supersession of the national norm as a result of the application of preference is especially clear when the later law—which must have priority over the prior one, in accordance with universal principles of law—is precisely the community norm.
>
> ...
>
> The [ECJ], in the previously cited decisions, has affirmed the absolute preeminence of community law over internal law, an argument that is also applicable to the judicial system of the Andean integration, in accordance with what was previously indicated.[8]

Taken together, these two early rulings revealed that the ATJ shared the ECJ's fundamental premise that Community law is different from other types of international law.[9] The two rulings also appeared to foreshadow the fact that the Tribunal would follow in the ECJ's audacious footsteps by adopting other legal doctrines to advance regional integration. As we now explain, however, ATJ has eschewed multiple opportunities to import such doctrines into Andean law and has instead developed its own distinctive jurisprudence that mediates the aspirations of the Community's founders against the foreseeable political objections of national actors.

Whether to constitutionalize the Community legal order

Perhaps most importantly, the ATJ has declined to emulate the ECJ in interpreting the Andean Community's founding treaty as a higher order charter for advancing legal integration. To illustrate this different and less ambitious trajectory, we first briefly review three instances in which the ECJ interpreted the Treaty of Rome as a mandate for judicial action to constitutionalize EC law. We then compare these

[7] F. Mancini, The Making of a Constitution for Europe. *Common Market Law Review* 1989, 26(4): 606. Chapter 3 discusses the ECJ's more directive approach to national judges in preliminary rulings.

[8] ATJ Preliminary Ruling 1-IP-88 point 2, 2–3.

[9] ATJ Preliminary Ruling 1-IP-87, 3. The ATJ reiterated this point in a later ruling, in which it held that Community law creates a "direct application effect" which transforms "states and citizens into subjects of a new system in which they both possess rights and obligations." This reality "distinguishes community law from international law." ATJ Preliminary Ruling 1-IP-96, Section III.

examples to cases in which the ATJ rejected similar opportunities to constitutionalize the Cartagena Agreement.

Three canonical doctrines reveal the ECJ's audacious strategy. First, the ECJ decided that treaty provisions prohibiting member states from raising tariffs or enacting new trade barriers were immediately binding.[10] Second, the court declared that the treaty and sufficiently detailed secondary laws created direct effects within domestic legal orders.[11] Third, it held that Community law was supreme to any conflicting prior or subsequent national rules and that national judges must not apply such rules.[12] In each instance, the ECJ justified its interpretation as necessary to realize the broad objectives of the EC legal order.

In developing these doctrines the ECJ used the rhetoric and decision-making style of a constitutional court.[13] Its rulings invoke principles found in many national constitutions, such as higher order legal norms, individual rights, and structural questions relating to delegated powers.[14] In addition, by elevating core provisions of the Treaty of Rome above laws and decisions adopted by member states and Community institutions, the court made the revision of those provisions far more difficult. This expanded supranational judicial power, since the only way to reverse an ECJ ruling interpreting the treaty was to convene an intergovernmental conference, adopt the new provisions by consensus, and then have every member state ratify them. The difficulty of this process, together with the recognition that intergovernmental conferences create opportunities for states to add other items to the agenda, meant that amendments were viewed as the "nuclear option—exceedingly effective, but difficult to use—and therefore a relatively ineffective and non-credible means of Member State control."[15]

The ATJ adopted strikingly different approaches when presented with similar legal issues. On several occasions private litigants asked the Tribunal to interpret the Cartagena Agreement to impose immediate constraints on member states. For example, litigants asked the ATJ to find that the treaty prohibited Colombia from imposing new duties on imports from Venezuela. Colombia argued that the Cartagena Agreement must be interpreted in conjunction with Andean secondary legislation, including those comprising the Andean Free Trade Programme, and suggested that these *Decisiones* effectively modified the treaty.[16] The ATJ agreed,

[10] ECJ Case 26/62, *Van Gend en Loos v. Nederlandse Administratie Belastingen* [1963] ECR 1.

[11] Ibid. See also ECJ Case 41/74, *Van Duyn v. Home Office* [1974] ECR 1337.

[12] Italian Constitutional Court, *Costa v. E.n.e.l. & Soc. Edisonvolta* [1964] CMLR 425, Decision 14 of March 7, 1964. ECJ Case 106/77, *Amministrazione delle Finanze dello Stato v. Simmenthal SpA (II)* [1978] ECR 629, [1978] CMLR 263.

[13] Many scholars have mined the constitutional origins and nature of the ECJ's doctrine. Examples include J. Weiler, The Transformation of Europe. *Yale Law Journal* 1991, 100 (8): 2403; Stein, 1981; M.P. Maduro, *We the Court: The European Court of Justice and the European Economic Constitution*. Oxford: Hart Publishers, 1998, 8; Vauchez, 2007, 139–66.

[14] For example, the ECJ, on its own authority, incorporated human rights protections into the EC. Weiler, 1991, 2417.

[15] M. Pollack, Delegation, Agency and Agenda Setting in the EC. *International Organization* 1997, 51 (1): 118–19.

[16] Saldías, 2007, 12.

reasoning that member states had free reign to exclude goods from the Free Trade Programme notwithstanding the fact that the treaty envisioned the eventual adoption of broader free trade rules.[17] In effect, the ATJ found that the Cartagena Agreement, unlike the Treaty of Rome, was not a fixed constitutional charter but only a starting point for integration that governments could amend by the less politically demanding process of adopting Andean secondary legislation.[18]

The ATJ also relinquished some of its interpretive authority to national courts. For example, in a case involving trade barriers that arose after a change in Andean law, the Tribunal identified three potentially applicable legal regimes governing the dispute. The ATJ defined the obligations under each regime,[19] but rather than selecting the relevant rules from among the three options, as the ECJ would have done, the ATJ left that key question for national courts to answer.[20]

In decisions involving Colombia's alcohol monopoly, the ATJ even appeared to back away from its earlier embrace of the ECJ's *Simmenthal* doctrine, which demanded that national judges treat European law as supreme over conflicting national laws. In an initial noncompliance judgment, the ATJ ruled that Colombia's implementation of alcohol monopoly violated Andean law.[21] The issue again reached the Tribunal in the form of a preliminary reference from the *Consejo de Estado*, a Colombian administrative court. The ATJ reaffirmed that Colombia was obligated to modify practices that conflicted with Andean law.[22] Yet, the Tribunal refused to follow the next logical step in *Simmenthal*—instructing national judges to do whatever was necessary to give effect to Community law. Instead, the ATJ simply reiterated what Andean law required without asking national judges to enforce that law. Although the ATJ did not explain its reluctance to follow the ECJ, its ruling may well reflect the very real concern that national judges lacked the legal authority or the political will to heed the ATJ's request.[23]

Why has the ATJ been more reticent than the ECJ in demanding immediate compliance with the Cartagena Agreement and Andean secondary legislation? There are some differences in the applicable legal rules, such as the Andean Free Trade Programme, but law alone cannot explain why the ATJ is less willing to constitutionalize the treaty. Both the Treaty of Rome and the Cartagena Agreement

[17] ATJ Preliminary Ruling 1-IP-90, conclusion point 1.

[18] Another example, is ATJ Preliminary Ruling 5-IP-89 in which the ATJ allowed governments to determine whether to prohibit foreign ownership in certain economic sectors.

[19] ATJ Preliminary Ruling 3-IP-93, point 2, at 7. The ATJ ruling suggested which legal regime applied, expecting the national judge would apply Andean law to the facts of the case as the ATJ had indicated. In contrast, the ECJ has been far more willing to direct national judicial discretion while paying "lip service to the language of the Treaty." Mancini, 1989, 606.

[20] ATJ Preliminary Ruling 3-IP-93, conclusions point 2: "It is for the [national court] to determine whether the product in question is part of the Free Trade Programme of the Cartagena Agreement, the *Nómina de Reserva* [which forms part of Andean Industrial Programmes,] or the list of exceptions of the member country."

[21] ATJ Noncompliance Judgment 3-AI-97.

[22] ATJ Preliminary Ruling 29-IP-98.

[23] Colombia remains in breach of Andean law (*Decisión* of November 11, 1999 regarding *Decreto* 244 of 1906). This case is discussed in greater detail in Chapter 6.

contain many similar features. They set broad and ambitious goals, such as promoting the well-being of citizens, contributing to development and prosperity, and building a common market. They define the competences of supranational legislative and administrative bodies and obligate states to work with these bodies to achieve the treaties' objectives. They incorporate timetables for future action as well as immediately binding promises not to create additional trade barriers, and they both include a vague provision that requires member states to ensure respect for Community rules within national legal orders.[24]

One possible explanation of the ATJ's greater reticence, notwithstanding these similarities, is that many Andean Pact policies, such as the Free Trade Programme, pre-dated the ATJ's existence. As a second-generation addition to the Andean integration project, the Tribunal's judges may have concluded that it would be too controversial to overturn these long-standing policies.

A second explanation relates to the basic premise of the region's early integration agenda. As explained in Chapter 2, the Andean Pact's early import substitution and regional industrial policies depended heavily on foreign investment that never materialized. The lack of progress in achieving these policies created a conundrum. Should a member state be held to the Community's market liberalization goals even if it had not received the quid pro quo of industrial development assistance? Seen in this light, establishing a "list of exceptions" from the Free Trade Programme was a transitional compromise that allowed member states to exempt politically sensitive products until the Common External Tariff existed and common industrial programs obviated the need for such protections.[25] The list of exceptions was clearly in tension with the Cartagena Agreement's free trade provisions, which prohibited new barriers to trade and required the progressive removal of existing barriers. But the political compromise that the Free Trade Programme embodied was arguably necessary to keep the troubled integration project afloat, and the ATJ may have been unwilling to challenge it without clear authorization to do so.

A third explanation relates to the relative ease of amending the basic ground rules of Andean integration. The settled constitutional status of the Treaty of Rome in part reflects the reticence of EC member states to reopen fundamental tenets

[24] Article 5 of the Original ATJ Treaty largely repeats Article 5 of the Treaty of Rome. The ECJ used this provision to suggest that member states had implicitly endorsed the notion that domestic courts should apply Community law over conflicting national law. See P. Pescatore, The Doctrine of "Direct Effect": An Infant Disease of Community Law. *European Law Review* 1983a, 8 (3): 155–77; P. Pescatore, La Clarence du Législateur Communautaire et le Devoir du Juge. In: *Gedächtnisschrift für L.-J. Constantinesco*. G. Lüke, G. Ress, and M.R. Will (eds), 559–80. Cologne: Carl Heymanns Verlag, 1983b, 559–80.

[25] Article 55 of the original Cartagena Agreement allowed member states to designate a "list of exceptions"—goods that were to be temporarily excluded from the trade liberalization program. The temporary exemptions continued for many years because the member states failed to adopt a Common External Tariff, which was to be a precursor to a total liberalization of goods within the Andean Community. F.V. García Amador, *The Andean Legal Order: A New Community of Law*. Dobbs Ferry, NY: Oceana Publications, 1978, 24–34.

of the treaty and the *acquis communautaire* developed by the ECJ.[26] In contrast, Andean governments have been more willing to revise the Cartagena Agreement.

In a 1996 nullification case (discussed in greater detail in Chapter 6), the ATJ established clear criteria for member states to revise the Agreement. The case involved temporary exemptions that national governments had given to Peru to derogate from certain free trade rules. The *Junta* challenged the derogations before the ATJ. The Tribunal received the case in late 1996 when the member states were reconsidering Peru's situation, which they resolved the following year with the adoption of the Sucre Protocol.[27] With Peru's status now settled, the *Junta* tried to withdraw its lawsuit. The ATJ, however, refused to dismiss the case. The judges found that the Peruvian exemption violated the Cartagena Agreement but that its illegality had been "purged" by the Sucre Protocol. In other words, the exemption did not need to be nullified because a valid law had already superseded it. In reaching this result, the ATJ distinguished *Decisiones*—Andean secondary legislation adopted by the member states sitting as the Andean *Comisión*—from treaty amendments such as the Sucre Protocol, which are agreed to at a "conference of plenipotentiaries" (*reunion de plenipotenciarios*).[28] The Tribunal thus suggested that states cannot adopt *Decisiones* that undermine the Cartagena Agreement, and that modifications of the treaty must be made via a different amendment procedure.

Formally speaking, the process of amending the Cartagena Agreement is the same as that for amending the EC's founding charter: the heads of the member states must meet to adopt the amendments, which must then be ratified by each country.[29] The ATJ thus appeared to be following the ECJ in enforcing more onerous procedures to amend the Community's founding charter. In practice, however, convening a *reunion de plenipotenciarios* does not appear to be very difficult. There are far fewer member states in the Andean Community than in the EC, no evidence of a reluctance to convene intergovernmental conferences, and no larger *acquis* of normative commitments that national governments view as inviolable.

Considering the ATJ's rulings in this wider political context reveals that the Tribunal has allowed the Cartagena Agreement's political masters far greater leeway to set the pace of regional integration rather than itself pushing to achieve that goal beyond what Andean law unequivocally requires. In doing so, the ATJ has also implicitly chosen not to build a broader base of support by signaling to attorneys, interest groups, and private litigants that it would be receptive to creative legal arguments to further the treaty's aspirational objectives.

[26] The *acquis communautaire* is the term used to describe the the entire body of legislation, legal acts, and court decisions that comprise EC law.

[27] Sucre Protocol of June 25, 1997, available at <http://www.sice.oas.org/trade/junac/Carta_Ag/sucre_e.asp>. For additional discussion, see J.L. da Cruz Vilaça and J.M. Sobrino Heredia, The European Union and the Transformation of the Andean Pact into the Andean Community: From the Trujillo Protocol to the Sucre Act. *European Foreign Affairs Review* 1998, 3 (1): 13–52.

[28] ATJ Nullification Decision 1-AN-1996, points 2.4 and 2.5. See Chapter 6 for more details.

[29] It is unclear what qualifies as a *reunion de plenipotenciarios*. Would any meeting of the heads of states suffice? One difficulty in answering this question is that the label *Decisiones* is attached to all Andean laws, and it often is unclear which type of meeting generated the *Decisión*.

Mediating between Community and national lawmaking

Another question faced by both the ATJ and ECJ was whether member states could adopt national regulations to address issues that Community law does not expressly regulate. The founding treaties did not answer this question. The ECJ developed the doctrine of implied powers, finding in favor of the EC authority and barring states from occupying regulatory space that fell within the purview of the Community.[30] The ATJ, in contrast, has been significantly more reluctant to restrict national rules where the power to regulate has not been expressly delegated to Andean institutions. The Tribunal has also allowed member states considerable leeway to adopt domestic rules in areas governed by Andean law, provided that such rules complement and do not undermine existing Community laws and objectives. The upshot of this difference is that the ECJ helped the European Community to expand into new legal domains, whereas the ATJ has been much more responsive to ebbs and flows in Andean secondary legislation.

Joseph Weiler has identified a number of ways in which the ECJ's recognition of implied powers furthered the European integration project. First, the court conferred authority on Community institutions where the Treaty of Rome was silent. Weiler referenced an ECJ decision that granted the EC the power to agree to treaties binding on member states. According to Weiler, "the full realization of many EC internal policies clearly depended on the ability of the Community to negotiate and conclude international treaties with third parties." To achieve this legal result, the ECJ "sidestep[ped] the presumptive rule of interpretation typical in international law, that treaties must be interpreted in a manner that minimizes encroachment on state sovereignty;" instead, it "favored a teleological, purposive rule drawn from the book of constitutional interpretation."[31]

Second, the ECJ barred states from enacting national legislation on issues deemed within the Community's exclusive competence. Weiler summarized the doctrine this way:

> In a number of fields, most importantly in common commercial policy, the [ECJ] held that the powers of the Community were exclusive. Member States were precluded from taking any action per se, whether or not their action conflicted with a positive measure of Community law. In other fields, the exclusivity was not an a priori notion. Instead, only positive Community legislation in these fields triggered a preemptive effect, barring Member States from any action, whether or not in actual conflict with Community law, according to specific criteria developed by the court. Exclusivity and pre-emption not only constitute an additional constitutional layer on those already mentioned but also have had a profound effect on Community decision making. Where a field has been pre-empted or is exclusive and action is needed, the Member States are pushed to act jointly.[32]

Weiler noted that the ECJ did not always find that Community power pre-empts national power. Sometimes the court waited for the adoption of EC legislation

[30] E.g., Case 22/70, *Commission v. Council (ERTA)* [1971] ECR 263.
[31] Weiler, 1991, 2416. [32] Ibid.

before claiming exclusive legislative authority in a contested domain.[33] For the time period that Weiler studied, however, the ECJ was notably reluctant to cede legislative authority to member states. The implied power and pre-emption doctrines were consistent with what Burley and Mattli observed as the ECJ's early tendency to create "one-way ratchets" that facilitated the participation of private litigants in the European litigation "only in a way that would advance community goals."[34] The ECJ has since developed these doctrines to define areas of exclusive and shared competence, as well as areas where subsidiarity leaves the issue to the member states.

The ATJ has approached similar questions about the relationship between Community and national lawmaking with substantially greater deference to member states. The Tribunal developed a distinctive legal doctrine, *complemento indispensable*, to modulate governments' discretion to adopt statutes, degrees, and regulations in areas where Andean law clearly governs and in areas where it does not. First articulated in a 1988 preliminary ruling,[35] the doctrine has been applied in dozens of cases and was recently summarized by the ATJ as follows:

> This principle implies that member states have the power to strengthen or complement, through internal rules or international agreements, the norms of the Andean Community system; but in the application of this principle, the domestic legislation of each country may not establish additional requirements or regulations that in one way or another conflict with Andean Community law or that restrict essential aspects covered by it …
>
> The principle measures the limits of regulatory innovations of domestic law, which are only legitimate if proven to be strictly necessary for the implementation of Community law, thus favoring its application and in no way detracting from it. [The Tribunal] has warned that domestic laws which are contrary to Community law are inapplicable and must be subtracted from the internal legislative competence for issues governed by Community legislation.[36]

The *complemento indispensable* doctrine gives the ATJ considerable flexibility to decide whether a domestic law is compatible with Andean law. A straightforward example where the Tribunal recognizes national complementary powers involves Community legislation that expressly delegates certain implementation or enforcement actions to the member states.[37] Also mostly uncontroversial are Andean *Decisiones*—such as those concerning certain regional tax regulations, interstate travelers' insurance, and transport of goods by road—that comprehensively regulate

[33] Ibid., 2417.

[34] Burley and Mattli were not discussing implied powers per se, but their comment applies more generally to how the ECJ allowed private actors to use the European legal system to promote their own agendas only so long as those agendas furthered the European integration project. A.-M. Burley and W. Mattli, Europe before the Court. *International Organization* 1993, 47 (1): 60.

[35] ATJ Preliminary Ruling 2-IP-88, point 3.

[36] ATJ Preliminary Ruling 15-IP-2014, paragraphs 45 and 46.

[37] E.g., the Andean *Decisión* on Harmonization of the Indirect Taxes as Incentives to Exports of Goods allows member states to set the deadlines for filing tax returns and to designate which documents are needed to comply with the *Decisión*'s requirements. ATJ Preliminary Ruling 2-IP-2008. Similarly, the *Decisión* on the Andean Declaration of Value for regionally traded goods provides that domestic law will establish sanctions for filing false or inaccurate information on valuation forms. ATJ Preliminary Ruling 117-IP-2010.

a topic.[38] In these domains, the Tribunal has pre-empted national laws that introduce restrictions, conditions, or requirements that reduce the protection of Andean law, or that "establish new rights or obligations or modify existing and planned community rules."[39] The ATJ has developed these principles mainly in preliminary rulings, but it has also applied them in noncompliance judgments finding that domestic regulations violate Andean law.[40]

Where the scope of Andean legal norms are less clear, however, the ATJ has declined to hold that member states have implicitly ceded power to the Community. The Tribunal signaled this deferential approach in a 1990 ruling in which it stressed that integration is a gradual, incremental process that limits the extent to which Andean rules pre-empt national authority:

> Especially when dealing with complex and vast issues, such as intellectual property ... it seems logical that many of these diverse issues, even if they have to be a matter of common regulation in the beginning, are still within the competence of the national legislator for an indefinite time until they are effectively covered by the Community norms.[41]

Our analysis of ATJ case law yielded no example where the Tribunal, unlike its European counterpart, has claimed exclusive competence for the Community. To the contrary, the ATJ regularly upholds national laws not only where "there is a vacuum or when Community legislation does not regulate a certain situation,"[42] but also where that legislation provides "a general rule and does not regulate exceptions," which states are free to develop in their respective domestic laws.[43]

The ATJ has coupled its recognition of shared legislative competence with significant deference to governments to determine the boundaries between Andean and national law.[44] In a 1989 preliminary ruling involving the revised Andean investment code, the ATJ underscored the fact that the member states could not change the ownership rules for industries that had been nationalized as part of Andean industrial programs. It did not, however, claim certain industrial sectors as

[38] E.g., ATJ Preliminary Ruling 114-IP-2009 (Andean *Decisión* on the registration and control of chemical pesticides for agricultural use prevents member states from creating a parallel register with different requirements or unilaterally modifying those requirements); ATJ Preliminary Ruling 133-IP-2007 (uniform insurance policy scheme for international passenger transport); ATJ Preliminary Ruling 001-IP-2008 (standard international cargo manifests for transport of goods by road).

[39] ATJ Preliminary Ruling 136-IP-2011, 7 (authors' translation).

[40] E.g., in ATJ Noncompliance Judgments 01-AI-2012 and 02-AI-2011, the Tribunal held that Peru's regulations regarding the registration of chemical pesticides violated Andean *Decisión* 436, which comprehensively addresses that topic. See Chapter 3 for additional discussion of these decisions.

[41] ATJ Preliminary Ruling 2-IP-90, point 1. As we discuss in greater detail in Chapter 5, the ATJ has given greater pre-emptive force to Andean intellectual property rules than to many other areas of Andean law. The Tribunal has relied on the extensive and detailed secondary legislation on patents and trademarks as indicating that the member states have "sovereignly transferred" their "exclusive authority" over intellectual property issues to the Community level. ATJ Preliminary Ruling 1-IP-96, Section III.

[42] ATJ Preliminary Ruling 136-IP-2011, 8.

[43] E.g., ATJ Preliminary Ruling 101-IP-2010 (interpreting Andean regulations on the qualification and certification of the origin of goods).

[44] T.A. O'Keefe, How the Andean Pact Transformed Itself into a Friend of Foreign Enterprise. *International Lawyer* 1996, 30 (4): 818.

principal domains of Andean law, nor did it assert exclusive Community competence over the regulation of foreign investment. Instead, it recognized that member states had "full authority" to decide which economic sectors were reserved for domestic ownership.[45]

Another example is the extensive litigation over the ownership of the "Belmont" trademark, discussed in Chapter 6. The case turned on national regulators' determination of whether Phillip Morris was using its registered trademark to block a rival cigarette company from marketing competing tobacco products under the regionally well-known Belmont brand. Andean law did not specify what constitutes use of a trademark, and the ATJ gave domestic decision-makers leeway to reach divergent outcomes. The Tribunal's rulings allowed Ecuadorian regulators to find that Phillip Morris' hasty decision to market a few products under the Belmont label was a use of the trademark. The rulings also allowed Colombian authorities to enact a law authorizing an importer to use a trademark that its competitor had not previously used. This, in turn, gave Colombian judges room to reject Phillip Morris' claim that domestic legal constraints, not the firm's strategic marketing decisions, caused its years of neglect of the Belmont trademark.

In sum, our analysis reveals that the ATJ has restricted domestic lawmaking only where Andean norms are unambiguous and comprehensive, offering evidence of the member states' intent that Andean rules occupy the field. In this respect, the Tribunal adheres to the traditional public international law practice of interpreting the absence of delegated competence as a retention of member state sovereignty. The result is that ATJ litigation has only modestly constrained the adoption of domestic rules relating to a wide range of subjects nominally regulated by Andean law.

Determining the degree of discretion to national judges in applying Community law

Chapter 3 compared the ECJ's engaged and guiding relationship with national judges with the Andean context, where national judges are mostly formalist and passive actors in the Community legal order. Jurisprudentially, this divergence is captured by another aspect of the ECJ's *Simmenthal* doctrine, discussed earlier in this chapter, and the ATJ's decision to walk back its earlier embrace of the doctrine.

In *Simmenthal*, the ECJ asserted the obligation of "every national court [to] apply Community law in its entirety and … accordingly set aside any provision of national law which may conflict with it, whether prior or subsequent to the Community rule."[46] In later cases, the ECJ went further, setting stringent limitations on national judges' ability to interpret EC law without first seeking the court's guidance.[47]

[45] ATJ Preliminary Ruling 5-IP-89.

[46] ECJ Case 106/77, *Amministrazione delle Finanze dello Stato v. Simmenthal SpA (II)* (1978) ECR 629, [1978] CMLR 263, 283.

[47] ECJ Case 283/81, *SRL CILFIT v. Ministry of Health (I)* [1982] ECR 3415. For an explanation of how the ECJ used this ruling to constrain national judges, see F. Mancini and D. Keeling, From

Although the ATJ cited *Simmenthal* in early preliminary rulings, it subsequently refused to endorse the full implications of the case. The key dispute involved various challenges to municipal alcohol regulations in Colombia. In one suit, opponents argued before the Colombian Constitutional Court that the regulations violated Andean law.[48] The court rejected the suit, concluding that Community law did not supplant national law. Unlike human rights treaties, which have quasi-constitutional status in Colombia,[49] Andean law was, according to the Constitutional Court, equivalent to domestic legislation. Because such laws "and the Constitution do not share the same hierarchy, nor are [they] an intermediate legal source between the Constitution and ordinary domestic laws ... contradictions between a domestic law and Andean community law will not have as a consequence the non-execution of the [domestic] law." The Colombian court accepted that Community law has "primacy" over conflicting national law, but it reasoned that primacy means that Community law "displaces but does not abrogate or render non-executable" conflicting national legislation.[50]

A later iteration of the dispute involved a preliminary reference from a Colombian administrative court, the *Consejo de Estado*, which arose after the ATJ upheld a separate noncompliance challenge to the alcohol regulations by two other member states. Had the Tribunal followed *Simmenthal*, it would have directed the national judges to invalidate the licenses as contrary to Andean law. Instead, the ATJ merely repeated its finding from the earlier noncompliance suit without indicating whether the *Consejo de Estado* was required to give effect to that finding.[51]

This deference is consistent with the ATJ's broader understanding of the division of legal authority between itself and domestic courts. Our review of all preliminary rulings up to and including 2014, discussed in more detail in Chapter 3, disclosed only a handful of cases in which the ATJ considered how its interpretation of Andean law applied to the facts presented.[52] In all other rulings, the ATJ explicated the meaning of Andean law in the abstract without suggesting how national judges should resolve the dispute. This deferential approach continued even after the adoption in 1996 of the Revised ATJ Treaty, which authorizes the Tribunal to

CILFIT to ERTA: The Constitutional Challenge Facing the European Court. *Yearbook of European Law* 1992, 11: 1–13.

[48] Colombian Constitutional Court, Sentencia C-256/98 of May 27, 1998. The licenses were also successfully challenged in an ATJ noncompliance suit. See ATJ Noncompliance Judgment 3-AI-97.

[49] International human rights agreements ratified by Colombia are part of a *bloque de constitucionalidad* which gives them a status superior to than national law. Article 93 of Colombia's 1993 Constitution states: "International treaties and agreements ratified by the Congress that recognize human rights and that prohibit their limitation in states of emergency have priority domestically."

[50] Colombian Constitutional Court, Sentencia C-256/98 of May 27, 1998, Section 3.1.

[51] ATJ Preliminary Ruling 29-IP-98, conclusions 1 and 2.

[52] For example, in ATJ Preliminary Ruling 19-IP-98, a case involving Venezuela's implementation of Community rules aimed at strengthening the competitiveness of the Andean shipping industry, the ATJ strongly implied that Venezuelan courts must exclude ships from countries that do not grant reciprocal access to ships from other Andean member states. Similarly, in ATJ Preliminary Ruling 103-IP-2000, the Tribunal concluded that only the General Secretariat, not national governments, can determine if imports from other member countries create temporary market disruptions that justify the imposition of safeguards.

consider the facts of preliminary references and thus, implicitly, guide domestic courts in the application of Andean law.[53]

Doctrinal Divergences Regarding the Relationship between Community Law and other International Law Obligations

Community courts as protectors of human rights

A fourth area of divergence between the ECJ and the ATJ concerns the place of international human rights norms in the Community legal order. There are several similarities between Andean and European institutions governing integration and human rights. In both systems, the development of human rights law instruments is primarily the responsibility of regional organizations (the Council of Europe and the Organization of American States) and the interpretation and enforcement of those instruments is carried out by regional judicial bodies (the ECtHR, the Inter-American Court of Human Rights (IACtHR), and the Inter-American Commission on Human Rights). In part for this reason, both founding Community integration treaties omit any references to human rights.[54]

Both the ATJ and the ECJ eschewed engaging with human rights in their early years. References to human rights were absent from preliminary rulings and non-compliance judgments in the ATJ's first two decades. Neither litigants nor the General Secretariat apparently gave much thought to whether Andean rules might violate human rights.[55]

In Europe, ECJ rulings in the 1950s and 1960s followed the prevailing view of the EC's founders, who rejected the idea that the Community had a human rights mandate. As de Burca has explained, European judges in these cases decisively rejected litigant claims "both that domestically protected fundamental rights constrained Community powers and that, more broadly, general principles of European law include human rights principles that should guide and shape the interpretation of the EEC Treaty."[56] Yet as early as the 1960s, German litigants and judges openly worried that Community law might violate the rights protections in the German Basic Law. The ECJ initially ignored these concerns. De Burca discusses a 1965

[53] Chapter 2 discusses the 1996 Cochabamba Protocol and its reform of the ATJ's jurisdiction and access rules as codified in the Revised ATJ Treaty.

[54] C. Heyns and M. Jillander, Toward Minimum Standards for Regional Human Rights Systems. In: *Looking to the Future: Essays on International Law in Honor of W. Michael Reisman*. M.H. Arsanjani, J.K Cogan, R.D. Sloane, and S. Wiessne (eds), Leiden: Brill, 2011, 555. G. De Burca, Roads Not Taken: The EU as a Global Human Rights Actor. *American Journal of International Law* 2011, 105 (4): 649–50.

[55] As Saldías has noted, "the A[T]J never undertook any measure that would link the establishment of a common market with the protection of individual rights." O. Saldías, *The Judicial Politics of Economic Integration: The Andean Court as an Engine of Development*. New York, NY: Routledge, 2013, 114.

[56] De Burca, 2011, 667.

ECJ ruling that rejected the relevance to EC law of German constitutional rights, as well as the arguments that Community law independently protected such rights.[57]

The status of human rights in the EC legal order changed in the 1970s, after the German Constitutional Court announced that it would not accept the ECJ's authority in cases involving constitutional rights due to the absence of a comparable system of rights protections in Community law. In a series of landmark rulings, European judges responded by radically shifting course:

> The ECJ defined a new role for human rights in the Community legal order. No longer were they to be treated as irrelevant or entirely peripheral to the common market project. Instead, respect for fundamental rights—inspired by the common constitutional traditions of the member states and the international human rights treaties on which they collaborated—was declared a general principle of Community law, and the ECJ would henceforth entertain claims that such rights had been adversely affected by Community acts and policies.[58]

EC member states went along with this doctrinal reversal. Formal political backing for adding human rights into the European integration agenda followed two decades later.[59] The ECJ, in turn, has become an increasingly active adjudicator of human rights issues, although it has yet to eclipse the influence of the ECtHR.[60]

The Andean Community's human rights trajectory has been far more modest. The first reference to human rights appeared in a 1980 Charter of Conduct, in which the region's presidents agreed that human rights "constitute a basic rule of the internal conduct of the States of the Andean Pact."[61] The Community took no further action on the topic until 2002, when it adopted the Andean Charter for the Promotion and Protection of Human Rights, a non-binding statement of principles that nevertheless includes many norms found in other international human rights instruments.[62] This was followed two years later by Andean legislation adopting a work program to disseminate and implement the Charter.[63] Although both documents endorse a wide range of national, regional, and international monitoring mechanisms, they make no mention of the ATJ.

During the heyday of Andean integration—the decade between the relaunch of the Community in 1996 and Venezuela's withdrawal in 2006—the ATJ continued to avoid human rights issues. The only reference to the topic appears in a 2005 judgment involving the protection of test data for pharmaceuticals, in which the Tribunal stated in passing that "granting exclusive rights for specified time periods may conflict with fundamental human rights such as health and life, since the

[57] Ibid. [58] Ibid., 668.

[59] The EU's human rights powers first appeared in the 1992 Maastricht Treaty, and were expanded in the 1997 Treaty of Amsterdam, the 2000 Treaty of Nice, EU Charter of Fundamental Rights, and the 2009 Lisbon Treaty.

[60] B. Schima, EU Fundamental Rights and Member State Action after Lisbon: Putting the ECJ's Case Law in Its Context. *Fordham International Law Journal* 2015, 38 (4): 1097–133.

[61] Charter of Conduct, signed at Riobamba, Ecuador, Article 3, September 11, 1980, 1301 UNTS 266, available at <https://treaties.un.org/doc/publication/UNTS/Volume%201301/v1301.pdf>.

[62] Carta Andina para la Promoción y Protección de los Derechos Humanos (July 26, 2002), available at <http://www.comunidadandina.org/documentos/actas/cart_DDHH.htm>.

[63] Andean *Decisión* 586.

consumption of drugs is related to its price and the monopoly price may make it impossible to access the medication, which can lead to illness and death of potential consumers."[64]

Human rights have, however, featured more prominently in two recent preliminary rulings. In a 2012 case from Colombia, the ATJ interpreted one of several ancillary regional treaties that aim to promote Andean industrial development. Article 6 of the Complementary Industrial Convention in the Automotive Sector prohibits the importation and trade of used cars and car parts, in part to "ensure minimum standards of safety, environmental protection, and the defense of consumers and industrial property." An administrative agency mistakenly granted a permit to import used car engines, which it later asked the Colombian *Consejo de Estado* to revoke. The *Consejo* asked the ATJ to interpret the purpose of the Convention. The Tribunal responded with a strikingly bold pronouncement: "The starting point of any plan or industrial program is the defense of human rights. Without it you cannot talk about development, let alone a proper integration process."[65] The judges then went further, linking human rights to consumer protection and asserting that human rights are a cornerstone of Andean integration:

> Human rights, among which are the right to life, health, physical integrity and a healthy environment are basic minimums without which it would be impossible to meet the objectives of the sub-regional integration process; they are general principles of Andean Community law. Therefore, these basic parameters are the basis for prohibiting the importation of used vehicles and auto parts into the sub-region. Consumer protection is also developed on the basis of these principles, as the minimum to be guaranteed in the market is that the acquisition of goods and services does not affect their fundamental rights.[66]

The ATJ left little doubt that the national court should nullify the import permits.

A second 2012 ruling, which interpreted the Andean Social Security Instrument,[67] is bold in a different respect. The Andean regulation protects migrant workers and their beneficiaries who are employed in more than one member state. Ignoring this law, the Colombian social security agency refused to award retirement benefits to a Colombian citizen who had worked for several years in Venezuela. The individual challenged the denial of benefits accrued in Venezuela and a domestic labor court referred the case to the ATJ.

In its ruling, the Tribunal—for the first time—cited the 2002 Andean Charter for the Promotion and Protection of Human Rights as one of several laws that seek to continuously improve the living standards of the region's inhabitants.[68] The judges then addressed two more difficult questions: whether the Social Security

[64] ATJ Noncompliance Judgment 114-AI-2004, 46.

[65] ATJ Preliminary Ruling 116-IP-2012, 8.

[66] Ibid. The ATJ quoted this passage with approval in a later case challenging health requirements for imported honey as contrary to Andean technical regulations. ATJ Preliminary Ruling 133-IP-2012. The Tribunal then expanded upon its prior analysis as follows: "The starting point therefore of any 'technical regulation' is the defense and protection of human rights. Without this we cannot speak of an adequate integration process." Ibid., 10.

[67] Andean *Decisión* 583.

[68] ATJ Preliminary Ruling 100-IP-2011, 7.

Instrument could be applied in the absence of implementing regulations, which the General Secretariat had failed to adopt, and whether it was permissible to include retirement benefits accrued in Venezuela, which had withdrawn from the Andean Community in 2006.

As to the first issue, the ATJ was unequivocal: "The General Secretariat's inactivity in issuing regulations ... cannot affect the efficacy of the rights enshrined in Community law, as the substantive rights of individuals, in this case the right to social security, cannot be disregarded by the lack of activity of the system's organs."[69] On the second question, the Tribunal reasoned that the Social Security Instrument had been adopted two years before Venezuela's withdrawal, and it buttressed that conclusion with the expansive statement that "fundamental rights prevail over historical, political, social, cultural and economic situations in which their exercise unfolds."[70] The ATJ's ruling thus made clear that the individual's retirement benefits in this case should be calculated based on his employment in both Andean countries.

The relationship between Andean law and international treaties

The previous sections analyzed four doctrinal divergences between the two Community courts, revealing that Andean judges have generally been less bold and expansive than their European colleagues. There is one area, however, where the ATJ appears to have been more assertive: conflicts between Andean law and treaties ratified by the member states. In the first noncompliance case, the Secretariat challenged a bilateral agreement between Ecuador and the United States that required Ecuador to grant patent protection to certain drugs previously patented elsewhere. Ecuador's parliament never ratified the treaty, but its president adopted a decree to implement it and Ecuador's intellectual property office relied on the decree to award a number of patents to foreign pharmaceutical companies.

When the Secretariat challenged these patents before the ATJ, Ecuador defended the decree as falling within the discretion reserved to member states to adopt domestic legislation and international agreements that "strengthen the industrial property rights provided for" in Andean law.[71] The Tribunal categorically rejected Ecuador's claim that "an international commitment [could] be invoked as a reason to validate noncompliance with a prior Community obligation."[72] Although the ATJ did not expressly address the supremacy of Andean rules, it strongly suggested that Community law—even Andean secondary legislation—trumps inconsistent bilateral agreements.

Several later cases considered the relationship between WTO treaty obligations and Andean law. In a 2001 noncompliance judgment, Ecuador and Venezuela invoked the Agreement on Trade-Related Aspects of Intellectual Rights (TRIPS) to

69 Ibid., 10. 70 Ibid., 11. 71 Article 143 of *Decisión* 344.

72 ATJ Noncompliance Judgment 1-AI-1996. See also ATJ Preliminary Ruling 1-IP-96, Section III (c), discussed in Conway, 2016, 14–15.

defend a decision to grant a "second-use" patent for Viagra. As discuss in Chapter 5, Andean IP rules categorically reject second use patents, stating that "[p]roducts or processes already patented and included in the state of the art … may not be the subject of new patents on the sole ground of having been put to a use different from that originally contemplated by the initial patent."[73] The ATJ reiterated that neither domestic nor international law can diminish or contradict Andean law, thereby indicating that Community rules prevail over multilateral as well as bilateral treaties.[74]

A later preliminary ruling involved a contract dispute between two private firms relating to foreign investment. The defendant invoked the General Agreement on Trade in Services as a defense, suggesting that this WTO treaty governed the dispute. An Ecuadorian judge asked the ATJ to decide which law to apply. The Tribunal again relied on the "autonomy of Andean law" to assert categorically that Community rules take precedence over international treaties:

> By virtue of its autonomy, it is confirmed that the Community legal order, both primary and secondary, is neither subordinate to domestic law nor to the international sources of such countries. Consequently, international treaties concluded by the member states on their own initiative, such as the TRIPS Agreement, do not bind the Community or have direct effect within it, without prejudice to the binding force of such instruments in the relationship between those member countries and third countries or international organizations.[75]

The ATJ's position makes eminent sense. Andean law could easily be undermined if international agreements trumped conflicting Andean rules. At the same time, the ATJ has stressed that "in today's interconnected and globalized world, Andean Community law is in constant dialogue with the multilateral legal system."[76] This statement suggests that the Tribunal may seek to resolve future treaty conflicts between Andean and WTO rules through interpretation rather than assertions of regional primacy.

The ECJ has also considered the relationship between EC and WTO law. In contrast to the ATJ, however, the ECJ has refused to decide whether WTO treaties trump Community rules. For example, when Germany invoked the General Agreement on Tariffs and Trade (GATT) to challenge the EC's banana imports regime, the ECJ did not resolve the compatibility of the two legal regimes.[77] Rather, it held that the GATT was generally not entitled to direct effect and could not be invoked to challenge the lawfulness of a Community act.[78] When private litigants

[73] Article 21 of Andean *Decisión* 486; Article 16 of Andean *Decisión* 344.

[74] ATJ Noncompliance Judgment 01-AI-2001, 39 (judgment against Venezuela); ATJ Noncompliance Judgment 34-AI-2001, 51–2 (judgment against Ecuador).

[75] ATJ Preliminary Ruling 158-IP-2006, Part C.

[76] ATJ Preliminary Ruling 117-IP-2010, 6. The ATJ made this statement in a case involving a "pass through" provision of the Andean Declaration of Value, which incorporates WTO rules by reference. In such situations, the Tribunal held that it "has no possibility of interpreting the multilateral rule," and instead will "give effect to the interpretation adopted by the multilateral organization." Ibid.

[77] ECJ Case 280/93, *Germany v. Council of the European Union* [1994] ECR I-4973. Germany raised the argument again in a later case, and the ECJ reaffirmed this position. See ECJ Opinion 3/94 on the Framework Agreement on Bananas, [1995] ECR I-4577.

[78] *Germany v. Council of the European Union*, paragraphs 109–112; see also Eeckhout 2002, 95.

later invoked GATT provisions to challenge the banana regime, the ECJ held its ground. The case also reached the German Constitutional Court, which refused to reverse the ECJ. The result was a stalemate. As a formal matter, the hierarchical relationship between EC law and multilateral trade treaties remains unresolved. As a practical matter, however, litigants are unable to invoke the treaties to challenge Community law (although they have successfully argued that the ECJ should interpret European law in conformity with WTO law).[79]

The hierarchy issue also featured prominently in the ECJ's 2008 ruling in *Kadi*, which involved a challenge to an EC regulation implementing a United Nations Security Council resolution ordering states to freeze the assets of certain suspected terrorists.[80] A key issue in the case was whether the ECJ was precluded from reviewing the validity of the regulation because, pursuant to the United Nations Charter, the Security Council resolution on which it was based trumped other international agreements.[81] Reasoning that "the obligations imposed by an international agreement cannot have the effect of prejudicing the constitutional principles of the EC Treaty," the ECJ further stated:

> [I]t is not a consequence of the principles governing the international legal order under the United Nations that any judicial review of the internal lawfulness of the contested regulation … is excluded by virtue of the fact that that measure is intended to give effect to a resolution of the Security Council adopted under Chapter VII of the Charter of the United Nations. What is more, such immunity from jurisdiction for a Community measure … as a corollary of the principle of the primacy at the level of international law of obligations under the Charter of the United Nations … cannot find a basis in the EC Treaty.[82]

Although scholars continue to debate the significance of *Kadi*, most agree that the judgment confirms the autonomous nature of European law. The ECJ asserted a higher order requirement that all Community acts and policies respect the core human rights and due process requirements inherent in EC law. The ECJ has not, however, gone as far as the ATJ by expressly concluding that Community law trumps conflicting international law.

Conclusion: Balancing Respect for Andean Law with Deference to National Actors

We conclude with a brief assessment of the legal and political implications of the doctrinal divergences analyzed in this chapter. Andean judges were unquestionably aware of analogous ECJ precedents when they considered whether to follow their colleagues in Europe. They nonetheless chose to diverge from the path that the ECJ

[79] These cases are discussed in Alter 2009, 222–23; and Alter 2001, 110–15.

[80] ECJ Joined Cases C-402/05 P and C-415/05 P, *Yassin Abdullah Kadi and Al Barakaat International Foundation v. Council of the European Union* [2008] ECR I-6351 (Kadi).

[81] UN Charter, Article 103.

[82] Kadi, paragraphs 299–300.

had previously trod. Chapter 8 returns to these divergences to explore why the ECJ is far more of an expansionist judicial lawmaker as compared to the ATJ.

Our initial review of ATJ case law reviewed preliminary rulings up to and including 2007. In the subsequent seven years, the ATJ has been modestly bolder in asserting the supremacy of Andean law over conflicting domestic regulations. This increased boldness does not, however, reflect a significant change in legal doctrine or strategy. The ATJ applies Andean law to its full extent when Community secondary legislation clearly pre-empts the discretion of national decision-makers. Recent rulings thus primarily reflect the fact that some cases involve Andean *Decisiones* that contain fewer legal loopholes. Such secondary legislation provides a justification for the ATJ to rule decisively against conflicting national laws and practices and to refine further the *complemento indispensable* principle.

The doctrinal divergences discussed in this chapter have allowed the ATJ largely to follow rather than to push against the collective preferences of the member states. When national executives are jointly committed to Community rules and greater Andean integration, the Tribunal allows private litigation to further those objectives. In contrast to the ECJ, however, the ATJ does not push the integrationist agenda beyond the limits indicated by national political leaders. This difference in approach has helped the Community and the Tribunal to weather significant political turmoil in the region and a generally weaker governmental commitment to Andean integration as a whole. We see the utility of this strategy in Chapter 6, which explores how governments used the Andean legal system to grant numerous temporary exemptions in response to the major economic challenges facing Peru in the early 1990s and Ecuador in the mid-2010s.

Andean member states are currently debating major retrenchments to the Community. As we explain in Chapter 7, for example, the member states in 2015 abrogated the Common External Tariff.[83] For a fully integrated economic union, such backtracking could create legal chaos. But the ATJ has long enforced common customs procedures while allowing domestic customs regulations in the absence of binding regional standards. The Tribunal's more permissive approach thus makes it comparatively less costly to abrogate the Common External Tariff.

In another recent publication, we extend the analysis in this chapter by investigating the relationship between the legitimacy of international courts and their propensity to engage in expansionist lawmaking.[84] We compare in greater depth the examples of lawmaking discussed here, which have contributed to the ECJ's legitimacy (including the doctrines of direct effect and the supremacy of European law, the role of national courts within the EC legal order, and the ECJ's insistence of that European law respect basic human rights) to the ATJ's lack of lawmaking in mostly technical disputes, and to the Community Court of the Economic Community of West African States' cautious application of international human

[83] *Decisión* 805, adopted April 24, 2015.

[84] L.R. Helfer and K.J. Alter, Legitimacy and Lawmaking: A Tale of Three International Courts. *Theoretical Inquires in Law* 2013, 14 (2): 479–503.

rights law in politically explosive cases. On the basis of this three-way comparison, we argue that:

> expansive judicial lawmaking is neither a necessary nor a sufficient condition for triggering challenges to [an international court's] legitimacy by powerful domestic actors. A court can engender such challenges simply by exercising the review functions that states have expressly and unambiguously delegated to it. Conversely, a court may, under the right conditions, boldly expand its power and receive a supportive or even laudatory response from governments.[85]

In other words, although legal circumspection has helped the ATJ to weather political storms, it has not enhanced the Tribunal's popularity or legitimacy in the region.

The upshot of these differences is that the ATJ has not replicated the ECJ's role as an engine of legal integration. To the contrary, Andean institutions, including the Tribunal, have given broad deference to the decisions of national executives. This perhaps reflects the absence of a hegemonic member state with the political and economic clout to dominate its neighbors. The inability of President Hugo Chavez to compel Colombia and Peru to abandon their preferred free market policies triggered Venezuela's 2006 denunciation of the Cartagena Agreement. What remained was a Community of four countries that have been deadlocked economically and politically. In a situation where Colombia and Peru—the two pro-integrationist member states—are unable to overcome the opposition of less integration-minded Ecuador and Bolivia, it would be foolhardy if not dangerous for the ATJ to attempt to fill political gaps in integration with bold legal doctrines.

[85] Ibid., 485.

5

Islands of Effective International Adjudication

Constructing an Intellectual Property Rule of Law in the Andean Community

with M. Florencia Guerzovich†

The previous three chapters explored the similarities and differences between the European Court of Justice (ECJ) and Andean Tribunal of Justice (ATJ). The two courts' formal designs are very similar because, as we explain in Chapter 2, the creators of the Andean legal system used the ECJ as a model for the Tribunal. Part of this institutional copying included ECJ doctrines regarding the direct effect and supremacy of Community rules, and the Tribunal continues to consult and cite ECJ case law. Similar also is the fact that the vast majority of ATJ rulings respond to questions posed by national judges via the preliminary reference mechanism. Yet Chapter 4's comparison of doctrinal developments found meaningful divergences in the jurisprudence of the two courts, and Chapter 3's analysis of the activation and content of ATJ preliminary references reveals that national judges are mostly passive intermediaries in cases involving intellectual property (IP) law that originate in domestic administrative agencies. In fact, IP rulings represent the vast majority of the ATJ's total judicial output.

This chapter explains why the ATJ became both active and effective with respect to IP disputes, and why IP remains an island of effective supranational adjudication in the Andean Community. Within the domain of IP, ATJ rulings have helped to establish a zone in which legal rules—rather than power, political influence, or bribery—govern decision-making by state actors.[1] Inside this rule-of-law island, national judges, agency officials, and private parties actively participate in ATJ litigation and conform their behavior to Andean IP rules.

† M. Florencia Guerzovich, Governance Consultant, florcig@gmail.com, <https://www.linkedin.com/in/m-florencia-guerzovich-9b3ab74>.

[1] We follow a narrow, formal definition of "rule of law" that requires "the government [to] be ruled by the law and subject to it." J. Raz, *The Authority of Law*. Oxford: Oxford University Press. 1979, 210, 212. Our definition stresses the "certainty and predictability of governmental action ... [and the] actual equality of legal treatment" in "relations between citizens[,] and between citizens and their government." R.S. Summers, A Formal Theory of the Rule of Law. *Ratio Juris* 1993, 6 (2): 127–42, 129, 131.

Transplanting International Courts: The Law and Politics of the Andean Tribunal of Justice. First Edition. Karen J. Alter and Laurence R. Helfer. © Karen J. Alter and Laurence R. Helfer 2017. Published 2017 by Oxford University Press.

The ATJ's success in creating and maintaining this island is surprising in three respects. First, the Tribunal's hegemony over the interpretation and application of Andean IP rules stands in sharp contrast to other domains of Andean law. In the vast seas surrounding the IP island, the majority of Andean rules remain riddled with exceptions, under-enforced and often circumvented by domestic actors. Second, litigation involving Andean IP issues has been largely impervious to the political vicissitudes that have hampered the progress of integration more generally. Andean countries have faced decades of economic and political instability, and they have generally lacked strong domestic rules of law or national judiciaries.[2] Even as the Community today experiences another round of political infighting (a topic we explore in Chapter 7), the IP rule of law island is stable and, arguably, expanding. Third, the highly professional international adjudication of IP disputes in the Andes stands in contrast to other parts of the world. Most regional integration systems that have copied Europe's legalized dispute settlement systems have laws on the books that are widely ignored. While not every Andean IP rule has elicited perfect compliance, firms and governments throughout the region generally support the enforcement of these rules via the Andean legal system.

The reality that the ATJ is effective almost entirely within a single issue area underscores the broader theoretical significance of the Andean experience. How did a region with weak legal institutions develop a stable rule of law for IP rights? Why have Andean judges and officials been able to induce widespread respect for Andean rules in IP but not in other areas of regional integration? What does the Andean Community's island of success portend for other international courts and dispute settlement bodies that exercise authority over countries whose legal, political, and economic conditions are roughly comparable to those prevailing in the Andes?

This chapter begins with a brief recap of the institutional and legal developments that set the stage for the IP rule-of-law island to emerge. A more detailed account of the Andean Pact's origins appears in Chapter 2. We then document litigation trends, case-law developments, and changes in administrative agency decision-making that are essential to the island's existence. The heart of the chapter analyzes the ATJ's effectiveness in creating and sustaining the IP island. We develop a broad yet measurable conception of an effective rule of law. We inquire, first, into the creation and protection of IP rights for private parties under the Andean legal system; second, into whether national actors—in particular, administrative agency officials—habitually implement Andean IP rules as interpreted by Andean judges; and third, into whether individual member countries comply with ATJ rulings in the face of pressure by foreign interests (principally the United States and American pharmaceutical companies).

[2] J.L. Esquiroi, The Failed Law of Latin America. *The American Journal of Comparative Law* 2008, 56 (1): 75–124; A. Solimano Political Instability, Institutional Quality and Social Conflict in the Andes. In: *Political Crisis, Social Conflict and Economic Development: The Political Economy of the Andean Region*. Andrés Solimano (ed.), 15–44, Edward Elgar Publishing: Cheltenham, 2005.

Next we offer three explanations for why the Andean legal system is effective with respect to IP but not for other areas of regional integration. First, other Andean rules are less precise and contain loopholes that limit their enforceability. This legal reality reflects the broader political reality that Andean governments are only weakly committed to integration because their most important trade relationships are with other countries. Second, the ATJ respects member state autonomy in areas where Andean law is less prescriptive, refusing to fill in gaps in Community rules to promote regional integration. The ATJ's cautious and restrictive interpretive approach reduces the incentives for litigants to mobilize to enforce Andean law. The third explanation is the absence of jurist advocacy networks and compliance constituencies whose professional interests motivate them to see that Andean laws on the books are respected in practice. We explore the implications of this explanation in Chapter 9.

This chapter closes by briefly considering why the IP rule-of-law island remains resilient notwithstanding the last decade of political tumult in the Andean Community. We identify the indicators of this resilience in Chapter 7, which focuses on the Andean legal system in a time of crisis. As we explain, the ATJ remains both active and effective within the IP island even as its authority in other domains of Andean law falters. Although this chapter does not use the categories of narrow, intermediate and extensive authority applied in Chapter 7, our analysis here provides a foundation for understanding how the ATJ extended its legal authority across a diverse range of audiences, including actual and potential litigants, IP law firms, domestic administrative agencies, and national judges. We also explain why the ATJ's authority with respect to IP has not spilled over into other issue areas regulated by Andean law.

The Legal and Institutional Framework of the Andean Community

Chapter 2 explains that the Andean Pact copied the European Community's legislative and executive institutions, but the substantive policies of the two integration projects were quite different. Whereas Europe focused on liberalizing trade and creating a common market, the Andean Pact's *raison d'être* was import substitution—promoting regional development as an alternative to purchasing goods and technologies from foreign firms. The Andean *Comisión* sought to achieve this goal by heavily regulating foreign investment, subsidizing domestic industries, and distributing jobs, factories, and infrastructure projects according to the needs of each member country.[3] The Andean Pact's distinctive policy orientation soon faltered. Member states counted on an influx of foreign capital to fund regional economic development. Few businesses, however, were willing to subject themselves

[3] S. Horton, Peru and Ancom: A Study in the Disintegration of a Common Market. *Texas International Law Journal* 1982, 17: 39–61.

to heavy-handed regulation.[4] In addition, frequent changes of government and economic instability made domestic officials reluctant to follow Andean policies.

The member states responded by creating a judicial mechanism to enforce Andean rules that was modeled on the design of the ECJ. Particularly relevant for our investigation of Andean IP issues is the inclusion of a noncompliance mechanism empowering the *Junta* (today known as the General Secretariat) to challenge a state's violations of Andean law, and a preliminary reference procedure for national courts to submit questions of Andean law to the ATJ.[5] Chapter 2 described how the Andean Pact's continuing problems hobbled the new judicial system when it began operating in 1984. During the Tribunal's first decade, national courts filed only thirty-two preliminary reference requests, private parties filed only three nullification complaints, and the *Junta* refrained from filing any noncompliance suits. All told, Chapter 3 explains in greater detail, it was not an auspicious beginning for the ATJ.

By the late 1980s, a pervasive debt crisis in Latin America had pushed the Andean Pact to the brink of failure. Using the substantial economic leverage that crisis engendered, the World Bank, the Inter-American Development Bank, and the International Monetary Fund (IMF) pressed Andean governments to adopt a broad array of liberalizing and deregulatory reforms. These reforms, known as the "Washington Consensus,"[6] engendered fundamental changes in how Andean countries regulated their economies. National governments—acting on their own and through Andean institutions—adopted major policy reforms to achieve open, market-based economies and created new institutions staffed by Western-educated professionals who endorsed these goals.[7] We focus on those reforms that contributed to building a rule-of-law island for intellectual property.

In response to the demands of international financial institutions and growing domestic dissatisfaction with the slow pace of regional economic growth, national governments relaunched Andean integration in the mid-1990s. They amended the Cartagena Agreement, jettisoned the import substitution policy, replaced it with a free trade model based on a common market, and rechristened the new integration system "the Andean Community."[8]

Major institutional changes accompanied this evulsive policy shift. Member states replaced the ineffectual *Junta* with a General Secretariat, increased the size of its budget, and appointed a new cadre of young lawyers eager to use the enhanced

[4] D.E. Hojman, The Andean Pact: Failure of a Model of Integration? *Journal of Common Market Studies* 1981, 20 (2): 139–59.

[5] Original ATJ Treaty, Articles 17–31. See Chapter 2 for more on these procedures.

[6] J. Williamson, What Washington Means by Policy Reform. In: *Latin American Adjustment: How Much Has Happened*. J. Williamson (ed.), 5–20. Washington, DC: Institute for International Economics, 1990, 7.

[7] For a discussion of the spread of the Washington Consensus, see Y. Dezalay and B.G. Garth, *Global Prescriptions: The Production, Exportation, and Importation of a New Legal Orthodoxy*. Ann Arbor, MI: University of Michigan Press, 2002a. For a discussion of its demise, see N. Serra and J. Stiglitz, *The Washington Consenus Reconsidered: Towards a New Global Governance*. Oxford: Oxford University Press, 2008.

[8] T.A. O'Keefe, How the Andean Pact Transformed Itself into a Friend of Foreign Enterprise. *International Lawyer* 1996, 30 (4): 818–24.

resources to promote regional integration.[9] The member states also expanded the ATJ's jurisdiction. They authorized private actors to challenge noncompliance with Andean laws by filing complaints with the General Secretariat, subject to a right of appeal to the ATJ, and they indicated that ATJ judges could address how Andean rules applied to the facts of preliminary references referred by national courts.[10]

These reforms, which were part of a wider effort to increase public access to Andean institutions,[11] made it more difficult for member states to block the enforcement of Andean laws. The General Secretariat could now credibly argue that its own failure to initiate a noncompliance suit would prompt private actors to file their own noncompliance actions. These institutional changes were thus prerequisites for the activation of the Andean legal system, including the overhaul of regional legislation governing intellectual property protection.

The evolution of Andean intellectual property rules

Regulation of IP has been an important part of Andean integration since the Andean Pact's founding. The Cartagena Agreement itself proclaims the need for "a common system for treatment of … trademarks, patents, licenses, and royalties."[12] The Andean *Comisión* has adopted numerous regional laws—*Decisiones* in Spanish—to achieve this goal. These *Decisiones*, summarized in Table 5.1, have direct effect in national legal systems. They are also precise and detailed, as befits regulations "intended to serve, not as broad-brush treaty norms, but as the domestic law of each of the five [member] countries."[13]

As Table 5.1 indicates, Andean IP rules have changed over the life of the Community. The earliest *Decisiones* subordinated the property rights of investors to the region's economic development goals, treating patents and trademarks as vehicles for transferring technology from foreign firms.[14] In the early 1990s, member states shifted course and adopted four *Decisiones* that mandated progressively higher levels of IP protection. These new regional laws reflected the market liberalization goals of the later phases of the Washington Consensus. However, other factors reinforced the impetus for change: the inclusion of IP rules in the Uruguay Round of multilateral trade negotiations and threats of trade sanctions by the United States.

Colombia and Peru, the two Andean countries that were members of the General Agreement on Tariffs and Trade, recognized that the soon-to-be-established World

[9] Interviews with former official (B) of the General Secretariat Legal Advisor's Office.

[10] Revised ATJ Treaty, Articles 25 and 34.

[11] Interviews with the former official (B) of the General Secretariat Legal Advisor's Office.

[12] Cartagena Agreement, Article 27 (now Article 55).

[13] R.M. Sherwood and C.A. Primo Braga, *Intellectual Property, Trade and Economic Development: A Road Map for FTAA Negotiations*. Miami, FL: North–South Center, University of Miami, 1996. As interpreted by the ATJ, Andean law permits member states to adopt national IP legislation and regulations, but only if such rules complement regional IP standards. We discuss the *complemento indispensable* doctrine in Chapter 4.

[14] F.M. Abbott, Bargaining Power and Strategy in the Foreign Investment Process: A Current Andean Code Analysis. *Syracuse Journal of International Law and Commerce* 1975, 3 (3): 349–50.

Table 5.1 Summary of Andean intellectual property *Decisiones*

Decision no	IP subjects covered	Dates in effect
Decision 24	Extensive regulation and licensing restrictions on IP protection for foreign investors	1970–91
Decision 85	Minimal protection of trademarks and patents	1974–91
Decision 291	Reduced regulation and licensing restrictions on intellectual property of foreign investors	1991–present
Decision 311	Modest expansion of trademark and patent protection (including some pharmaceuticals)	1991–92
Decision 313	Same protection as Decision 311, with shorter transition periods	1992–94
Decision 344	IP rules mostly consistent with multilateral standards in WTO/TRIPS Agreement	1994–2000
Decision 486	Similar to Decision 344, with more detailed procedures and enforcement mechanisms	2000–present
Decision 632	Interpretation of data protection provision of Decision 486	2005–present
Decision 689	Adjusting ten specific patent and trademark provisions of Decision 486	2008–present

Trade Organization would include a treaty on intellectual property rights. Andean states opposed strong IP protection, but they realized that the Agreement on Trade-Related Aspects of Intellectual Property Rights (TRIPS) would be the price of admission to the new global trading system.[15]

TRIPS was attractive for other reasons. First, it offered a way to end the threat of US trade sanctions. By adapting regional rules to emerging multilateral standards, Andean governments hoped to end the US Trade Representative's practice of placing them on "priority watch lists" for refusing to recognize the IP rights demanded by foreign businesses.[16] Adopting these standards would also alleviate pressure by the World Intellectual Property Organization (WIPO), whose officials had long attempted to persuade Andean governments to follow the multilateral IP rules that TRIPS later incorporated.[17]

Yet even as member states agreed to TRIPS, they retained an awareness from the Andean Pact's import substitution days that IP regulation could be tailored to achieve other economic and social objectives important to developing countries. For example, early Andean patent rules did not protect pharmaceuticals. Later *Decisiones* did so, but with important exceptions that restricted the IP rights of foreign drug companies. These exceptions nurtured a thriving regional generics industry that

[15] L.R. Helfer, Regime Shifting: The TRIPS Agreement and the New Dynamics of International Intellectual Property Making. *Yale Journal of International Law* 2004, 29 (1):1–82, 18–24.

[16] S. Sell, *Power and Ideas: North-South Politics of Intellectual Property and Antitrust*. Albany, NY: State University of New York Press, 1998, 113–40.

[17] R.S. Manrique, The Andean Community's Intellectual Property Regime. In: *The Andean Community and the United States: Trade and Investment Relations in the 1990s*. M. Rodríguez Mendoza, P. Correa, and B. Kotschwar (eds), 212–19. Organization of American States, 1998.

produced low-cost medicines.[18] Analogous provisions had been included in the region's trademark laws. For example, Andean legislation required all trademark owners to use their trademarked goods and services in Andean commerce or risk losing them to local competitors.

By 1994 Andean law was consistent with TRIPS, but it still fell short of the demands of US IP industries. The United States and its IP industries responded by putting pressure on individual Andean countries to negotiate bilateral treaties and to enact domestic laws containing enhanced IP rules. These strategies caused some national executives to defect from Andean rules, but, as we explain later in this chapter, the ATJ and the General Secretariat proved to be hospitable forums for the region's generic drug industry to challenge these defections as violations of Andean law. Compliance with the ATJ rulings upholding these challenges would not have occurred, however, without the support of domestic IP agencies, whose restructuring was also part of the Washington Consensus reforms.

Restructuring domestic IP administrative agencies

The international financial institutions that promoted the liberalization of Andean markets did not expect that adopting market-friendly policies would on their own generate significant economic growth. Proponents of the Washington Consensus thus called for new legal and regulatory institutions to facilitate the working of national markets. To meet this objective, the multilateral development banks supported a second wave of reforms asking governments to restructure and strengthen administrative agencies in areas such as consumer protection, competition, bankruptcy, transparency, and intellectual property.

These pressures dovetailed with ongoing efforts of Andean governments to reform the domestic administrative state. In 1992 Peru established the National Institute for the Defense of Competition and the Protection of Intellectual Property (commonly referred to by the Spanish acronym INDECOPI, for *Instituto Nacional de Defensa de la Competencia y de la Protección de la Propiedad Intelectual*), an agency that cobbled together subjects, including intellectual property, consumer protection, and bankruptcy, that had previously been unregulated or scattered across several ministries.[19] In that same year, the Colombian government established a Superintendent of Industry and Commerce (SIC, for *Superintendencia de Industria y Comercio*) and entrusted the office with a similar array of competences.[20] Other Andean countries also created or restructured their domestic IP agencies over the next several years.[21]

[18] Interview with retired official (C) of the General Secretariat Legal Advisor's Office and a negotiator of early Andean IP *Decisiones*.

[19] On the origins of INDECOPI, see M.R. Ryan, Intellectual Property Institutions and the Public Administration of Knowledge in Developing Countries: The Case of INDECOPI in Peru. In: *The Role of the State in Competition and Intellectual Property Policy in Latin America: Towards an Academic Audit of INDECOPI*. Beatriz Boza (ed.), 319–29 Lima: INDECOPI, 2000.

[20] See <http://www.sic.gov.co/drupal/>.

[21] Bolivia created the National Intellectual Property Service (known as SENAPI, an abbreviation of *Servicio Nacional de Propiedad Intelectual*) in 1996; Venezuela created a similar agency, the Autonomous

INDECOPI, SIC, and the other IP agencies in the region were logical recipients of aid from the international financial institutions and from the WIPO. The institutions helped the agencies to improve their efficiency and transparency, providing funds and technical assistance to modernize their operations, train personnel, and adopt new technologies to disseminate information. This external funding helped to transform the agencies into relatively well-resourced institutions able to carry out their mandates free from domestic political pressures. It especially benefited agencies like INDECOPI, whose organization as a public corporation "exempts it from civil service personnel rules" and "insulates it from the day-to-day managerial control of the executive branch."[22]

The key factor setting domestic IP agencies apart from other government bodies, however, is their funding source: IP registration fees and fines. Firms must apply to register patents and trademarks, and many foreign businesses that own intellectual property are quite wealthy. With an independent funding source, the IP agencies are able to attract and retain high-quality officials and staff to provide the services that IP rights holders expect. Compared to other administrative entities, INDECOPI, SIC, and the other IP agencies were well off financially and highly professionalized. Many officials made their careers advancing in the agencies' ranks and worked hard, and in most cases successfully, to protect their resources and institutional culture.

When reviewing applications to register patents, trademarks, and other IP rights, agency administrators applied Andean IP *Decisiones* and, in the process, identified gaps and ambiguities in the law. Since all of the agencies applied the same regional rules, their officials and staff naturally sought the advice of their peers in other member states. These consultations engendered an informal regional network of IP agency officials and staff who shared information, developed criteria to resolve common legal problems, and came to view themselves as engaged in highly skilled and technical activities.[23] Several of the new agencies were also tasked with protecting consumers, a mandate that informed their views as to the proper balance between private economic rights and the public interest.

The Andean General Secretariat supported this nascent regional network. It also consulted the agencies during the revisions of Andean IP *Decisiones* in the late 1990s. The next iteration of Andean IP rules (*Decisión* 486, adopted in 2000) drew on the agencies' expertise to close lacunae and clarify ambiguities while maintaining many distinctive features of Andean IP law. These consultations gave agency

Intellectual Property Service (known as SAPI, for *Servicio autónomo de la propiedad intelectual*), one year later; and in 1998 Ecuador established the Ecuadorian Institute of Intellectual Property (EIIP, for *Instituto Ecuatoriano de la Propiedad Intelectual*), a public juridical entity with its own assets and administrative, economic, financial, and operative autonomy.

22 D.G. Becker, Justice for Peruvian Consumers? INDECOPI and Consumer Protection. In: *Paper presented at the XXIII Int'l Congress of the Latin American Studies Association.* Washington DC, 2001, 11 (stating that "about 70 percent of INDECOPI's annual expenditures is covered by fines and the fees it earns from trademark registrations").

23 Interview with official (B) of INDECOPI. Meetings funded by WIPO encouraged the formation of these networks.

officials a voice in Andean rule-making and, as a result, a stake in implementing those rules.[24]

In sum, the emergence of domestic administrative agencies with a professional interest in enforcing Andean rules was an important catalyst for the development of a rule-of-law island for intellectual property. As we explain later in this chapter, the agencies' registration of trademarks and patents generated a demand by private actors for Andean litigation that enabled the ATJ to clarify the content of regional IP rules and to resolve disputes on the basis of those rules.

Activating the Andean Tribunal of Justice

As the IP agencies began to issue more trademark and patent registration decisions, appeals to national courts challenging those decisions also increased. Yet businesses and their counsel had little faith that national judges, most of whom were generalists, could master the specialized and technical issues IP law often involves. They thus preferred to have the ATJ interpret the Andean IP rules rather than leave it to national courts to review the agencies' decisions on their own.[25]

Chapter 3 documents the rise in Andean litigation and the predominance of IP disputes on the ATJ's docket. Of the 1338 ATJ preliminary rulings issued up to and including 2007, 1,303 (97%) concerned intellectual property: 1,165 (87%) interpreted Andean trademark legislation; 103 (8%) involve Andean patent rules; 11 (less than 1%) dealt with copyrights; and 24 (less than 2%) concern other types of IP, such as industrial designs and utility models. Over the next seven years, the Tribunal has addressed a broader range of legal issues, but the prevalence of IP references remains overwhelming—in percentage terms, 96% of the 2,679 preliminary rulings issued between 1985 and 2014 involve IP issues, primarily trademarks and patents.

Chapter 3 also explains that national courts initially ignored their obligation to refer questions of Andean law to the Tribunal. In response, IP attorneys personally lobbied judges, and, when that failed, filed noncompliance actions with the General Secretariat challenging the refusal to refer cases. Once judges were made aware of their obligations and realized that referring cases to the ATJ would not undermine their decision-making power, they began to refer a large number of IP cases to the Tribunal.[26] Although efforts to overcome national judicial skepticism varied across the member states, the success of these efforts was akin to uncorking a tap. Beginning in the mid-1990s, each uncorking produced a sharp increase in the ATJ's docket.

[24] Interviews with former official (B) of the General Secretariat Legal Advisor's Office.

[25] Interview with attorney (C) from IP law firm in Peru; Interview with attorney (D) from IP law firm in Colombia; Interview with attorney (A) from commercial and administrative law firm in Colombia.

[26] Chapter 3 analyzes efforts to activate national court referrals to the ATJ. Chapter 9 discusses attempts by pro-integration lawyers to encourage references to the Tribunal in its early years.

Constructing an Effective IP Rule of Law in the Andean Community

Many legal scholars evaluate whether or not a legal system is effective by considering the extent of compliance with its rules. International relations theorists determine effectiveness by assessing whether states behave differently than they otherwise would have done because international rules or institutions exist. We incorporate both of these assessments into our analysis of how the ATJ helped to construct and bolster the rule of law in the Andean Community. We also consider elements that are taken for granted in well-functioning legal systems: whether decisions by state actors are made pursuant to legal rules rather than power, political influence or bribery.

Our analysis proceeds in three parts. First, we ask whether Andean IP rules influence the expectations and behavior of private actors. We document a growing demand for trademarks and patents, an increase in disputes over IP ownership, and the rise of a specialized bar devoted to the registration and enforcement of intellectual property rights. These trends reveal that businesses and their counsel are voting with their feet; rights holders file and defend applications for trademarks and patents because IP rights have economic value and because agency proceedings and litigation can effectively secure that value.

Second, we ask whether ATJ litigation has contributed to the reasoned, even-handed, and transparent application of Andean rules by domestic IP agencies and has shaped substantive legal doctrines. We evaluate the ATJ's case law and, drawing on interviews with lawyers and agency officials, demonstrate that the ATJ has created the kind of procedures and standards that one would expect in well-functioning legal systems.

Third, we investigate compliance with ATJ rulings, focusing on how the ATJ and the General Secretariat induced governments to reverse policies that violated Andean IP rules. The cases we discuss show how the ATJ helped to rebuff pressure by the United States and multinational corporations to circumvent Andean IP rules, leading to behavior by national actors different from what it would have been in the absence of the Andean legal system.

The rising demand for and economic value of Andean IP rights

At the most basic level, an effective rule of law creates rights protected by enforceable legal rules that apply equally to similarly situated actors. Several indicators reveal that Andean IP rights meet this standard. Statistics gathered from domestic IP agencies and interviews with attorneys indicate that trademarks and patents are economically valuable and that the procedures governing their acquisition and adjudication are effective.

Figures 5.1 and 5.2 exhibit a growing demand for trademark and patent protection in the Andean Community through 2007. Applications for patents and trademarks rose immediately after the restructuring of domestic IP administrative

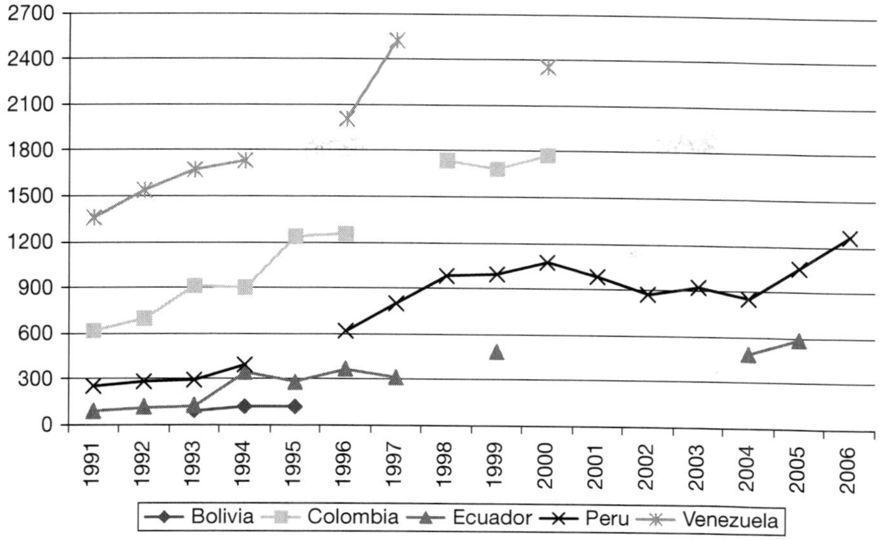

Figure 5.1 Total patent applications by country and year

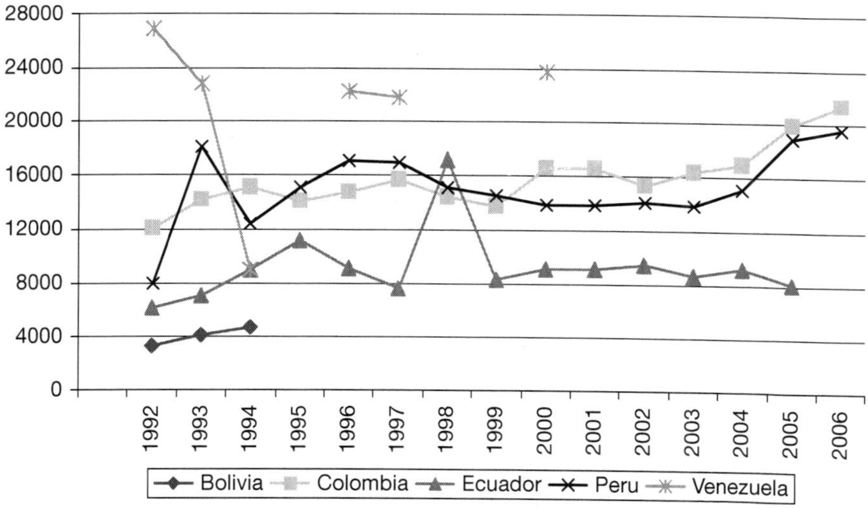

Figure 5.2 Total trademark applications by country and year

agencies and the revision of Andean IP *Decisiones* in the early and mid-1990s.[27] In Colombia, for example, patent applications increased nearly threefold between

[27] Data for Figures 5.1 and 5.2 were provided by WIPO, Statistics Data and Indicators, available at <http://www.wipo.int/ipstats/en/>. In Figures 5.1 and 5.2, trademark and patent application data for Peru from 1998 to 2006 were provided by INDECOPI; and trademark application data for Colombia were provided by SIC. No data were available for some countries in some years.

1991 and 2000, and trademark applications rose more than 76% between 1992 and 2006. Data from the IP agencies also record the nationality of the applicants for IP rights. In the case of patents, foreign firms were responsible for between 85% and 95% of all filings. Between 50% and 60% of trademark applications, however, emanated from domestic businesses.[28]

Another indicator of the growing regional interest in IP is the number of private parties that oppose applications to register trademarks and patents. Oppositions are usually filed by business competitors that own trademarks or patents similar to those that applicants seek to register, or by firms, such as generic drug producers, that benefit from the lack of IP protection in a particular industry. That these businesses take the time and expense to oppose IP applications is one indication of the economic value of registering a trademark or patent.

The available evidence reveals a marked increase in IP oppositions. Figure 5.3 shows the number ATJ preliminary references through 2007 that involved IP registration disputes. In the early and mid-1990s, most patent and trademark applications were uncontested. Over the next decade, however, private parties lodged a substantially larger number of oppositions to IP applications at the administrative level. By the middle of the next decade, cases involving oppositions outnumbered uncontested cases by a ratio of greater than two to one.

Officials in the patent and trademark divisions of INDECOPI and SIC confirmed that the number of oppositions grew beginning in the late 1990s, a trend

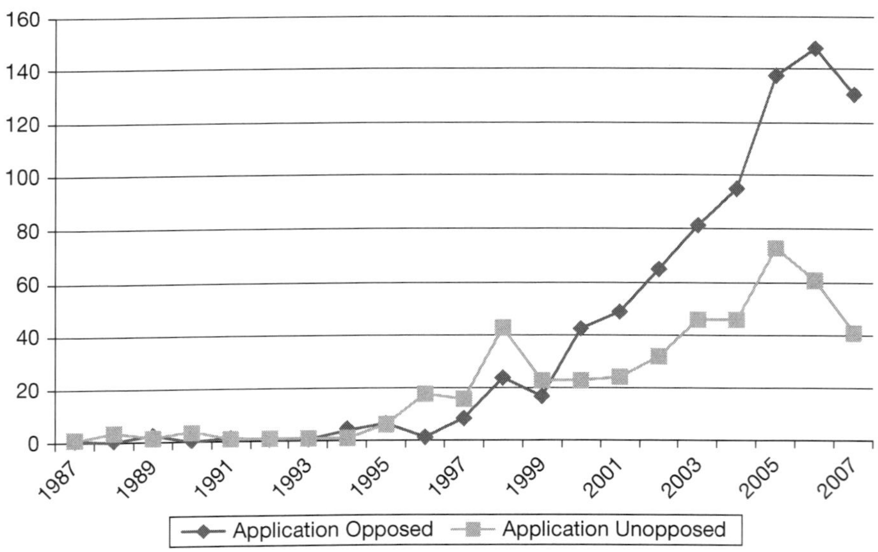

Figure 5.3 ATJ preliminary rulings involving oppositions to IP registrations

[28] Patent and trademark applications filed by individuals or businesses in other Andean countries are counted as nonresident applications.

that they attributed to the growth of IP industries and IP-related investment in the region and wider societal recognition of the economic value of patents and trademarks.[29] Many IP holders are also repeat players in Andean litigation, suggesting that they have found the legal system to be an effective way to protect their rights.[30]

The growing demand for IP rights has also fueled an expansion of legal specialists in the region. For example, a lawyer in Ecuador estimated that while in the past there were ten lawyers or firms in the country whose practices included IP issues, by 2004 approximately 200 single lawyers or firms were practicing in the area.[31] In Peru, a leading IP lawyer told us that his firm had added intellectual property to its corporate law practice in 1997. In 2007 the firm decided to focus exclusively on intellectual property.[32] A Colombian lawyer estimated that by 2007 twenty law firms in Bogotá specialized in the field, whereas there were perhaps five firms ten years earlier.[33]

For most areas of Andean law, neither litigation nor jurisprudence is reported in scholarly publications. Intellectual property is a striking exception. Many IP law firms publish newsletters in which they review recent developments and tout the firms' accomplishments, seeking to attract new clients in an increasingly competitive market for legal services.[34] By 2004, interest in intellectual property among the region's legal community was strong enough to merit the creation of a new specialized journal, the *Anuario andino de derechos intelectuales*.[35] These developments suggest that the audience for information about Andean IP law has achieved a critical mass.

Interviews provided additional evidence that statistics alone cannot show. We asked every attorney with whom we spoke whether the empirical picture just described reflected reality; that is, whether applications for and oppositions to IP rights were increasing, whether agency and judicial decision-making reflected rules on the books, and whether attorneys could protect the trademarks and patents registered by their clients. The answer was a uniform yes, regardless of whether the attorney worked for the government, an industry association, a local family-owned law firm, or a branch of a global law firm with multinational corporate clients.[36]

[29] Interview with official (C) of the *Superintendencia de Industria y Comercio* (SIC); Interview with official (C) of INDECOPI.

[30] For example, the US shipping giant UPS, the European food conglomerate Nestlé, and the Colombian food producer Alpina each participated in more than ten agency registration proceedings—as both applicants and opponents—as well as national court appeals and ATJ preliminary rulings to protect their respective trademarks in the region. E.g., ATJ Preliminary Ruling 223-IP-2005; ATJ Preliminary Ruling 146-IP-2005; ATJ Preliminary Ruling 238-IP-2005.

[31] Interview with two attorneys (I) from IP law firm in Ecuador.

[32] Interview with attorney (C) from IP law firm in Peru.

[33] Interview with attorney (F) from IP law firm in Colombia.

[34] See, e.g., Latin American Intellectual Property Newsletter (Baker and McKenzie), March 2004; Intellectual Property Update (Olarte Raisbeck and Frieri Ltd), September 2007; Interview with attorney (C) from IP law firm in Peru.

[35] *Anuario andino de derechos intelectuales*, available at <http://anuarioandino.com/>.

[36] E.g., Interview with attorney (C) from IP law firm in Peru; Interview with four attorneys (H) at Colombian branch of a multinational law firm; Interview with official (C) of INDECOPI; Interview with official (C) of the *Superintendencia de Industria y Comercio* (SIC); Interview with official (B) of

This answer is itself remarkable. The attorneys we interviewed were pessimistic about the Andean Community as a whole. They repeatedly stated that for many subjects the region's legal system did not work, that rules were drafted to allow for domestic derogations, and that ATJ and General Secretariat rulings often enabled governments to do as they pleased. Yet the attorneys largely took for granted that the Andean IP system functions as a rule of law should, through the habitual application of legal rules and procedures.

The domestic IP agencies received much of the credit for this result. Attorneys interviewed in 2005 and 2007 commented favorably on the quality of agency officials' legal and technical analysis. This was not always the case. Prior to the creation of the domestic IP agencies in the 1990s, commentators claimed that IP disputes were often resolved through political connections, "back channels," and even bribery. Our interviews with agency officials and the private companies who are their clients strongly suggest that the use of these extralegal means diminished with the creation of independent and professionalized administrative agencies.

Bolstering the rule of law in domestic administrative agencies

Chapter 3 explained that ATJ preliminary rulings are highly repetitive. This is especially true for rulings in IP cases. Appeals from administrative agencies often raise the same legal issues, such as whether two trademarks for similar products are likely to cause confusion, whether a trademark is famous, and whether an invention satisfies the requirements for patentability.[37] National judges, in turn, repeatedly ask the ATJ to interpret the same provisions of Andean law even when the Tribunal has already interpreted those provisions.[38] The ATJ responds to these requests in kind, regurgitating its analysis and sometimes cutting and pasting paragraphs from its earlier rulings.[39]

This repetition is a source of frustration for the Andean intellectual property bar. Attorneys complain that many ATJ rulings are "elementary and repetitive; substantively there is little new" because the Tribunal rarely indicates how Andean rules, as it has interpreted them, should be applied to the facts of the case.[40]

Yet repetition also serves a different function: it helps to overcome judicial resistance. Our coding and interviews revealed that national judges were reluctant to cede authority to the ATJ or to provoke political controversy by challenging domestic statutes or decrees.[41] The sameness of preliminary references and of the ATJ's

INDECOPI; Interview with attorney (D) from IP law firm in Colombia; Interview with attorney (A) from commercial and administrative law firm in Colombia.

[37] E.g., ATJ Preliminary Ruling 90-IP-2004, 3, 5, 6–8 (likelihood of confusion); ATJ Preliminary Ruling 162-IP-2004, 7, 11 (famous trademarks); ATJ Preliminary Ruling 49-IP-2005, 5 (patentability).

[38] As discussed in Chapter 3, the ATJ does not follow *acte clair*, an ECJ doctrine that directs national judges to refrain from referring cases involving previously decided legal issues and instead to apply earlier ECJ rulings.

[39] E.g., ATJ Preliminary Ruling 4-IP-2001; ATJ Preliminary Ruling 45-IP-2006.

[40] E.g., Interviews with attorneys (C) and (D) in IP law firms in Bogotá and Lima.

[41] Several attorneys, who requested anonymity, stated that they would not use a preliminary reference to challenge a domestic law as contrary to an Andean secondary legislation or to the Cartagena

responses made national judges more accepting of the preliminary reference mechanism, eventually engendering habituation that made referrals in IP cases unremarkable. Clear and repetitive rulings also helped to expedite the disposition of cases and facilitate compliance. For example, the judges of the *Consejo de Estado*—the Colombian administrative court that is the ATJ's first and most frequent domestic judicial interlocutor—explained that they "accept the interpretation" of the ATJ in every referred case, but that "[w]hen the Tribunal is clearer, it makes the application easier and quicker."[42]

By far the most favorable assessment of ATJ preliminary rulings, however, came from the lawyers and professional staff of domestic IP agencies—the administrators who interpret and apply Andean law on a daily basis. As a member of the INDECOPI administrative tribunal and former head of the agency's Trademark Office stated:

> We [the members of the INDECOPI administrative tribunal] expect and await the [ATJ] rulings. We read the rulings and they help us to clarify the procedures and substantive issues in the law. We apply the rulings as soon as they come down from the tribunal, and we reference the rulings in the texts of our decisions about registrations.[43]

The head of the Industrial Property Division at SIC in Colombia concurred, stating that ATJ "rulings certainly help" the division's work. "We read all the decisions, and discuss the important points," especially now that the Internet makes it possible to "review cases immediately" after the Tribunal decides them.[44] The IP agency's *Compendio de Doctrina* confirms the influence of Andean jurisprudence in the agency's work. This 2005 publication comprehensively catalogues the procedural rules and substantive standards that SIC applies when reviewing trademark and patent applications. It is peppered with quotes from ATJ preliminary rulings.[45] While Venezuela was a member of the Andean Community, its *Servicio autónomo de la propiedad intelectual* (SAPI) followed a similar practice. According to SAPI's former legal counsel, the agency viewed ATJ rulings as persuasive authority and referred to them in hundreds of IP registration decisions.[46]

The generally favorable impression of ATJ case law reported by national judges and administrators suggests that the repetitiveness of the Tribunal's judgments has a value that has eluded the private IP bar. Attorneys appear to be frustrated by the Tribunal's repetition precisely because they have internalized the validity of regional IP rules and are seeking more specific guidance from Andean judges. As recently as the late 1990s, however, attorneys, national courts, and administrative agencies

Agreement. Instead, they would bypass national judges and file a noncompliance action with the General Secretariat and then, if that body rejected the case, with the ATJ. For a more detailed discussion of the choice to use the noncompliance procedure, see Chapter 3.

[42] Interview with five judges (A) of the *Sala Primera del Consejo de Estado de Colombia*.
[43] Interview with official (B) of INDECOPI.
[44] Interview with official (C) of the *Superintendencia de Industria y Comercio* (SIC).
[45] SIC, *Compendio de Doctrina: Propiedad Industrial* (2005) (on file with authors).
[46] Interview with former official (A) of SAPI.

had not fully accepted the supremacy of Andean law or the ATJ's authority.[47] Seen from this perspective, a high degree of repetition may be a rational strategy for an international court to inculcate habitual compliance with its rulings in countries where the domestic rule of law is weak.

A deeper analysis of ATJ rulings provides further support for this position. In tracking the evolution of Andean case law in our coding, we identified four trends that suggest that repetition has strengthened adherence to the rule of law in the region's domestic IP agencies.

First, the quality of information in preliminary references has improved markedly over time. Early referrals omitted basic facts and procedural histories. In case after case, the ATJ responded by calling for a complete factual record.[48] Administrative agencies and national courts reacted, in turn, by furnishing details about the parties, the history of the dispute, and the legal issues at stake. Eventually, the ATJ standardized preliminary reference requests. Colombian and Peruvian judges showed us request forms that require them to provide specific items of information. This standardization has reduced many basic errors that IP agencies committed in early registration proceedings.[49] More important, it has facilitated the systematic application of legal rules to similarly situated applicants—an essential feature of the rule of law.

Second, the ATJ has adopted procedures to protect private actors who oppose applications to register trademarks and patents. An early and influential decision involved a challenge by an association of generic drug manufacturers to the registration of pipeline patents—an issue we analyze later in this chapter. The Ecuadorian IP agency rejected the opposition, stating that a presidential decree required it to approve such patents. The ATJ disagreed. It reasoned that "an association of pharmaceutical laboratories has a prima facie legitimate interest in the subject of pharmaceutical patents" that may violate Andean norms.[50] Over the next several years, the Tribunal clarified and repeated the procedures that agency officials were required to follow when reviewing contested IP applications. These procedures included strict adherence to Andean rules regulating oppositions,[51] the obligation to justify the rejection of oppositions,[52] the responsibility to apply Andean IP standards with particular care when applications are contested,[53] and the duty to provide adequate facts and legal analysis to enable both parties to challenge the agency's registration decisions.[54] These procedures fostered a hospitable climate for the fair and even-handed adjudication of IP disputes.

[47] For example, in ATJ Preliminary Ruling 9-IP-99, the ATJ stated that it was "required" to repeat its analysis because the Colombian SIC continued to refer to the Tribunal's preliminary rulings as merely persuasive authority. ATJ Preliminary Ruling 9-IP-99, 5.

[48] E.g., ATJ Preliminary Ruling 1-IP-87; ATJ Preliminary Ruling 3-IP-88; ATJ Preliminary Ruling 1-IP-91; ATJ Preliminary Ruling 2-IP-91; ATJ Preliminary Ruling 4-IP-93; ATJ Preliminary Ruling 6-IP-93; ATJ Preliminary Ruling 7-IP-96.

[49] E.g., ATJ Preliminary Ruling 9-IP-95, 2–4; ATJ Preliminary Ruling 9-IP-97, 2.

[50] ATJ Preliminary Ruling 39-IP-98, 6.

[51] ATJ Preliminary Ruling 5-IP-99, 6–7.

[52] Ibid., 7–8.

[53] ATJ Preliminary Ruling 16-IP-2003, 7.

[54] ATJ Preliminary Ruling 44-IP-2006, 10.

Third, the Tribunal has required IP agencies to justify their decisions with reasons. In any legal system, reasoned decision-making cabins the discretion of public officials. But in countries where the rule of law is weak, the obligation to give reasons has a more powerful effect: it deters officials from circumventing or perverting the law by deciding cases on the basis of bribes, political influence, or "intuition."[55] The ATJ expressly recognized that domestic agencies were not free from political pressure.[56] By repeatedly insisting that agency lawyers and administrators justify and explain their registration decisions in writing, the Tribunal not only bounded their discretion. It also helped to insulate the agencies from domestic politics and to create a constituency for compliance with its rulings.

The previous examples describe important procedural dimensions of the rule of law. The ATJ has also drawn upon its close relationship with the administrative agencies to fill gaps in substantive Andean IP rules. One striking example involves "coexistence agreements," contracts that allow two or more trademark owners to set rules for the peaceful coexistence of their marks in the same market. In many countries, such privately brokered agreements are presumptively valid. If two businesses consent to coexist in the same territory, the trademarks of both are likely to be registered regardless of whether consumers would be confused by such parallel legal protection.[57]

Originally, Andean law was silent on coexistence agreements. The ATJ filled this gap by requiring IP agencies to review all such agreements to protect the interests of consumers. A subsequent Andean *Decisión* appeared to contradict this doctrine,[58] but the ATJ distinguished the potential conflict and reaffirmed its earlier position. Colombian and Peruvian agencies—whose mandates, as explained earlier, include both consumer protection and intellectual property—were sympathetic to the Tribunal's position. Although the agencies' pro-consumer orientation initially triggered some grumbling by the trademark bar, resistance subsided after repeated rulings by the ATJ that were followed by national judges and administrators.[59] Chapter 3 further explains how the IP agencies have shaped ATJ jurisprudence.

The foregoing analysis reveals how the registration decisions of domestic IP agencies, appeals to national courts, and preliminary references to the ATJ, taken together, generated a positive feedback mechanism that helped build an effective IP rule of law. Early ATJ rulings improved the agencies' procedures, promoted reasoned decision-making, clarified ambiguities in Andean rules, and helped to insulate officials from domestic politics. The resulting favorable legal climate for

[55] ATJ Preliminary Ruling 28-IP-96, 11–12.

[56] In ATJ Preliminary Ruling 27-IP-95, the ATJ stressed the need for "administrative and economic autonomy to free officials from any kind of pressures or influences that derogate from the ends or purposes of the defense of a trademark for the owner as well as for the public or consumer." Ibid., 15.

[57] See, e.g., M. Moss, Trademark "Coexistence" Agreements: Legitimate Contracts or Tools of Consumer Deception? *Loyola Consumer Law Review* 2005, 18 (2): 197–222, 209–13. For additional discussion of trademark coexistence agreements, see Chapter 3.

[58] Andean *Decisión* 486, Article 136.

[59] Interview with official (B) of INDECOPI. For examples of cases invalidating coexistence agreements, see SIC, *Compendio de Doctrina: Propiedad Industrial* (2005), 398–401.

IP protection encouraged an increase in IP applications and appeals to national courts. The judges on those courts referred a growing number of cases to the ATJ, which further clarified Andean IP rules and administrative procedures. The cycle was completed when the Tribunal's case law was consumed by the same agencies whose registration decisions had spawned the first wave of ATJ litigation. This positive feedback mechanism was an important component of establishing IP rights as an effective rule-of-law island in the Andean Community.

Enforcing Andean IP rules in response to national violations

A third feature of an effective rule of law is inducing changes in state behavior that would not otherwise have occurred. Although the individuals we interviewed sometimes expressed disagreement with the ATJ's reasoning, they all attested that national judges and agency officials habitually comply with preliminary rulings, most of which interpret Andean legislation in the abstract without applying the law to the facts of the case at hand. However, the ATJ has also been effective in politically high-profile cases challenging national laws as a violation of Andean IP rules. Three disputes in particular merit analysis, each of which involves the Tribunal's jurisdiction to review noncompliance complaints filed by private parties and the General Secretariat.

In the "pipeline" patent case, decided in 1996, the ATJ invalidated a bilateral agreement between Ecuador and the United States that granted patent protection to foreign pharmaceutical firms. In the "second-use" patent case of 2001, the ATJ overturned a Peruvian decree—adopted in response to pressure by the US pharmaceutical giant Pfizer—that authorized domestic IP agencies to grant second-use patents, including the lucrative second-use patent for Viagra, in contravention of Andean rules. The ATJ later overturned Ecuadorian and Venezuelan agency decisions awarding patents for Viagra. Last, in the "data protection" case, decided in 2005, the Tribunal found fault with a Colombian decree—adopted under pressure from the United States—that protects the test data submitted by pharmaceutical manufacturers to national health agencies when seeking approval to market new medicines.

We describe these cases in detail to demonstrate that national courts and IP agencies initially followed government decrees that were contrary to Andean law. These actors changed course, however, after the ATJ found the decrees to be in violation of Andean law and ordered the agencies to reverse decisions based on the decrees. In two of the three disputes, national governments acquiesced in these reversals. The third case—data protection—was more contentious. Colombia argued that the ATJ's interpretation of Andean law was erroneous. However, rather than defy the Tribunal's ruling, Colombia orchestrated the adoption of an interpretive decision using a procedure for legislative revision that the Tribunal itself had previously approved.

The essential point that ties all three cases together is that ATJ rulings have made it more difficult for individual member states to defect from Andean policies in response to demands by the United States and US corporations for stronger IP protection rules. Such pressures are unrelenting, and over time the United States has won some concessions, especially relating to data protection. Yet Andean countries have successfully resisted pressures to which many of their regional neighbors have succumbed. As a result, the Andean Community has been more adept at maintaining key elements of the region's distinctive and balanced approach to reconciling the social and economic needs of consumers in developing countries with the interests of IP rights holders.

Our focus here is on how litigation before the ATJ changed state behavior. All three cases involve the legal protection of patented drugs, a topic of intense interstate negotiation and lobbying by the pharmaceutical industry. Chapter 6 analyzes a different branch of Andean intellectual property law—a trademark dispute between two multinational tobacco companies over control of the Belmont cigarette brand. In that dispute, which spanned multiple Andean countries, the ATJ performed a different function. It clarified vague provisions of Andean law regarding the use of a trademark in a way that facilitated the resolution of the controversy, allowing administrative agencies and national judges in each country to make different factual determinations regarding the use of the Belmont mark.

Enforcing the ban on "pipeline" patents

During the first two decades of the Andean Pact, its member states did not award patents for pharmaceutical products, a position shared by most developing countries.[60] In the early 1990s, however, the member states lifted this ban as part of their broader effort to conform Andean rules to multilateral IP standards. Rather than fully embracing patents for drugs, Andean governments phased in protection incrementally. They recognized patents for new drugs developed after the revision of Andean rules. However, adopting a doctrine known as "absolute novelty," the member states refused to protect medicines patented in other countries during the years when it was impossible to apply for a pharmaceutical patent in the Andean countries. Although many of these foreign drugs were in the production "pipeline" before the change in Andean law, the region's governments nevertheless refused to recognize them.[61]

The United States took a position that favored the pharmaceutical companies. It pressured Andean countries to recognize so-called pipeline protection for these pre-existing patented drugs. Most Andean member states resisted this pressure.[62]

[60] Sell, 1998, 191–2.

[61] Pipeline patents protect inventions that were ineligible for protection under prior domestic legislation:

> For example, if a country begins granting pharmaceutical patents in 1995, a drug that was invented in 1991 would not have been eligible for a patent at the time it was new. Strict interpretation of novelty would make such a drug ineligible for patents in 1995 too, because by the time the patent scope was changed to make drugs patentable the drug in question did not satisfy the novelty requirement. Yet some countries opted to grant patents to older drugs in the "pipeline," provided they were not already on the market.

K.C. Shadlen, The Politics of Patents and Drugs in Brazil and Mexico: The Industrial Bases of Health Activism. *Global Development & Environmental Institute Working Paper No. 07-05*, 2007, 6, available at <https://www.ciaonet.org/attachments/13604/uploads>.

[62] Manrique, 1998, 217.

In 1993, however, Ecuador and the United States signed a bilateral treaty granting pipeline protection. Ecuador's Congress never ratified the treaty, but the country's president adopted a decree to implement it. Relying on this decree, over the next two years the Ecuadorian IP agency awarded twenty-three pipeline patents to foreign pharmaceutical manufacturers such as Pfizer and Novartis.

In response, several domestic producers of generic drugs challenged the presidential decree. An Ecuadorian administrative court referred the case to the ATJ, which issued a preliminary ruling holding that Andean law follows the absolute novelty requirement.[63] The administrative court responded by rejecting the ATJ's ruling and upholding the national decree instead.

Attorneys on the staff of the General Secretariat were following the litigation in Ecuador closely. After the administrative court's decision, the Secretariat filed a noncompliance action against Ecuador before the Tribunal alleging that the pipeline decree and the court's ruling violated Andean law's absolute novelty requirement. This was the first noncompliance action that the Secretariat brought to the ATJ.[64]

Ecuador defended the domestic decree as falling within the discretion granted to member states to adopt domestic legislation or international agreements that "strengthen the industrial property rights provided for in" Andean *Decisión* 344.[65] The General Secretariat countered that the Ecuadorian decree contradicted an unambiguous limitation on Andean IP protection and created an incentive for foreign firms to seek pharmaceutical patents in Ecuador but not in other member states. The ATJ sided with the Andean officials.[66] It interpreted the word "strengthen" in a teleological fashion, reasoning that national laws and treaties must complement the regional IP system, not contradict it. Ecuador had thus violated Andean IP rules "by establishing an exceptional regime … granting advantages to patenting in its own country, in a manner that was unfair under the common regime applied in the other Andean countries."[67] The Tribunal also categorically rejected Ecuador's claim that "an international commitment [could] be invoked as a reason to validate noncompliance with a prior Community obligation."[68]

Compliance with the ATJ's judgment played out over the next decade in several venues. Within weeks of the ruling, the government adopted a new decree revoking the prior law recognizing pipeline patents. Relying on the new decree, the domestic IP agency rejected at least 120 pending applications from foreign businesses seeking to register pipeline patents.

Frustrated foreign patent applicants challenged the agency's rejections. When national judges referred these cases to the ATJ, the Tribunal supported the agencies. It also reaffirmed its prior ruling, stating: "[t]he 'pipeline' principle is not part of Andean law and is contrary to that of 'absolute novelty,' which must be applied by

63 ATJ Preliminary Ruling 6-IP-94.

64 General Secretariat officials chose this case to demonstrate their support for the ATJ. They also wanted the Tribunal to penalize a clear violation of Andean rules and thereby to affirm the supremacy of the Andean Community's balanced approach to IP protection in the area of pharmaceutical patents. Interviews with former official (B) of the General Secretariat Legal Advisor's Office.

65 Andean *Decisión* 344, Article 143.

66 ATJ Noncompliance Judgment 1-AI-96.

67 Manrique, 1998, 217.

68 ATJ Noncompliance Judgment 1-AI-96, 30.

the competent authorities. Any patent requested on the basis of the pipeline principle must be denied or, if granted, nullified."[69]

Since the first ATJ pipeline ruling in 1996, Ecuadorian IP agencies have not granted any additional pipeline patents. Nor, our interviews disclosed, have the administrative agencies of the other four member countries. The agencies thus played a key role in enforcing Andean law.[70] Without the ATJ's intervention, Ecuador would likely have succumbed to demands from the United States to protect pipeline patents. For example, Mexico and three of the four members of MERCOSUR—Argentina, Brazil, and Uruguay—acceded to US pressure to recognize such patents during roughly the same period.[71]

Enforcing the ban on second-use patents

The Andean requirement of absolute novelty for inventions also bars recognition of second-use patents—patents initially granted for one purpose but later found to be beneficial for an unrelated purpose. Andean *Decisiones* 344 and 486 categorically reject second-use patents, stating that "[p]roducts or processes already patented and included in the state of the art ... may not be the subject of new patents on the sole ground [that the product was] put to a use different from that originally contemplated by the initial patent."[72]

In the 1990s, the American pharmaceutical company Pfizer discovered that its heart medication, pyrazolpyrimidinones (Viagra), had the side effect of treating male impotence. Latin America promised to be a lucrative market for Viagra. Notwithstanding clear Andean rules to the contrary, Pfizer filed second-use patent applications in all Andean countries in an effort to prevent the sale of generic copies of the drug throughout the region.

In Peru, the INDECOPI patent office applied Andean law and rejected three applications by Pfizer. A few months later, in June 1997, President Alberto Fujimori issued a decree that purported "to facilitate the proper application of" various articles of *Decisión* 344.[73] Article 4 of the decree recognized second-use patents, including new uses of existing drugs.[74] Several officials and attorneys we

69 ATJ Preliminary Ruling 25-IP-2002, 18.

70 The situation with respect to the twenty-three pipeline patents registered prior to the ATJ's ruling was more complex. In 1998 the Ecuadorian director of industrial property confirmed the validity of these patents. In response, the ATJ concluded that the director's decision upholding the registrations was a further infringement of Andean law, and it imposed sanctions on Ecuador. ATJ Noncompliance Judgment 1-AI-96, at 1-2. The following year, an Ecuadorian administrative court ruled that the government was required to nullify all acts that violated the ATJ's ruling. ATJ Preliminary Ruling 25-IP-2002, at 19. We have been unable to confirm that the IP agency has revoked these twenty-three pipeline patents. However, we infer from the fact that the ATJ continues to receive occasional preliminary references concerning these patents that not all of them have been nullified.

71 C.S. Harrison, *The Politics of the International Pricing of Prescription Drugs*. Westport, CT: Praeger, 2004, 103–10.

72 Andean *Decisión* 486, Article 21; Andean *Decisión* 344, Article 16.

73 Supreme *Decreto* No. 010-97-ITINCI, El Peruano, June 6, 1997, 149,830.

74 Article 4, Andean *Decisión* 344, provided that "a distinct use included in the state of the art shall be the subject of a new patent if it complies with" the normal patent requirements of novelty, inventive

interviewed indicated that they were suspicious of the decree's origins, stating that the law "appeared out of nowhere."

Immediately thereafter, Pfizer asked INDECOPI to re-examine its applications to patent Viagra. Relying on the new law, the agency granted the applications in January 1999. Pfizer then threatened to sue Peruvian drug companies that were manufacturing or selling generic copies of Viagra. With domestic litigation looming, the Association of Pharmaceutical Industries of National Origin (known by its Spanish acronym ADIFAN, for *Asociación de Industrias Farmacéuticas Nacionales*) filed a complaint with the General Secretariat alleging that Peru had violated *Decisión* 344's ban on second-use patents. The General Secretariat upheld the complaint and, after Peru failed to overturn the decree, submitted the case to the ATJ. In a reflection of the case's high political salience, ADIFAN participated as an interested third party in support of the General Secretariat, while Pfizer and the Association of National Pharmaceutical Laboratories joined the case in support of Peru. In a 2001 judgment, the ATJ upheld the complaint and the Andean ban on second-use patents. As a result, it directed Peru "to leave without effect the patent granted to" Pfizer.[75]

ADIFAN then asked INDECOPI to revoke the Viagra patent. Following its normal procedures, the agency did so several months later. According to INDECOPI officials, adhering to the Andean Tribunal's judgment was a straightforward matter: "When the ATJ tells us what the supreme interpretation of the law is, then our own interpretation is void." Since the Viagra case, the agency has not granted any second-use patents.[76]

INDECOPI officials stated that they were dismayed by the political interference in their decision-making. Nevertheless, before the ATJ's ruling, the officials refused to ignore the Peruvian decree. The Peruvian government never repealed the law, but neither did it pressure INDECOPI to enforce it,[77] suggesting that government officials had been willing to circumvent Andean law yet unwilling to fight Andean officials or repudiate the ATJ on behalf of Pfizer.

Litigation in Venezuela and Ecuador followed a similar pattern. The IP agency in each country registered a second-use patent for Viagra prior to the ATJ ruling against Peru, and national associations of generic drug manufacturers turned to the Andean legal system to challenge the registrations. When the General Secretariat and the ATJ reaffirmed their prior rulings, the administrative agencies reversed their positions and invalidated the patents.[78] In Colombia, the administrative agency was bolder. It

step, and industrial applicability. See also P. Boulet, Patents and Medicines in Peru 4 (Campaign for Access to Essential Medicines, November 2001) (on file with authors); *Ena Matos Jaqui, Las patentes de segundo uso*, LA Hora (Ecuador) (undated), available at <http://www.dlh.lahora.com.ec/paginas/judicial/PAGINAS/D.Autor.4.htm>.

[75] ATJ Noncompliance Judgment 89-AI-2000, 40.

[76] Interviews with officials (B) and (C) of INDECOPI.

[77] Ibid.

[78] See ATJ Noncompliance Judgment 01-AI-2001, 39 (judgment against Venezuela); ATJ Noncompliance Judgment 34-AI-2001, 51–52 (judgment against Ecuador); see also C. Pacheco and M. Milagros Nebrada, Venezuela: How to Protect Inventions of Use. *Managing Intellectual Property—Supplement*, 2006, available at <http://www.managingip.com/Article/1321317/Venezuela-How-to-protect-inventions-of-use.html>.

rejected Pfizer's application, leading the company to appeal to the *Consejo de Estado*, which sent a reference to Quito. The Tribunal reiterated its interpretation of Andean law and the Colombian court implemented the ATJ's ruling.[79]

The ATJ's response to one argument in favor of second-use patents highlights its insistence on the pre-eminence of Andean IP rules not only over conflicting national laws and bilateral treaties but also over multilateral agreements—a topic also discussed in Chapter 4. In the noncompliance suit against Venezuela, Pfizer argued that the Andean countries, as members of the WTO, were obligated to interpret the region's IP rules in harmony with the TRIPS Agreement, which, it claimed, required protection of second-use patents.[80] The ATJ categorically rejected this argument. It reasoned that the member states had transferred regulatory authority to the Andean Community to establish common regional IP rules whose application is mandatory and "neither depends on, nor is subject to compatibility with, other international laws."[81]

The end result of this wave of litigation was that all domestic IP agencies in the Andean Community denied or annulled patents for Viagra.[82] This region-wide refusal to recognize second-use patents remains a major irritant to the US pharmaceutical industry. The industry's 2008 Special 301 Report to the Office of the US Trade Representative places the blame for this state of affairs squarely on the ATJ:

> The Andean Court of Justice (ACJ) [has] issued several legal opinions … forcing Andean Community members to refuse recognition of patents for second uses … Such decisions constitute law in Bolivia, Colombia, Ecuador, and Peru. Andean member countries have either been compelled by the ACJ not to grant second use patents or chosen to honor Andean Community obligations … The failure to provide patents for second uses particularly affects the pharmaceutical industry, which has dedicated substantial research dollars to evaluating additional therapeutic benefits of known molecules (second uses) in order to provide effective solutions for unsatisfied medical needs. The ACJ position is dispositive on the issue and no further domestic appeals/remedies are possible.[83]

Without the ATJ's interventions, Andean countries would likely have succumbed to external pressures to grant second-use patents. Indeed, the legal landscape looks quite different elsewhere in Latin America. El Salvador, Guatemala, Honduras, Mexico, and Paraguay recognize second-use patents; Chile, Panama, and Uruguay do so in certain instances; and the status of such patents in Brazil is uncertain. Only Argentina, Costa Rica, the Dominican Republic, and Nicaragua share the Andean Community's prohibition of all second-use patents.[84]

[79] See *Multinacional Pfizer no puede patentar principio activo del potenciador sexual Viagra en Colombia*, El Tiempo.com, January 6, 2009, available at <http://www.eltiempo.com/archivo/documento/CMS-4743402>.

[80] ATJ Noncompliance Judgment 01-AI-2001, 11.

[81] Ibid., 36–7 (quoting ATJ Noncompliance Judgment 89-AI-2000).

[82] Pacheco and Milagros Nebrada, 2006, 3.

[83] Pharmaceutical Research and Manufacturers of America (PhRMA), Special 301 Submission, 236 (2008) (on file with authors).

[84] The enactment dates of the relevant national laws are as follows: Argentina (2000), Chile (2005), El Salvador (2005), Guatemala (2000), Honduras (1999), Mexico (1994), Nicaragua (2000), Panama

The politics of data protection and the reversal of an ATJ ruling

The third Andean IP noncompliance dispute concerns the test data that drug companies submit to domestic health ministries when seeking approval to market new medicines.[85] The pharmaceutical industry favors laws that give the companies an exclusive right to control such data. Absent such protection, the industry claims, competitors can unfairly rely on the drug companies' data without expending the time and resources to conduct their own safety tests.[86]

Contentious disputes over data protection have been waged in the Andean Community.[87] *Decisión* 344, adopted in 1993, prohibited the disclosure of unpublished test data—a form of legal protection mandated by the TRIPS Agreement.[88] However, the *Decisión* also made this protection exclusive for five years, exceeding TRIPS' requirements.[89] In this respect, the protection of test data contrasted with other Andean IP rules, which incorporated many of the flexibilities that TRIPS provides for developing countries.

During negotiations to revise *Decisión* 344, governments were sharply divided over whether to modify the region's data protection rules. On the one hand, the region was home to a large generics industry that sold drugs at prices substantially lower than patented medicines.[90] On the other, the United States and US pharmaceutical firms were exerting strong pressure on Andean states to provide for a five-year period of exclusivity for test data in a draft US–Andean trade treaty and in the proposed Free Trade Agreement of the Americas.[91] Indeed, the US Trade Representative characterized exclusive data protection as "one [of its] key implementation priorit[ies]."[92]

Colombia, which faced strong pressure to accede to US demands, pushed for a provision permitting member states to grant a period of exclusive protection for test data. The four other countries countered that Andean IP rules should not exceed TRIPS standards.[93] In the end, the new legislation—*Decisión* 486 of 2000—tracked

(1998), Paraguay (2001), and Uruguay (1999). See M. Basso, Intervention of Health Authorities in Patent Examination: The Brazilian Practice of the Prior Consent. *International Journal of Intellectual Property Management* 2006 1 (1): 54–74, 56–7.

[85] D. Cullen, Data Protection: The New IP Frontier—An Overview of Existing Laws and Regulations. *Journal of Generic Medicines* 2007, 5 (1): 9–10.

[86] R. Dinca, The "Bermuda Triangle" of Pharmaceutical Law. *The Journal of World Intellectual Property* 2005, 8 (4): 520–1.

[87] As a result of these contestations, the current and former governmental officials whom we interviewed requested anonymity.

[88] Andean *Decisión* 344, Article 78; TRIPS, Article 39.3.

[89] Andean *Decisión* 344, Article 79.

[90] Interviews with official (A) of the Colombian Ministry of Trade, Industry and Tourism; Interview with official (B) of the *Asociación de Industrias Farmacéuticas de Colombia* (ASINFAR).

[91] G.P. Krikorian and D.M. Szymkowiak, Intellectual Property Rights in the Making: The Evolution of Intellectual Property Provisions in US Free Trade Agreements and Access to Medicine. *Journal of World Intellectual Property* 2007, 10 (5): 388–418.

[92] Office of the US Trade Representative, 2003 Special 301 Report—Executive Summary, 6 (on file with authors).

[93] The ATJ described this negotiating history in detail in ATJ Noncompliance Judgment 114-AI-2004, 36–41.

the language of its predecessor and required protection of "undisclosed test or other data … against unfair commercial use." This language was followed, however, by an ambiguous final sentence to the effect that member states "may take steps to guarantee the protection provided for under this article."[94]

Relying on this sentence, Colombia enacted a decree in 2002 that granted up to five years of exclusive protection for test data.[95] The Association of Colombian Pharmaceutical Industries (commonly known as ASINFAR, for *Asociación de Industrias Farmacéuticas de Colombia*) promptly challenged the decree, but the General Secretariat upheld the law as permitted under the sentence just quoted.[96] ASINFAR appealed to the ATJ, which rejected the Secretariat's interpretation and held that the Colombian decree violated *Decisión* 486.[97] The ATJ's disagreement with the Secretariat is itself noteworthy. In all prior IP noncompliance cases, the Secretariat had found national laws to be incompatible with Andean rules, and the ATJ had upheld its findings. The data protection ruling thus placed the two Community actors in opposition to each other for the first time.

In its analysis of the decree, the Tribunal reasoned that the member states had made a deliberate choice to abolish the period of exclusivity that had previously existed in Andean law.[98] It also reasoned that data protection, like other forms of intellectual property, must be interpreted in light of the Community's broader interests in public health.[99] These interests precluded Colombia from enacting data protection rules that deviated from the regional standard.[100]

The fallout from the ATJ's ruling was immediate. As noted earlier, all Andean countries (except Bolivia) were in the midst of negotiating a regional trade treaty with the United States, which had demanded a five-year period of exclusivity for test data. Ecuador and Venezuela opposed the provision, but Peru and Colombia had accepted it.[101] After the ATJ ruling, government officials told us that this provision was "off the table." In response, the Colombian Ministry of Foreign Trade issued a press release defending the decree. It also asked the other governments—acting in

[94] Andean *Decisión* 486, Article 266.

[95] Supreme *Decreto* 2085 of 2002, *Diario Oficial*, September 19, 2002 (Colom.), available at <http://www.presidencia.gov.co/prensa_new/decretoslinea/2002/septiembre/19/dec2085190902.pdf>.

[96] *Resolución* 817, General Secretariat *Decreto* No. 10 (April 14, 2004).

[97] ATJ Noncompliance Judgment 114-AI-2004. The case drew widespread attention from the pharmaceutical and generics industry associations, which participated in the case as interested third parties. The National Association of Pharmaceutical Laboratories (known by the Spanish acronym ALAFAR, for *Asociación Nacional de Laboratorios Farmacéuticos*) supported the petitioner ASINFAR, and the Association of Pharmaceutical Research Laboratories of Colombia (AFIDRO, an acronym of *Asociación de Laboratorios Farmacéuticos de Investigación y Desarrollo*) supported Colombia.

[98] Our interviews revealed this to be a particular point of contention and criticism of the Tribunal. According to Colombian IP attorneys and officials in the Ministry of Trade, Colombia had agreed to the cryptic final sentence of Article 266 only after it received assurances from the other member states that it could adopt a five-year exclusive right to protect test data. This tacit understanding was not, however, reflected in the drafting history, which indicated that Colombia's efforts to retain a period of exclusive data protection were unsuccessful. See ATJ Noncompliance Judgment 114-AI-2004, 41.

[99] Ibid. [100] Ibid., 49.

[101] See Disagreement over Data Protection Holding up Andean-US FTA, 9 Bridges Weekly Trade News Digest, September 28, 2005, 4.

their capacity as members of the Andean *Comisión*—to affirm that the decree was consistent with Andean law.[102]

All prior *Decisiones* had been approved by consensus, but on this issue the member states were deadlocked. After several attempts to reach agreement failed, the *Comisión* scheduled another meeting for April 2006. Bolivia and Venezuela were unable to vote at that meeting because they had not paid their membership dues. In their absence, the remaining three countries agreed to adopt *Decisión* 632. The legislation "clarifies the intent of the legislators … by establishing that each Member Country shall have the authority to choose the means for protecting test data, including the possibility of establishing time periods" of exclusive protection[103]—a retroactive validation of the Colombian data protection decree.

Whether the *Comisión*'s action should be seen as a rebuke to the Tribunal is a different matter. A document issued by the US pharmaceutical industry asserts that *Decisión* 632 "quashed the decision of the Court."[104] But there is evidence to the contrary. Colombia never contemplated ignoring the ATJ's ruling. In interviews, officials emphasized that "Colombia is a country that obeys Andean Tribunal decisions" and that, as a result, they considered only lawful means to preserve the data protection decree. They also feared that noncompliance might lead the ATJ to impose sanctions, as it had done in the pipeline case against Ecuador.[105] *Decisión* 632 reflects this concern for legality. It never mentions the Tribunal's 2005 ruling. Instead, it refers to an earlier case in which the ATJ stated that

> only the [Andean] *Comisión* … is authorized to make what is known in legal doctrine as an "authentic interpretation," by issuing another legal norm at the same level or with the same hierarchy … This later legislative effort is intended to clarify the material content of a law that in the legislators' opinion was unclear or that had been subject to differing interpretations.[106]

The member states thus emphasized that the precedents of the ATJ itself authorized them to correct its interpretation of *Decisión* 486's ambiguous text and drafting history.

Whatever its consequences for the Tribunal's authority, the data protection dispute exacerbated an already tense political climate in the region. Trade negotiations broke down in late 2005 when first Peru and later Colombia negotiated bilateral treaties with the United States, both of which require a five-year period of exclusivity for test data.[107] Two weeks after the *Comisión* adopted *Decisión* 632, Venezuela

[102] Interview with official (A) of the Ministry of Trade, Industry and Tourism of Colombia, Bogotá, Colombia.

[103] Andean *Decisión* 632.

[104] Pharmaceutical Research and Manufacturers of America (PhRMA), Special 301 Submission 2007, 257.

[105] Interview with official (A) of the Colombian Ministry of Trade, Industry and Tourism.

[106] Andean *Decisión* 632 (quoting ATJ Noncompliance Judgment 7-AI-99, 18).

[107] R.C. Bernieri, Intellectual Property Rights in Bilateral Investment Treaties and Access to Medicines: The Case of Latin America. *Journal of World Intellectual Property* 2006 9 (5): 548–72, 563–4. The most recent Andean IP legislation, *Decisión* 689, adopted in 2008, gives the member states greater leeway to revise domestic IP protection standards. Colombia and Peru advocated for this *Decisión* to allow them to adopt IP protection rules required by bilateral free trade agreements with

withdrew from the Andean Community. "President Chavez stated publicly that the reason for the withdrawal was the entry of other member countries into free trade agreements with the United States."[108] An official in Colombia's foreign trade ministry concurred, but characterized *Decisión* 632 as the "last straw" in precipitating Venezuela's break with the regional integration pact.[109]

Decisión 632 brings Andean countries closer to the United States' preferred position, in that it permits—but does not require—member states to grant a term of exclusive protection for test data. In the remainder of Latin America, however, a five-year period of exclusivity is rapidly becoming the norm, as countries have capitulated to US pressure or have ratified bilateral treaties mandating such protection. In contrast, Bolivia, Ecuador, and Venezuela do not provide for exclusive protection, nor have they negotiated bilateral treaties with the United States.[110]

The ATJ's contribution to building a balanced IP rule-of-law island in the Andean Community

We highlight four facets of the IP rule-of-law island raised in our previous discussion. First, we have shown that the Andean legal system creates valuable and enforceable property rights that are enhanced by the ability of private parties to seek ATJ rulings that interpret Andean IP laws. Second, ATJ rulings have changed national court and administrative practices relating to IP by requiring agency officials to create an adequate factual record, justify their decisions with reasons, and provide clear and fair procedures for contesting parties. Third, the ATJ has acted as a bulwark against powerful foreign interests that have put pressure on individual governments to defect from Andean IP *Decisiones*. Fourth, the symbiotic relationship between the Tribunal and domestic administrative agencies have enabled Andean countries to maintain a balanced approach to IP protection that limits the economic interests of private businesses in the name of preventing consumer confusion and expanding access to medicines.

These four facets are interrelated and mutually reinforcing. Early ATJ litigation clarified the content of Andean IP rules and improved the quality of agency decision-making. These advances made the acquisition of IP rights more attractive for private parties, who filed a growing number of applications for trademarks and patents. These filings, in turn, increased the agencies' revenue, and thus their autonomy. Over time, agency officials came to rely on Andean jurisprudence to carry out their core functions. Consultations with the General Secretariat over revisions of

the United States. Bolivia opposed the dilution of regional IP standards but was outvoted by the other three member states. Erin Kelechava, Andean IP Changes Allow Peru to Sign US FTA, Managing Intellectual Property, August 28, 2008, available at <http://www.managingip.com/Article/2001721/Andean-IP-changes-allow-Peru-to-sign-US-FTA.html>.

[108] US Trade Representative, National Trade Estimate Report on Foreign Trade Barriers 621 (2007), available at <https://ustr.gov/archive/assets/Document_Library/Reports_Publications/2007/2007_NTE_Report/asset_upload_file855_10945.pdf>.

[109] Interview with official (A) of the Colombian Ministry of Trade, Industry and Tourism.

[110] Cullen, 2007, 9–10 and Table 5.1.

Andean IP rules, and ATJ rulings that tempered IP rights in the name of consumer protection, further bolstered the agencies' fidelity to the Andean legal system.

Disputes between trademark applicants and opponents were principally responsible for these developments, but these disputes between private businesses laid the groundwork for the agencies to act as compliance constituencies in high-profile cases challenging domestic patent decrees as contrary to Andean law. The agencies' actions increased the cost of noncompliance in these cases. To flout the ATJ, national executives would have been required to do more than simply ignore the Tribunal's rulings: they would have been compelled to interfere with the settled rules and decision-making procedures of the domestic agencies themselves.

The noncompliance judgments discussed earlier concerned Andean laws that restrict IP to achieve public interest and public health objectives. The TRIPS Agreement does not obligate states to recognize pipeline or second-use patents, nor does it require five years of exclusivity for pharmaceutical test data. Commentators describe a government that chooses to deny these and other optional IP protections as exercising the "flexibilities" in TRIPS to tailor domestic IP laws in light of other policy goals.[111] In contrast to most other developing countries, the Andean Community treated these restrictions on IP as mandatory. When adopting IP *Decisiones*, member states made a collective decision to capitalize on TRIPS' flexibilities as a way to protect consumers and promote public health. After these regional laws were adopted, however, the United States, pharmaceutical companies, and some trademark owners lobbied for stronger IP protections contrary to Andean law. The ATJ provided a hospitable forum for generic drug companies and other opponents of such protection to push back against these efforts, with the result that Andean law today retains limitations on intellectual property that most other Latin American countries abrogated in response to pressure from the United States and foreign IP industries.

To be sure, the ATJ's effectiveness in the IP rule-of-law island is not unlimited. The data protection dispute may reveal one outer edge of the island. The case is exceptional, however, in several ways. The first concerns the content of Andean law. Andean *Decisiones* are very clear in disallowing second-use patents; for data protection, the rules were undeniably cryptic and subject to conflicting interpretations. Second, the General Secretariat sided with the Colombian government, but the ATJ—unlike in earlier IP noncompliance cases—disagreed with the Secretariat's conclusion. Third, the ATJ handed down its ruling during a period of sharp ideological divisions in the region, as three of the five member states—Bolivia, Ecuador, and Venezuela—were distancing themselves from the liberalizing policies of the Washington Consensus, and the other two—Colombia and Peru—which were negotiating trade agreements with the United States, were coming under increasing pressure to protect test data. Fourth, unlike the pipeline and second-use-patent litigation, the data protection case involved an issue within the purview of national

[111] N. Pires de Carvalho, *The TRIPS Regime of Patent Rights*. Alphen aan den Rijn: Kluwer Law International, 2010, 62.

health ministries. Unlike the IP agencies, these ministries had no prior relationship with the Tribunal and no professional stake in enforcing Andean law. For all of these reasons, the data protection dispute is different from other IP cases where ATJ rulings successfully rebuffed political efforts to circumvent Andean IP rules.

A second outer edge of the IP rule-of-law island involves Bolivia and Venezuela, whose courts have referred only a handful of preliminary references to the ATJ. Chapter 3 discussed the reasons for the dearth of cases from these two countries and the recent increase in IP-related referrals from Bolivia. In Venezuela, the government created a new IP agency, SAPI, in 1997. According to a former legal counsel for the agency, SAPI applied Andean IP law to review patent and trademark applications.[112] Although the agency initially granted a second-use patent to Pfizer, it complied with the ATJ's decision rejecting such patents.[113] This record is similar to those of IP agencies in other member states. The practice of the national courts, however, is quite different. As in Peru and Ecuador, Venezuelan courts initially refused to refer appeals of agency decisions to the ATJ. However, in contrast to those two countries, in Venezuela no private actor complained about this refusal to the General Secretariat. The prospect of such complaints diminished with the election of President Hugo Chavez in 2001, and it vanished with Venezuela's withdrawal from the Andean Community in 2006. Strikingly, however, SAPI and some Venezuelan judges have continued to apply Andean IP law following the withdrawal, suggesting that, under different political conditions, they might eventually have referred IP cases to the ATJ.[114]

Why Andean Litigation Has Not Spilled Over to Other Issue Areas

Our coding of ATJ cases indicates that more than 95% of preliminary rulings involved IP issues. Although references involving non-IP issues have increased in the last seven years (as further described in Chapter 3), the dominance of IP references has remained constant over time. It is thus still true that private actor litigation has not spilled over to other issue areas. The existence of such spillovers is critical to explanations of the ECJ's success.[115] Why has litigation of IP disputes not extended to other areas regulated by the Andean Community? To answer this question, we must investigate "dogs that did not bark," an inquiry that is inherently more suggestive than definitive.

We identify four principal arguments for why intellectual property remains an island. First, Andean IP rules (see Table 5.1) are detailed and precise; in other areas,

112 Interview with former official (A) of SAPI.

113 ATJ Noncompliance Judgment 01-AI-2001; Pacheco and Milagros Nebrada, 2006.

114 US Department of State, 2007 Investment Climate Statement—Venezuela, available at <http://2001-2009.state.gov/e/eeb/ifd/2007/80762.htm>.

115 See, e.g., A.-M. Burley and W. Mattli, Europe before the Court. *International Organization* 1993, 47 (1): 60.

Decisiones often contain loopholes or hortatory language that preserve national discretion. For example, the Andean telecommunications policy, which requires governments to create access to scarce frequencies, is "without prejudice to such national provisions as each member country may establish," allowing governments to privilege national carriers owned by politically powerful families.[116] Agricultural and livestock legislation permits member states to decide whether applying Andean rules is feasible and efficacious.[117] In addition, the secondary legislation harmonizing value-added taxes is replete with transitory provisions, exemptions for certain sectors and actors, and rules that grandfather pre-existing national tax systems.[118]

A few exceptions to this pattern exist, including common rules for taxing intra-regional trade, tariffs, customs, and transportation issues. As we discuss in Chapter 3, the ATJ's non-IP preliminary rulings generally involve these highly technical Andean rules. Chapter 3 also explains the ATJ's insistence that Colombia and Peru adhere to Andean pesticides rules that prioritize the protection of public health and the environment. Yet as we discuss in Chapter 7, governments later revised the pesticides regulation to permit greater national discretion. On the whole, however, the differences between Andean IP rules and other Andean laws reveal that governments have a shared interest in maintaining a common policy for trademarks and patents but only weakly support other areas of regional integration.[119]

Second, competing trade regimes sap member states' commitment to Andean integration. Latin American countries have negotiated free trade agreements for at least half a century. MERCOSUR, a South American customs union initially comprising Argentina, Brazil, Paraguay, and Uruguay, has acted as a powerful centrifugal force that pulls Andean member states away from each other. Andean countries have sought to manage this competition through a strategy of "open regionalism."[120] All Andean countries became associate members of MERCOSUR, which has provided some tariff reductions, and in 2002 the two regional initiatives entered

[116] Andean *Decisión* 462, Article 23; see also Articles 20 and 22; Interview with attorney (A) from commercial and administrative law firm in Colombia.

[117] Andean *Decisión* 328, Articles 15 and 20.

[118] Andean *Decisión* 599, Articles 7, 13, 14, 16, 17, 28, 30, 32, 33, 37, and 39.

[119] This tepid commitment reflects the reality that trade with nonmembers (especially the United States, the EC, China, Brazil, Argentina, and Mexico) is far more economically important than inter-Andean trade, which has accounted for roughly 10% of total trade since the 1990s. See Rodríguez Mendoza, Low, and Kotschwar, 1999. A related factor is that intra-regional trade consists primarily of low value-added finished goods, as opposed to intermediary products used in the production of high value-added goods. Producers of these finished goods may gain from lowering intra-Andean trade barriers, but they may also face increased competition from producers of similar products in neighboring Andean countries, and thus be less enthusiastic about lowering market barriers. M. Kuwayama, Latin American South-South Integration and Cooperation: From a Regional Public Goods Perspective. In: *Comercio Internacional Series No. 50*, Division of Trade and Integration: United Nations Economic Commission for Latin America and the Caribbean, 2005, 33; W.P. Avery and J.D. Cochraine, Innovation in Latin American Regionalism: The Andean Common Market. *International Organization* 1973 27 (2): 181–223, 191–2.

[120] C. Brummer, The Ties That Bind? Regionalism, Commercial Treaties, and the Future of Global Economic Integration. *Vanderbilt Law Review* 2007, 60 (5): 1349–409; M. Baquero Herrera, Open Regionalism in Latin America: An Appraisal. *Law and Business Review of the Americas* 2005, 11 (2): 139–84.

into their own free trade pact.[121] Open regionalism promotes member states' trade interests, but it also diminishes incentives to deepen Andean integration and favors building closer economic relations with other countries. Chapter 7 describes how leftist governments in Latin America are championing the creation of UNASUR—a merger of the Andean Community and MERCOSUR—and Ecuador is pushing for a "re-engineering" (a code word abolishing or scaling back) of Andean institutions in preparation for the merger.

A third explanation for why intellectual property remains a rule-of-law island is that the ATJ has been reluctant to interpret vague Andean rules purposively. The Tribunal has included some purposive analysis in several recent non-IP preliminary references concerning human rights and the environment, but it has done so in dictum so that the effect on the outcome of the cases is unclear. We discuss these issues further when comparing doctrinal divergences between the ATJ and the ECJ in Chapter 4, and analyzing politically fraught cases in the Andean legal system in Chapter 6.

When it comes to IP, however, the ATJ has not been nearly as reticent. Instead, it has acted more like the ECJ by drawing upon national practices to build Andean legal doctrines and defend regional IP rules against conflicting national and international standards. For example, the ATJ case law on trademark coexistence agreements, discussed earlier in this chapter, is entirely judge-made and reflects the influence of domestic IP agencies whose mandate includes consumer protection. Chapter 3 discusses other IP issues for which the ATJ fashioned legal doctrines that reflect the concerns of the administrative agencies, such as the need to avoid consumer confusion.

The fourth explanation for the persistence of IP as an island is that the ATJ is not supported by a broader set of private or public constituencies. Our comparison of the role of advocacy movements in Europe and the Andes (Chapter 9) explains that, with the exception of IP issues, the ATJ lacks a jurist advocacy network that identifies test cases and rallies behind pro-integration Tribunal rulings. As a result, awareness of the Andean legal system remains limited. Most attorneys do not view the system as relevant to their practice, and activists, scholars, and most non-governmental organizations do not perceive Andean litigation as having strategic value or providing meaningful advocacy opportunities.[122]

The ATJ also lacks broad support in national judiciaries. Our discussion of the Tribunal's judicial interlocutors (Chapter 3) explains the reluctant and mostly passive nature of national court interactions with the Tribunal. Even after being persuaded to send references to Quito, national judges have hesitated to expand their involvement with the ATJ beyond areas exclusively governed by Andean

[121] *Acuerdo de complementación económica* No. 56, CAN-MERCOSUR, December 6, 2002, available at <http://www.sice.oas.org/Trade/MRCSR/acMerAns.asp>.

[122] E.g., Interview with two attorneys (I) from IP law firm in Ecuador; Interview with attorney (C) from IP law firm in Peru; Interviews with former official (B) of the General Secretariat Legal Advisor's Office; Interview with attorney (A) from commercial and administrative law firm in Colombia. Private litigants can also file noncompliance suits with the General Secretariat, and, through it, reach the ATJ, a possibility we discuss in Chapter 3.

law.[123] In interviews, judges emphasized that the member states and the General Secretariat were responsible for ensuring compliance with Community law. They further claimed that they need not refer cases that concern only domestic legal issues.[124] This limited conception of the national judicial role is at odds with the ATJ Treaty, which requires referrals not only of cases in which an Andean rule "is litigated," but also of those in which Andean law "should be applied."[125]

Another missing compliance constituency is a broader set of autonomous domestic actors within the state that are committed to following Andean rules. The IP agencies were differently situated than other administrative agencies in important respects.[126] First, the IP agencies were either wholly new or substantially reinvented. With no entrenched habits or established track record, and few domestic actors with knowledge of IP law, the agencies were open to drawing on Andean Community expertise. Second, IP agencies were fairly well resourced. They received initial funding from the international financial institutions that promoted market liberalization, and they benefited from the material and technical support of WIPO. Several agencies also have an independent funding source: fees paid by firms applying to register IP. Finally, intellectual property is a specialized area of legal practice with international career prospects. It attracts ambitious lawyers and trade negotiators who study outside the region and thus themselves become part of a global community of actors who believe in the rule of law for the subject. These resources and actors give the IP agencies the know-how, incentive, and opportunity to do their job well. They also provide agency administrators with the autonomy to embed Andean IP rules in their administrative practices.

In sum, there appears to be a wholesale lack of demand for enforcing Andean law outside of the intellectual property island. In addition, the factors undermining broader support for integration are self-reinforcing, creating a negative feedback loop that inhibits the penetration of Andean rules into national legal systems. The lack of governmental commitment to expand intra-regional economic ties decreases the incentives of private actors to build those ties, and it allows national judicial and administrative reticence to act as a barrier to litigants using the Andean legal system to promote their interests.

Conclusion: The Stability of the IP Rule-of-Law Island in Challenging Political Times

Our initial analysis of the IP rule-of-law island was based on coding of ATJ case law up to and including 2007. At the time, the economic and political crisis in

[123] Interview with attorney (G) practicing tax law in Colombia.

[124] E.g.,, Interview with five judges (A) of the *Sección Primera del Consejo de Estado de Colombia*; Interview with judge (A) of the *Sala de Derecho Constitucional y Social de Justicia de Peru*.

[125] Revised ATJ Treaty, Article 33.

[126] See Annual Review: The Twelfth Annual International Review of Trademark Jurisprudence, 2005, 67.

the Andean Community, which we discuss in Chapter 7, was just beginning to emerge. We thus ended our analysis on a cautionary note. We recognized that, with Venezuela's then recent departure, the political and ideological divisions among the member states were greater than at any time since the Andean Pact's founding. Yet we also predicted that domestic IP agencies in the Andes would continue to follow Andean IP legislation regardless of the fate of the larger regional integration initiative.

Nearly a decade later, we can say two things with confidence. First, the Andean Community today faces existential challenges, both from within (deadlocks produced by a membership of two neoliberal-leaning governments and two leftist regimes) and from without (the pull of more economically and politically consequential regional cooperation projects and efforts to subsume Andean institutions within those projects). Second, and surprising in light of this first finding, is that the island of effective international adjudication for intellectual property disputes remains robust and is arguably flourishing, nurtured by the same symbiotic relationship between Andean judges and administrative agency officials that engendered the island in the first instance.

Chapter 7 describes the numerous indicators of the IP island's resilience and situates them within a broader discussion of how the ATJ and the Andean legal system are faring in a time of regional crisis. We end this chapter by considering a different topic: how the broader legal and institutional contexts within which regional IP rules are embedded help to bolster the island's stability and protect it from significant meddling by national governments.

The remarkable constancy of the IP rule-of-law island reflects the reality that Andean IP *Decisiones* are dually embedded within national legislation and domestic institutions that register trademarks and patents and adjudicate disputes relating to IP applications. This dual embedding reinforces adherence to those rules by domestic actors. Intellectual property issues are also governed by a WTO treaty—the TRIPS Agreement—that limits the ability of Andean governments to modify IP rules if doing so runs afoul of WTO obligations. The WIPO is another anchor of stability, providing capacity building, networking, and technical support that enhance the professionalism and independence of domestic IP agencies and their staff. As a result of these nested institutional structures, national political leaders—whose short-term political interests sometimes favor deviating from Andean *Decisiones*—recognize that local and foreign businesses and their attorneys view harmonized regional IP legislation as a source of economically valuable and legally enforceable entitlements that help to promote investment across the region.

These nested legal and institutional attributes give the IP island an existence separate and apart from the Andean Community itself. When we first published our findings regarding the island, we noted that the Venezuelan IP agency SENAPI continued to apply Andean rules on trademarks and patents even after President Hugo Chavez had denounced the Cartagena Agreement. This was hardly surprising given that, in the absence of *Decisión* 486, the only relevant domestic legislation was the woefully outdated and TRIPS-incompatible 1955 National Industrial Property Law.

One might reasonably expect the influence of Andean IP rules to diminish in Venezuela over time. Recent reports by the US government confirm this prediction, finding a "deteriorating environment for the protection and enforcement of [IP] in Venezuela."[127] Yet there remains "uncertainty regarding the impact of Venezuela's withdrawal ... on existing laws that implemented Andean Community norms, including those related to intellectual property rights."[128] Moreover, as recently as 2011 Venezuelan judges continued to invoke Andean IP legislation and ATJ judgments in support of limiting the protection of pharmaceutical patents to achieve public health goals—precisely the same policy balance that Andean judges have long wrestled with.[129] The continuing influence Andean IP rules in one member state long after the domestic abrogation of those rules and the formal disengagement from Community institutions suggests that even if the Andean integration project is abandoned or merged into UNASUR, the IP rule-of-law island is likely to have lingering effects and will not so easily be displaced.

What is less clear is how much the ATJ's role as a centralized interpreter of regional IP rules contributes to Andean IP law's legacy effect. American and European governments continue to lobby for national patent and data protection rules that favor their respective IP industries. This chapter discussed the ATJ's central role in overturning national decrees in the pipeline and second use patent cases. In both controversies, national administrators preferred the Andean IP rules that they had helped to draft. These rules were nonetheless altered by political leaders under pressure from the US government and multinational drug companies. In the future and without the ATJ's backing, the IP agencies are unlikely to be able to defend the balanced approach to IP that Andean law codifies. This could eventually lead to IP rules that either are less accommodating of public health or consumer protection or, conversely, rules that follow Venezuela's example in falling far below global minimum IP norms.

[127] US Department of State, 2014 Investment Climate Statement—Venezuela, available at <http://www.state.gov/e/eb/rls/othr/ics/2014/229093.htm>.

[128] US Department of State, 2012 Investment Climate Statement—Venezuela, available at <http://www.state.gov/e/eb/rls/othr/ics/2012/191262.htm>.

[129] *Eli Lilly & Co. v. Laboratories Leti, S.A. V, Juzgado Superior Octavo en lo Civil, Mercantil, Tránsito y Bancario de la Circunscripción Judicial del Área Metropolitana de Caracas* (March 23, 2011) (quoting ATJ Noncompliance Judgment 114-AI-2004), available at <http://caracas.tsj.gob.ve/decisiones/2011/marzo/2145-23-8998-.html>.

6

The Judicialization of Andean Politics

Cigarettes, Alcohol, and Economic Hard Times

Most cases that come before the ATJ involve narrow or technical legal issues that have limited resonance beyond the parties to the dispute. The four cases we discuss in this chapter are atypical; they are among the most politically fraught legal controversies that the ATJ has adjudicated in its thirty-year life span.

The first two cases concern struggles between powerful private economic interests seeking to force their way into new national markets. The second two disputes examine the terms by which states can deviate from Andean free trade rules to manage major economic shocks and market disruptions.[1] The four disputes were politically fraught not because they involved expansionist judicial lawmaking (a topic we explore in Chapter 8), but rather because they were linked to wider political fights among national leaders and Community officials, were carefully monitored by influential foreign actors, and had the potential to establish precedents with far reaching consequences for Andean integration. The four cases also allow us to explore how private actors and governments use litigation to pursue their preferred policy objectives, and how the ATJ navigates politically challenging terrains.

As a group, the four cases reveal how governments, interest groups, and private litigants mix adjudicatory and policy-making strategies to achieve desired outcomes. These actors use litigation to challenge Andean secondary legislation as well as to invalidate national laws, administrative decisions, and practices that conflict with Andean law. The actors use policy-making to clarify or revise interpretations of ambiguous rules and to preserve or expand national autonomy. The Tribunal plays the role of legal referee, ensuring that actors adhere to the rules of the Community legal system. Where national governments agree to revise Andean law to resolve the dispute, ATJ judges respect the political compromise. But they also ensure that policy-making follows formal rules of procedure.

The ATJ's legal referee role is especially important in a region where corruption is all too common, where the executive can create binding law through unilateral decrees, and where national judges may lack the independence or courage to

[1] Earlier versions of three of the case studies were previously published in K.J. Alter, *The New Terrain of International Law: Courts, Politics, Rights*. Princeton, NJ: Princeton University Press, 2014. The fourth case study, involving the economic crisis in Ecuador, is discussed in this book for the first time.

challenge government actions that violate laws on the books. The Tribunal provides legal and political cover for national courts to challenge these decisions. The ATJ's support is important because the challenged decisions were lawful but for the fact that they violated or circumvented Andean law. The ATJ noncompliance findings allowed national judges to justify their rejection of these decisions as necessary to enforce Andean law.

Yet when courts enter into "mega-politics"—defined as "matters of outright and utmost political significance that often define and divide whole polities"[2]—serving as a legal referee can be especially challenging and risky. The ATJ has little ability to pressure, let alone compel, national governments to change their policies, especially when compliance would be politically costly. Andean judges have developed a distinctive response to these fraught situations. They are legally cautious, in that they stick closely to the letter of the law and eschew expansive rulings, but are also politically bold, in that they do not shy away from openly condemning illegal national and Community acts even if they do not expect compliance.

Process-tracing these four disputes across legal and political venues also reveals the importance of multiple access points in the Andean legal system—the different judicial forums and decision-making choices available to supranational, government, and private litigants to challenge and revise national and Community rules. It is a marker of the relatively sophisticated judicialization of politics in the Andes that different actors challenge contested policies in multiple venues and use domestic and international legal procedures in tandem and sequentially. As we explain, however, litigants have a mixed record of success in deploying these strategies.

A key finding of this chapter is that the ATJ protects itself by serving as a policeman of good governance practices while giving national political leaders the last word on Andean law. The Tribunal condemns legal violations, but member states can fairly easily revise Community rules to preserve national autonomy and the ATJ respects their decision to do so. Changing the law is not necessarily a rebuke of the ATJ, a point we also emphasize in Chapter 5 when discussing the data protection litigation. Rather, the Tribunal's preferred approach is to apply legal rules as written and put the onus on the member states to act collectively to amend Andean rules. This give and take between the political and legal branches breaks down, however, when governments are deeply divided and unable to reach consensus on revisions. When such schisms occur—as has been the case for the last decade—the ATJ's involvement may exacerbate political and legal conflicts. The Tribunal's ability to police good governance and the rule of law thus depends, paradoxically, on political cooperation.

In the remainder of this chapter, we first outline the different legal procedures that litigants can use to challenge national and Andean laws and policies. We then provide a process tracing account of the four disputes over time and through

[2] R. Hirschl, The Judicialization of Mega-Politics and the Rise of Political Courts. *Annual Review of Political Science* 2008, 11: 93–118, 94.

multiple legal and political venues. We conclude by assessing the limits of the ATJ's ability to shape the outcomes of highly politicized disputes.

The Andean Legal System Provides Multiple Access Points for Litigants to Challenge Regional and National Laws and Policies

Scholars tend to study litigation patterns by focusing on a single legal procedure. Such studies usefully compare similar cases and provide a convenient way to analyze large numbers of suits. However, single-procedure studies have an important limitation: they obscure how litigants use different legal mechanisms and raise claims in multiple venues simultaneously or sequentially.

Chapter 2 explains that ECJ-style tribunals differ from other international courts in that they establish multiple mechanisms for states, private litigants, and supranational officials to challenge decisions, policies, actions, and non-actions at both the national and regional levels. Table 6.1 below summarizes four different Andean legal procedures established by the Revised ATJ Treaty. Each procedure has its own access rules, and each offers different potential remedies to prevailing litigants. The treaty further specifies the time limits, standing requirements, and other restrictions on the use of these procedures.[3]

Multiple means to challenge member state violations of Andean law

The noncompliance procedure authorizes member states (and after 1996, private litigants) to file complaints alleging that the domestic laws, policies, or actions of another member state are contrary to Andean law.[4] The General Secretariat investigates the complaint and issues a *Resolución*—a reasoned determination as to whether the challenged measure violates Andean law.[5] Most disputes end at this stage. If noncompliance persists, however, the Secretariat must refer the dispute to the ATJ. Either party may also refer the case to the Tribunal if it disagrees with the Secretariat's determination.[6]

If the ATJ rules in favor of the complainant, it declares a violation of Andean law that obligates the violating state to remove or revise its offending national policy. In

[3] Revised ATJ Treaty. For additional discussion of the Treaty, see Chapter 3. We omit two other Andean legal procedures: The ATJ can adjudicate labor disputes involving Andean employees (Article 40), and it can arbitrate disputes involving private actors who have contracted with Andean institutions (Article 38).

[4] Ibid., Articles 24 and 25. Chapter 2 describes the adoption of the 1996 Cochabamba Protocol that revised the ATJ Treaty to enable private actors to file noncompliance suits with the General Secretariat and the ATJ.

[5] The General Secretariat can also initiate its own investigations of noncompliance. Ibid., Article 23.

[6] Ibid., Articles 24 and 25.

Table 6.1 Legal procedures in the Andean Community

Legal procedure	Who can initiate litigation?	Legal remedies
Noncompliance procedure *To challenge member state violations of Andean law*	Private litigants, the General Secretariat, and member states can challenge national laws and practices that allegedly violate Andean law.[8] or Private litigants may raise noncompliance suits in national courts.[9]	The ATJ can order a temporary suspension of the challenged law or practice while the suit is pending.[7] The ATJ determines whether noncompliance has occurred and, if it has, declares which laws have been violated. After the ATJ rules, the violating state must "take the necessary steps to execute the judgment" within ninety days.[10] Private litigants may enforce ATJ noncompliance judgments by seeking compensation for violations of Andean law in national courts.[11] For inter-state suits, the ATJ may, after consulting with General Secretariat, authorize the prevailing state to restrict or suspend benefits enjoyed by the violating state.[12]
Preliminary Reference Procedure *To interpret Andean law in suits arising in national courts*	Private litigants file suits in domestic courts; national judges refer questions of Andean law to the ATJ.[13]	After the ATJ interprets the law and issues a preliminary ruling, the case returns to national court for further proceedings. National court must adopt the ATJ's interpretation.[14] Any remedies awarded by national court thus indirectly enforce Andean law as interpreted by the ATJ.
Nullification procedure *To challenge illegal actions by an Andean institution*	Private litigants, member states, and Community institutions can challenge Andean agreements, legislation, or resolutions of the General Secretariat.[15] or Private litigants may raise nullification suits in national courts.[16]	The ATJ may order a temporary suspension of the challenged measure while the suit is pending.[17] The ATJ determines whether the measure should be nullified in whole or in part. The ATJ must indicate the process for phasing out or replacing the illegal measure; such remedies can apply prospectively and retrospectively.[18]

Omissions procedure *To challenge an Andean institution's failure to act*	Private litigants, member states, and Community institutions can challenge the failure of another Community institution to fulfil a legal obligation.[19]	ATJ specifies "the form, way and period" in which the Community institution shall take the required action.[20]

[7] Revised ATJ Treaty, Article 28.

[8] Ibid., Articles 23 and 25.

[9] Ibid., Article 31.

[10] Ibid., Article 27(1).

[11] Ibid., Article 30.

[12] Ibid., Article 27(2).

[13] Ibid., Article 33.

[14] Ibid., Article 35.

[15] Ibid., Article 17. Member states may only bring nullification claims in "Cases of Decisions or Agreements that were approved without their affirmative vote." Ibid., Article 18. This prevents a state from challenging decisions adopted by previous government of that state.

[16] Ibid., Article 20.

[17] Ibid., Article 21.

[18] Ibid., Article 22. ATJ report *Informe Estadistico 1984–2014*, at 7–8 provides a discussion of the temporal application of ATJ nullification rulings in practice, available at <http://www.tribunalandino.org.ec/sitetjca/index.php?option=com_wrapper&view=wrapper&Itemid=80>.

[19] Revised ATJ Treaty, Article 37(1).

[20] Ibid., Article 37(3).

practice, however, this declaratory remedy is mostly a symbolic victory. For inter-state disputes, the Revised ATJ Treaty specifies an enforcement mechanism—trade retaliation—that has proven to be generally ineffective in inducing compliance.[21] For suits raised by private litigants, the prevailing firm or individual can seek to enforce an ATJ noncompliance judgment by asking national judges to nullify the contested legislation or administrative decision, or by seeking compensation for damages resulting from the violation.[22]

In principle, noncompliance allegations can also be raised in domestic courts via the preliminary reference procedure. Legal victories in domestic courts (following a reference to the ATJ) may result in different remedies with more direct and immediate benefits for private litigants than the Andean noncompliance procedure. For example, litigants might receive an injunction against enforcement of the challenged national law, regulation, or agency decision, as well as damages or compensation for the violation.

In Chapter 3, however, we show that private litigants rarely use the preliminary ruling procedure to challenge violations of Andean law. Rather, ATJ preliminary rulings overwhelmingly involve the application of regional trademark and patent rules in IP agency registration disputes and, less frequently, violations of other technical Andean secondary legislation, such as customs valuations and tax refunds. These rulings are no doubt important to litigants, but they have limited legal or political significance beyond the facts of each case.

The domestic suits we discuss in this chapter are different. They involve efforts to enforce a legal victory at the Andean level by filing a separate suit asking a national judge to compel the government to give effect to an ATJ judgment. Because this follow-on litigation begins and ends in a domestic court, private litigants can harness the legal and remedial power of national judges in the service of enforcing Andean law. Judicial support is crucial for this tandem litigation strategy. Yet, as we discuss later in this chapter, national judges have only sometimes been willing to act as compliance partners for the ATJ.

Procedures for challenging the legality of Andean decisions and inactivity

The nullification and omissions procedures can be seen as flip sides of the same coin: namely, procedures to force Andean officials to act as required by Community law. Nullification suits target decisions by a Community institution that arguably violate Andean law; omissions cases challenge a Community institution's failure to act.

The nullification procedure provides a mechanism to challenge Andean secondary legislation, policy decisions, and political bargains. Private litigants, member

[21] For an analysis of how this remedy is applied in practice, see M.A. Sasaki Otani, El Sistema de Sanciones por Incumpliemiento en el Ámbito de la Comunidad Andina. *Anuario Mexicano de Derecho Internacional* 2012, 15: 301–37.

[22] Revised ATJ Treaty, Article 30.

states, and the Secretariat can ask the ATJ to review the legal validity of these actions, and they have done so in more than fifty cases.[23]

The omissions procedure, added in 1996, is designed to compel Community institutions to act where they have a legal obligation to do so. The ATJ has adjudicated only a handful of omissions proceedings.[24] We cannot definitively explain the paucity of these cases. On the one hand, if the General Secretariat is responsive to complaints challenging inaction by Community institutions, there is no need for ATJ review. On the other, litigants may refrain from filing omissions suits because the procedure is ineffective at forcing Andean institutions to act. If the threat of an omissions suit incentivizes the Secretariat to act, the omissions procedure would be useful yet there would still be a paucity of ATJ omissions suits.

Multiple access points in the four case studies

Table 6.2 on the next page summarizes how litigants used different regional and national legal procedures in the four fraught cases discussed in this chapter to pressure governments to comply with Andean rules.

Tobacco and Alcohol Litigation: Forcing Open National and Regional Markets

Regulations of alcohol and tobacco products have frequently been litigated before global and regional international courts and dispute settlement bodies.[25] The reasons are specific to the two products yet common to countries around the world. Both alcohol and tobacco are easy to produce, highly substitutable, and very profitable. Since many alcoholic beverages and tobacco products are quite similar, producers and distributors acquire and retain market share by developing brand loyalty

[23] As of 2014, the ATJ had adjudicated 55 nullification suits—20 raised by member states, 33 by private actors, and two by Community bodies. Of these, 16 rulings nullified the contested Andean decision or action. *Informe Estadístico* 1984–2014, 4 and 5, available at <http://www.tribunalandino.org.ec/sitetjca/index.php?option=com_wrapper&view=wrapper&Itemid=80>.

[24] The ATJ has heard six omissions cases through 2014, all of which were raised by the General Secretariat. The ATJ found three of the six cases to be inadmissible. Ibid., 30.

[25] Well-known ECJ decisions involving alcohol and tobacco include: Case 8/74 *Procureur du Roi v. Benoît and Gustave Dassonville* [1974] ECR I-837; Case 120/78, *Rewe-Zentral AG v. Bundesmonopolverwaltung für Branntwein* [1979] ECR I-649 ("Cassis de Dijon"); Case C-491/01, *The Queen v. Secretary of State for Health, ex parte British American Tobacco (Investments) Ltd.; and Imperial Tobacco Ltd.*, 2002 CJEU 1-11453. The WTO dispute settlement system has also adjudicated several cases involving import restrictions on and regulation of alcohol and tobacco products. For a list of cases and an analysis of potential conflicts between EU and WTO law, see L. Gruszczynski, The New Tobacco Products Directive and WTO Law: Much Ado About Nothing? *Asian Journal of WTO and International Health Law and Policy* 2015, 10 (1): 115–50. For a broader discussion, see B. McGrady, *Trade and Public Health: The WTO, Tobacco, Alcohol, and Diet*. New York, NY: Cambridge University Press, 2011.

Table 6.2 Andean and domestic litigation in the four fraught cases

Name of dispute (years of litigation)	Andean litigation	Domestic litigation
Cigarette dispute (1996–2007) *Venezuelan cigarette companies are the principle litigants, aided by the Venezuelan government*	*Ecuador*: Noncompliance suit for blocking cigarette imports from Venezuela	*Ecuador*: Unsuccessful attempt to invalidate Phillip Morris' ownership of Belmont trademark. *Colombia*: Successful attempt to cancel Phillip Morris' ownership of Belmont trademark
Alcohol dispute (1996–2001) *Venezuela and Ecuador challenge municipal alcohol regulations in Colombia*	*Colombia:* Noncompliance suit alleges that alcohol regulations discriminate against foreign producers *Ecuador:* Noncompliance suit challenges Ecuador's unilateral retaliation against Colombia.	*Colombia:* Constitutional Court refuses to enforce ATJ rulings, but Council of State (*Consejo de Estado*) refers a case to the ATJ *Ecuador:* National court enforcement of ATJ noncompliance judgments, but without a preliminary reference
Economic hard times: Peru (1992–95) *Peru restricts imports from other Andean states during "economic shock therapy"*	*Junta* raises nullification suit challenging member state decisions granting repeated derogations to Peru	*None that we know of*
Economic hard times: Ecuador (2011–16) *Ecuador creates a health certification scheme that effectively blocks imports from Peru and Colombia* *Ecuador imposes temporary safeguards restricting imports in response to currency devaluations and to stabilize balance of payments*	Secretariat upholds private litigant noncompliance suits against Ecuador; Ecuador seeks to nullify Secretariat decision finding violations Secretariat rules against currency devaluation safeguards, but upholds balance of payments safeguards; Peru and Colombia seek to nullify balance of payments ruling	*None that we know of*

among consumers and lobbying public officials to exclude competitors from entering the market.

Governments have long regulated the sale and consumption of both products in recognition of their adverse health and social consequences. "Sin taxes," for example, increase prices with the goal of discouraging consumption. They also provide welcome revenue for cash-starved governments. Alcohol and tobacco firms seek to influence these regulations and taxes, at times supporting seemingly neutral restrictions and tax rules that have the effect of limiting rivals' market access.

A growing body of health-based restrictions in the United States and Europe have led multinational producers of cigarettes and alcohol to seek out new foreign markets. Producers have used international test cases to try to force their way into developing countries whose markets were previously closed or captured by local firms. Litigation in the Andean Community was part of that strategy. Big wins in Andean cigarette and alcohol test cases, it was hoped, would provide a roadmap for other firms to enter Andean markets, and perhaps more importantly, provide a strategy to open developing countries in other regional integration systems to foreign tobacco and alcohol products. The financial stakes in these cases were thus quite high. And although the principal economic actors were foreign firms, the nature of the challenged regulations pitted Andean governments against each other.

Our discussion of these cases demonstrates the artful dance of legal actors at every level of the Andean legal system. Judges adhered to the law, while governments maneuvered to protect the status quo. As a result, multinational firms ultimately failed in their effort to enter previously closed markets. The ATJ's role in these cases was to apply legal rules as written. The Tribunal reversed several national-level decisions that were politically attractive yet legally dubious, but it also avoided plausible legal interpretations that might have generated political heat among governments.

In the cigarette litigation, the ATJ and the General Secretariat helped to broker a political compromise that maintained the integrity of the Andean legal system while allowing governments to "agree to disagree" about which cigarette company could use the Belmont trademark in different national markets. In the alcohol cases, the ATJ avoided issuing a demand for compliance that was unlikely to be met, dodging a direct confrontation with the Colombian Constitutional Court and backtracking on its earlier doctrine suggesting that national judges must ensure respect for Community law. As a result, noncompliance persisted in Colombia—an outcome that was perhaps politically unavoidable given the entrenched nature of the country's alcohol monopoly. By contrast, Ecuadorian judges who prioritized Andean law over conflicting national administrative acts overturned Ecuador's illegal retaliation against Colombia. This outcome is especially interesting in light of this chapter's fourth contested case, where litigants have not turned to Ecuador's courts to challenge serious violations of Andean law.

Cigarette wars: The Belmont trademark dispute

The Belmont trademark dispute involves contestations over well-known cigarette brands. The litigation is one of the most politically salient Andean legal disputes to date. Each side marshaled teams of local and international lawyers who challenged decision-making at every step as the litigation unfolded. Both major cigarette companies also mobilized domestic support, leading the member states to disagree with each other about what constituted "use" of the Belmont trademark under Andean IP rules. The ATJ's contributions to resolving the controversies were significant. The Tribunal filled in gaps in the relevant Andean *Decisiones*, developed new legal doctrines, resolved a dispute about ownership of an economically valuable brand name, and facilitated the uniform application of Andean rules.[26]

In 1963, British American Tobacco (BAT) through a subsidiary (Cigarrera Bigott) registered the trademark "Belmont" for marketing tobacco products in Venezuela. The company later attempted to register the same trademark in Ecuador, but its competitor, Philip Morris (PM), secured the trademark instead. This was not an isolated occurrence. PM had claimed trademarks that included BAT brands in numerous countries, leading Bigott to file multiple legal challenges. Notwithstanding the fact that PM was not using the trademark in Ecuador, the company convinced Ecuadorian officials to uphold their ownership claim. Table 6.3 below provides general information about the companies and trademark claims at the time of this dispute. The multinational tobacco firms listed have more extensive political influence in countries where they have established subsidiaries.

Conflicts over the Belmont trademark began to heat up in 1989. The reinvigoration of regional integration projects around the world offered new opportunities to use regional free trade rules to penetrate previously closed national markets. BAT saw the Andean Community as "being in the vanguard" of regional integration processes and thus ripe for developing a new legal and marketing strategy.[27] The tobacco giant also attempted to influence the content of Andean IP rules, which, as we explain in Chapter 5, member states redrafted several times in the 1990s in anticipation of joining the WTO.[28]

At the outset of the Andean conflict, BAT had registered rights to the Belmont trademark in Bolivia, Peru, and Venezuela while PM had registered the Belmont

Table 6.3 Basic facts in the Andean cigarette wars (as of 1989)

	British American Tobacco (BAT)	Phillip Morris (PM)
Headquarters	United Kingdom	United States
Location of Latin American subsidiaries	Argentina, Brazil, Chile, Venezuela	Argentina, Colombia, Dominican Republic, Mexico
Location of ownership of Belmont trademark	Bolivia, Peru, Venezuela	Colombia, Ecuador

[26] The ATJ decisions in the Belmont cases include the following: ATJ Preliminary Ruling 11-IP-96, ATJ Noncompliance Judgment 2-AI-96; ATJ Preliminary Ruling 15-IP-99, ATJ Preliminary Ruling 44-IP-2002, ATJ Preliminary Ruling 17-IP-2004, ATJ Preliminary Ruling 47-IP-2004, ATJ Preliminary Ruling 04-IP-2006, ATJ Preliminary Ruling 80-IP-2009. A later round of litigation involving the Belmont trademark concerned a dispute over labels used by Greenmint that were similar to Belmont cigarette labels. ATJ Preliminary Ruling 26-IP-2012 and ATJ Preliminary Ruling 164-IP-2012.

[27] C. Holden, K. Lee, G. J. Fooks, and N. Wander, The Impact of Regional Trade Integration on Firm Organization and Strategy: British American Tobacco in the Andean Pact. *Business and Politics* 2010, 12 (4): 2.

[28] Ibid., 20–2.

mark in Colombia and Ecuador. Notwithstanding these registrations, Colombia and Peru effectively closed their respective national markets to foreign tobacco products to favor local cigarette brands. This made it all but impossible for either global tobacco firm to sell their tobacco products lawfully in either country. But their cigarette brands were regularly smuggled into these closed markets, stoking brand loyalty.

A significant aspect of the cases involved the commercial use of the Belmont trademark. Although PM owned rights to Belmont in both Ecuador and Colombia, it did not actually use the trademark until 1989, when a PM subsidiary started to export Belmont tobacco products from Ecuador.[29] Andean IP law requires businesses to use trademarks to retain ownership, allows national administrative bodies to determine what constitutes use, and permits cancelation of trademarks for non-use.[30] But Andean law also specifies that exports of branded products are evidence of use.[31] PM's sudden decision to export small amounts of Belmont cigarettes from Ecuador—while not selling the Belmont brand in that country—suggested that the company was primarily interested in blocking access to its rivals' tobacco products.

In 1992 BAT filed applications to register the Belmont trademark in Bolivia, Colombia, and Peru. It also began an extensive lobbying campaign to influence the revision of Andean IP rules and bolster support for interpretations of Andean law that favored its trademark claims.[32] In 1993, a new set of regional IP rules entered force. *Decisión* 344 continued to allow exports to serve as evidence of use, but a new provision stated that a product with the same trademark could be imported from other Andean countries if "the mark is not being used *on the territory* of the importing country."[33] This provision—which significantly narrowed the "export as use" rule of prior Andean law—provided a way to circumvent PM's strategy of blocking rival products in countries where it owned the Belmont trademark. Bigott (BAT's subsidiary) immediately invoked this new provision, securing a certificate from the Ecuadorian Patent and Trademark office that recognized its right to import products with the Belmont brand. Bigott then began legally importing Belmont cigarettes from Venezuela into Ecuador.

PM responded immediately. The company had not used the Belmont trademark on products sold in Ecuador for over thirty years. But acting via local subsidiaries,

[29] These facts are discussed in Andean Noncompliance Judgment 2-AI-96, at 4, point 12.

[30] Early Andean IP legislation left it entirely to domestic IP administrators to determine when trademarks could be registered and what constituted use. Over time, Andean rules shortened use requirements from five to three years and specified what constituted use in greater detail. But the rules continued to allow administrators to determine whether or not a mark was being used. See Andean *Decisión* 344, Article 108.

[31] E.g., Article 111 of Andean *Decisión* 344 stated: "A mark shall otherwise be deemed to be used when it distinguishes products exclusively intended to be exported from any of the Member Countries."

[32] The strategy is described in Holden, et al., 2010, 20–2.

[33] Andean *Decisión* 344, Article 107(3) (emphasis added). Article 107 resolves conflicts where identical or similar trademarks are registered to different owners in different member states. In general, each owner is limited to its respective national market. However, the third paragraph of Article 107 permits imports of one company's trademarked products into the territory of its rival "where the mark is not being used on the territory of the importing country ... except where the owner of the said mark satisfies the competent national office that the non-use of the mark is justified by legitimate factors."

PM successfully demanded that several Ecuadorian administrative agencies—the Duties Office, Ministry of Industries, Intellectual Property Office, and Central Bank—ban imports of Bigott tobacco products. BAT responded by appealing to other Ecuadorian agencies, and asking a first-instance judge to find that, under Andean law, PM no longer had rights to the Belmont name because of nonuse of the mark.

Before the judge could rule on this claim, however, PM pre-empted BAT's nonuse argument by creating new facts on the ground. Ten days after Bigott's Belmont cigarettes from Venezuela entered the Ecuadorian market, PM began to market its own Belmont products in Ecuador. PM also lobbied the government of Ecuador to undertake an aggressive public campaign, announcing that "illegal" Venezuelan Belmont cigarettes would be confiscated and that individuals and businesses involved in the trade or marketing of Belmont "contraband" would be prosecuted.[34]

Venezuelan officials then took up Bigott's claims, turning to the Andean legal system to stop Ecuador from restricting imports of Belmont products from Venezuela. At the time, the *Junta* avoided bringing cases to the ATJ, instead arguing that its own *Resoluciones* responding to noncompliance suits were legally binding. In this case, Andean officials found that Ecuador initially violated Andean law by restricting BAT imports, but that once PM began to use the trademark on tobacco products sold locally, Bigott lost the right to import Belmont-branded products for sale in Ecuador.[35] Venezuelan officials, who believed that free trade principles should prevail over a hastily constructed and opportunistic trademark use claim, decided to pursue a noncompliance suit before the Andean Tribunal.[36]

In litigation before the ATJ, Bigott argued that Ecuador's IP office had no authority to ban imports of its Belmont cigarettes. The tobacco company further argued that it had made a larger investment in developing the Belmont name, that Andean IP rules were intended to resolve conflicts when the same mark is used in multiple member states, and that the ATJ should prioritize Andean free trade principles over PM's warehousing of a trademark it never actually used prior to the revision of Andean IP rules.[37]

These arguments did not, however, win the day. The claims were in tension with Andean law's deference to domestic decision-makers on the issue of trademark use. Rather than trench on that discretion, the ATJ affirmed the compromise position of the *Junta*. The judges found that the Ecuadorian agencies violated Andean law because their decision to ban imports failed to consider whether PM was using the Belmont trademark in the national market, as *Decisión* 344 required. The Tribunal also clarified that exports may be sufficient to avoid cancellation of a mark for

[34] These facts are summarized in Andean Noncompliance Judgment 2-AI-96, 4–5, points 12–23.

[35] This decision was discussed in G. Mancero-Bucheli, Intellectual Property and Rules on Free Movement: A Contradiction in the Andean Community. *NAFTA: Law and Business Review of the Americas* 1998, 4: 125–36.

[36] This dispute is a relatively rare early example of one Andean member state circumventing the *Junta* and initiating a noncompliance suit against another member state before the ATJ.

[37] These arguments are discussed in the Andean Noncompliance Judgment 2-AI-96, 1.b, *La Demanda*.

nonuse, but that Andean law allows for the importation of trademarked goods where another firm's similar trademarked products are not being marketed in the importing country.[38] The Tribunal dismissed, however, the most important alleged violation—the continued refusal to allow imports from Venezuela—because PM had in fact begun to use its trademark in Ecuador.[39] Thus, PM preserved its trademark rights in Ecuador, but only because national administrators had accepted the company's use as valid.

Follow-on litigation over PM's Belmont trademark continued in Ecuador, but the real prize to be fought over was Colombia's larger cigarette market, where PM also held an unused Belmont trademark. The ATJ's noncompliance judgment created a problematic precedent for that dispute. The decision rewarded what many saw as a bad faith effort by PM to hinder Bigott's valid use of the Belmont mark. More problematic was that the suggestion that other firms could mimic PM's strategy of registering the trademarks of their competitors to block their entrance into new markets. *Decisión* 344 permitted competitors to import products using the same or similar brands in this situation, but businesses would have no incentive to do so because their rivals could block future imports by hastily starting to sell or market the branded product locally.[40]

The root problem, however, lay in Andean IP legislation, which was ambiguous about what constitutes trademark use. Its silence on this issue allows each country's officials the final say in determining use in any particular instance. Thus, the ATJ required the Ecuadorian IP agency to make a factual finding about use of the Belmont trademark but accepted without question its determination that PM had in fact used the mark in Ecuador.

The Colombian government responded by closing the legal loophole. According to the ATJ's *complemento indispensable* doctrine (discussed in Chapter 4), member states may adopt domestic rules on issues regulated by Andean law so long as the rules complement rather than conflict with regional rules. The President of Colombia, invoking the doctrine, adopted a decree directing administrators to protect an importer's right to a use trademark registered by another business but not previously used on products sold in Colombia.[41]

With this decree in place, the Colombian phase of the litigation battle between the two tobacco companies began. In a pre-emptive move, Bigott filed a petition asking the Colombian Trademark Office to cancel PM's Belmont registration on grounds of nonuse.[42] PM responded that Colombian import restrictions—rather than a business decision to focus on its Marlboro brand—justified its nonuse of the Belmont mark in Colombia. When the Trademark Office sided with PM, Bigott

[38] Mancero-Bucheli, 1998, 134.
[39] Andean Noncompliance Judgment 2-AI-96.
[40] Mancero-Bucheli, 1998, 135.
[41] *Decreto* No. 698 of March 14, 1997, on file with the author. Article 1 states: "The right established in Article 107 of *Decisión* 344 ... to import products or services will *not* cease if, after an import, the right holder of the trademark in Colombia started to use the trademark in national territory" (emphasis added).
[42] Bigott relied on local rules that allow the trademark agency to cancel a trademark abandoned through nonuse. Interview with 4 attorneys (H) at Colombian branch of a multinational law firm.

appealed to the *Consejo de Estado*, a Colombian administrative court, which sent a preliminary reference to the Tribunal.

The ATJ used the opportunity to interpret Andean rules on trademark cancellations and respond to the gap in the law that had led to criticism of its earlier noncompliance judgment. The Tribunal reasoned that in order to avoid cancellation of a trademark, use of the mark had to be real and effective before a cancellation petition is filed. An intention to use the trademark, or a merely symbolic use, were insufficient.[43]

As required under Andean law, the Tribunal left it for the *Consejo de Estado* to apply its interpretation to the facts of the case. The *Consejo* determined that PM's failure to use the trademark occurred prior to the import restriction and, as a result, that the restriction did not justify the nonuse of the mark. Based on this finding, the *Consejo* canceled PM's registration and its right to the Belmont trademark in Colombia. This cancellation opened the way for BAT to claim the trademark.[44]

National and regional litigation involving the Belmont trademark has continued,[45] but the brand is much less popular in the region today.[46] Corporate acquisitions have supplemented litigation as a strategy for tobacco companies to enter and dominate national markets. In 2009, for example, PM attempted to purchase Protabaco, the second largest cigarette company in Colombia. Colombia's IP agency rejected the purchase because it would have given PM an 80% share of the country's tobacco market.[47] After the deal collapsed, BAT acquired Protobaco.

In sum, the ATJ made useful interventions to help resolve the Belmont cigarette wars. The Tribunal clarified the steps needed to demonstrate use of a trademark, while respecting the latitude that Andean law affords to national agencies to make factual assessments regarding such use. In doing so, the ATJ helped national judges and administrative agencies navigate a linked set of suits in multiple venues involving two major multinational firms and their legal teams, while facilitating the uniform application of Andean rules.[48]

[43] Andean Preliminary Ruling 15-IP-99. Andean *Decisión* 486, adopted in 2000 to replace *Decisión* 344, clarifies what constitutes use of a trademark (see Article 166), but ATJ case law continues to provide more specific instructions for how domestic agencies should determine use.

[44] World Trademark Law and Practice, § 6.05, n.5 (2011); German Cavelier Associates, The Belmont Trademark Case, Managing Intellectual Property, November 1, 2000.

[45] These cases involved issues such as whether similar names and pictures infringed the Belmont trademark, and whether PM's registration of the mark was properly canceled.

[46] An Internet website that lists popular cigarette brands in different countries indicates that Belmont cigarettes still dominate the market in Chile and Venezuela, but not in any of the other Andean countries See Best Selling Cigarette Brand in each Country, available at <http://www.tobacco-facts.net/trends-in-tobacco-use/best-selling-cigarette-brand-in-each-country>. PM continues to dominate the cigarette market in Ecuador through its subsidiary Tabacalera Andina, which produces Lider Suave, the most popular brand in that country.

[47] See B. Borkin, Philip Morris fails to buy Colombian tobacco firm, *Colombia Reports* (June 16, 2010), available at <http://colombiareports.com/philip-morris-fails-in-bid-to-buy-colombian-tobacco-company/>.

[48] The ATJ's resolution of the Belmont cigarette wars continues to cast a shadow. We found 12 subsequent preliminary rulings involving the Belmont brand and six additional rulings involving other cigarette brands.

Challenges to Colombia's alcohol marketing regulations

In the cigarette wars, the *Consejo de Estado*—the Colombian administrative court that, as we explain in Chapter 3, has sent more preliminary references to the ATJ than any other judicial body in the Andes—applied the Tribunal's interpretation of Andean law to resolve an economically significant trademark dispute between two tobacco firms. In the alcohol litigation, in contrast, Andean judges did not receive similar support from Colombian courts. The case study is thus especially revealing of the ATJ's role in judicializing politics in economic disputes where the Tribunal lacks faithful domestic compliance partners.

For more than a century, the Constitution of Colombia has authorized the central government to create monopolies over alcohol products that enable municipalities to raise revenue for health and social services.[49] The municipalities carried out the monopoly by adopting a complex system of permits, marketing rules, price controls, and local purchasing requirements that discriminated against alcohol products from other Andean member states.

Disputes challenging these municipal policies unfolded over many years in several different legal venues. Ecuador first challenged the policies in 1991. At the same time, it unilaterally retaliated by restricting imports of Colombian alcohol products. Venezuela filed a separate complaint against the municipal alcohol restrictions in 1996. The Venezuelan complaint led to *Resolución* 453, a reasoned opinion by the *Junta* condemning Colombia for violating Andean law. When Colombia ignored the *Resolución*, the *Junta* filed a noncompliance suit with the Tribunal.[50] A parallel case challenged Ecuador's retaliation against Colombia. The *Junta* refused to link the two cases, and instead issued a separate reasoned opinion condemning Ecuador's unilateral restriction on Colombian imports.[51] The upshot of these investigations was that both Colombia's municipal alcohol regulations and Ecuador's retaliation violated Andean law.

While the noncompliance suit against Colombia was pending, a private citizen (Maria Carolina Rodriguez Ruiz) challenged the laws authorizing the government monopoly on alcohol before the Colombian Constitutional Court. As noted above, the monopoly is based on the Colombian Constitution and as such it fell under the court's purview. But the constitution does not define the terms of the monopoly, and it was generally understood that the monopoly did not in itself violate Community rules.[52] Rather, Colombia's noncompliance stemmed from municipal practices that set minimum price and licensing requirements, undercutting price advantages of alcohol produced in other countries and making it more onerous to

[49] The history of the Colombian alcohol monopoly is discussed in ATJ Noncompliance Judgment 03-AI-97.

[50] For a number of years the *Junta* insisted that its *Resoluciones* had the same legal effect as an ATJ judgment. The case was filed with the ATJ on October 20, 1997.

[51] *Resolución* 454, *Gaceta Oficial del Acuerdo del Cartagena*, Año XIII—Número 249.

[52] This view was upheld in the *Junta*'s reasoned opinion (*Resolución* 453) and in the ATJ judgment. This position is similar in the EC and the WTO, both of which permit monopolies so long as they do not discriminate against foreign producers.

sell those products in Colombia. Under established principles of state responsibility, international law violations by municipal actors are attributable to the nation as a whole. It would thus have been reasonable for the Constitutional Court to use Rodriguez Ruiz' lawsuit to ensure that the alcohol monopoly, as implemented, was consistent with Andean law.[53]

Instead, the Constitutional Court not only failed to send a preliminary reference to the ATJ as required by Andean law,[54] it also issued a ruling that undermined the status of Andean rules in the domestic legal order. In its May 1998 ruling, the court reasoned that, unlike human rights treaties that have quasi-constitutional status in Colombia, Andean laws were equivalent to domestic legislation. Because such laws "and the Constitution do not share the same hierarchy, nor are [they] an intermediate legal source between the Constitution and ordinary domestic laws ... contradictions between a domestic law and Andean community law will not have as a consequence the non-execution of the [domestic] law." The Constitutional Court accepted, however, that Andean law has "primacy" over domestic law, a concept that the court interpreted to mean that Community law "displaces but does not abrogate or render non-executable" conflicting national legislation.[55]

Two weeks before this decision, the Ecuadorian Supreme Court had issued a ruling in a case brought by a private litigant challenging Ecuador's unilateral retaliation against Colombia. The Supreme Court also failed to make a preliminary reference to Quito as required by Andean law. But in contrast to the Colombian colleagues, the Ecuadorian judges accepted the "preeminence of Community over national law," which it interpreted as "requir[ing] that national regulations not conflict with higher-level legal norms."[56] The result was conflicting high court precedents regarding the supremacy of Andean law in substantively related cases.

The ATJ issued its noncompliance judgments several months later, in September and December 1998.[57] The Tribunal quoted from both high court rulings, although it refrained from condemning the judges for failing to refer the cases. The ATJ was

[53] Article 35 of the Revised ATJ Treaty codifies this principle of state responsibility in the following terms: "The Andean Community Member Countries shall ensure the fulfillment of the provisions of this Treaty and particularly the observance by national judges of the stipulations in this section."

[54] The Revised ATJ Treaty provides that, in cases involving an issue of Andean law heard by domestic courts from which no appeal is possible, the national judge "shall suspend the proceeding and directly request the Tribunal's interpretation." Ibid., Article 33(2).

[55] Article 93 of Colombia's the 1993 Constitution of Colombia states: "International treaties and agreements ratified by the Congress that recognize human rights and that prohibit their limitation in states of emergency have priority domestically." The Constitutional Court ruling notes that international human rights agreements ratified by Colombia are part of a *bloque de constitucionalidad*, which gives them a status superior to the national law. See Colombian Constitutional Court, Sentencia C-256/98 of May 27, 1998, Section 3.1.

[56] Judgment of May 15, 1998, cited in ATJ Noncompliance Judgment 02-AI-97: section XIII. Chapter 9 explains that Gallo Pico Mantilla, an entrepreneurial pro-integration Ecuadorian judge, served on that country's Supreme Court from 1997 to 2004. His presence may help to explain the Supreme Court's support of the ATJ in this case.

[57] ATJ Noncompliance Judgment 02-AI-97 (September 24, 1998) (finding violations by Ecuador); ATJ Noncompliance Judgment 3-AI-97 (December 8, 1998) (finding violations by Colombia).

unequivocal, however, in condemning both Ecuador and Colombia for the substantive violations of Andean law. With regard to Colombia, the Tribunal accepted the Constitutional Court's position that there was no inherent conflict between the alcohol monopoly and Andean law. However, because the municipalities' implementation of the monopoly continued to discriminate against foreign alcohol products in violation of Andean free trade rules, Colombia was under an obligation to correct the problem.[58]

The two states ignored the respective ATJ judgments against them. In Colombia, the litigant who had instigated the earlier constitutional challenge returned to court, asking the *Consejo de Estado* to nullify a Presidential degree clarifying details of the alcohol monopoly. As required, the *Consejo* referred the case to the ATJ. The legal issues in the case were complex. Rodriguez Ruiz argued that that the President lacked the power to issue the decree, although the Parliament had since adopted legislation on the issue. This claim involved domestic law issues outside the ATJ's purview. With regard to Andean law, the plaintiff argued that the decree created an encumbrance to the distribution of foreign alcohol products, although the decree itself had not created the municipal price supports and other restrictions that burdened those products.

The preliminary reference gave Andean judges an opportunity to speak directly to the Colombian courts about a Community law violation that it had explicitly condemned. As we explain in Chapter 4, the ATJ had earlier embraced the ECJ's *Simmenthal* doctrine, which requires national judges to take whatever steps are necessary to give effect to Community law—including abrogating the conflicting domestic legislation. In the reference from the *Consejo*, however, the Tribunal declined to follow the full implications of this decision. Specifically, the ATJ did not require the *Consejo* to ensure the application of the ATJ's noncompliance ruling.[59] Avoiding a confrontation with the court, the Tribunal merely reiterated that the Colombian government was legally bound to modify the municipal practices that conflicted with Andean law.

In Ecuador, the government also did not respond to the ATJ's noncompliance judgment against it. The government had, however, accepted the earlier ruling of its own Supreme Court that overturned the retaliatory quotas and tariffs as contrary to Andean free trade rules. A different Ecuadorian agency later issued new restrictions on Colombian alcohol imports in explicit contravention of the ATJ ruling.[60] This new restriction triggered a fresh judicial challenge, which this time was appealed to the Constitutional Court of Ecuador. Although the Constitutional Court did not refer the case to the ATJ, it embraced the supremacy of Andean law and invalidated the illegal administrative regulation. The ruling was the deathblow to Ecuador's unilateral retaliation efforts. The government thus complied with the

[58] The Tribunal acknowledged a Colombian statute, *Ley 223 de 1995 sobre Racionalización Tributaria,* had attempted to address the problem. ATJ Noncompliance Judgment 3-AI-97, 12.

[59] ATJ Preliminary Ruling 29-IP-98, conclusions 1 and 2.

[60] *Resolución* No. 004, Ecuador Board of Foreign Trade and Investment (COMEX), published in *Gaceta Oficial* No. 372 of July 30, 1998.

ATJ judgment against it, but only because its national high courts had themselves invalidated the regulations as contrary to Andean law.

Meanwhile, Colombia continued to ignore the ATJ's noncompliance judgment, leading the Andean General Secretariat (which by then had replaced the *Junta*) to initiate a new suit against the government. In March 2000 the ATJ found that Colombia had not complied with its earlier ruling, and in November 2001 the Tribunal approved retaliatory sanctions, authorizing the other member states to "impose an additional tax of 5% on up to five products" of Colombian origin—sanctions that were to remain in effect until Colombia provided "clear evidence" that it has "strictly complied" with the noncompliance judgment.[61] There is no evidence that any Andean country imposed these penalties, however. As of 2011, the General Secretariat indicated that Colombia still had not complied with the 1998 ATJ judgment,[62] and a 2014 analysis by Spirits Europe, a trade association, indicated that the discriminatory municipal policies remain in force.[63]

The multiple lawsuits challenging the Colombian alcohol monopoly raise a number of questions about judicial strategy. Most importantly, why did the ATJ decline to follow the logical implication of its earlier case law and refuse to instruct national judges to enforce its noncompliance ruling? Perhaps the Tribunal feared that any edict along these lines would be ignored. It seems plausible that neither the Colombian Constitutional Court nor the *Consejo de Estado* would have nullified the legislation and degrees in question, especially because the real culprits—the municipal practices—were not directly at issue in the cases. Rectifying the breach would likely have required a complete overhaul of longstanding municipal alcohol policies that provided a steady source of revenue to local governments. In other words, compliance with Andean free trade rules would have been especially difficult.

The domestic legal status of Andean law in both Colombia and Ecuador remains unsettled in the wake of the alcohol litigation. Both before and after the litigation, the Colombian *Consejo de Estado* has assiduously referred all cases involving Andean law to the ATJ, and the Colombian Constitutional Court's 1998 decision recognized that Andean law has primacy over national law. Yet the former court mostly sends cases involving disputes between private firms over trademarks and patents, while the latter has not explained the practical consequences of Andean law's primacy.

In Ecuador, the two high courts were bolder, endorsing the supremacy of Andean law and invaliding conflicting administrative regulations. These rulings occurred

61 ATJ Noncompliance Judgment 3-AI-97, paragraphs 1 and 2.

62 In 2011, the General Secretariat issued a report listing all cases in which member states had failed to comply with ATJ noncompliance judgments. *Secretaria General Comunidad Andina, Estado de Dictamenes y Sentencias Pendientes de Cumplimiento y Relación de Acciones de Incumplimiento ante el Tribunal de Justicia de la Comunidad Andina, Documentos de Trabajo* SG/dt 452, E.5, November 29, 2011.

63 Spirits Europe—Position Summary, *Anti-competitive Practices of Colombian Departments' Alcohol Monopolies* (September 2014) (on file with authors).

during an unusual period for the country's judiciary. In the late 1990s, Ecuador's Supreme Court was renowned for its independence and opposition to corruption.[64] The government orchestrated "purges" of the Supreme and Constitutional Courts in 2004 and 2005, ousting the judges and replacing them with jurists subservient to the government.[65] The executive intervention in the courts continued under President Rafael Correa, who implemented a series of "reforms" that further undermined the independence of the judiciary[66] and that may explain the lack of domestic judicial challenges to the import restrictions we discuss in the fourth case study in this chapter.

The limited willingness or ability of national judges to enforce Community rules presents a challenge for the Tribunal. The ATJ responded with a dual strategy in the alcohol cases. It did not shy away from reiterating settled legal doctrines and past findings of Andean law violations, but it avoided directly confronting domestic courts that failed to enforce its judgments or ignored their obligation to send references to Quito. Given the politically fraught environment in which the Tribunal operates, this prudential approach may be the most Andean judges can reasonably do to cajole states toward compliance.

The ATJ and Mega-Politics: National Autonomy during Economic Hard Times

The cigarette and alcohol cases were of greatest economic and political interest to private firms and, to a lesser extent, the administrative agencies that regulated their brands and products. The next pair of disputes, in contrast, raised high-level questions of national and Andean policy that were of deep interest to the region's political leaders, making the ATJ's intervention far riskier.

The Peru exceptions and Ecuador import restrictions cases have interesting parallels. The governments of both countries used trade and financial policies to reorient their respective national economies. In 1990, President Fujimori of Peru introduced neoliberal "shock therapy" reforms, while President Correa of Ecuador pursued state-led development projects beginning in the late 2000s. Although these policy goals and the strategies for implementing them differed, the two fraught

64 See Ecuador: The Politics of Justice, *The Economist* (July 31, 1997), available at <http://www.economist.com/node/152840> and Carlos de la Torre, Populist Playbook: The Slow Death of Democracy in Correa's Ecuador, *World Politics Review* (March 19, 2015), available at <http://www.worldpoliticsreview.com/articles/15335/populist-playbook-the-slow-death-of-democracy-in-correa-s-ecuador>.

65 S.G. Edwards, Outside the Rule of Law: Ecuador's Courts in Crisis, Washington Office on Latin America (April 2005), available at <https://www.wola.org/sites/default/files/downloadable/Andes/Ecuador/past/ecuador_memo_april_1_2005.pdf>.

66 See O. Reich and E. Vázquez Ger, How to Destroy a Judicial System in Three Easy Steps, *Foreign Policy Online* (June 13, 2012), available at <http://foreignpolicy.com/2012/06/13/how-to-destroy-a-judicial-system-in-three-easy-steps/>; Independence in Ecuador's Judicial Reform Process (2014), available at <http://www.dplf.org/sites/default/files/indjud_ecuador_executivereport_eng.pdf>.

cases raised the same basic dilemma. Economic restructuring warped prices, making imported goods significantly cheaper than comparable domestic products. Yet exposing local producers to foreign competition would have had devastating economic consequences.

As we explain below, Peru requested and obtained from its fellow member states a formal derogation from Andean free trade rules, enabling it to implement an economic program endorsed by the International Monetary Fund and foreign creditors while avoiding violations of Andean law. When faced with a balance of payments crises exacerbated the rising value of the dollar and the falling price of oil, Ecuador, in contrast, did not seek a formal derogation. Instead, it adopted a shifting series of certification requirements and tariffs to limit imports, triggering numerous complaints by private firms. The General Secretariat rejected most of the government's restrictions but upheld the balance of payments safeguards. Both sides have appealed the rulings or sought to nullify the Secretariat's decisions and, at the time this book went to press, the cases were pending before the ATJ.

It is tempting to praise Peru for seeking a collective solution while criticizing Ecuador for acting alone. Yet the reality is that Peru's reforms had international backing, so that the other member states were likely to grant its derogation request. President Correa, in contrast, relishes challenging the United States and the international financial institutions that it supports. As we explain in Chapter 7, Correa also favors weakening or dismantling the Andean Community and replacing it with other Latin American initiatives that capture the symbolic resonance of a regional integration project while escaping the legal straightjacket of Andean law. In this context, seeking the permission of external actors is not part of the political playbook.

Another commonality of the two cases is that the severe economic crises that Peru and Ecuador faced were well beyond what Andean institutions could address using ordinary legal and political tools. Some more fundamental accommodation or conflict was thus inevitable. An important difference between the two situations, however, concerns the evolution of the Andean integration project. Peru's economic disruptions occurred before private litigants could access the noncompliance procedure, facilitating an intergovernmental resolution of the dispute. In addition, all of the Andean member states shared a pro-market policy agenda at the time of Peru's economic shock therapy, whereas today Peru and Colombia's more neoliberal governments are ideologically at odds with the leftist-populist regimes in Bolivia and Ecuador.[67]

We discuss Ecuador's economic hard times in greater detail in Chapter 7, asking whether the ATJ's involvement is helpful or an irritant to resolving mega-politics disputes. That chapter also situates the Andean litigation against Ecuador within ongoing debates about reforming or retrenching the Andean Community or subsuming the Andean integration process within MERCOSUR or UNSAUR.

[67] Chapter 1, footnote 9 explains our use of the term "leftist-populist" with respect to the Chavez, Morales, and Correa regimes in Venezuela, Bolivia, and Ecuador, respectively.

Peru's economic hard times: A politically sanctioned derogation from regional free trade rules

A cornerstone of a common market is the commitment to eliminate internal barriers to trade. The Andean Community has struggled with this commitment, in part because member states have faced a series of severe economic disruptions that have limited the political feasibility of opening markets to intra-regional trade. The *Junta* and its later incarnation, the General Secretariat, have navigated these economic crises by allowing exceptions to Andean free trade rules while trying to ensure that these exceptions are limited in scope, temporary, and sanctioned by supranational agreement.

Beginning in August 1992, the member states adopted a series of *Decisiones* that temporarily exempted Peru from the Andean Free Trade Area. At the time, President Fujimori was pursuing an economic policy known as *Fujishock*, which involved eliminating price and exchange rate controls and reducing subsidies. When prices for basic commodities skyrocketed, the government imposed trade restrictions to stop low-cost products from other Andean countries from displacing demand for more expensive domestic products. The International Monetary Fund encouraged these structural adjustments, rewarding Peru with significant loans. Over time, capital investment flowed into Peru, seemingly vindicating the decision to impose economic shock therapy.

Fujimori's import restrictions would have unequivocally violated Andean law unless Peru received temporary exemptions from regional free trade rules. The supranational officials of the *Junta* did not like the *Decisiones* granting Peru such exemptions, but they tried to work within the political process to address this exceptional situation. After the *Junta*'s efforts to encourage member states to "correct the legal situation" repeatedly failed, the *Junta* challenged the most recent derogation, codified in Andean *Decisión* 387, before the ATJ.

The *Junta* raised several arguments to support its request that the Tribunal nullify *Decisión* 387. They included a concern that the member states had supplemented the *Decisiones* with a series of bilateral agreements with Peru that undermined the Andean Pact's requirement of multilateral policymaking, that *Decisión* 387 was inconsistent with the Tariff Liberalization Program's promise of an irreversible lowering of internal trade barriers, that the *Decisión* violated the most-favored-nation principle, and that the Cartagena Agreement did not give the Andean *Comisión* the competence to grant an exemption from Andean free trade rules.[68]

The outgoing President of the *Comisión*, Ecuador's Minister of Foreign Trade, Industrialization and Fisheries, and the *Comisión*'s incoming President, Peru's Minister of Industry, Tourism, Integration and International Trade, both defended the *Decisiones* granting Peru temporary exemptions from Andean free trade rules. The incoming President noted that that the suspensions were "adopted by unanimous decision" only after an "extensive discussion" and "tireless efforts to advance

[68] Andean Nullification Decision 1-AN-1996, Points 1.1 and 1.1.2.

[an] economic program designed to overcome problems affecting the economy of the country."[69]

When the nullification case appeared on the ATJ's docket in November 1996, Peru's relationship to the Andean Community was under active discussion. Several months later, the member states adopted the Sucre Protocol, re-launching the Andean integration project.[70] Most of the Protocol's provisions advanced the integration process. But the agreement also included a transitory provision that explicitly authorized the *Comisión* to renew Peru's exceptional status for eight more years—until the end of 2005.[71]

After the Sucre Protocol's adoption, the *Junta* then tried to withdraw its suit, since its legal challenges were now moot.[72] The member states also argued that the ATJ could not review *Decisión* 387, since so many similar *Decisiones* granting Peru a temporary derogation had been enacted using the same legal process without being challenged. It would undermine legal certainty, government officials argued, if the ATJ now questioned legislation adopted many years earlier with the support of the member states.[73]

The Tribunal, however, refused to dismiss the suit, reasoning that the repeal of *Decisión* 387 did not annul the alleged violation of the Andean legal order, and that its adjudication of the suit furthered a general public interest in ensuring the legality of Andean laws on the books. This interest remained even after the *Junta*'s attempt to withdraw the case.[74] A related issue was that the series of *Decisiones* granting the temporary exemptions were ad hoc, repeatedly revising Peru's free trade obligations without setting a clear end date for the measures. In addition, some of the earlier *Decisiones* allowed Peru to participate in discussions of Community rules that would not bind it because of the exemptions.[75]

Having explained why it would review the claims on the merits, the ATJ then declared that *Decisión* 387 violated the Cartagena Agreement because it "introduce[d] substantial modifications [of the treaty] … by an agency, the *Comisión*, that does not have the power to modify the treaty."[76] However, the Tribunal also concluded that any illegality had been "purged" by the Sucre Protocol. In other words, *Decisión* 387 did not need to be nullified because a valid treaty amendment had superseded it. In reaching this result, the ATJ distinguished between *Decisiones*, which are legislative

[69] Ibid., Point 1.2.2.

[70] Sucre Protocol of June 25, 1997, available at <http://www.sice.oas.org/trade/junac/Carta_Ag/sucre_e.asp>.

[71] The relevant transitory clause provides in full: "Notwithstanding the stipulation of Article 75 of the Cartagena Agreement [governing the Trade Liberalization Program], the Andean Commission shall define the terms of the Liberalization Program to be applied to the trade between Peru and the other Member Countries, so that the Andean Free Trade Area will become fully operational by December 31, 2005 at the latest. Peru shall not be obliged to apply the Common External Tariff until the Commission has decided upon the time limits and methods for Peru's incorporation into this mechanism."

[72] Andean Nullification Decision 1-AN-1996, Point 1.4.1.

[73] Ibid., Point 1.2.

[74] Ibid., Point 2.2.

[75] Andean *Decisión* 353 (April 4, 1994) allowed Peru to participate in harmonization negotiations. The law was superseded a few months later by *Decisión* 377.

[76] Andean Nullification Decision 1-AN-1996, Point 2.4.

acts adopted by the member states acting as the Andean *Comisión*, and a Protocol, which is approved during a conference of plenipotentiaries (*reunión de plenipotenciarios*), and which is thus more akin to a constitutional convention.[77]

The politically astute ruling used a judicial tactic pioneered by the US Supreme Court in *Marbury v. Madison*.[78] The ATJ defended its jurisdiction and its power to nullify illegal *Decisiones* while finding that the particular situation did not require the exercise of this power, since it was clearly within the member states' competence to adopt a formal revision of the Cartagena Agreement.

The ruling means that governments must meet at the presidential level and agree upon a protocol to amend the Community's founding charter. Such a meeting and formal revision are not difficult to orchestrate because there have been only four or five member states in the Community's history, and it appears to be fairly easy for national executives to convince their respective legislative bodies to ratify treaty amendments. When members states are ideologically divided, however, approval of a treaty revision is far more difficult. The precedent set by the ATJ in the Peru derogations case thus makes a collective response to Ecuador's financial and economic crisis, discussed below, far more challenging.

Ecuador's economic hard times: Deterring imports through unilateral certification requirements and safeguards

Ecuador's Andean law violations are linked to the combination of a strong US dollar (Ecuador's currency) and falling prices for petroleum, one of the country's principal exports. These two events generated a balance of payments crisis and a lack of dollars needed to pay for imports and to service debts. Ecuador's economic woes also stem from President Correa's state-led development strategy, a component of the leftist economic agenda that he has followed since his election in 2007.

Until recently, Correa's reforms were economically successful and politically popular, leading to his reelection to a third term as President in 2013. By 2014, however, a rising dollar and falling oil prices created an acute liquidity crisis. One way the government has attempted to protect national producers and retain dollars is by adopting regulations to reduce imports into Ecuador.

Chapter 7 discusses Ecuador's COMEX regulations, which created an onerous certification process ostensibly to ensure the quality of imports and protect the health of consumers. The Peruvian Chamber of Commerce, a Peruvian paint company, the Colombian commerce and trade ministries, and Ecuadorian businesses dependent on imports challenged the regulations before the General Secretariat. In a 2014 *Resolución*, the General Secretariat concluded that the COMEX regulations restricted trade, was not justified as a public health measure, and violated Andean

[77] Ibid., Points 2.4 and 2.5.

[78] *Marbury v. Madison*, 5 US (1 Cranch) 137 (1803). This technique has also been used by the ECJ and other national courts.

administrative regulations.[79] Disagreeing with these findings of noncompliance, Ecuador asked the ATJ to review the Secretariat's determination.

The COMEX certification scheme proved insufficient to stabilize Ecuador's balance of payments. Chapter 7 also discusses Ecuador's invocation of a currency safeguard to justify corrective measures applied to Peruvian and Colombian goods to counteract the rising value of the dollar and the devaluation of both countries' currencies. The Secretariat rejected Ecuador's safeguard because it was enacted without prior approval and because the government failed to prove that the devaluations had changed the terms of trade with Peru and Colombia.[80]

Ecuador initially sought a reconsideration of the Secretariat's decision, but it later shifted tactics, imposing import surcharges on a broad range of capital and consumer goods that it justified on balance of payment grounds.[81] This time, the Secretariat approved Ecuador's safeguards over the objections of Peru and Colombia. Ecuador presented ample evidence of its balance of payments difficulties and ensured that the corrective measures applied to a broad range of countries at levels proportionate to Ecuador's trade with those nations. Peru and Colombia asked the ATJ to annul the Secretariat's authorization,[82] and the validity of Ecuador's safeguards are also being reviewed by the WTO. At the time this book went to press, the ATJ had not yet ruled on the various appeals of the Secretariat's decisions.[83]

Given that Ecuador's economic measures impose real and immediate financial hardship on Peruvian and Colombian firms, these legal challenges are understandable.[84] Yet one can reasonably ask why the member states have not granted Ecuador a politically sanctioned derogation from Andean free trade rules, as they did for Peru, given Correa's extensive efforts to invest in and restructure Ecuador's economy.

Unlike Fujimori, Correa has, until recently, been unwilling to admit that his policies were creating economic hardship. Instead, the government justified the COMEX regulations as necessary to protect the health of Ecuador's citizens, and the safeguards as a reasonable response to Colombia and Peru's currency devaluations. Yet government officials also expressed anger at their Andean counterparts for refusing to recognize the structural factors generating the economic challenges that Ecuador faces. A trained economist, Correa has repeatedly stressed how the prior government's decision to adopt the US dollar as Ecuador's currency has harmed the economy. As the leftist president argued in defense of the safeguards: "We would not do any of this if we had control of our own exchange rate. If Colombia and Peru devalued ... we would do the same, to avoid problems in the external sector."

[79] General Secretariat *Resolución* 1695, Article 1.

[80] *Resolución* 1762 (February 6, 2015), available at <http://www.andi.com.co/cse/PublishingImages/Paginas/Informacion_de_Interes/RESO%201762.pdf>.

[81] WTO 2015 News Item, WTO members consult with Ecuador on its import surcharges imposed on balance-of-payment grounds (June 29–30, 2015), available at <https://www.wto.org/english/news_e/news15_e/bop_29jun15_e.htm>.

[82] 0003-AN-2015 and 0004-AN-2015.

[83] See Chapter 7 for additional details.

[84] In assessing the economic impact of Ecuador's COMEX measures, the Secretariat found that Andean imports into Ecuador had grown by over 10% in the three years preceding the imposition of the COMEX regulations, and had then shrunk by over 40% following the regulation's adoption.

Instead, he continued, the country faces "problems in the balance of payments due to the collapse of oil prices; the U.S. dollar has appreciated, and our neighbors' currencies are depreciating."[85] Pro-business actors in the region have no sympathy for these arguments, however, and they have used Andean litigation to question the legality of Ecuador's trade restrictions and the extent of its economic difficulties.

Conclusion: A Judicial Strategy to Navigate Fraught Political Terrains

All four cases discussed in this chapter involve domestic and foreign firms mobilizing to advance their strongly held policy preferences by litigating in multiple venues and (with the exception of the Peru derogations case) lobbying governments to advocate on their behalf. How should the ATJ respond when the member states adopt conflicting and arguably illegal policies in response to pressure from these powerful economic interests? In Chapter 5 we explain that in most IP-related disputes the ATJ enjoys the active support of domestic administrative agencies and the tacit support of national judges. National judicial support is more tepid, in part because leftist-populist governments with authoritarian leanings often "reform" the judiciary into subservience. In the Belmont trademark cases, the ATJ received the support of its most frequent domestic judicial ally—the *Consejo de Estado*, and in the alcohol dispute Ecuador's two high courts enforced an ATJ noncompliance ruling. Where the Tribunal lacks compliance partners in the national judiciary—as was the case for the Colombian side of the alcohol dispute and for Ecuador's recent import restrictions—the ATJ has issued judgments identifying noncompliance and requesting that states change their behavior while allowing national judges to decide for themselves whether and how to contribute to this goal.

Our central objective in analyzing these four case studies was to understand how the ATJ navigates politically fraught legal disputes. In all of these disputes, Andean judges and officials adhered closely to the letter of the law. The ATJ and the General Secretariat condemned violations of settled legal rules. But they also identified mechanisms for governments to circumvent legal constraints and they respected political decisions to invoke those mechanisms.

In the Belmont cases, for example, the ATJ upheld Andean secondary legislation authorizing imports of trademarked goods from other member states when the same registered mark was not being used in the country of importation. But the Tribunal also allowed each country's administrative agencies to determine whether such use had in fact occurred. This approach validated Ecuador's decision to uphold Phillip Morris' ownership of the Belmont brand *and* Colombia's contrary decision to cancel Phillip Morris' trademark registration. In the alcohol monopoly cases,

[85] R. Morla, Ecuador Abandons "Safeguard" Currency Controls for an Array of Tarriffs, *Pan Am Post* (February 12, 2015), available at <https://panampost.com/rebeca-morla/2015/02/12/ecuador-abandons-safeguard-currency-controls-for-array-of-tariffs/>.

the ATJ repeatedly condemned Colombia's violation of Andean law (although it implicitly tolerated continued noncompliance by refusing to order national judges to end the violation), and it demanded that Ecuador impose retaliatory trade sanctions within the Andean system rather than unilaterally. In the two economic hard times case studies, Andean officials accepted the possibility of using derogations and safeguards during periods of economic turmoil. But they required the states invoking those escape mechanisms to follow established legal procedures, enhancing the rule of law in a region in which backroom deals, political connections, and even outright corruption often prevail.

The steadfast commitment of Andean judges and supranational officials to enforcing the law on the books is noteworthy. In Europe, the ECJ and EC officials also demand respect for Community legal rules. The same cannot always be said, however, of other regional integration systems in developing country contexts.

The economic hard times cases also raise a distinct question: can and should the Andean legal system be part of a political process to addresses major economic crises? In other words, is it helpful to judicialize the management of these crises? Even the most neoliberal governments recognize that economic and political exigencies must sometimes take precedence over free trade rules. Most regional integration systems include provisions for states of emergency, temporary market disruptions, balance of payments crises, and protection of essential security interests. The invocation of these provisions is (at least in principle) subject to international review to deter opportunistic uses of these temporary escape mechanisms and impose constraints on governments. Domestic legal systems also have provisions that suspend the application legal rules to deal with economic disruptions. These flexibility provisions, however, are designed to deal with temporary market discontinuities and small-scale economic shocks, such as weather-related crop failures, supply bottlenecks, and various macroeconomic fluctuations. One can reasonably question, however, whether strict legal review makes sense for major economic turbulence of the sort faced by Peru in the 1990s and Ecuador in the mid-2010s.

In principle, the member states could have granted a politically sanctioned derogation to Ecuador, as they did for Peru. As best as we can determine, Correa did not ask for one. Our best guess as to why is that, given the ideological divisions in the Community and the fundamental "reengineering" of Andean integration that is currently under discussion (topics we discuss in Chapter 7), there was no political consensus for formally modifying the Cartagena Agreement to grant a temporary derogation. Yet a key difference between the two economic hard times cases is that Peru continued to profess a commitment to the policies of Andean integration while arguing that an exception from free trade rules would help to avoid Peru's formal exit from the regional integration project.[86] Ecuador's President Correa,

[86] Andean Nullification Decision 1-AN-1996, Points 1.2.2. and 1.2.2.1.

by contrast, has publicly maligned the Andean integration process, arguing that it "serves very little."[87]

The adjudication of Ecuador's trade restrictions has contributed to the hardening of political differences. The adversarial nature of litigation, with governments on each side seeking to discredit the claims of opponents, led Peruvian and Colombian officials to question Ecuador's claims of economic hardship from a fall in the price of oil, the appreciation of the US dollar, and a devaluation of Peruvian and Colombian currencies.[88] In sum, Andean litigation did not help to diffuse and may even have exacerbated the larger political crisis, although it did push Ecuador to follow Community procedures for adopting unilateral safeguards.

The legal fights over Ecuador's trade restrictions are ongoing. Ecuador has appealed the Secretariat's noncompliance findings in the COMEX certification case, and Peru and Colombia have appealed the Secretariat's approval of Ecuador's balance of payments safeguards. Ecuador has also twice extended its promised end-date for the safeguards. The next chapter situates these heated legal disputes within political discussions about reengineering the Andean integration system. If litigation is exacerbating conflicts among the member states, the ATJ cannot play the role of legal referee whose rulings help to broker a political compromise. To the contrary, litigation may actually make difficult conversations about the future of Andean integration all the more contentious.

[87] L. Vergnaud, Ecuador Cconsiders Leaving Trade Bloc Admist Currency Disputes, *Blouinnews* (February 12, 2015), available at <http://blogs.blouinnews.com/blouinbeatbusiness/2015/02/12/ecuador-considers-leaving-trade-bloc-amidst-currency-disputes/>.

[88] See Secretariat General *Resolución* 1784, 41.

7

The Authority of the Andean Tribunal of Justice in a Time of Regional Political Crisis

While working on this book, we began another collaborative project that investigates the variable authority of international courts.[1] The goal of that project is to better understand the challenges that international judges face in transforming delegations of formal legal authority (de jure authority) into legal authority that influences the actions of different audiences (de facto authority, or authority in fact). The authority project develops a theoretical framework to facilitate comparative assessments of de facto authority along multiple dimensions—between tribunals, over time, across issue areas, and among different countries. We create metrics to assess and compare how institutional, political, social, and other contextual factors affect the de facto authority of international judges. The metric includes five types of authority in fact—no de facto authority, narrow authority, intermediate authority, extensive authority, and public authority.

This chapter applies the authority framework to consider how consensus versus disagreement among the member states about the Andean integration project's objectives affects the de facto authority of the ATJ. Beginning in the mid-1990s, the close working relationships that Andean judges developed with several administrative agencies and some national courts helped the Tribunal to establish authority vis-à-vis litigants in specific disputes (narrow authority), similarly-situated litigants (intermediate authority), and the broader legal community (extensive authority) with respect to intellectual property (IP) law. These three dimensions of ATJ authority together created the island of effective international adjudication that we analyze in Chapter 5, a zone in which legal rules rather than power, political influence, or bribery govern decision-making by state and private actors.

Here we consider whether political and economic crises in the Andes have diminished the ATJ's de facto authority. The consensus favoring economic liberalization, open markets, and intellectual property (IP) protection that existed among

[1] The project was spearheaded by iCourts, the Danish National Research Foundation's Center of Excellence for International Courts at the University of Copenhagen Faculty of Law. It is published as K.J. Alter, L.R. Helfer, and M.R. Madsen, The Variable Authority of International Courts. *Law and Contemporary Problems* 2016, 79 (1): 1–36; and K.J. Alter, L.R. Helfer, and M.R. Madsen, *International Court Authority*. Oxford: Oxford University Press, 2017. These publications provide detailed analysis of the differences between de jure and de facto authority, the different levels of de facto authority, and the distinction between authority and power.

Transplanting International Courts: The Law and Politics of the Andean Tribunal of Justice. First Edition. Karen J. Alter and Laurence R. Helfer.
Published 2017 by Oxford University Press.

Andean governments in the 1990s eroded sharply beginning in the mid-2000s following the election of leftist-populist political leaders in Bolivia and Ecuador and the decision of another leftist-populist president—Hugo Chavez—to withdraw Venezuela from the Andean Community.[2] The remaining four member states are ideologically split between the neoliberal-leaning governments of Colombia and Peru—both of which entered into free trade agreements with the United States that precipitated Venezuela's departure—and the leftist-populist regimes of Evo Morales in Bolivia and Rafael Correa in Ecuador. These divisions, together with the pull of competing regional projects such as MERCOSUR and UNASUR, have impeded the long-standing goal of creating an Andean common market and have significantly reduced government support for the Andean integration project as a whole. Our primary objective in this chapter is to understand what happened to the ATJ's authority as a result of these developments.

We begin by dividing the Andean integration project into three phases—the developmentalist period between the Andean Pact's founding in 1969 and 1989, the Washington Consensus period between 1990 and 2005, and the crisis period from 2006 and the present. The discussion of the Washington Consensus period recaps our discussion in Chapters 3 and 5 of how, beginning in the early 1990s, the ATJ forged alliances with domestic administrative agencies to build narrow, intermediate, and extensive authority in IP cases, while having little if any impact in other areas regulated by Andean law. We then investigate how the island of effective international adjudication for IP disputes has fared during the last decade of political crisis in the Andes. We find that the island has remained resilient. The total output of ATJ decisions has doubled, the number of non-IP rulings has increased, and Andean judges have solicited references from courts and administrative bodies that had not previously referred cases. Our data and analysis thus suggest an unexpected result: that an international court can maintain its de facto authority even in a politically fraught environment in which governments are questioning the foundations of the international legal project that provides the court's *raison d'etre*.

Later sections of the chapter consider the ATJ's influence beyond the IP island during the crisis period. We discuss three examples where member states narrowed the scope of Andean law to allow greater national discretion, the most important of which was the abrogation of the Common External Tariff in 2015. To understand the ATJ's authority during this period, we also consider high-profile noncompliance and nullification complaints challenging Ecuador's economically consequential violations of Andean free trade rules. We situate this litigation alongside ongoing high-level political discussions regarding the future of Andean integration and the ATJ.

[2] The term "leftist-populist" is controversial in Latin America. See, e.g., R.S. Jansen, Populist Mobilization: A New Theoretical Approach to Populism. *Sociological Theory* 2011, 29 (2): 75–96. We nevertheless believe that the label applies to the governments led by Presidents Chavez, Correa, and Morales in Venezuela, Ecuador, and Bolivia, respectively. Each regime, albeit to different degrees, has made anti-establishment public appeals, organized referenda to circumvent constitutional limits, employed extra-legal tactics to thwart opponents, and dismantled institutional checks and balances within each national legal system.

The chapter's conclusion considers how recent events in the Andes illuminate the differences between the concepts of authority and power of international courts. As we have shown in several chapters of this book, the ATJ depends on the support of government officials, agency administrators, and private actors across the region. Within the IP island, the ATJ has long enjoyed the backing of administrative agencies and the businesses and law firms whose financial livelihood depends on intellectual property. This support—which has enabled the Tribunal to push back against government deviations from Andean IP rules—makes Andean law and the ATJ legally and politically powerful, albeit only within a narrowly circumscribed policy domain.

The ATJ's support among substate actors is much weaker beyond the IP island, and the Tribunal has been far less powerful as a result. Yet the Andean legal system—backstopped by the overlapping legal constraints of the World Trade Organization—pushed Ecuador to search repeatedly for legally plausible grounds to defend the imposition of new import restrictions designed to ease its economic and financial crisis. The result is that Rafael Correa's leftist-populist government—even as it openly distained the Community and pushed to retrench some Andean rules and institutions—did not have a free hand in responding to the crisis.

A final note before proceeding. The first sections of this chapter refer to the ATJ as a free-standing judicial body and do not discuss the other institutions of the Andean legal system, in particular the General Secretariat. This focus on the ATJ alone makes sense when discussing the preliminary ruling system and its impact on IP agency decision-making—legal procedures in which the Secretariat plays no part. When the chapter turns to considering the Tribunal's authority beyond the IP island, the focus shifts to noncompliance suits challenging safeguards and other emergency measures. Because the General Secretariat first adjudicates these cases, we assess the Andean legal system as a composite of the General Secretariat, operating in the shadow of potential ATJ review, and the Tribunal itself.

The ATJ in its Global and Regional Context

We begin with an overview of forty years of political struggle over economic policy in the Andes. We return to the beginning of the Andean integration project because, in many respects, the current crisis harkens back to the challenges that initially stymied regional integration and respect for Andean law. During these early years—which we label the developmentalist period—there was no Tribunal and national political leaders professed lofty integration goals with little follow-through. As Chapter 2 explains in greater detail, the creation of the ATJ was a response to the failures of this period. The second era, which we call the Washington Consensus period, was the heyday of Andean integration. The expansion of regional secondary legislation and a more muscular and well-resourced Andean administrative body—the General Secretariat—contributed to the activation of the ATJ and to the creation of its narrow, intermediate, and extensive authority in IP cases. Finally, we summarize the current crisis period, which was triggered by the schism between the Community's leftist-populist and neoliberal oriented member states.

The developmentalist period (1969–89): The ATJ struggles to establish authority in fact

The Andean Pact began in 1969 as a union of left-leaning governments committed to state-led development based on the principle of import substitution. Andean governments sought to parcel out economic projects across the member states, and they adopted stringent regulations to transfer technology from multinational firms to local businesses and to retain profits within the region. To achieve these goals, Andean political leaders created supranational institutions and adopted common legal rules, and for this reason some observers saw the Andean Pact as progressing further than other Latin American integration projects.[3] However, the Pact's economic development strategy depended on foreign investment, and few multinational firms would accept such stringent regulations of their local subsidiaries.

Pro-business actors particularly disliked the Andean investment code (*Decisión* 24), which limited the repatriation of profits. Controversies over the investment code delayed Venezuela's entry into the Andean Pact until 1973, provoked the legal and political challenges to the code in Colombia and Chile in the early 1970s, and precipitated Chile's withdrawal from the Pact in 1976.[4] As Chapter 2 explains, these controversies provided the impetus to create the ATJ. Political leaders hoped that a regional court, together with an agreement to give direct effect and supremacy to Andean law, would facilitate domestic implementation of regional rules and protect the Pact's initiatives from domestic legal and political challenges.

The Andean Pact's second decade included a series of initiatives to revive the stalled integration project. In 1979, political leaders created a regional Parliament, a Council of Foreign Ministers, and a Tribunal (which was not actually constituted until 1984). These efforts, however, had did little to promote regional integration. For example, the 1987 Quito Protocol set firm timetables for establishing a Free Trade Area and a Common External Tariff, but governments soon ignored these deadlines.[5]

The ATJ began operating during this period, but its early rulings were legally and politically timid. As we explain in Chapter 4, the ATJ eschewed several opportunities to follow the European Court of Justice's path and adopt expansionist doctrines to advance Andean integration. For example, the Tribunal rejected a private litigant's attempt to file a noncompliance suit, which at the time only member states could raise. The ruling adhered to the letter of Andean law, but the predictable result was that the Tribunal received no noncompliance cases until the major

[3] See, for example, R. French-Davis, The Andean Pact: A Model of Economic Integration for Developing Countries. *World Development* 1977, 5 (1): 137–53.

[4] T.A. O'Keefe, How the Andean Pact Transformed Itself into a Friend of Foreign Enterprise. *International Lawyer* 1996, 30 (4): 811–24.

[5] These reforms are discussed in O'Keefe, 1996, 817–19.

restructuring of Andean institutions discussed later in this chapter.[6] In another early ruling, the ATJ refused to investigate the compatibility of national regulations with the Andean Free Trade Programme, concluding that the regulations fell within a "list of exceptions" that, in effect, allowed member states to do as they pleased.[7] Overall, as we explain in Chapter 8, the ATJ generally thwarted efforts by private litigants to use Andean law to dismantle national policies contrary to their economic interests. This refusal set up a vicious circle that inhibited litigants from filing additional complaints that might have expanded Community law.

This cautious and deferential approach reveals that the Tribunal had little if any de facto authority during the developmentalist period. Most ATJ preliminary rulings were abstract legal interpretations that gave national courts wide discretion to apply Andean rules to the facts before them. In addition, the Tribunal did little if anything to move governments beyond paper endorsements of regional integration goals.[8]

The Washington Consensus period (1990–2005): Establishing narrow, intermediate, and extensive authority within the intellectual property island

Chapter 5 describes how a consensus among the five member states in favor of free trade and open markets created the political, legal, and institutional conditions for the activation of the ATJ and the development of a rule-of-law island for intellectual property disputes in the Andean Community. The lynchpin of this island was the symbiotic relationship between Andean judges and IP agency administrators, which we analyze in detail in Chapters 3 and 5.

As a result of this relationship between supranational and substate actors, the ATJ acquired first narrow authority (respect for its decisions by the litigating parties) and then intermediate authority (respect for its decisions by IP agencies, national judges, and similarly situated litigants). Evidence of narrow authority is found in the recognition by agency officials of an obligation to comply with each preliminary ruling. As a member of the INDECOPI administrative tribunal, who previously led the Peruvian agency's Trademark Office, recounted in an interview: "We apply the rulings as soon as they come down from the Tribunal, and we reference the rulings in the texts of our decisions about registrations."[9] The ATJ's interpretation of Andean law thus determined whether the agency would grant or deny a patent or trademark application. That registration decision, in turn, was binding on the

[6] The case was 1-AI-1987. The ATJ held that private litigants had no standing to file noncompliance suits.

[7] ATJ ruling 1-IP-90, conclusion point 1.

[8] Writing in 1996, O'Keefe finds that that only "Colombia and Venezuela came close to meeting the deadlines for implementation of the intraregional free trade area and the CET [Common External Tariff] .... In theory, nontariff barriers have also been eliminated among the four countries, although recent actions by Colombia and Venezuela indicate that this is still not always the case in practice." O'Keefe, 1996, 819.

[9] Interview with official (B) of INDECOPI.

business that submitted the application, and the decision determined whether the firm received legal protection for its brand or invention.

Over time, the quality of the agencies' decisions and procedures improved as they internalized the ATJ's guidance. These improvements, in turn, led to an increase in applications for trademarks and patents by both foreign and domestic businesses. The rise in applications generated a growing demand for Andean litigation. Our coding of ATJ case law reveals that more than 95% of preliminary rulings began as challenges to agency IP registration decisions. The increase in preliminary references—together with the testimonies of lawyers and industry associations representing IP industries—provide compelling evidence of intermediate authority. In particular, the Tribunal cast a legal shadow that covered similarly situated litigants across the Andes, including the private firms whose businesses depended on IP protection, the attorneys who filed or opposed trademark and patent applications, and the administrators in all five member states who applied Andean IP rules as interpreted by the ATJ to review those applications.

Later in the Washington Consensus period, the ATJ gained the support of the larger legal community of IP lawyers and scholars, thus achieving extensive authority within the island of Andean IP law. One indicator of this extensive authority, also discussed in Chapter 5, is the growth of a specialized bar of IP lawyers who repeatedly appeared before the administrative agencies, national courts, and the ATJ. Additional evidence can be found in specialized publications devoted to Andean IP law. These include law firm newsletters explaining new ATJ decisions and touting courtroom victories; a legal journal, the *Anuario andino de derechos intelectuales*; and detailed practice digests that collect and synthesize ATJ rulings relevant to the IP agencies' registration decisions.

The ATJ's de facto authority outside of the IP island was strikingly different. As a formal matter, Community officials viewed the Tribunal's jurisdiction as extending to all areas governed by Andean law. Yet the Tribunal received only twenty-six preliminary references concerning taxes, tariffs, customs duties, taxes, and other integration law topics from its inception through 2005. Our interviews also disclosed a broadly shared sense that violations of Andean *Decisones* on these issues were rarely challenged, and that important Secretariat and ATJ noncompliance findings remained unaddressed.

One reason for the paucity of cases outside of the IP island, as we note in Chapter 5, is that Andean secondary legislation often included loopholes or ambiguities that preserved domestic discretion and reflect member states' tepid commitment to regional integration. Private actors had few incentives to challenge violations of Andean *Decisiones* that national governments could easily defend in court. A related explanation concerns the ATJ's reticence to construe Andean rules purposively, either to close gaps or give greater precision to vague commitments. With little to gain from an ATJ preliminary ruling, there was little reason to file suit in a national court in the first instance. A third reason relates to the absence of Tribunal compliance constituencies—whether among national judges, administrative agencies, or private industry—whose professional or economic interests favored the application of Andean law and the referral of cases to Quito. The three factors were broadly self-reinforcing, creating a negative feedback loop that inhibited the emergence of ATJ authority in fact outside of the IP issue area.

The crisis period (2006–present): Political threats to ATJ de jure and de facto authority

The return in the mid-2000s of leftist-populist governments in several Andean countries triggered a rejection of the Washington Consensus and its legal and policy reforms. This section discusses the political and institutional manifestations of this rejection, focusing on Venezuela's withdrawal from the Andean Community, the ideological schism among the remaining four member states, and the championing of other regional cooperation projects by leftist-populist political leaders. We defer until the next sections a discussion of the ATJ's activities during this period and of the impact of the crisis on the Tribunal's de jure and de facto authority.

The first signs of rejecting the Washington Consensus arose with the election of Venezuelan President Hugo Chavez in 1999. Buoyed by high oil prices, Chavez sought to return Andean integration, and Latin American politics more generally, to state-led development. Consistent with this vision, in 2003 Venezuela supported a MERCOSUR–Andean Community Trade Agreement that the country's Vice-Minister of Commerce described as "a first generation agreement … which goes much beyond the commercial component" to encompass "physical, political, cultural, social, and economic integration."[10] Chavez also sought to diminish United States influence in the region. His grand vision included the creation of regional alternatives to the Organization of American States, the World Bank, and the International Monetary Fund—which are all based in Washington and in which the United States plays a central role.[11]

This vision was not shared by Peru and Colombia, whose continuing commitment to reducing trade barriers and liberalizing markets was reflected in the negotiation of bilateral free trade agreements with the United States. These free trade treaties precipitated Venezuela's withdrawal from the Andean Community in April 2006.[12] At the time of Venezuela's exit, Chavez had only one ally in the Community, the newly elected populist President of Bolivia, Evo Morales. Just over a year later, Rafael Correa, another leftist-populist leader, was elected as Ecuador's President. Had Chavez remained in the Community, there would have been a majority of three member states in favor of returning to a more statist economic development policy. Instead, Venezuela's withdrawal resulted in a two–two split between the

10 S. Baribeau, Chavez: Venezuela to Withdraw from the Andean Community of Nations, *Venezuelanalysis.com* (April 21, 2006), available at: <http://venezuelanalysis.com/news/1706>.

11 This radical view has its origins in the *Alianza Bolivariana para los Pueblos de Nuestra América* (ALBA), a socialist-oriented regional integration system created in 2004 at the initiative of Chavez and Cuban President Fidel Castro. ALBA's members include Venezuela, Bolivia, Ecuador, Cuba, Nicaragua, and several small island nations.

12 C. Malamud, Venezuela's Withdrawal from the Andean Community of Nations and the Consequences for Regional Integration. ARI 54/2006 Real Institute Elcano, 2006, 1.

remaining countries, creating a nearly insurmountable obstacle to adopting new secondary legislation or advancing any vision of Andean integration.

This schism also exacerbated competition between the Andean Community and other Latin American initiatives that offer different ideological visions of economic and political cooperation. Unlike the European Union, the Andean Community has long followed an open regionalism model that permits member states to join other regional ventures. During the crisis period, open regionalism created opportunities for advocates of both neoliberal and populist-leftist visions for Latin America to advance their objectives. Both types of initiatives sapped government support for the sharply divided four-member Andean Community.

For proponents of neoliberalism, open regionalism is a device "to accelerate the progress toward global liberalization and rule-making."[13] In the early 2000s, for example, the United States advocated stitching together preexisting trade treaties and integration projects into a trans-continental Free Trade Area of the Americas (FTAA). The United States abandoned this initiative in 2005, and redirected its efforts toward negotiating the Trans-Pacific Partnership (TPP), a plurilateral treaty that sought to link the free trade-oriented countries of the Pacific Rim. Among Latin American countries, this neoliberal vision is reflected in the Pacific Alliance, an integration pact endorsed by Chile, Colombia, Mexico, and Peru.[14]

The counter-liberal alternative is embodied in the Union of South American Nations (UNASUR), which seeks to merge MERCOSUR and the Andean Community.[15] When Venezuela left the Andean Community in 2006, Chavez announced his intention to join MERCOSUR.[16] Bolivia's Evo Morales later followed Chavez's lead. Although Bolivia remains a member of the Andean Community, it became an associate member of MERCOSUR in 2013 and a full member in 2015.

Ecuador, although not a part of MERCOSUR, is a strong proponent of subsuming the Community into UNASUR. Ecuador's President Correa has attempted to co-opt the Andean legislative process to achieve this goal. *Decisión* 792, nominally described as an effort to "reengineer" Andean integration, was in fact a critical review of all Community institutions.[17] In the end, the member states decided to retain all of these institutions except the Andean Parliament, which has been suspended and will be merged into a proposed UNASUR legislative body—the South American Parliament.

[13] C.F. Bergsten, Open Regionalism. *The World Economy* 1997, 20 (5): 545–65, 549 (italics omitted).

[14] M. Baquero Herrera, Open Regionalism in Latin America: An Appraisal. *Law and Business Review of the Americas* 2005, 11 (2): 139–84. The contest among "open regionalism" and "post-liberal regionalism" is discussed in J.A. Sanahuja, Post-Liberal Regionalism in South America: The Case of UNASUR. Series/Report No. EUI RSCAS: 2012/05 Fiesole, 2012, 1–8.

[15] Support for UNASUR has been strongest among political leaders in Brazil, Ecuador, and Venezuela. See also note 11, which discusses the socialist regional alternative ALBA.

[16] With Brazil as Advocate, Venezuela Joins Trade Bloc, *New York Times* (July 31, 2012), A6.

[17] *Decisión* 792—Reengineering Implementation the Andean Integration System (September 19, 2013), available at <http://www.sice.oas.org/trade/junac/Decisiones/DEC792s.pdf>.

If leftist-populist political leaders eventually succeed in merging all Andean institutions into UNASUR, the move would shift the focus of regional cooperation away from free trade and economic integration toward other development goals.[18] UNASUR's "character would be eminently political [with] a specific focus on cooperation and common policies in non-trade areas."[19] The extent and significance of this shift is somewhat obscured by vague references to the Andean Community and MERCOSUR in the UNASUR Treaty,[20] and by the focus on grand political gestures—such as plans for a South American passport that would give citizens "the right to live, work and study in any UNASUR country"—rather than concrete policies.[21] To many observers, however, this strategic ambiguity masks a concerted effort by leftist-populist leaders to create a continent-wide pact in which the fiction of interstate cooperation and a figleaf of economic integration obscure a reality that places national priorities over common regional objectives.

To date, UNASUR remains mostly a paper initiative with a handful of symbolic achievements, such as the high-profile opening of UNASUR's headquarters in Quito. Meanwhile, the Andean Community continues to limp along, hamstrung by the ongoing schism between the two neoliberal and two leftist-populist member states. For most of the crisis period, this schism has resulted in a lack of progress towards stated Andean goals rather than open conflict. More recently, however, a move to scale back Andean integration objectives, together with multiple legal suits challenging Ecuador's flagrant violation of Andean free trade rules, have threatened to end that détente. Before we describe these make or break legal controversies and parallel developments regarding retrenchment of Andean rules and institutions, we first explain how the ATJ has managed over the last decade to defend—and in some instances even expand—its de facto authority in IP cases.

The Persistence of the ATJ's de facto Authority in the IP Island During the Crisis Period

Our initial research on the Andean legal system ended in 2007, early in the crisis period. This book's analysis includes seven additional years of ATJ preliminary rulings and additional interviews with Andean and national judges and IP agency officials. To our surprise, we found that the ATJ's narrow, intermediate, and extensive authority within the island of effective international adjudication for IP disputes has not only survived, it is flourishing.

[18] Thus far, UNASUR has remained more promise than reality, in large part due to its "low demands and flexibility concerning trade and development." Sanahuja, 2012, 12.

[19] Ibid., 1–8.

[20] Treaty Establishing the Union of South American Nations (May 23, 2008).

[21] Sanahuja, 2012. See UNASUR: Specific Goals, available at <http://www.unasursg.org/en/node/180>. Regarding the announced passport plan, see Ewan Robertson, UNASUR Moves toward Continental Freedom of Movement, Venezuela Makes 'Equality' Call, available at <https://venezuelanalysis.com/news/11057>.

One suggestive piece of evidence is the increase in the number of IP preliminary references during the crisis period. As we detail in Chapter 3, references, after falling from about 200 to about 125 per year between 2006 and 2010, began to rise sharply, reaching 325 in 2014 and an all-time high of 691 in 2015—the latest year for which figures are available.[22] As has been true throughout the Tribunal's history, the overwhelming majority of cases involve disputes over trademark and patent registrations and other topics relating to intellectual property.[23]

Other indicia of ATJ authority have also carried over from the Washington Consensus era. Interviews we conducted in late 2014 revealed that the parties to individual cases, prospective litigants, national judges, IP agency administrators, and IP lawyers all recognize ATJ rulings as legally binding interpretations of Andean IP legislation. As before, the IP agencies are the vehicle by which these actors demonstrate their recognition of the Tribunal's authority. Agency administrators incorporate the Tribunal's interpretations of Andean law into the their policies and practices. Businesses and their legal counsel, in turn, frame their applications to register trademarks and patents—or their opposition to those applications—in light of these interpretations. In addition, the *Anuario andino de derechos intelectuales* continues to publish analyses of noteworthy ATJ rulings and agency decisions. An observer who compared these sources in 2005 and in 2015 would likely conclude that little had changed in the ensuing decade.

Even more surprising, however, are indications that the ATJ's de facto authority within the IP island is expanding to encompass new domestic actors. First, to improve the quality of judicial rulings on economic matters, including intellectual property, in 2012 Peru established a specialized intermediate appellate court to review decisions of the INDECOPI administrative tribunal. The judges appointed to the new court received training in IP law and met with ATJ judges to familiarize themselves with the preliminary reference procedure and the Tribunal's jurisprudence. In its first two years, the specialized court referred dozens of cases to the ATJ, accounting for much of the increase in ATJ preliminary rulings in 2013 and 2014.[24]

Second, in a pair of rulings in November 2014, the ATJ permitted administrative agencies to submit preliminary references.[25] In the past, the Tribunal approached this issue in a highly formalistic way, concluding that only true judicial bodies could refer questions of Andean law. The 2014 rulings accepted referrals from INDECOPI and from Bolivia's IP agency, SENAPI. The rulings articulated a multifactor functional test that considers an entity's powers and the types of activities it

[22] *Tribunal de Justicia de la Comunidad Andina, Interpretaciones Prejudiciales 1985–2015*, available at <http://www.tribunalandino.org.ec/sitetjca1/index.php?option=com_wrapper&view=wrapper&Itemid=24>.

[23] *Tribunal de Justicia de la Comunidad Andina, Informe de Labores Gestión 2015*, 70–2, available at <http://www.tribunalandino.org.ec/sitetjca1/INFORME%20TOTAL%202015%20final.pdf>.

[24] Interview with judges (B) of the *Octavo Sala Especializada en lo Contencioso Administrativo de Peru*.

[25] ATJ Preliminary Ruling 121-IP-2014 (reference from INDECOPI); ATJ Preliminary Ruling 105-IP-2014 (reference from SENAPI).We discuss these decisions in Chapter 4.

performs. The result has been an increase in direct references from other IP agencies in the Andes.[26] The functional test also suggests the possibility that administrative agencies responsible for other subjects relevant to Andean law could refer cases to the Tribunal.

Third, the ATJ's authority has expanded geographically to include preliminary references from Bolivia. As we explain in Chapter 3, Bolivian courts had submitted only three references between 1984 and 2013. One reason for the paucity of cases is that the Bolivian Constitution lacks a provision authorizing the delegation of lawmaking powers to the Andean Community. Recognizing the supremacy of Andean law and sending references to the ATJ thus poses greater political risk for Bolivian judges than for jurists elsewhere in the region. This judicial reluctance, combined with the ATJ's formalist definition of which actors could refer cases, meant that SENAPI officials had no way to communicate with Andean judges. The ATJ's 2014 rulings opened up a direct pipeline to the Tribunal. That year Bolivian courts referred three cases and SENAPI referred an additional three cases, more than doubling the total number of references from the country in a single year. In 2015, Bolivian courts and administrative bodies made thirty-four preliminary references, all but one of which concerned intellectual property.[27]

How has the ATJ managed to retain its de facto authority within the IP island, notwithstanding the collapse of the commitment to neoliberal policies that supported the Andean Community during the Washington Consensus era? Part of the answer is surely the extensive outreach efforts of Judge Luis José Diez Canseco Núñez—a former member of the INDECOPI administrative tribunal—who, as President of the ATJ in 2015, traveled across the region to meet with national judiciaries and administrative agencies, encourage the referrals of new cases, and explore opportunities for deeper cooperation.[28]

A few distinctive features of the IP island have also aided its survival. First, a diverse group of stakeholders—the officials in IP agencies, the businesses that own IP, and the lawyers who represent them—support Andean IP law and the ATJ preliminary reference mechanism. In addition, trademark and patent registrations (other than those for pharmaceuticals) are mainly private disputes that do not raise politically contentious legal or policy issues, whether the parties are foreign firms, domestic businesses, or local subsidiaries of multinational corporations. There is thus little reason for governments to pick a fight over the ATJ's exercise of de facto authority in these cases.

Second, the funding source of the domestic IP agencies—registration fees and fines—sets them apart from other administrative bodies. Firms must apply to register patents and trademarks, and many foreign businesses that depend

[26] The most recent ATJ annual report notes the following referrals from IP agencies in 2015: Colombia's Unfair Competition and Industrial Property Working Group (twenty-five cases); Colombia's Directorate of Distinctive Signs (two cases); Bolivia's SENAPI (six cases); Peru's INDECOPI (three cases). *Tribunal de Justicia de la Comunidad Andina, Informe de Labores Gestión, 2015*, 9.

[27] *Tribunal de Justicia de la Comunidad Andina, Informe de Labores Gestión 2015*, 70.

[28] Ibid., 52–65 (describing these activities); Interview with ATJ judge H.

on IP rights are quite wealthy. The agencies retain the revenue from these registrations, which has enabled them to attract and retain high-quality and professionalized officials and staff who protect their resources and institutional culture. Yet, the agencies' independence is not especially of concern to governments, especially in comparison to the tax and customs agencies that provide a more lucrative and politically important revenue stream, as well as a tool to police national borders.

Third, the island does not depend on national judicial support. Many scholars, ourselves included, have argued that such support greatly enhances the authority of international courts.[29] Yet, authoritarian leaders may seize control of the judiciary, as has occurred in Venezuela and Ecuador.[30] The recent ATJ decisions accepting references directly from the IP agencies have created a way to circumvent any national judicial reticence or opposition that may arise now or in the future. Moreover, the fact that domestic IP agencies regularly request ATJ interpretations of Andean IP law makes it less politically risky for sympathetic national judges to refer cases and apply Tribunal rulings. Finally, the general satisfaction of most stakeholders with the existing system suggests another reason why Andean political leaders have left the IP island alone.

The ATJ Beyond the IP Island During the Crisis Period: Changing de jure and de facto Authority

This section focuses on the ATJ's authority and power outside of the IP island during the crisis period. We discuss two legal and political developments affecting the ATJ's de jure and de facto authority:

1. decisions to scale back Andean legislation, including eliminating the Common External Tariff; and
2. suits challenging Ecuador's pervasive restrictions on imports in response to a severe financial crisis that raised fundamental challenges to the Community.

Overall, we find that the crisis period has seen a diminution of the ATJ's de jure authority—that is, the scope of the Tribunal's formal jurisdiction—which has correspondingly reduced the ATJ's de facto authority.

[29] K.J. Alter, Who Are the Masters of the Treaty?: European Governments and the European Court of Justice. *International Organization* 1998, 52 (1): 125–52; L.R. Helfer, Overlegalizing Human Rights: International Relations Theory and the Commonwealth Caribbean Backlash against Human Rights Regimes. *Columbia Law Review* 2002, 102 (7): 1832–911.

[30] E.g., Human Rights Watch, Rigging the Rule of Law: Judicial Independence Under Siege in Venezuela, 2004, available at <http://www.hrw.org/reports/2004/venezuela0604/index.htm>; Human Rights Watch, Ecuador: Supreme Court Purged: President and Congress Thwart Judicial Independence, 2004, available at <https://www.hrw.org/news/2004/12/16/ecuador-supreme-court-purged>; Due Process of Law Foundation, Judicial Independence in Ecuador's Judicial Reform Process, 2014, available at <http://www.dplf.org/sites/default/files/indjud_ecuador_executivereport_eng.pdf>.

Contracting Andean law: Does restricting the ATJ's de jure authority also diminish its authority in fact?

The crisis period has witnessed a scaling back of Andean law. Contracting the reach of Community legal norms necessarily constricts the ATJ's de jure authority. If Andean legislation no longer governs a particular topic or issue, the ATJ has nothing to interpret nor can member states be condemned for domestic laws and practices that conflict with Andean rules. Do these changes also diminish the Tribunal's de facto authority? The answer may seem obvious, but if the ATJ decided few cases concerning the more expansive but now repealed regional rules, then Andean judges may not have lost authority in fact in any meaningful sense.

In at least two instances, the member states revised Community secondary legislation following ATJ noncompliance judgments that found states in breach of *Decisiones* that were more prescriptive or expansive. The contested *Decisiones* were created during the Washington Consensus period when member states favored enhancing the regional integration process. The revisions introduced legal loopholes that allowed the member states to retain or adopt domestic laws and practices previously proscribed by Andean law.

The first instance of retrenchment involved Andean rules regulating the test data that drug companies submit to domestic health agencies when seeking approval to market new medicines. We discuss this example in detail in Chapter 5. In brief, Andean *Decisión* 486, adopted in 2000 protected undisclosed test data "against unfair commercial use," but did not resolve whether this protection would be exclusive—a legal feature sought by multinational drug companies. In 2002, Colombia—under pressure from the United States, with which it was then negotiating a bilateral free trade agreement—adopted a decree granting drug companies five years of exclusive data protection. Local generics companies sued. The General Secretariat sided with the government, finding no violation of Andean law. The generic companies then appealed to the ATJ, which upheld their noncompliance complaint in late 2005. This was a rare case in which the Secretariat and the ATJ took opposing positions.[31]

Following the judgment, Colombia lobbied the other four member states to adopt new secondary legislation affirming that its more IP-protective domestic decree was in fact consistent with Andean law. After several failed attempts to reach agreement, Colombia forced the approval of *Decisión* 632 at a meeting where the two opponent states—Venezuela and Bolivia—were ineligible to vote because they had not paid their Community membership dues. The legislation retroactively validated the domestic decree and, by facilitating Colombia's free trade negotiations with the United States, contributed to Venezuela's withdrawal from the Andean Community soon thereinafter.[32]

A second retrenchment involved Andean secondary legislation that regulates chemical pesticides for agriculture.[33] This legislation, adopted in 1998, was part of

[31] ATJ Noncompliance Judgment 114-AI-2004, 41.

[32] This dispute is discussed in depth in Chapter 5.

[33] Chapter 8 provides additional discussion of these cases.

a set of policies introducing environmental protection rules into the Community.[34] In two preliminary rulings from Colombia and three noncompliance judgments against Peru, the ATJ became increasingly forceful in challenging the failure to follow the legislation in full. In the Colombian cases, the ATJ ruled that member states could neither enact parallel requirements nor allow exemptions to Andean rules.[35] In the Peruvian suits, the Tribunal found violations involving the adoption of more favorable registration procedures for chemical pesticides imported by farmers and the granting of automatic import licenses if the government did not evaluate registration requests within a certain time.[36] Peru responded with a half-hearted measure, creating a simplified registration process that circumvented the review of imported pesticides required by Andean law. The persistent litigants returned to the ATJ a third time. The Tribunal once again ruled against Peru and warned that the prevailing litigants could file suit in national courts seeking damages, an enforcement mechanism envisioned in the ATJ Treaty but never previously utilized.[37]

Member states responded to the ATJ rulings by relaxing Andean pesticides rules to give greater leeway for domestic regulations.[38] In interviews we were told that the prior regional rules were highly restrictive, to the point that only a handful of importers could pass muster. Although environmentalists supported the strict regulations, farmers wanted more relaxed rules for importing chemical pesticides, and governments sided with the farmers.[39]

The retrenchments following the data protection and pesticide litigation realigned Andean legislation with the contested national laws and practices. How do these sorts of retrenchments affect the ATJ's de jure and de facto authority? Since the ATJ can still interpret and enforce the revised Andean legislation, one might argue that the ATJ's authority is unaffected. The data protection case supports this view. Privately, Colombian officials insisted that the original Andean legislation, although ambiguous and poorly written, permitted national variation in the extent of data protection.[40] The Secretariat's position in the litigation supports this claim. Member states reversed the ATJ's contrary position, issuing an "interpretive decision" that kept the legislation intact while clarifying the contested provision. Given that this clause was but one small piece of a larger set of rules, it is plausible that the reversal did not meaningfully constrict the ATJ's authority.

The pesticides cases are different. The ATJ stringently applied Andean law against both Peru and Colombia, but this forceful approach led member states to add the sort of legal loopholes that have long hindered the growth of ATJ authority outside

[34] See T.A. O'Keefe, *Latin American and Caribbean Trade Agreements: Keys to a Prosperous Community of the Americas*. Leiden: Martinus Nijhoff Publishers, 2009.

[35] See ATJ Preliminary Rulings 114-IP-2009 and 115-IP-2009.

[36] See ATJ Noncompliance Judgments 05-AI-2008 and 02-AI-2010.

[37] ATJ Noncompliance Judgment 01-AI-2012, at 20. Article 30 of the Revised ATJ Treaty provides: "A verdict of noncompliance issued by the [ATJ], in the cases envisaged in Article 25, shall constitute legal and sufficient grounds for the party to ask the national judge for compensation for any damages or loss that may be due."

[38] *Decisión* 804, adopted April 28, 2015.

[39] Interview with ATJ judge H.

[40] Interview with official (A) of the Ministry of Trade, Industry and Tourism of Colombia.

of the IP island. As a formal legal matter, the ATJ retains de jure authority vis-à-vis the contested Andean pesticides rules, but litigants may conclude from this experience that efforts to enforce Andean law are counterproductive. We find evidence supporting this contention in the rise and fall of noncompliance suits over time. During the height of the Washington Consensus period (1996–2005), the ATJ adjudicated 94 noncompliance suits, an average of 9.4 per year. In the crisis period (2006–14), the filing of noncompliance suits dropped sharply, eventually falling to zero. The ATJ adjudicated only 23 noncompliance case in this period, an average 2.3 per year.[41] The decline may have been an implicit recognition of the decreasing legal capacity of the Andean General Secretariat. Potential litigants may also have wondered if there was any point in turning to the Community legal system if national governments would simply respond to adverse rulings by overturning Andean rules.

The third and arguably the most important constriction of the ATJ's de jure authority concerns the 2015 abrogation of the Common External Tariff (CET).[42] The 1969 Cartagena Agreement listed the CET as one of the Andean Pact's founding objectives, but it was not adopted until 1995.[43] The date for full implementation of the CET was subsequently pushed back several times, but the member states took numerous steps to adopt harmonized procedures that applied to both intra-Andean and external trade. These legislative enactments expanded the ATJ's de jure and de facto authority over these aspects of the CET.

During the Washington Consensus and crisis periods, the ATJ interpreted this secondary legislation and highlighted the CET's central place in the Andean integration process. In a 1999 ruling, for example, the Tribunal identified the common tariff as a key element of the Andean integration project:

> Without it we cannot speak of common market and ... little or nothing serious in the integration process could be considered effective. [The CET] is, together with the Trade Liberalization Program, indispensable for the construction of the expanded market area, in other words a substantial part of the existence of the Andean market .... [The *Decisión* adopting CET] begins to fulfill the obligations agreed to in [the Cartagena Agreement]. The *Decisión* sets tariff levels based on the rules of the Cartagena Agreement and the procedures and conditions for introducing amendments to such instruments. [It is] noteworthy that in no case can such amendments be adopted unilaterally by any country.[44]

In 2005, toward the end of the Washington Consensus era, the ATJ twice applied the CET, condemning Colombia for lowering the tariff on rice,[45] and castigating Ecuador for changing tariffs on paper products.[46] During the crisis period, an ATJ

[41] Chapters 3 and 8 provide additional detail.

[42] *Decisión* 805, adopted April 24, 2015.

[43] See Cartagena Agreement, Articles 80 to 86. The Andean *Comisión* adopted the CET in *Decisión* 370, and subsequently modified it in *Decisiones* 465 and 535.

[44] ATJ Noncompliance Judgment 7-AI-98 (quoted in ATJ Preliminary Ruling 115-IP-2005, 11).

[45] ATJ Preliminary Ruling 115-IP-2005. The Colombian *Consejo de Estado* enforced the ATJ's ruling in a 2010 decision, *Dorian Rocha Avila v. Decreto* 635 of 2001 (on file with the authors).

[46] ATJ Noncompliance Judgment 200-AI-2005.

preliminary ruling strongly suggested that the Colombian customs agency contravened the common tariff classification system—known as NANDINA—and that national judges should overturn its decision.[47] These are only three cases, but we do not know how often the General Secretariat adjudicated complaints involving the CET and adopted *Resoluciones* finding violations of Andean law that were not appealed to the ATJ.

Given the importance that Andean judges attached to the CET as a pillar of the Community, the decision in 2015 to abrogate its core legislative instruments (*Decisiones* 370, 465, and 535) must be seen as a significant diminution of the ATJ's de jure and de facto authority. Yet, the Andean rules harmonizing customs procedures were not repealed. These harmonized rules, which mostly concern procedural and technical requirements, have been the primary focus of the ATJ's customs and tariff-related rulings. It is also noteworthy that the conflict with Ecuador, discussed later in this chapter, is unrelated to the CET's abolition, revealing that the Secretariat and the ATJ retain considerable de jure authority over free trade, tariffs, and customs rules governing Andean markets.

The ATJ and mega-politics: Ecuador challenges fundamental common market precepts

We previously noted that the number of noncompliance suits dwindled to zero during the crisis period. The dearth of Andean noncompliance cases ended in late 2013 when Ecuador adopted a series of administration regulations and trade restrictions to discourage imports and improve its balance of payments situation. Ecuador's domestic measures raised serious questions about the country's continuing commitment to Community law and the Andean integration project more generally. This section reviews three high-stakes legal disputes related to Ecuador's efforts to manage its current financial crisis: an import certification regulation that hindered the importation of hundreds of products into Ecuador, a safeguard applied to Peruvian and Colombian imports to compensate for those countries' currency devaluations, and far more significant balance of payments safeguards applied to a broad range of imports from Andean and non-Andean countries.

When faced with litigation, Ecuador at first seemed poised to quit the Community entirely or to accelerate its merger with MERCOSUR or a transition to UNASUR. Much to our surprise, however, Ecuador participated in and respected Andean legal processes. Peruvian and Colombian economic interests remain dissatisfied with the General Secretariat's approval of Ecuador's balance of payments safeguards, and suits relating to all three disputes remain on the ATJ's docket. As of now, however, Ecuador appears to have found a legal way to achieve its economic objectives within the Andean Community's institutional structure.

[47] ATJ Preliminary Ruling 17-IP-2008, 7–8.

Challenges to Ecuador's COMEX import certification regulations

In November 2013, the Committee on Foreign Trade ("COMEX"), the policy-making arm of Ecuador's Ministry of Foreign Trade, established a certification requirement for 200 to 450 imported products, ostensibly to ensure the quality of the imports and protect the health of domestic consumers.[48] The certification scheme angered actors involved in intra-regional trade—including the Peruvian Chamber of Commerce, a Peruvian paint company, the Colombian commerce and trade ministries, and Ecuadorian businesses dependent on imports—which challenged the COMEX regulations as contrary to Andean law.[49]

In a 2014 *Resolución*, the General Secretariat concluded that the COMEX regulations restricted trade, were not justified as a public health measure, and violated Andean administrative procedures.[50] The Secretariat also condemned Ecuador for applying more permissive certification rules to imports from the European Union but not from other Andean countries.[51] After the Secretariat refused to reconsider its initial findings,[52] Ecuador asked the ATJ to review the Secretariat's determination.

The COMEX litigation is one facet of a broader controversy linked to Ecuador's dollar liquidity crisis. Since his election as the country's President, Rafael Correa has pursued an aggressive plan of state-led economic development and social policies. Correa financed these policies using foreign loans that offered significant financial benefits to bondholders, most notably high interest rates.[53] These actions make the US dollar—Ecuador's official currency—extremely valuable. Yet the recent rise in the value of the dollar and the decrease in the price of oil (one of the country's key industries) has increased the price of Ecuadorian exports while making goods imported from the country's Andean neighbors (who do not use the US dollar) much cheaper.

One way to cushion the economic shock for domestic producers and stem the exodus of much-needed dollars has been to stop imports into Ecuador. Many observers thus suspect that trade protectionism is the true goal of the COMEX regulations.[54] Some government officials have obliquely confirmed this suspicion

[48] COMEX *Resolución* 116, Article 1, adopted November 19, 2013. In 2014, COMEX extended the certification requirement to additional classes of imported goods.

[49] General Secretariat *Resolución* 003-2014. Although the COMEX regulations nominally apply to all imports, a US agency reports that the EU secured an exemption for European imports, which require only a sworn statement to satisfy the regulations. See <https://ustr.gov/sites/default/files/files/reports/2015/NTE/2015%20NTE%20Ecuador.pdf>. Thus, in practice, the certification scheme primarily burdens intra-Andean trade.

[50] General Secretariat *Resolución* 1695, Article 1, adopted June 6, 2014.

[51] General Secretariat *Resolución* 003-2014, adopted November 7, 2014.

[52] General Secretariat *Resolución* 1716, Article 1, adopted August 18, 2014.

[53] For more on how the search for funds is driving a broad range of Ecuador's economic policies, see K. Porzecanski, Ecuador's Bond Slump Is Just Beginning to Stone Harbor, *Aberdeen Bloomberg Business* (May 20, 2015), available at <http://www.bloomberg.com/news/articles/2015-05-20/ecuador-s-bond-slump-is-just-beginning-to-stone-harbor-aberdeen>.

[54] See C. Espinosa, Las Empresas Nacionales Crecieron por la Apertura, no por la Protección Estatal, *ElComercio.com*, available at <http://www.elcomercio.com/actualidad/negocios/cristian-espinosa-empresas-nacionales-crecieron.html>, ("*Creo que el Gobierno tomó esa decisión viendo el déficit de la balanza commercial*"; "*Un aumento de los precios de los productos importados, sin que necesariamente*

by acknowledging that the regulations are part of a wider program to spur the domestic economy.[55]

As far as we know, Ecuador never complied with the Secretariat's legal ruling and the country's nullification challenge to Secretariat's noncompliance *Resolución* remains on the ATJ's docket. Peruvian and Colombian businesses also remain upset that Ecuador continues to apply more permissive certification rules to imports from EU. Ecuador negotiated bilateral agreements with Peru and Colombia that give imports from those countries some of the procedural benefits it affords to EU imports. This relieved some of the pressure to pursue the litigation. However, a violation of the Cartagena Agreement's most-favored nation rule persists because only EU imports can be certified under the technical regulations of the country of origin, whereas Andean imports must be certified as complying with Ecuadorian regulations. Thus, it is possible that the suits will be reactivated and eventually be the subject of ATJ noncompliance judgments.

Meanwhile, as the COMEX litigation unfolded, discussions regarding the Andean Community's future accelerated. A few years earlier, in 2011, Andean officials had created a working group to study the possibility of a transition to UNASUR. In May 2012, the member states commissioned two non-Andean consulting groups to make recommendations regarding the transition.[56] A year later, with the consultants' recommendations in hand, the working group suggested a "new vision" for the Community, which asserted that the expansion of the goals of Andean integration had undermined the project's effectiveness.[57]

In September 2013, the member states' Ministers of Foreign Affairs adopted the working group's recommendations. They authorized the drafting of a protocol to eliminate the Andean Parliament and created a High Level Group comprising Deputy Foreign Ministers and Deputy Ministers of Trade, coordinated by the Secretariat. Appended to this decision was the working group's "new vision" and a set of slides from a presentation by Ecuador's Foreign Ministry. The slides suggested four areas where the Community's competence should be rescinded—the CET, the negotiation of commercial relationships with non-Andean countries, corruption, and initiatives relating to municipal development.[58] With respect to the Andean Tribunal, the Foreign Ministry suggested modifying the ATJ Treaty with the goal

suba la calidad"); see also No hay Vuelta Atrás a la Aplicación de la Resolución 116, *ElComercio*, available at <http://www.elcomercio.com/actualidad/negocios/no-hay-vuelta-a-aplicacion.html>.

[55] Richard Espinosa, the Coordinating Secretary of Production, Employment and Competition, stated that the certificate system is a strategic move intended to foster domestic production. La Resolución 116 es Estratégica para Cambiar la Matriz Productive, *ElComercio*, available at <http://www.elcomercio.com/actualidad/negocios/resolucion-116-estrategica-cambiar-matriz.html>.

[56] *Decisión* 773, May 3, 2012, Article 1, at 2. The two consulting groups are the Economic Commission for Latin America and the Caribbean, a regional commission based in Santiago, Chile that works in conjunction with the United Nations, and the Getulio Vargas Foundation, a Brazilian think-tank that, according to its website, is "dedicated to promoting Brazil's economic and social development." <http://portal.fgv.br/en/about-1>.

[57] *Decisión* 792, September 19, 2013, 5–8. The recommendation regarding the ATJ is item "h" on page 7.

[58] Ibid., 15.

of "adapting [it] to the new needs and realities of the Andean integration process."[59] The Foreign Ministers instructed the High Level Group to consider these Ecuadorian recommendations "as input" in its decision-making.

In October 2014—in the midst of the General Secretariat's review and condemnation of Ecuador's COMEX regulations—the Andean Council of Foreign Ministers established a number of ad hoc committees to review twenty-seven different aspects of the Andean integration project.[60] These groups have continued to meet while the litigation against Ecuador has proceeded.

Challenges to Ecuador's currency safeguards

The COMEX certification scheme soon proved insufficient to stabilize Ecuador's financial crisis. In January 2015, Peru and Colombia devalued their respective currencies, leading Ecuador to impose safeguards on thousands of imports from both countries. Ecuador justified these levies as "temporary corrective measures" under Article 98 of the Cartagena Agreement, which creates a procedure for the Secretariat to review and authorize remedies for competitive shocks caused by currency devaluations.[61] One month later, the Secretariat admonished Ecuador's government for applying the safeguards without prior approval, and it rejected the safeguards because the government had failed to prove that the currency devaluations caused what were in any event only modest changes in the terms of trade with the two Andean countries.[62]

The Secretariat's decision incensed the government, which initially sought a reconsideration of its ruling. Ecuadorian officials were deeply annoyed that the other member states and Andean officials refused to acknowledge the severe economic difficulties their country faced due to the strong dollar and the low price of oil. Shortly after the Secretariat issued the ruling, President Correa openly speculated about leaving the Andean Community, which he suggested "serves very little" purpose.[63]

Challenges to Ecuador's balance of payments safeguards

As the country's financial crisis deepened, the government shifted tactics. It abandoned the currency safeguards[64] and notified the Secretariat that it would impose a

[59] Ibid., 18. [60] *Decisión* 797 (October 14, 2014).

[61] Rebecca Moral, Imports, Investments on Chopping Block in Ecuador: Trade Partners, Consumers Feel Brunt of Austerity Plan, *PanAm Post* (January 6, 2015), available at <https://panampost.com/rebeca-morla/2015/01/06/imports-investments-on-the-chopping-block-in-ecuador/>.

[62] *Resolución* 1762 (February 6, 2015).

[63] M. Lerner, Ecuador Considers Leaving Trade Bloc Amidst Currency Dispute, *Blouin News Blogs* (February 12, 2015), available at <http://blogs.blouinnews.com/blouinbeatbusiness/2015/02/12/ecuador-considers-leaving-trade-bloc-amidst-currency-disputes/>.

[64] Ecuador Lifts Tariffs on Peruvian and Colombian Imported Goods Following Pressure from the Community of Andean Nations, *Cuenca High Life*, available at <https://www.cuencahighlife.com/ecuador-lifts-new-tariffs-on-peruvian-and-colombia-goods-following-pressure-from-the-community-of-andean-nations/>.

more extensive set of safeguards to restore its global balance of payments. This time, Ecuador suggested that the safeguards were provisional and it requested permission to impose the restrictions.[65] A different safeguards provision in Andean law allows a member state to adopt "measures to correct the imbalance of its global balance of payments" if the measures are found to be temporary and nondiscriminatory.[66]

Over the objections of Peru and Colombia, the Secretariat approved the balance of payments safeguards for one year. The approval came two months after the initial application, thus three months after the Secretariat's disapproval of the currency measures. In defending its decision, the Secretariat noted that the safeguards were proportional in size (applying to 30% of Ecuador's imports) and in geographic scope. Colombian and Peruvian products comprised only 10% and 4%, respectively, of the targeted goods, whereas the safeguards also applied to 35% of Chinese imports, 14% of US imports, and 9% of EU imports.[67] The Secretariat thus accepted Ecuador's claim that the balance of payments crisis justified a temporary trade-restrictive response. Peru and Colombia filed annulment proceedings challenging the Secretariat's authorization, which remain on the ATJ's docket.[68]

The global orientation of the new safeguards helped Ecuador to defend the measures before the General Secretariat. But this same orientation also gave rise to a WTO complaint. The WTO Committee on Balance of Payments Restrictions met in June and October 2015 to review the surcharges. At the latter meeting, Ecuador announced that it would end the surcharges by June 2016.[69] In April 2016, however, Ecuador notified the WTO that it would delay compliance until April 2017, explaining that "the prevailing macroeconomic conditions show a severe deterioration in the balance of payments which the country has been unable to resolve fully." Urgent humanitarian and economic needs created by a powerful recent earthquake in Ecuador provided a further justification for delay.[70]

The state of play as at the end of 2016

As the next section explains, the situation in the Andes is entering an even more difficult period of political and economic turbulence. It is thus unsurprising

[65] WTO News Item, WTO Members Consult with Ecuador on its Import Surcharges Imposed on Balance-of-payment Grounds (June 29–30, 2015), available at <https://www.wto.org/english/news_e/news15_e/bop_29jun15_e.htm>.

[66] *Decisión* 389, expanding on Article 95 of the Cartagena Agreement. See especially Article 1.

[67] General Secretariat *Resolución* 1784 (June 2, 2015) authorized Ecuador's safeguards for a period of one year beginning on March 11, 2015, the date that Ecuador adopted the safeguards. Trade import figures appear on page 54.

[68] ATJ Nullification Proceedings 0003-AN-2015 and 0004-AN-2015.

[69] WTO News Iitem, Ecuador Starts Phasing Out Import Surcharge (February 17, 2016), available at <https://www.wto.org/english/news_e/news16_e/bop_17feb16_e.htm>.

[70] Communication from Ecuador to the Chairman of the Committee on Balance of Payment Restrictions WTBOP/G/24 (May 4, 2016). WTO review of balance of payments safeguards tends to be fairly pro-forma, and safeguards are generally not challenged in the WTO dispute settlement system. See F. Roessler, *The Legal Structure, Functions and Limits of the World Trade Order: A Collection of Essays*. London: Cameron May, 2000, 171–3.

that the legal challenges to Ecuador's trade-restrictive measures also remain in flux. A recent report by the ATJ notes that ten noncompliance and five nullification suits were filed in 2015.[71] As of late 2016, the Tribunal had yet to issue noncompliance or nullification rulings in these cases. Unless the suits are withdrawn or settled, it seems plausible that the ATJ will find at least some of Ecuador's measures contrary to Andean law. Even if the Tribunal upholds the Colombian and Peruvian challenges to the Secretariat's decisions, and even if it rejects Ecuador's appeal of the Secretariat's COMEX rulings, Correa will have succeeded in buying several months of balance-of-payments relief. If Ecuador loses one or more of the suits, however, Correa may well openly flout the ATJ and perhaps escalate the conflict by pursuing his threat to withdraw from the Andean Community.

How the Andean Legal System Channels Responses to Systemic Noncompliance

The filing of these noncompliance and nullification suits and Ecuador's participation in the litigation suggests that firms, business associations, governments, and the Andean Secretariat all recognize the ATJ's de jure authority, and have some faith in the Andean legal system's ability to fairly adjudicate the cases. But is it wise to encourage supranational adjudication of these sorts of high politics disputes? During the COMEX litigation, Ecuador justified its more favorable treatment of European products by implicitly questioning the competence and trustworthiness of the Peruvian and Colombian regulatory systems to ensure the safety and quality of their exports. During the safeguards litigation, Colombia and Peru raised numerous procedural and legal arguments against Ecuador's emergency measures, suggesting that they had no sympathy for the very real economic problems that Ecuador is facing.

In principle, there were three plausible responses to Ecuador's measures: ignore them, bring them within the system via a politically sanctioned derogation, or confront them as violations. As we now explain, the strengthening of the Andean legal system during the Washington Consensus period has combined with the current ideological dissensus among the member states to take the first two options off the table. This leaves confrontation, a response that creates grave and foreseeable risks to the Community's future.

Under the Andean legal system's original design, the Secretariat most likely would have ignored the complaints against Ecuador's trade measures.[72] Ignoring violations seems to be the strategy of choice for MERCOSUR. Indeed, when Argentina

[71] See *Tribunal de Justicia de la Comunidad Andina, Informe de Labores Gestión* 2015, 69.

[72] As we explain in Chapter 2, during the developmentalist period, only member states could initiate noncompliance suits, and the *Junta* did not bring those suits to the Tribunal if it could not resolve a dispute diplomatically.

adopted trade-restricting legislation that was very similar to Ecuador's COMEX regulations, none of the other MERCOSUR member states challenged the legislation before MERCOSUR's Permanent Tribunal.[73]

After the reforms of the 1996 Cochabamba Protocol, however, the Secretariat can sit on a noncompliance case for at most two months; thereafter, complaining private actors and governments can challenge the Secretariat's inaction before the ATJ.[74] This institutional structure creates an incentive for the Secretariat to act, since the Tribunal's review of the dispute on the merits is all but inevitable. In fact, the Secretariat did not shy away from investigating and condemning the COMEX suits against Ecuador or from quickly reviewing both of the country's safeguards measures.

A second way to avoid the conflict would have been for member states to grant Ecuador a derogation from Andean free trade rules. As Chapter 6 explains, precedent exists for this approach: the member states' political decision to grant Peru multi-year exemptions from Andean free trade rules to enable President Alberto Fujimori to carry out his economic program of neoliberal shock therapy. Creating a similar derogation for Ecuador to mitigate the severe economic pain of the country's dollarized economy and the slump in oil prices could have provided a politically sanctioned exit within the system that would have mooted the noncompliance suits and legalized Ecuador's actions. When we asked why the member states had not granted a similar derogation for Ecuador, we were told that the government had not requested an exemption.

With these two options effectively off the table, the only alternative was confrontation, which in the short term led to legal condemnations by the General Secretariat and in the longer term may lead to definitive ATJ noncompliance judgments condemning one or more of the Ecuadorian trade measures. This result risks a collision course that may lead Correa to ramp up his opposition to the Andean Community, to undermine or even dismantle its institutions, or to replace them with more politically malleable regional alternatives.

It is possible, however, that national and regional politics will intervene before the ATJ issues definitive rulings. In November 2015, Correa announced that he will not seek reelection in 2017 (although news reports suggest that he is maneuvering to control the government from behind the scenes).[75] In February 2016, Bolivian voters rejected President Morales' bid to change the constitution to allow

[73] Argentina's restrictions are also designed to protect a fragile dollar liquidity. See Argentina's current import restrictions forecasted to continue during 2015, *Merco Press* (January 28, 2015), available at <http://en.mercopress.com/2015/01/28/argentina-s-current-import-restrictions-forecasted-to-continue-during-2015>. This legislation was recently condemned by the WTO Appellate Body in response to a suit by the EU, Japan, and the United States. See WTO Appellate Body condemns Argentina's import restrictions (January 15, 2015), available at <http://trade.ec.europa.eu/doclib/press/index.cfm?id=1235>.

[74] These reforms also granted private litigants the right to raise and pursue noncompliance cases. Articles 24 and 25 of the Revised ATJ Treaty.

[75] Ecuador: Wily Correa, *The Economist* (November 21, 2015), available at <http://www.economist.com/news/americas/21678835-even-if-he-does-not-stand-re-election-president-may-still-run-country-wily-correa>.

him to run for a fourth term.[76] In addition, the defeat of Argentina's President Cristina Fernández de Kirchner in November 2015 and the explosive impeachment trial and corruption investigations unfolding in Brazil in 2016 cast grave doubt not only on the future of UNASUR but the very survival of leftist-populist regimes in Latin America. The situation took a further turn for the worse as 2016 was coming to a close. Venezuela faces a disastrous economic and social crisis that continues to deepen since the 2013 death of Hugo Chavez, and Brazil's political system teeters on the brink of collapse.[77]

The political and economic landscape in the two neoliberal-leaning Andean member states is less volatile, but the prospects for creating a neoliberal alternative to the Community now appear increasingly unlikely. The election of President Trump in the United States has undermined propects for the TPP and the Pacific Alliance, and the near-revolutionary unrest in several Latin American countries makes it highly unlikely that an global or regional financial organization will push for economic austerity that a return to neoliberalism implies.

Given this unpredictable climate, the ATJ would be advised to defer ruling on the Ecuadorian suits until the political winds have shifted. Such an approach would not only avoid a direct confrontation with Ecuador but also prevent the Tribunal from issuing a judgment that could exacerbate the schism among the member states and perhaps trigger the collapse of the Community. Although the situation remains in flux, it is not too early to consider what the events of the crisis period suggest about the ATJ's authority and power.

Conclusion: Reflections on the Power of the ATJ in the Andean Legal System

This chapter has demonstrated that the ATJ's narrow, intermediate, and extensive authority within the intellectual property island remains resilient. More surprisingly, we have also shown that the Tribunal has solidified and expanded its de facto authority within this island during the current crisis period. We emphasize, however, that these expansions are modest. Overall, the Andean Community has mostly failed to achieve its broader economic integration objectives.

Viewing the Andean legal system in a wider perspective reveals that the ATJ's authority and power are inextricably linked to the fate of the regional integration project as a whole. The ATJ's de facto authority depends on support of national governments, substate actors such as IP administrative agencies, or both. Within the IP island, firms, lawyers, agency officials, and national judges support Andean IP law as interpreted by the ATJ. When Andean governments issued decrees that

[76] Bolivian voters reject fourth term for Morales, *BBC News* (February 24, 2016), available at <http://www.bbc.com/news/world-latin-america-35647852>.

[77] M. O'Brien, Venezuela is on the Brink of a Complete Economic Collapse, *Washington Post* (January 29, 2016); S. Romerodec, Who's Taping Whom? Paranoia Infuses Brazil's Scandal-Ridden Politics, *New York Times* (December 2, 2016); N. Casey, Hungary Venezuelans Flee in Boats to Escape Economic Collapse, *New York Times* (November 25, 2016).

diverged from Andean IP law, IP stakeholders filed suits to challenge them. When administrative agencies took the side of the ATJ in these disputes, the governments backed down. The support of domestic agencies in these cases translated de facto authority into a source of political power for the Tribunal—albeit within a confined policy space.

The problem arises when the ATJ has the support of neither substate actors nor governments. This is the situation the Tribunal now faces. Member states have not shied away from retrenching the Andean integration process. They abrogated the Andean Parliament and renounced the goal of a Common External Tariff (but have retained harmonized customs procedures for intra-regional trade). The ATJ navigates this difficult territory by enforcing the letter of the law. In the data protection suit, Andean legislation was ambiguous and Community actors disagreed as to its meaning. Following the Tribunal's ruling and seizing on a moment when Bolivia and Venezuela could not vote, Colombian officials reimposed their preferred interpretation of the relevant *Decisión*. With respect to Andean pesticides legislation, the ATJ's insistence that states respect Andean legal rules led to changes in regional rules to give greater discretion to the member states.

The current disputes involving Ecuador are in a different category. Ecuador's policies are at odds with core principles of the common market, including the extension of national and most-favored-nation treatment to goods within the region, and the requirement to seek Secretariat authorization before imposing temporary safeguards. Yet it is also true that Ecuador faces grave economic problems. The Secretariat is trying to find a legal compromise, but Peruvian and Colombian economic actors remain unhappy with some of its rulings.

The fact that major political disputes are resolved via the Andean Community's established legal processes suggests that the ATJ and the Secretariat exert real power—albeit to a limited degree. Ecuador has participated fully in the litigation and provided a wealth of economic and policy information to support its actions. The Secretariat's rulings are based on a deep analysis of law and fact, allowing for a nuanced and substantive review of the issues at stake. In addition, even heated objections to Ecuador's actions have not triggered unauthorized retaliation by Peru or Colombia.

At the same time, Ecuador does not appear to be greatly constrained by common market rules and or the Community's longer-term aspirations. Ironically, the relative effectiveness of the region's legal system may actually be exacerbating the conflict, propelling efforts to cut back on Andean rules and Andean institutions.[78]

Ran Hirschl warns that judicializing controversies of high political significance will inevitably politicize courts and the legal process in general.[79] We see

[78] For more on how international litigation can exacerbate conflict, see K.J. Alter, Resolving or Exacerbating Disputes? The WTO's New Dispute Resolution System. *International Affairs* 2003, 79 (4): 783–800.

[79] R. Hirschl, The Judicialization of Mega-Politics and the Rise of Political Courts. *Annual Review of Political Science* 2008, 11: 93–118.

this politicization in the debate over merging the Andean Community with MERCOSUR. The drive for a merger is not inspired by economic gains from a larger regional market. Rather, the chief attraction of UNASUR is the prospect of weaker and more politically malleable regional institutions, including institutions involved in dispute settlement. Embedding adjudication into this wider and shifting political context reveals that the ATJ's de facto authority and power are more fragile than is suggested by an examination of its formal legal architecture, a quantitative assessment of its judicial output, or a doctrinal analysis of its decisions.

Many consider the International Monetary Fund to be a powerful institution because it can force governments to adopt painful and highly unpopular economic policies. The Andean Community is clearly not this powerful. Ecuador's government would rather violate Andean law than compromise on domestic policies that it sees as necessary for the country's economic health and development. Perhaps, in a democracy, this is how it should be.

Ecuador is facing major economic uncertainty. In this context, the government is unlikely to be focused on the Andean Community because trade with Andean neighbors is not very significant. By contrast, Ecuador remains constrained by its dependence on trade beyond the region and its need to borrow capital from foreign lenders. For now, President Correa is mostly following Andean legal procedures, if only because violations of Andean rules are packaged together with violations of WTO rules, and Ecuador cannot afford to antagonize its major trading partners, all of which are WTO members. So long as Andean laws and procedures are not more demanding than those of the WTO, and Andean officials are willing to authorize derogations from common market rules when given plausible reasons to do so, adhering to the Andean legal system is not too onerous, even for a recalcitrant government.

Stepping back to a comparative perspective, it is worth pointing out a few features specific to the Andean context that will guide the ATJ as it considers how to proceed. The Andean Community has only four member states. This small number, the low political salience of Andean integration, and strong presidential systems in each country make changing Andean legal rules relatively easy. In other words, the Andean Community is not like the WTO or the EU, where it is nearly impossible to renegotiate legal rules or the revise the institutional architecture every time an international court issues an interpretation that one or two countries dislike.

How do these insights help us to assess the ATJ's authority and power? The Tribunal exercises de facto as well as de jure authority where it can count on the support of substate interlocutors to enforce or voluntarily embrace its rulings. Where there is a transnational consensus in favor of international adjudication among these actors, as exists for intellectual property, the ATJ can exercise narrow, intermediate, and extensive authority. It can even exercise political power within a confined policy domain, casting a shadow over national policies and international negotiations.

For most areas regulated by Andean law, however, the ATJ lacks such compliance partners, and the most it can hope to do is push states toward following procedures that are not especially constraining. In fact, where member states are ideologically divided, strict enforcement of Andean law can be counterproductive, exacerbating underlying political and economic disputes. These are treacherous waters for the Andean judges to navigate. Thus far, they have managed to avoid meaningful backlashes by relying on the support of the IP community, support that raises the costs of a decision to abandon the ATJ or mount a fundamental challenge to its rulings.

PART III

RECONSIDERING INTERNATIONAL ADJUDICATION IN EUROPE IN LIGHT OF THE ANDEAN EXPERIENCE

8

Nature or Nurture? Judicial Lawmaking in the European Court of Justice and the Andean Tribunal of Justice

One often hears concerns that international judges may run amok, actively expanding international law in ways not explicitly based on state consent. There is a lot more rhetoric than reality to these concerns. In practice, all judges make law. Indeed, a key reason that states delegate authority to international adjudicators is because governments know that agreements are incomplete and that legal commitments will need to be interpreted and gaps filled in.[1] Yet some international courts and tribunals extend international legal rules in ways that constrain national sovereignty beyond what states intended. For governments and commentators concerned with such expansive judicial lawmaking, the European Court of Justice (ECJ) represents this problem in the extreme.

Decades of ECJ rulings transformed the Treaty of Rome into a de facto constitution of the European Community (EC).[2] The ECJ achieved this remarkable result by expanding the reach and scope of EC law and by enabling litigants to use the European legal system to promote key objectives. For example, the ECJ has condemned Germany's exclusion of women from combat-related military roles, Ireland's censoring of a student brochure about abortion clinics in Britain, and the EU's implementation of a United Nations program freezing the assets of alleged terrorists.[3] Proponents of effective international adjudication see the ECJ as an exemplar for other international courts.[4] Those dedicated to maintaining state sovereignty, by contrast, criticize the ECJ as riding roughshod over national

[1] D. Hawkins, D. Neilson, M.J. Tierney, and D.A. Lake, *Delegation and Agency in International Organizations*. Cambridge: Cambridge University Press, 2006, 17.

[2] E. Stein, Lawyers, Judges and the Making of a Transnational Constitution. *American Journal of International Law* 1981, 75 (1): 1–27; T. Hartley, *Constitutional Problems of the European Union*. Oxford: Hart Publishing, 1996; J. Weiler, The Transformation of Europe. *Yale Law Journal* 1991, 100 (8): 2403–83.

[3] ECJ Case 159/90, *Society for the Protection of Unborn Children Ireland v. Grogan* [1991] ECR 4685. ECJ Case C-285/98, *Tanja Kreil v. Bundesrepublik Deutschland* [2000] ECR I-69. ECJ Joined Cases C-402/05P & C-415/05P, *Kadi and Al Barakaat International Foundation v. Council* [2008] CMLR 41 [2008].

[4] L.R. Helfer and A.-M. Slaughter, Toward a Theory of Effective Supranational Adjudication. *Yale Law Journal* 1997, 107 (2): 273–391.

autonomy,[5] suggesting a cautionary lesson in why states should avoid creating independent international courts.

This chapter revisits the history and early decisions of the ECJ to explore how context shapes international judicial lawmaking. We do so by comparing the ECJ with its Andean counterpart, the Andean Tribunal of Justice (ATJ or Tribunal). Chapter 2 of this book explains the structural similarity of the ECJ and the ATJ. The two courts have nearly identical designs; they were both tasked with interpreting very similar framework agreements; and they were created to help further ambitious regional integration projects. Although there are important differences between the two judicial bodies—differences that we explore in other chapters in this book—the many legal and structural parallels allow us to examine how context shapes the behavior of similarly designed institutions with similar mandates.

We focus on the strikingly more modest judicial lawmaking of the ATJ as compared to that of the ECJ. The Tribunal has incorporated the key ECJ doctrines of the supremacy and direct effect of Community law. But unlike the ECJ, the ATJ overwhelmingly respects the discretion that Andean law leaves to state actors. Even when provided with opportunities to adopt broad legal rulings, the ATJ generally adheres to formalist interpretive techniques and refrains from expanding its own authority or the reach of Andean rules in ways that constrain national sovereignty.[6]

The ECJ/ATJ's comparison reminds one of the "nature" versus "nurture" debate in child rearing. Is it the genes or the environment that shapes how an actor develops? Most international relations and international law scholars favor the nature side of this debate. They assume that judges are hardwired to increase their power. It is only limited opportunities or the fear of being sanctioned that inhibits judges' natural tendency to expand their authority. By contrast, nurture-based explanations assume that international courts typically apply the law in fairly straightforward and circumscribed ways. Expansionist lawmaking—which we define as judicial decisions that broaden the reach or scope of international law at the expense of national political discretion—requires, according to this view, special care and encouragement.

We investigate the relative influences of nature versus nurture by comparing the first twenty-five years of ATJ and ECJ decisions, periods when the regional organizations that created both courts had smaller memberships, nascent supranational institutions, and lower trade volumes.[7] We study lawmaking in different time periods, exploring how state support for integration interacts with a court's penchant

5 E.A. Posner and J.C. Yoo, A Theory of International Adjudication. *California Law Review* 2005, 93 (1): 1–72; H. Rasmussen, *On Law and Policy in the European Court of Justice*. Dordrecht: Martinus Nijhoff Publishers, 1986; Lord Denning, Introduction to *The European Court of Justice: Judges or Policy Makers?* London: Bruge Group Publication, 1990.

6 We recognize that judges can use formalist or textualist interpretive techniques to expand the meaning and scope of law in ways that constrain national sovereignty and government discretion. Our essential point is that the ATJ uses formalist interpretations as a judicial strategy to build support for its rulings, and, in addition, that the Tribunal eschews expansionist lawmaking by strictly adhering to the letter of Andean legal texts and by allowing member states to define the pace and scope of regional integration.

7 For additional details, see Chapter 1.

for judicial lawmaking. We show that the ATJ has generally refrained from the sort of expansionist lawmaking that is the hallmark of its European cousin, and we offer a new explanation of why the ECJ has engaged in that practice.

Our analysis of the divergence of expansionist lawmaking has three wider implications. First, we call into question the notion that international judges are power-seeking by nature. This assumption lies at the heart of international relations theories that focus on how specific judicial design features facilitate or hinder expansionist lawmaking. Our analysis of two nearly identically structured regional tribunals suggests that scholars have placed too much emphasis on formal institutional design and state control of judges.

Second, we argue that international courts are more likely to be expansionist where substate and societal interlocutors—government officials, national judiciaries, advocacy networks, administrative agencies, or the public more generally—encourage lawmaking and facilitate compliance with judicial rulings. In emphasizing the preferences of these actors, we implicitly reject the dominant international relations approach that views the preferences of states as the primary factor shaping decision-making by international judges.

A third broad policy implication of our analysis is that politically independent international courts can, contrary to sovereigntists' fears, be active but not activist, interpreting and completing international contracts while avoiding expansive judicial lawmaking that significantly narrows state discretion.

This chapter is organized as follows. The first sections define expansionist international judicial lawmaking, situate our analysis in existing scholarship, and briefly recap Chapter 2's explanation of how the ECJ and ATJ are nearly identically designed institutions. We then document key trends in ATJ decision-making across time, creating three time periods characterized by varying levels of elite and popular support for regional integration. This temporal analysis reveals that while the Tribunal has copied several key ECJ doctrines, Andean judges, unlike their European counterparts, are generally deferential to governments except in the domain of intellectual property (IP) law. Next, we draw on seven years of additional data since the publication of an earlier version of this chapter to assess whether a number of recent ATJ rulings have sown the seeds for future expansionist lawmaking. The chapter concludes by considering and rejecting several claims that international courts are expansionist-by-nature, setting the stage for a discussion in Chapter 9 of nurture-based theories of expansionist lawmaking.

Theories of Expansionist Judicial Lawmaking by International Courts

Judging often involves lawmaking.[8] When faced with controversies involving indeterminate rules, judges must interpret those rules to resolve the parties' disputes.

[8] M. Shapiro, *Courts: A Comparative Political Analysis*. Chicago, IL: University of Chicago Press, 1981, 29.

Most lawmaking by international courts fills gaps in existing legal rules, or, using the terminology of rational choice, completes incomplete contracts. Our focus, however, is on expansionist judicial lawmaking, which we define as occurring when international courts identify new legal obligations or constraints not found in treaty texts nor supported by the intentions of their drafters, and when these obligations or constraints narrow states' discretion. Typically, expansionist lawmaking significantly broadens the substantive reach of international law and asserts the court's competence to interpret that law.[9] We do not include in this definition a requirement that international judges rule against governments. Courts can expand international law without ruling against governments; conversely, they can rule against governments without expanding international law.

Most international relations theories begin from the premise that judges are power-seeking by nature, using empowerment to explain why international courts expand judicial authority at the expense of state discretion. This assumption also underpins most claims about how institutional design contributes to expansionist lawmaking.

There are two variants of these expansionist-by-nature theories. One group of scholars focuses on how access rules shape opportunities to litigate, and thereby opportunities for expansionist lawmaking. Posner and Yoo claim that where states must consent to submit disputes to international adjudication, courts will strive to make their rulings politically palatable to governments. By contrast, international courts that do not require state consent to hear a particular dispute (that is, tribunals with compulsory jurisdiction) and those that allow private parties to initiate litigation are more independent and therefore more likely to issue expansionist rulings that displease states.[10] Other scholars concur that compulsory jurisdiction and private access lead to more active and independent courts that are more likely to expand the reach and scope of international law.[11] For example, Keohane, Moravcsik, and Slaughter argue that "transnational dispute resolution seems to have an inherently more expansionary character." They note that "a steady flow of cases … allows a court to become an actor on the legal and political stage," and that "a court gains political capital from a growing caseload by demonstrably performing a needed function."[12]

A second set of scholars focuses on the tools states use to thwart expansionist lawmaking. Building on the insights of principal-agent theory, these scholars argue that international courts are less expansionist where states can easily revise

[9] This definition differs slightly from Steinberg, who focuses on judicial lawmaking by the WTO Appellate Body, R.H. Steinberg, Judicial Lawmaking at the WTO: Discursive, Constitutional and Political Constraints. *American Journal of International Law* 2004, 98 (2): 250–7.

[10] Posner and Yoo, 2005, 6–7.

[11] R. Keohane, A. Moravcsik, and A.-M. Slaughter, Legalized Dispute Resolution: Interstate and Transnational. *International Organization* 2000, 54 (3): 457–88; Helfer and Slaughter, 1997; D. Hawkins and W. Jacoby, Agent Permeability, Principal Delegation and the European Court of Human Rights. *The Review of International Organizations* 2008, 3 (1): 1–28.

[12] Keohane, Moravcsik, and Slaughter, 2000, 459, 482.

international rules, where judicial terms are short or subject to reappointment, and where design features allow states to punish judges for decisions that political leaders dislike.[13] According to this view, judicial lawmaking should increase with the number of parties to an agreement and the difficulty of amending the treaty or overruling judges, and decrease with the ease of exit from the regime.[14]

This book's comparison of the ECJ and ATJ holds international court design features constant, allowing us to explore how environmental factors and political context shapes judicial behavior. As we explain in Chapter 2, Andean governments replicated most aspects of the ECJ's design, hoping to copy its success in enhancing respect for Community rules. The ATJ's founders were aware of the ECJ's history of expansionist lawmaking, and they embraced some of the resulting legal doctrines. Although neither the Cartagena Agreement nor the treaty establishing the ATJ explicitly stated that Andean law has direct effect in national legal systems or that it is supreme to national law, negotiators accepted that the Andean legal system would replicate these judge-made EC doctrines. However, the drafters also sought to curtail the ATJ's expansionist lawmaking by allowing only member states to bring noncompliance complaints, and by explicitly stating that the Tribunal could not delve into the facts of preliminary rulings. The ATJ's faithful respect of these limitations contributed to the dearth of cases in its early years. In 1996, member states relaxed both these restrictions, so that after 1996, the ATJ resembles the ECJ's design even more closely.

As Chapters 1 and 2 of this book explain, the ECJ and the ATJ provide the same mechanisms for challenging government behavior that conflicts with Community rules. Both systems contain a noncompliance procedure that enables private actors and member states to inform the Community secretariats about rule violations. The secretariats investigate the alleged violation, and, if necessary, file noncompliance complaints with the ECJ/ATJ. Both systems also contain a preliminary ruling mechanism in which private actors invoke Community law in domestic litigation and national judges refer questions of interpretation to the regional court. National judges then apply the ECJ/ATJ ruling to the case at hand. In both systems, sanctions can be imposed if a state fails to comply with the court's ruling.[15] As of 1996, the Andean system has one feature the ECJ lacks: if the Secretariat refuses to pursue a noncompliance suit, a private actor can bring the suit directly to the ATJ.

[13] G. Tsebelis and G. Garrett, The Institutional Foundations of Intergovernmentalism and Supranationalism in the European Union. *International Organization* 2001, 55 (2): 357–90; R. Vaubel, Principal-Agent Problems in International Organizations. *Review of International Organizations* 2006, 1 (2): 125–38; P.B. Stephan, Courts, Tribunals and Legal Unification—The Agency Problem. *Chicago Journal of International Law* 2002 (3): 333–52.

[14] T. Ginsburg, Bounded Discretion in International Judicial Lawmaking. *Virginia Journal of International Law* 2005, 43 (3): 631–73. Steinberg (2004) offers a more nuanced version of this argument, suggesting that the WTO Appellate Body considers how its rulings will affect the attitudes of WTO member states.

[15] The Andean legal system has always allowed for retaliatory sanctions (Article 25 of the Original ATJ Treaty; Articles 27 and 30 of the Revised ATJ Treaty). In 1989—after the period of time we study—the EC added a system of fines for noncompliance with ECJ rulings. See J. Tallberg, *European Governance and Supranational Institutions: Making States Comply*. London: Routledge, 2003, 73–84.

Although the Andean Pact and the EC initially had different substantive goals,[16] the Cartagena Agreement contained the same key elements in the Treaty of Rome that the European judges used to expand the legal reach of EC law and the ECJ's central role adjudicating the line between state and supranational legal authority. Both treaties prohibit member states from creating new barriers to trade, require national treatment for products from other member states, and allow supranational bodies to adopt directly applicable secondary legislation.[17]

Both regional systems also provide governments with the same formal opportunities to sanction expansionist lawmaking: judges are appointed to fixed, renewable terms;[18] member states can redefine each court's jurisdiction by unanimously amending its founding charter;[19] and they may in theory withdraw from both Communities.[20] As a practical matter, exit has been—at least until very recently—highly unlikely in Europe, whereas Chile and Venezuela have exited from the Andean regime (for reasons unrelated to the ATJ). Notwithstanding these nearly identical design features, the ATJ, unlike the ECJ, has not become an expansionist lawmaker.

The literature on international judicial lawmaking overwhelmingly reflects the prevalence of nature-based assumptions and the tendency of scholars to theorize from a US and Euro-centric perspective. There continues to be a dearth of scholarship on whether judicial behavior differs in fundamental ways in developing country contexts. Although revising Community law and unilaterally exiting the Community are easier in the Andes than in Europe, these two features are insufficient to explain the ATJ's more circumscribed judicial lawmaking. Instead, the ATJ's more circumspect approach reflects an understanding of the political realities that Andean judges face given the greater economic and political turbulence in the region. Chapter 10, the book's conclusion, revisits this issue and offers a broader assessment of how international courts operate in developing country contexts. We suggest that a more targeted and circumspect approach to lawmaking may aid the survival of international judges who regularly face apathy, or even open hostility, from the governments that appear before them.

[16] The Andean Pact was focused on building regional industrial programs to replace reliance on imports. With this goal in mind, the Pact's secondary legislation controversially regulated foreign investment and the transfer of intellectual property and technical knowledge to Andean countries.

[17] In the Andes, revisions to secondary legislation require the support of all member states; in Europe, unanimity was required during the period we investigate. As of 1989, some secondary EC legislation can be changed by a qualified majority vote.

[18] Andean judges serve six-year terms, as do their European equivalents. Whereas ECJ judges can be reappointed numerous times, ATJ judges can only be reappointed once. Judges on both courts can only be removed for serious misconduct. We are unaware of any attempt by states to remove an ATJ or ECJ judge.

[19] For the ECJ, member states amended the Consolidated Treaty on a European Union. For the Andean Tribunal, member states amended the Original ATJ Treaty. Both treaties have been revised to expand, rather than limit, each court's jurisdiction. On changes to the ATJ's jurisdiction, see Chapter 2.

[20] Hartley, 1999, 164–5.

Does Active Mean Activist? ECJ and ATJ Lawmaking Compared

This section compares ATJ and ECJ lawmaking over staggered twenty-five-year periods when each court was establishing its legal and political authority. Chapter 1 explains why our original study chose these time periods. Contrasting the ATJ's first twenty-five years of operation (1984–2007) to the ECJ's quarter-century in the common market (1958–83) allows us to place side by side periods when each court faced a similar challenge of defining its legal role in its respective Community. Similar too is the fact that member states were unsure during these years what they wanted each regional integration project to become. Our comparison with the ECJ ends in the mid-1980s, when EC member states recommitted to the goal of regional integration. Our analysis of the ATJ continues beyond 2007 to investigate the Tribunal's lawmaking during a decade of political and economic crisis in the Andes.

During time periods we compare, both regional courts were similarly active, with a steadily increasing diet of preliminary references. Between 1960 and 1985, the ECJ issued 305 noncompliance judgments and 1,808 preliminary rulings (an average of 86.1 cases per year), whereas the ATJ, with a geographically and demographically smaller region to oversee, issued 85 noncompliance judgments and 1,338 preliminary rulings between 1984 and 2007 (an average of 71.5 per year).[21] Notwithstanding the large number of cases, European and Andean governments were only weakly committed to economic and legal integration. Pro-integration litigants urged the courts to overcome these political impediments with teleological interpretations that furthered the treaties' integrationist goals. The ECJ responded eagerly to these entreaties by engaging in expansionist lawmaking, whereas the ATJ was more circumspect.[22]

We give greater attention to the ATJ, drawing on our coding of 1,338 ATJ preliminary rulings from the Tribunal's founding through 2007. Where the ATJ broke new legal ground, we analyze its decisions in depth. We focus on preliminary rulings because most ECJ lawmaking occurred in such rulings. However, we also consider a number of noncompliance decisions. Our analysis of the case law is supplemented by interviews with lawyers, judges, and government officials in Peru, Ecuador, and Colombia. Finally, we include a discussion of post-2007 developments based on seven additional years of case coding and follow-up interviews in the region.

Our account of ECJ lawmaking relies heavily on Joseph Weiler's seminal legal analysis, and on Anne-Marie Burley (now Slaughter) and Walter Mattli's political

[21] See Chapter 3 for a more detailed analysis of these patterns.

[22] Chapter 4 discusses the legal aspects of these doctrinal divergences in greater detail.

analysis, both of which argue that judges are power-seeking by nature.[23] Following Weiler, we group our study into time periods that correspond to varying levels of support for regional integration to capture the dynamics between political and legal integration.

The foundational period: The ATJ during the Andean Pact (1984–95)

For purposes of this chapter, we use the term "foundational period" to refer to the years when the ECJ/ATJ were defining for themselves, litigants, national judges, Community bodies, and member states what their legal role would be within the context of their respective common markets. Weiler, who first used this label, noted that ECJ lawmaking was most expansive during the court's foundational period from 1962 to the mid-1970s. There was significant political turmoil in Europe during these years. Consumed by internal problems and divergent objectives, European governments seemingly turned away from supranationalism and the goal of building a common market.[24] Weiler argued that the ECJ responded to this political impasse by being remarkably activist, building through law what supporters of integration could not achieve through politics. In this period, the ECJ established the core doctrines of regional integration: the direct effect, supremacy, and pre-emption of Community law over national law, and the implied powers of supranational institutions.[25]

The ATJ's genesis shares some elements of the ECJ's experience, but not others. As in Europe, early on a handful of motivated litigants turned to the court to promote the objectives inscribed in the Cartagena Agreement.[26] The ATJ responded by following the ECJ's lead. The Tribunal's first preliminary ruling did not involve an actual or potential conflict between Andean and national law. Nevertheless, Andean judges used the case to declare the supremacy and preemptive power of Andean law (the direct effect of Andean law was assumed). It cited the ECJ's *Costa v. Enel* decision establishing the supremacy of European law and its *Simmenthal* ruling that obligated national courts to enforce the primacy of Community law.[27] The ECJ had framed its analysis in constitutional

[23] Weiler, 1991 at 2426; A.-M. Burley and W. Mattli, Europe before the Court. *International Organization* 1993, 47 (1): 41–76. Burley and Mattli cite Weiler as evidence for their empowerment thesis, and add that self-interested empowerment explains scholarly and national judicial support for ECJ expansionist lawmaking. Ibid., 63–5.

[24] S. Hoffmann, Obstinate or Obsolete? France, European Integration, and the Fate of the Nation-State. *Daedalus* 1966, 95 (3): 881–95.

[25] Weiler, 1991, 2445–50.

[26] The first ATJ case was raised by Germán Cavelier, who had served as Secretary General of Colombia's Ministry of Foreign Affairs in 1968 and 1969 when the Andean Pact was negotiated. According to attorneys in Cavelier's law firm, Cavelier viewed Andean integration and the ATJ as mechanisms to strengthen international law. Interview with two attorneys (J) of a Bogotá law firm.

[27] See ATJ Preliminary Ruling 1-IP-87 (points 2 and 3.5) (citing ECJ Case 6/64, *Costa v. Ente Nazionale per L'Energia Elettrica (Enel)*, [1964] ECR 585, [1964] CMLR 425 and ECJ Case 106/77, *Amministrazione delle Finanze dello Stato v. Simmenthal SpA (II)* (1978) ECR 629, [1978] CMLR 263, 283).

terms, boldly asserting that "the Community constitutes a new legal order of international law for the benefit of which the states have limited their sovereign rights."[28] The ATJ, however, stressed the functional necessity and implicit state support for supremacy.[29]

The ATJ's second preliminary ruling raised the question of what becomes of a national law that conflicts with Andean rules yet remains on the books. In *Simmenthal*, the ECJ had resolved this conflict with an unyielding rule: "Every national court must apply Community law in its entirety and ... must accordingly set aside any provision of national law which may conflict with it, whether prior or subsequent to the Community rule."[30] The ATJ, athough citing *Simmenthal*, ultimately interpreted Andean law more modestly as "firstly settl[ing] for [a rule of] preferential application." National law remains valid and on the books but it is not applied. The incompatible national law can be reactivated, however, if Andean law is later modified to remove the conflict.[31]

A comparison of the two courts' pre-emption doctrines provides another example of the ATJ's greater deference to state autonomy. Without any textual support in the Treaty of Rome, the ECJ asserted that in fields such as the common commercial policy, Community powers were exclusive and precluded member states from legislating regardless of whether their actions conflicted with Community law. In other areas regulated by European law, the ECJ concluded that member states could not legislate even where there is no EC rule on point. Not only do these rulings diminish state discretion, it is the ECJ that determines whether a particular EC rule or policy space is exclusive and pre-eminent.[32]

In striking contrast, the pre-emptive force of Andean law is far more modest. In an early ruling, the ATJ announced the principle of *complemento indispensable*: even in areas where Andean law clearly governs, member states may enact domestic laws necessary to implement a Community rule provided that the laws do not obstruct or nullify that rule.[33] Stated differently, whereas the ECJ both implied powers not explicitly delegated to the EC and asserted pre-emptive authority even where EC law was silent, the ATJ has not implied powers for the Andean Community, and it has held that states retain the power to legislate with the exception of national laws that directly conflict with extant Community rules.

[28] This famous quote is from the *Van Gend en Loos* decision, ECJ Case 26/62, [1963] ECR 1, 12. Commentators have stressed that the ECJ's constitutional framing was an important political move. See M.P. Maduro, *We the Court: The European Court of Justice and the European Economic Constitution*. Oxford: Hart Publishers, 1998, 8; A. Vauchez, Judge-Made Law. Aux Origines du Modèle Politique Communautaire (Retour Sur Van Gend en Loos et Costa c. Enel). In: *Une Europe des Élites? Réflexions sur la Fracture Démocratique de L'Union Européenne*. O. Costa and P. Magnette (eds), 139–66. Brussels: Presses de l'Université libre de Bruxelles, 2007b; Weiler, 1991, 2413–15.

[29] The Tribunal stated that supremacy "is the essential characteristic of Community Law and a basic requirement for building integration." The ATJ cited a 1980 declaration in which member states had agreed that "the legal system of the [Cartagena] Agreement prevails within the framework of its competences over national norms." ATJ Preliminary Ruling 1-IP-87, point 2.

[30] *Simmenthal* [1978] CMLR, 283.

[31] ATJ Preliminary Ruling 2-IP-88, point 2.

[32] On the ECJ's doctrine of implied powers, see Weiler, 1991, 2415–19.

[33] ATJ Preliminary Ruling 2-IP-88, point 3. For the subsequent development of this doctrine, see Chapter 4.

In a 1990 decision, the ATJ further cabined the pre-emption doctrine. Although citing the ECJ to reaffirm that Andean laws can displace national rules, the ATJ also stressed that integration is a gradual, incremental process that limits the extent to which Andean rules pre-empt national authority:

> Especially when dealing with complex and vast issues, such as intellectual property ... it seems logical that many of these diverse issues, even if they have to be a matter of common regulation in the beginning, are still within the competence of the national legislator for an indefinite time until they are effectively covered by Community norms.[34]

Other ATJ rulings during the foundational period exhibited even greater deference. Consider, for example, the multi-year *Reynolds Aluminum* dispute. The ATJ first dismissed the case in 1987 because private actors at the time lacked standing to raise noncompliance suits.[35] The case reappeared in 1990 as a preliminary ruling with facts strikingly similar to the ECJ's landmark *Van Gend en Loos* decision of 1962. As in *Van Gend en Loos*, the plaintiff claimed that the common market treaty created an immediate bar to increasing tariffs on imports from other member states. However, Andean governments had previously adopted, via secondary legislation, a Free Trade Programme that allowed broad exemptions from regional free trade rules. The plaintiff nevertheless argued that the Cartagena Agreement should be read as freezing existing tariffs for products exempted by the Programme. Colombia countered that the Free Trade Programme should be interpreted as effectively amending the treaty.[36] The ATJ sided with the government, ruling that member states had free reign to decide which products to include on the Free Trade Programme's list of exceptions.[37] The ECJ's *Van Gend en Loos* ruling made the Treaty of Rome a constitutional document that created immediately enforceable rights for private actors and higher-order legal obligations for governments. By contrast, the ATJ in effect interpreted the Cartagena Agreement not as a fixed constitutional charter but only as a starting point for integration, one that member states could amend fairly easily.[38]

The ATJ has also given more deference to national judges than its European counterpart. In a later iteration of the *Reynolds Aluminum* dispute, the Tribunal considered which of three potentially applicable legal regimes governed the dispute. The ATJ defined the obligations under each regime, one of which gave states complete control over certain products "as long as exception and reserve lists exist."[39]

34 ATJ Preliminary Ruling 2-IP-90, point 1.

35 ATJ Noncompliance Judgment 1-INCULP-1987. This early ruling used a the term "INCULP" that was replaced by AI (*Acciones de Inculpiementos*).

36 O. Saldías, Supranational Courts as Engines of Disintegration: The Case of the Andrean Community (Free University of Berlin Working Paper on European Integration No. 5, 2007, 12, available at <http://citeseerx.ist.psu.edu/viewdoc/download?doi=10.1.1.588.9948&rep=rep1&type=pdf>.

37 ATJ Preliminary Ruling 1-IP-90, conclusion point 1.

38 Another example is case ATJ Preliminary Ruling 5-IP-89, in which the ATJ allowed governments to determine whether to prohibit foreign ownership in certain economic sectors.

39 ATJ Preliminary Ruling 3-IP-93, point 2.

Rather than selecting the relevant rules from among the three options, however, the ATJ left that key question for national courts to answer.[40]

In striking contrast, the ECJ has a long tradition of reserving to itself the power to determine the scope of national exceptions to free trade rules.[41] The ECJ also directs national judges regarding the application of EC rules. ECJ Judge Federico Mancini acknowledged that the ECJ formally refrains from overstepping its authority to rule on whether a national law violates European law. However,

> having clarified the meaning of the relevant Community measure, the court usually indicated the extent to which a certain type of national legislation can be regarded as compatible with that measure. The national judge is thus led hand in hand as far as the door; crossing the threshold is his job, but now a job no harder than child's play.[42]

In contrast, as we explain in Chapter 2, Andean governments initially limited the ATJ from similarly guiding national courts on the application of preliminary rulings by instructing the Tribunal not to consider the facts of referred cases, and later providing that it could only consider the facts "when essential for the requested interpretation."[43]

There is thus some textual support for the ATJ's reticence, but the extent of its deference to national governments and judges is surprising. There were a number of ways that the ATJ could have used the *Reynolds Aluminum* cases to expand the reach and scope of Community law as well as to create a larger role for itself in overseeing the Andean legal system. The ATJ could have found that Andean industrial programs pre-empted national discretion; it could have declared the exemption list a part of Andean law and itself determined which goods were included on the list; or it could have allowed national judges to decide individual cases subject to well-defined Andean guidelines for determining the validity of government exemptions. Instead, the ATJ handed to national judges both the task of ascertaining which regime governed and whether a product was included on the list of exceptions, effectively removing itself from determining whether member states were complying with Andean free trade rules.

ATJ lawmaking during a period of political consensus: 1996–2005

Would the ATJ have become more of an expansionist lawmaker if there were greater political consensus among Andean member states over building a common market?

[40] ATJ Preliminary Ruling 3-IP-93, conclusions point 2: "It is for the [national court] to determine whether the product in question is part of the Free Trade Programme of the Cartagena Agreement, the *Nómina de Reserva* [which forms part of Andean industrial programs] or the list of exceptions of the member country."

[41] Maduro, 1998, 122–8; A. Stone Sweet, *The Judicial Construction of Europe*. Oxford: Oxford University Press, 2004.

[42] F. Mancini, The Making of a Constitution for Europe. *Common Market Law Review* 1989, 26 (4), 606.

[43] Revised ATJ Treaty, Article 34.

The ATJ faced just such an environment beginning in the mid-1990s, during what we label as the Washington Consensus Period. As we explain in Chapter 7, during the first decade of the Andean Pact's existence, actors both within and across the member states disagreed vehemently about the import substitution policy at the center of regional integration efforts. By the 1990s, the import substitution theory had come into disrepute. Andean governments decisively embraced the neoliberal Washington Consensus, adopting sweeping legislative and institutional reforms at the national and regional levels with the renewed goal of building a common market.[44]

In 1993, the Free Trade Zone became fully effective for Bolivia, Colombia, Ecuador, and Venezuela. In 1994, Andean countries agreed to create the Common External Tariff. In 1997, they adopted the Sucre Protocol, which resembled the EC's Single European Act in that it committed member states to finally complete the common market.[45] Member states also reformed Andean institutions, replacing the ineffectual *Junta* with a General Secretariat, increasing the size of the Secretariat's budget, and appointing a cadre of young lawyers eager to use those enhanced resources to promote regional integration.[46]

Andean integration still faced challenges, such as Peru's withdrawal from the Common External Tariff and its delay until 2003 in ratifying the Sucre Protocol, but using the Andean legal system to promote compliance with Andean rules was not among them. On the contrary, revisions of the Tribunal's jurisdiction in the 1996 Cochabamba Protocol suggested that member states wanted the ATJ to be more assertive in interpreting and enforcing Andean law.[47]

We observe a marked change around this time in ATJ rulings concerning Andean intellectual property law. New Andean secondary legislation (*Decisiones* 311, 313, and 344) revised the region's IP rules, which led to an increase in applications to register trademarks and patents with national IP agencies. Although detailed, the regional IP legislation contained ambiguous provisions and lacunae that the agencies and private litigants sought to clarify in numerous references to the ATJ.

As we explain in Chapter 5, Andean judges responded to these repeated requests by interpreting regional IP rules in ways not dictated by the texts of the *Decisiones*. Some of the Tribunal's rulings were relatively modest extensions of established legal principles. For example, the ATJ created judge-made doctrines concerning trademark coexistence agreements and pharmaceutical trademarks that instructed

[44] Y. Dezalay and B.G. Garth, From the Cold War to Kosovo: The Renewal of the Field of International Human Rights. *Annual Review of Law and Social Science* 2002b, 2: 231–55; J. Williamson, What Washington Means by Policy Reform. In: *Latin American Adjustment: How Much Has Happened.* In: J. Williamson (ed.), 5–20 Washington, DC: Institute for International Economics, 1990.

[45] T.A. O'Keefe, How the Andean Pact Transformed Itself into a Friend of Foreign Enterprise. *International Lawyer* 1996, 30 (4): 811–24. For example, the 1997 Sucre Protocol envisioned the phase out of all exceptions to the common market.

[46] Interviews with former official (B) of the General Secretariat Legal Advisor's Office.

[47] See the discussion of the Cochabamba Protocol and the Revised ATJ Treaty in Chapter 2.

agency officials to balance the private rights of IP owners against preventing consumer confusion and promoting public health.[48]

Other decisions were far bolder and substantially cabined government discretion. The first ATJ noncompliance ruling in 1996, which upheld a General Secretariat challenge to a bilateral agreement between Ecuador and the United States, provides an apt illustration. Adopted under pressure from the US pharmaceutical industry, the bilateral treaty protected drugs in the production "pipeline" before an Andean law recognizing patented medicines took effect.[49] Ecuador defended the agreement by citing a clause authorizing member states, "in their own domestic legislation or under international treaties, [to] strengthen the intellectual property rights provided for in this Decision."[50] The ATJ rejected Ecuador's reliance on this seemingly unambiguous text. It reasoned that Andean IP rules were "one of the fundamental pillars for economic harmonization" and "an essential instrument" to "promote well-balanced, harmonious, and equal development" in the region. It then adopted a teleological interpretation of the word "strengthen" that allowed member states to enhance—but not contradict—Andean rules and precluded them from invoking bilateral treaties "as a reason to validate noncompliance with a prior Community obligation."[51]

In the same year, the ATJ was equally bold in a case referred by the Colombian Constitutional Court concerning the relationship between Andean IP legislation and the Paris Convention—a multilateral patent and trademark treaty. In this ruling, the ATJ addressed the contested issue of national sovereignty. Whereas the ECJ found that EC member states had transferred entire domains of sovereign authority to the European level by ratifying the Treaty of Rome, the ATJ reasoned that Andean member states retained control over the pace and scope of the transfer via secondary legislation. The ATJ was unequivocal in stating that sovereignty had in fact been shifted to the Andean Community, but it also reasoned that the more extensive the secondary legislation at issue, the more the "exclusive authority of the member countries" had been "sovereignly transferred" to the Andean level. Turning to the case before it, the ATJ relied on the existence of extensive and detailed regional IP legislation to rule that significant national authority had been delegated to the Community in that domain. The ATJ then asserted its exclusive authority to interpret Andean IP rules and to define their relationship to IP treaties, making it clear that member states cannot deviate from "the common interests" of the Community except by acting together through Andean institutions.[52]

The ATJ extended this approach again in a 2001 judgment involving second-use patents, another intellectual property right sought by foreign pharmaceutical

[48] E.g., ATJ Preliminary Ruling 104-IP-2002 (holding that trademark coexistence agreements do not create an automatic basis for registration, since it is always necessary to place the public interest of consumers over the private interests of the contracting parties); ATJ Preliminary Ruling 50-IP-2001 (stressing that consumer confusion regarding pharmaceutical products could create irreversible damage to human health).

[49] ATJ Noncompliance Judgment 1-AI-96.

[50] Andean *Decisión* 344, Article 143.

[51] ATJ Preliminary Ruling 1-IP-96, sections X, XI, and XII.

[52] ATJ Preliminary Ruling 1-IP-96, section III.

companies.[53] The plaintiff argued that the World Trade Organization (WTO) Agreement on Trade-Related Aspects of Intellectual Property Rights (TRIPS) required second-use patents. Adopting a position arguably bolder than analogous European rulings, the ATJ concluded that Andean law is supreme even over multilateral treaties such as those adopted in the WTO.[54]

In litigation unrelated to intellectual property issues, by contrast, the shift in ATJ decision-making was less pronounced. The Tribunal became more scrupulous in finding violations of clear Andean rules, in enforcing Andean procedures, and in reviewing the facts of preliminary references. However, it did not issue expansionist rulings that limited state discretion or pushed member states toward deeper levels of legal integration.

The Colombian alcohol monopoly cases, discussed in more detail in Chapters 4 and 6, illustrate the ATJ's approach during this period. In May 1991, Ecuador complained to the Andean *Junta* that municipal rules in Colombia impeded competition and discriminated against Ecuadorian alcohol products. The *Junta* settled the dispute out of court, but it reappeared in 1996 in a complaint by Venezuela. This time the *Junta* adopted *Resolución* 453, a legally binding decision that found fault with the Colombian municipal policies and required Colombia to fix the problem. When the country ignored the decision, the General Secretariat (which by then had replaced the *Junta*) brought the noncompliance case to the ATJ.[55]

Meanwhile, in 1997, a private citizen had asked the Colombian Constitutional Court to review the state's alcohol monopoly. One of the plaintiff's arguments was that the monopoly was incompatible with the Cartagena Agreement as interpreted in *Resolución* 453. In a 1998 judgment, the Colombian court declined to enforce the *Resolución*. It reasoned that, unlike human rights treaties that have quasi-constitutional status in Colombia, Andean laws were equivalent to domestic legislation. Because such laws "and the Constitution do not share the same hierarchy, nor are [they] an intermediate legal source between the Constitution and ordinary domestic laws ... contradictions between a domestic law and Andean community law will not have as a consequence the non-execution of the [domestic] law." The court also noted that Andean Community law has "primacy" over conflicting national law—a concept that the Constitutional Court interpreted to mean that Andean law "displaces but does not abrogate or render non-executable" conflicting national legislation.[56]

The ATJ issued its noncompliance judgment six months later. The situation was remarkably similar to the landmark *Costa v. Enel* decision, in which the ECJ asserted the supremacy of EC law. There was, however, a key difference: *Costa v. Enel* had been simultaneously referred both to the Italian Constitutional Court and to the ECJ. The constitutional court ruled first, finding that European law was

[53] ATJ Noncompliance Judgment 1-AI-2001. [54] Ibid., section 7.6.
[55] The case was referred on 20 October 1997. ATJ Noncompliance Judgment 3-AI-97.
[56] Colombian Constitutional Court, Sentencia C-256/98 of May 27, 1998.

inapplicable to the case at hand and not supreme over national law.[57] The ECJ, by contrast, found that European law is supreme and that national courts were obliged to apply it instead of conflicting national law, but that the Italian law at issue did not conflict with EC law. The ATJ was less politically fortunate in that the case involved a Colombian practice that had been challenged by two member states and condemned by a General Secretariat *Resolución*. Thus, whereas the ECJ found Italian law compatible with EC law, in the alcohol case, the law and facts were such that the ATJ could not avoid ruling against Colombia.

In the noncompliance judgment, the ATJ went out of its way to agree with the Colombian Constitutional Court that there was no inherent conflict between the Colombian alcohol monopoly and Andean law. The implementation of the monopoly was a different matter, however. Although the national government had tried to introduce a common system of alcohol taxation, local policies that created barriers to trade persisted. Colombia remained in violation of Andean law because of these municipal practices.

The same litigant who had filed the Constitutional Court challenge later asked another Colombian court—the *Consejo de Estado*—to review the municipal policies. To nullify municipal acts, especially after the Constitutional Court ruling, would have been a radical step. National courts in Europe had taken just such a step when they embraced the supremacy of European law. As of 1999, however, no court in the Andean Community had shown much willingness to overturn domestic statutes or doctrines to help enforce Andean law. The *Consejo* referred the case to the ATJ as required under Andean law. The ATJ reiterated that Colombia was obliged to modify practices that conflict with Andean law.[58] Yet the Tribunal refused to extend its earlier reliance on the European supremacy doctrine and, as the ECJ had done, instruct national judges to do whatever was necessary to give effect to Community law. Instead, the ATJ simply declared (again) what Andean law required without asking national judges to help it to enforce that law. Although the ATJ did not explain its reluctance to follow the ECJ, its ruling is difficult to divorce from the very real concern that national judges might find that they lacked the legal authority or the political will to heed the ATJ's request.[59]

The ATJ in times of crisis: 2006 to the present

In the mid-2000s, the Andean Community entered a period of crisis triggered by political and economic schisms between the member states. As we explain in Chapter 7, the crisis began when Peru and Colombia announced their intention

[57] Indeed, initially the Italian Constitutional Court suggested that Italian statutes take precedence over the EC Treaty. *Costa v. Enel. & Soc. Edisonvolta*, Italian Constitutional Court Decision 14 of March 7, 1964, [1964] CMLR 425, [1964] I Il Foro It. 87 I 465.

[58] ATJ Preliminary Ruling 29-IP-98.

[59] The *Consejo de Estado* found against the plaintiff in the case. Decision of November 11, 1999, regarding *Decreto* 244 of 1906. Colombia has remained in breach of Andean law. Chapter 3 discusses the reticence of national judges to enforce ATJ rulings.

to negotiate free trade agreements with the United States, leading leftist-populist President Hugo Chavez to withdraw Venezuela from the Community in April 2006. At the time of Venezuela's exit, Chavez had only one ally in the Andes, the recently elected President of Bolivia, Evo Morales. Just over a year later, Ecuador elected President Rafael Correa, with a similar policy agenda. When judges questioned their policies, all three political leaders pursued reforms of their respective national judiciaries that, according to critics, undermined judicial independence.[60]

These events led to a two–two split among the remaining member states that continues to hobble the Andean integration project. Chapter 7 details the geopolitical reasons for and manifestations of this decline. The Andean Community's "open regionalism" approach allows countries to join or propose other Latin American initiatives—such as MERCOSUR and UNSASUR—that offer different visions of economic and political cooperation. Within the Community, the two–two schism sapped the General Secretariat of resources and staff, diminishing the incentives for litigants to challenge violations of Andean law. The split also triggered proposals to "re-engineer" (a euphemism for restructure or abolish) Community institutions, such as the Andean Parliament and, potentially, the ATJ. Finally, political leaders acknowledged the reality of the region's political stalemate by eliminating Andean policies that had little hope of being achieved, most notably the Common External Tariff. Chapter 7 further explores how these institutional reforms create a potential existential threat to the Andean Community and the Tribunal.

The central question we now examine is how the crisis has affected ATJ lawmaking. An earlier version of this chapter, published in 2010, relied on data that ended in 2007. The domestic and regional transformations that Correa would undertake were not yet evident, and we also lacked information on how the crisis was affecting the ATJ. Our findings were therefore tentative. The analysis in this book is based on nearly a decade of additional research, which provides further examples and nuance but essentially confirm our prior findings.

The Tribunal has for the most part continued to follow the doctrinal path charted during its early years and solidified in the Community's heyday. Chapter 7 explains that within the rule-of-law island for intellectual property disputes, where the Community is widely accepted as the primary source of legal rules, the ATJ continues to issue expansive interpretations of Andean law. Indeed, the island is flourishing. Beyond the island, however, the ATJ enforces unequivocal and detailed

[60] The Inter-American Commission on Human Rights criticized Venezuela's judicial reforms in Case No. 12.724, *Brewer Carías v. Venezuela* (2012). The Inter-American Court of Human Rights condemned Ecuador's dismissal of members of its Constitutional Tribunal in 2004, before President Correa took office. *Constitutional Tribunal (Camba Campos et al.) v. Ecuador*, Inter–Am. Ct. H.R. (ser. C) No. 268 (2013). For a discussion of Correa's judicial reforms, see O. Reich and E. Vázquez Ger, How to Destroy a Judicial System in Three Easy Steps, *Foreign Policy Online* (June 13, 2012), available at <http://foreignpolicy.com/2012/06/13/how-to-destroy-a-judicial-system-in-three-easy-steps/>. For a critique of judicial reforms in Bolivia, see Due Process of Law Foundation, Judicial Elections in Bolivia: An Unprecedented Event (March 5, 2015), available at <http://www.dplf.org/en/resources/judicial-elections-bolivia-unprecedented-event>; IBAHRI concerned at threats to the independence of the judiciary and legal profession in Bolivia (March 29, 2010), available at <http://www.ibanet.org/Article/Detail.aspx?ArticleUid=C8707609-35AC-4235-AAE6-3C1081E8813F>.

Community rules. But it also assiduously respects the discretion that Andean law reserves to national governments.

Chapter 4 describes how in 2014 the ATJ reversed its earlier practice and accepted preliminary references from the IP administrative agencies in Bolivia and Peru.[61] The Revised ATJ Treaty refers to "national judges" in describing the preliminary reference mechanism. The Tribunal's 2014 rulings interpreted this phrase as an "autonomous concept of Andean Community law to be defined by the Tribunal in accordance with criteria that take into account the purposes of the prejudicial interpretation mechanism."[62] The ATJ reasoned that the IP agencies also interpret and apply Andean law and thus the ATJ's guidance was important to the uniform application of that law. The Tribunal then developed a functional test for referrals that considers, among other factors, whether offices and bureaus within an agency exercise quasi-judicial functions. This approach is similar to the ECJ's long-standing practice of stretching the relevant EC treaty clause to accept references from a broad array of administrative and quasi-judicial adjudicatory bodies that are not courts in a traditional sense.[63]

The ATJ's functional approach creates a direct link between Andean judges and the IP agencies that are their primary interlocutors and compliance partners. Agency administrators and IP lawyers prefer direct referrals, which allow the agencies to ask more detailed and relevant questions, avoid appeals to national judges with limited IP expertise, and cut the cost and time of litigation. This consensus in favor of direct agency referrals suggests that the Tribunal's legal innovations have few if any political costs and thus do not meet the second element of our definition of expansionist judicial lawmaking: a broad interpretation of the law that limits state discretion.

If, however, references from administrative agencies come to be perceived as circumventing national judiciaries, what seems like an efficiency device could be reframed as expansionist lawmaking. This possibility is real. The extension of direct access for IP agencies unblocked a legal barrier in Bolivia to the application of Andean IP legislation. Chapter 3 explains that the absence of a supranational delegation clause in the Bolivian Constitution made it politically riskier for national judges to refer cases to the ATJ. Bolivian courts submitted only three references

[61] ATJ Preliminary Rulings 104-IP-2014 and 105-IP-2014 are referrals from the Bolivian IP agency, SENAPI; ATJ Preliminary Ruling 121- IP-2014 is a referral from the Directorate of Distinctive Signs in the Peruvian IP agency, INDECOPI.

[62] ATJ Preliminary Ruling, 121- IP-2014, at paragraph 17 ("*El concepto de 'juez nacional' … constituye un concepto autonomo, propio del Derecho Comunitario Andino que debe ser definido por el Tribunal de acuerdo con criterios propios y tomando en cuenta el objeto del institute de la interpretación prejudicial*").

[63] Article 267 of the Treaty on the Functioning of the European Union (previously Article 234 of the EC Treaty) describes the preliminary reference procedure as applying where a question of EC law is raised before "any court or tribunal of a Member State." To determine whether a body making a reference is a "court or tribunal," the ECJ "takes account of a number of factors, such as whether the body is established by law, whether it is permanent, whether its jurisdiction is compulsory, whether its procedure is *inter partes*, whether it applies rules of law and whether it is independent." Case C-210/06, *Cartesio Oktató és Szolgáltató bt*, 2008 I-09641(2008) at paragraph 55. The ECJ has acknowledged that these factors are not found in text of the treaty. Ibid., paragraph 56.

between 1984 and 2013. In the two years following the ATJ's interpretation, Bolivian courts requested preliminary rulings in forty cases.[64] It is also plausible that the ATJ's new and more flexible referral standard will engender references from administrative agencies in other legal domains. Under either scenario, the Tribunal's legal innovation could be seen as compromising state sovereignty or the proper functioning of the national legal order.

The decision to allow direct agency referrals is the clearest example during the crisis period of a judicial interpretation that has the potential to become expansionist. In other cases, however, the ATJ used bold language to explicate its rulings without applying them in ways that circumscribe national discretion. We summarize the findings from our analysis of ATJ rulings between 2006 and 2014, focusing on legal issues that may someday lead to expansionist lawmaking. Chapter 4 further develops this analysis, also discussing the evolution of the *complemento indispensable* doctrine and the Tribunal's bold pronouncements regarding the supremacy of Andean law over competing international law, including WTO treaties.

First, the ATJ has asserted, albeit only in dictum, the pre-eminent place of human rights in the Andean legal system. The most forceful articulation of this view appears in a 2012 preliminary ruling that, for the first time, identified fundamental individual rights as central to Andean integration: "Human rights, among which are the right to life, health, physical integrity and a healthy environment, are basic minimums without which it would be impossible to meet the objectives of the sub-regional integration process; they are general principles Andean Community law."[65] Taken to its logical conclusion, this bold pronouncement has the potential to infuse public interest values into the economic goals of Andean integration. To date, however, the ATJ has not applied these statements in ways that constrain government discretion at the supranational or national level.

Second, the ATJ has not shied away from bold pronouncements in preliminary references interpreting Andean secondary legislation that creates common regional policies. In a 2007 ruling, for example, the ATJ proclaimed the supremacy, direct applicability, and pre-emptive effect of Community rules governing intra-regional transport. It did so using forceful language, stating that "there is only one Andean policy in relation to passengers, equipment and transportation."[66] The Tribunal has adopted a similar approach when interpreting Andean *Decisiones* involving other narrow and technical subjects, such as customs valuations, value-added taxes, and information required on official forms.[67]

Third, the ATJ has been equally forceful in noncompliance judgments. Chapter 7 discusses suits challenging Andean rules regulating agricultural pesticides with

64 Data from our coding of ATJ preliminary rulings from 1984–2014. Data for 2015 are from *Tribunal de Justicia de la Comunidad Andina, Informe de Labores Gestión* 2015, 69.

65 ATJ Preliminary Ruling 116-IP-2012, 8.

66 ATJ Preliminary Ruling 133-IP-2007, conclusions 1 and 2.

67 E.g., the ATJ did not allow Colombia to add requirements to the International Cargo Manifest (ATJ Preliminary Ruling 1-IP-2008), or to use a minimum valuation when setting the price of certain imported good (ATJ Preliminary Ruling 44-IP-2009).

the aim of protecting the environment. The Tribunal found violations stemming from Peru's adoption of more permissive registration procedures for pesticides imported by farmers, and from the country's decision to grant automatic import licenses if the registration requests were not evaluated within a certain time.[68] In the third case, the Tribunal once again ruled against Peru and warned that the prevailing litigants could file suit in national courts seeking damages.[69] This enforcement mechanism is mentioned in the ATJ Treaty, but it has never been utilized. Given the Tribunal's general reluctance to instruct national judges in the application of Andean law, the suggestion that private litigants could turn to those same judges to help enforce Andean noncompliance judgments is a comparatively bold stance.[70]

The ATJ's legal assertiveness in the face of opposition to Andean integration is noteworthy. The Tribunal has thus far hewed to its past practice of enforcing Andean legislation that clearly indicates an intent to transfer legislative competence to the regional level and pre-empt conflicting national law and policy. The only real difference between the Washington Consensus and the crisis periods is that the ATJ has adjudicated a wider range of legal issues. As Chapter 3 documents, preliminary references during the crisis period dipped but then grew in number. References relating to IP still dominate the ATJ's docket, but if we analyze reference patterns based on the level of political commitment to integration, we see that the number of non-IP preliminary references quadrupled in the crisis period as compared to the twenty-two preceding years (from twenty-six non-IP preliminary rulings submitted during the Washington Consensus period to eighty-eight submitted during the crisis period). Most of the legal developments discussed above emerged from these non-IP preliminary rulings.

Chapter 3 also documents a sharp decline in the filing of noncompliance cases during the crisis period. Figure 8.1 below repeats Figure 3.7, adding the three time periods applied in this chapter.

The decline in noncompliance cases is attributable to several factors. Most notable among them is the political crisis in the Andean Community. Venezuela's departure in 2006 resulted in a sizeable diminution of the Community' budget. In the ensuing decade, the Andean integration project has been hobbled by conflicts between the two neoliberal-leaning states (Colombia and Peru) and two countries (Ecuador and Bolivia) whose leftist-populist policies are at odds with the Community's economic integration goals. When Ecuadorian and Bolivian officials were appointed to lead the General Secretariat, financial and institutional support decreased, transforming the organization from a competent administrative body into a mostly empty building occupied by a skeletal staff.[71] In addition,

[68] ATJ Noncompliance Judgments 05-AI-2008 and 02-AI-2010.

[69] ATJ Noncompliance Judgment 01-AI-2012, 20.

[70] We explain in Chapter 7 that the member states changed Andean law in response to these rulings, creating a loophole that gives member states greater discretion in granting licenses and registering pesticide products.

[71] Ecuadorian official Freddy Ehlers served as Secretary General from 2006–2010. Since then, three Bolivian officials have been appointed to that office: Adalid Contreras Baspineiro (2011–13), Pablo Guzmán Laugier (2013–16), and Walker San Miguel (2016 to the present).

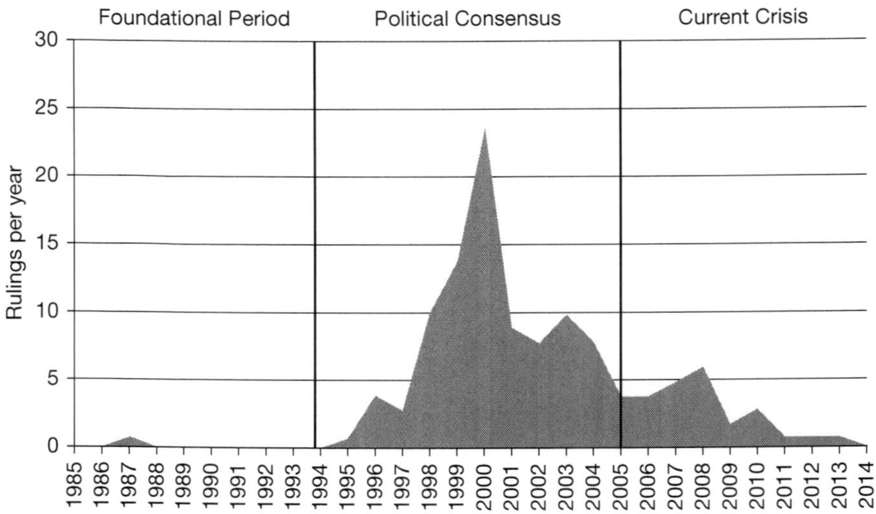

Figure 8.1 Three time periods of ATJ noncompliance judgments 1984–2014 (*N* = 113)

the production of Andean secondary legislation declined, limiting the number of new legal rules for the ATJ to interpret and enforce. Finally, the decline of noncompliance suits also signaled that litigants had lost faith that the Secretariat either would or could independently assess whether the member states were complying with existing Andean laws.

Comparing twenty-five years of expansionist judicial lawmaking by the ATJ and ECJ

The analysis in this chapter reviews ATJ lawmaking across the universe of preliminary rulings and important noncompliance judgments issued between 1984 and 2014. Our primary focus is comparing lawmaking by the ATJ and ECJ during the first twenty-five years of each regional common market. To recap our main findings: early ATJ rulings mostly emulated key ECJ doctrines, making Andean law directly effective and supreme over national law and pre-empting national governments from enacting conflicting domestic legislation. The ATJ stressed that governments had agreed to these developments. The ATJ also enforced clear Andean laws and required national judges to give priority to those laws, particularly in the area of intellectual property. In these ways, the ATJ generally followed in the ECJ's footsteps as a builder and strong defender of a supranational legal order.

In numerous other ways, however, the ATJ has exhibited far more deference to national authority. It has reiterated that Andean legal commitments are a product of member state consent and has scrupulously respected the discretion that Andean secondary legislation reserves to national governments. The ATJ has also eschewed opportunities to expand the reach and scope of Andean law. While the Tribunal formally treats the Cartagena Agreement as higher-order law, the judges readily defer to political decisions to modulate the scope and pace of integration when interpreting the treaty. This approach gives member states broad discretion to revise Andean rules to reflect the waxing and waning of their collective commitment to the Community.

The ATJ has generally adhered to this pattern during the crisis period. The Tribunal enforces common Andean rules, mainly in low-stakes technical cases, and it is occasionally bolder in dictum. Because Andean legislation expanded during the Washington Consensus period and that legislation has remained in effect over the last decade, there are more policy areas in which the ATJ has ruled against national violations of clear Andean rules. Most of these decisions do not, however, qualify as expansionist lawmaking because they do not broaden the substantive reach of Community law in ways that constrain member state discretion.

In contrast to the ATJ, the ECJ has been pervasively expansionist even though member states have often been only weakly committed to the European integration project. Stone Sweet has examined ECJ decision-making involving three substantive areas of European law: the environment, sex discrimination, and free movement of goods. He concludes that "through its rulings [the ECJ] has acted—relatively systematically—to reduce the domain of national autonomy, to expand supranational modes of governance to the detriment of intergovernmental modes, and to create the conditions for the gradual Europeanization of national administration and judging."[72]

Analyzing ATJ and ECJ lawmaking in discrete historical periods reveals another important difference between the two courts. Weiler observed that in Europe, legal supranationalism advanced furthest when political steps toward integration were in retreat.[73] The ATJ also developed its key doctrines during its foundational period, but the Tribunal's lawmaking tends to reflect rather than counterbalance political support for integration. We return to this issue in this chapter's conclusion.

Explaining the Divergent Supply of Expansionist Lawmaking

What explains the striking differences between ECJ/ATJ lawmaking? The two courts possessed the same potent combination of wide access rules, self-interested litigants, swelling dockets, and repeat-player legal entrepreneurs who sought out cases to promote legal integration.[74] In other words, both courts contained the ingredients needed for judicial empowerment, but unlike the ECJ, the ATJ often

[72] Stone Sweet, 2004, 232.

[73] J. Weiler, The Community System: The Dual Character of Supranationalism. *Yearbook of European Law* 1981, 1 (1): 257–306; Weiler, 1991.

[74] Repeat players are litigants who raise multiple suits. Scholars assert that repeat players are advantaged in litigation because of their experience and are prevalent in suits aimed at influencing policy. On the role of repeat players in European integration, see R. Rawlings, The Eurolaw Game: Some Deductions from a Saga. *Journal of Law and Society* 1993, 20: 309–40; W. Mattli and A.-M. Slaughter,

thwarted litigants' efforts to use Andean law to dismantle national policies contrary to their economic interests. The ATJ's refusal to help litigants achieve their goals set up a vicious circle that has inhibited the filing of cases that might have expanded Community law.

When we first published the findings in this chapter in 2010, we were skeptical that structural or political factors could explain the ECJ's greater penchant for expansionist lawmaking and the ATJ's contrasting reticence. We noted that it was too soon to say what Venezuela's departure might mean for the Andean Community, and we could not anticipate that Rafael Correa would be repeatedly re-elected as Ecuador's President, enabling a fundamental reorientation of that country's economy, politics, judiciary, and relationship to the Community.

Our central claim—which remains unchanged—is that international courts are not expansionist by nature and that expansionist judicial lawmaking requires the nurturing support of substate actors. However, recent political developments in the Andes, discussed in greater depth in Chapter 7, have created a threat to the future of the Andean integration process and the ATJ. These events provide an opportunity to refine our original analysis.

We first discuss and reject three potential explanations of the divergent approaches to expansive judicial lawmaking during the time periods we examine—the appointment processes for ECJ and ATJ judges, the different levels of trade in the two regions, and the fact that EC member states are (almost all) stable liberal democracies. We then discuss two plausible explanations that are more difficult to dismiss: the threat of exit in response to political turbulence, and variation in the extent of regional secondary legislation.

Nature-based theories of international judicial behavior would explain the differences in lawmaking by looking for judicial design features and political constraints that inhibit judges from issuing expansionist rulings in response to litigant demands. During the periods we examined, the appointment process for the ECJ and ATJ were similar. In the Andes, as in Europe, member states nominated judges whom they expected to have some expertise in the legal issues the court would hear. Andean governments submit a ranked list of three nominees, which, like their European counterparts, typically hail from government, academia, the foreign service, and the national judiciary. Other member states choose from this list. None of our interviews suggested that governments seek out nominees with particular judicial philosophies or approaches to their job.[75] Once appointed, ATJ judges appear no more vulnerable to retribution than are ECJ judges. Both courts issue

Revisiting the European Court of Justice. *International Organization* 1998, 52 (1): 186–9. In the Andes, we found small clusters of repeat players in cases involving the aluminum and alcohol industries and second-use patents. Our subsequent studies revealed repeat players in cases involving tobacco trademarks, taxes, and customs.

[75] Governments often nominate political allies, although these allies are not always selected by other states. A former ATJ judge recounted his unusual appointment. The government put him third on the list, hoping that one of the two diplomats placed ahead of him would be selected. It later tried to scuttle his candidacy by failing to communicate that he had been selected. (Interview with former ATJ judge (B).) We also find examples of ATJ judges with clear pro-integration backgrounds. For example, Gallo Pico Mantilla was a committed integrationist with an extensive background in Ecuadorian politics

rulings unanimously.[76] In neither context have governments attempted to remove judges from office, although they have elected new judges at the end of their terms rather than reappointing them. Judges rotate in Europe and in the Andes mostly for personal or professional reasons and because new governments want to exercise their power of appointment.[77]

Recent efforts by national executives to control the domestic judiciary complicate this picture. The previous section mentioned judicial "reforms" instigated by the leftist-populist leaders of Bolivia, Ecuador, and Venezuela. Our recent interviews suggested that these domestic practices have carried over to the Andean level, with the result that only politically loyal judges from Bolivia and Ecuador were appointed to the ATJ. If true, the instances of bold decision-making by Andean judges during the crisis period are all the more surprising. Yet most of the Tribunal's forceful rulings involved cases against or referred from Peru and Colombia, which makes it difficult to draw firm conclusions about whether politicized appointments have affected ATJ decision-making.

Second, some scholars may seek to explain the variation in expansive judicial law-making by focusing on the extent to which each Community is comprised of stable liberal democracies.[78] Andean countries scored reasonably well on measurements of democracy during the years in our study, although there has been significant slippage over the last decade.[79] Andean member states have also experienced significant economic and political turmoil during this period. We discuss two of these crises in Chapter 6, contrasting the response to Peru's economic "shock therapy" in the early 1990s with its handling of Ecuador's current economic travails, brought on by a rising dollar and declining oil prices.[80]

and the diplomatic corps. More recently, ATJ Judge Luis José Diez Canseco Núñez actively promoted Andean legal integration. Judge Canseco Núñez had the support of the IP lawyers and agency administrators, whose activities we discuss in Chapter 5, but there is no evidence that member states appointed him with the purpose of enhancing the ATJ's profile or expanding its jurisprudential reach.

[76] In 2015, then ATJ President Diez Canseco Núñez introduced the practice of individually-authored decisions and the possibility of filing dissenting opinions. As far as we are aware, however, dissenting opinions are not published.

[77] On ECJ judges, see S. Kenney, The Members of the Court of Justice of the European Communities. *Columbia Journal of European Law* 1998, 5 (1): 101–33. Kenney finds no indication that political factors influence the selection of ECJ judges. Ibid., at 128–30. Our survey of ATJ judges appointed from its founding up to and including 2007 was less systematic, but we discerned no clear appointment pattern across countries or time.

[78] A. Moravcsik, *The Choice for Europe*. Ithaca, NY: Cornell University Press, 2000.

[79] Polity scores rate the level of democracy around the world, with 10 being the highest democratic score. European countries mostly scored a 10 during the period of time we study, though France had a score of 5 from 1958–68, rising to 8 from 1969–85, after which it has remained at a score of 9. Andean countries' Polity scores have been more variable. During the early Washington Consensus period, Colombia rose to a ranking of 9, but then fell to a 7 where it has remained since 1997. Peru plunged to −3 in 1992, and remained at 1 until 2000 when it returned to a 9 rating. Ecuador achieved a ranking of 9 in 1988, but it began falling in 2000. Under President Correa, Ecuador's Polity score has fallen to 5. Bolivia rose to a rank of 9 in 1986. Under President Morales, Bolivia's score fell to a 7. Under Chavez's presidency, Venezuela's score fell from 9 to −3. Venezuela's departure from the Andean Community coincided with a major inflection; Venezuela's Polity score fell from a 5 into the negative numbers.

[80] The ECJ has also confronted political turmoil and fraught cases, engaging in expansionist law-making in the 1960s and 1970s in the face of waning political support for integration, student and labor protests, and mass labor unrest.

A third potential explanation for the divergence in expansionist lawmaking is the differing levels of intra-Community trade in the two regions. At the start of European integration, intra-European trade was relatively small, constituting less than 3% of the member states' gross domestic product.[81] Although perhaps not as economically central to European countries in the 1960s, trade among EC member states has always constituted a larger proportion of the total trade as compared to intra-regional trade in the Andes. In 1958, between 23.7% and 27.5% of French, Italian, and German trade went to other European member states. By 1972, intra-European trade constituted between 40% and 60% of total member states' trade.[82]

Trade among Andean countries increased from the founding of the Andean Pact through 2007, beginning from a low of 3% of total trade during the Andean Pact, peaking at about 10% of total trade in 2002. For Bolivia and Ecuador, common market trade was relatively more important (between 15% and 24%).[83] Nevertheless, internal trade has never been as significant in the Andean region as in Europe. A recent Secretariat report notes that in 2015, intra-Andean trade constituted 8% of all exports by the four member states. In terms of relative importance, the United States accounted for 24% of Andean exports, followed by China (10%), the European Union (15%), and MERCOSUR (9%).[84]

Economic realities certainly influence the extent to which European and Andean governments invest in their respective Communities. Nonetheless, we find it implausible that different trade levels explain the divergent lawmaking by the two regional courts. It is far from clear, for example, that European governments in the 1960s and 1970s saw economic integration as vital to their economies. One could easily argue that these governments saw maintaining national trade barriers as necessary for the larger project of protecting the embedded liberal compromise of post-war European societies.[85]

We next consider two more plausible explanations for the divergence in ECJ/ATJ expansionist lawmaking. Until very recently, there was no evidence suggesting that the ATJ was institutionally more vulnerable than the ECJ. Both European and Andean judges have been criticized for decisions governments did not like, but member states have only rarely overturned unwanted legal rulings.[86] In Europe, exit from the European Union was considered to be inconceivable until the United

[81] Stone Sweet, 2004, 57.

[82] Figures compiled by the authors in 2010 from IMF Direction of Trade Statistics, accessed through the Inter-University Consortium for Political and Social Research (ICPSR).

[83] See Evolucion del Proceso de Integracion 1969–1999, CAN document SG/di 219/Rev.1, 28 (April 26, 2000) (on file with authors).

[84] The export figures reflect the economic turbulence in Ecuador based on the falling price of oil and the rise of the US dollar. Imports from Andean countries comprise 6.5% of total regional imports. *Comercio Exterior des Bienes* 2006–15, 1, available at <http://intranet.comunidadandina.org/Documentos/DEstadisticos/SGDE732.pdf>.

[85] Milward makes this claim with respect to European integration. A. Milward, *The European Rescue of the Nation-State*. London: Routledge, 1992.

[86] Chapter 5 analyzes the member states' reversal of an ATJ judgment against Colombia involving data protection. Chapter 7 discusses a revision of Andean pesticide legislation following ATJ noncompliance judgments against Peru, as well as the decision to eliminate the Common External Tariff.

Kingdom's vote for Brexit in June 2016. The Andean Community has experienced exits: Chile in 1976 and Venezuela in 2006. As Chapter 7 notes, Ecuadorian officials recently voiced the possibility of unilateral withdrawal while also exploring a merger with MERCOSUR into UNASUR. This greater threat of exit has not cowed the ATJ, but the larger political turbulence within member states and the Community reinforces the sagacity of the ATJ's legal strategy; namely, its willingness to enforce clear Andean rules while respecting national discretion where Andean law so allows.

Differences in regional legislation offer another plausible explanation. Compared to the Andean Community, the EC has far more secondary legislation concerning the free movement of goods, services, capital, and people. Litigation tends to rise as the number and scope of enforceable Community rules increase. In addition, some Andean legislation contains loopholes that make it difficult for litigants to challenge conflicting national policies.[87] These differences affect our dependent variable, since the ATJ is more willing to assert its authority in domains where Andean rules are clear and precise.

Although political realities reinforce the ATJ's reticence to interpret Andean law expansively, nothing the crisis period undermines our prior claim that nature-based arguments are wrong in viewing expansionist lawmaking as the norm for courts, both national and international. When we shed this nature-based assumption, the ATJ's prudent decision to let member states set the pace of integration seems rather unsurprising. What is more unexpected is that the ECJ repeatedly chose to serve as an engine of regional integration even when European governments appeared to have all but abandoned the integration project.

Jettisoning the assumption that international judges are power-seeking by nature thus calls into question existing explanations of the ECJ's origins. Chapter 9 explores this issue in greater depth, contrasting the organization and behavior of Euro-law associations with the actions of a handful of legal entrepreneurs in the Andes. In Europe, jurist advocacy movements were ideologically committed to the goal of regional integration. They generated test cases, connected European judges with pro-integration national lawyers and judges, encouraged bold ECJ legal rulings, and promoted the validity of controversial ECJ decisions within the legal community. We argue that ideology rather than narrow economic interests motivated these actors, and explain that beyond the area of intellectual property, the ATJ has not received the support of jurist advocacy networks. In this respect, the ATJ also differs markedly from the Inter-American human rights system, where advocacy groups regularly mobilize across borders and file cases in national and regional judicial venues, including the Inter-American Court of Human Rights.[88]

[87] E.g., the Andean telecommunications policy requires governments to provide access to scarce frequencies. However, the requirement is "without prejudice to such national provisions as each Member Country may establish," *Decisión* 462, Article 23, allowing governments to privilege national carriers owned by politically powerful families. Interview with attorney (A) from commercial and administrative law firm in Colombia. Chapter 5 discusses these and other loopholes in Andean legislation.

[88] J.L. Cavallaro and S.E. Brewer, Reevaluating Regional Human Rights Litigation in the Twenty-First Century: The Case of the Inter-American Court. *American Journal of International Law* 2008, 102 (4): 768–827; M.E. Keck and K. Sikkink, *Activists Beyond Borders: Advocacy Networks in*

Conclusion: Expansive Judicial Lawmaking at the Interface of Regional Law and Politics

International judicial decisions that clarify ambiguities and fill gaps in treaties are an inherent part of judging. Chapter 4 provides many examples of the ATJ engaging in this form of judicial lawmaking. By contrast, expansionist lawmaking—in which judges broaden the reach of international legal rules at the expense of state discretion—is a distinctive and more politically consequential judicial activity.

Although many scholars presume that international courts are hardwired to issue expansive decisions, our findings in this chapter and in Chapter 9 suggest that such behavior may well be the exception not the rule. In particular, the ATJ's experience demonstrates that international jurists can be active without being activist. We thus suggest that the dominant presumption may be wrong. International judges have many reasons to act with political prudence, especially where they lack nurturing by substate and societal actors, which may—but need not—include government officials.

A few conclusions follow from this chapter's analysis. First, our comparison of two identically structured international courts suggests that too much weight has been placed on judicial design as an explanation of judicial behavior. The conclusion of this book (Chapter 10) places the ATJ's experience in a wider context, comparing the ATJ to the other international courts modeled on the ECJ. If design were destiny for international judges, we would expect all copies of the ECJ to develop in ways that at least roughly track the rise of supranational litigation in Europe. In fact, when compared to its ECJ-style cousins, the Andean legal system stands out in multiple respects: its level of activity, the number of preliminary references, diversity of national judges referring cases, the breadth of legal issues adjudicated, the willingness of states and private actors to file noncompliance suits with the General Secretariat, and the Secretariat's willingness to investigate and pursue these complaints, including by challenging member states before the ATJ.

These distinctions make the ATJ the most likely of all of the ECJ copies to follow the path of its progenitor. Yet even at the height of the Washington Consensus, a ten-year period of time when Andean governments and international institutions all supported the free market orientation of Andean rules, the ATJ did not engage in expansionist lawmaking. Instead, in good times and bad, the ATJ has been constant in its willingness to enforce the supremacy of clear Andean law while allowing governments to set the pace and extent of regional integration.

Second, although judicial power seeking and self-interest may be necessary for expansionist lawmaking, they are not sufficient. Chapter 9 serves as a companion to this chapter, showing how jurist advocacy movements nurtured ECJ lawmaking.

International Politics. Ithaca, NY: Cornell University Press, 1998; K. Sikkink and E. Lutz, The Justice Cascade: The Evolution and Impact of Foreign Human Rights Trials in Latin America. *Chicago Journal of International Law* 2001, 2: 1–33.

We also document the lack of a jurist advocacy movement in the Andes. If we are right that expansionist lawmaking requires nurturing by advocacy movements, we should expect international courts to supply expansionist decisions when they anticipate that domestic advocacy networks and compliance constituencies will pressure states to change their conduct. The support of these domestic interlocutors facilitates judicial lawmaking, while the lack of support and the prospect that states may exit from a court's jurisdiction provide a counterweight.[89] The reality that advocacy movements and substate actors can encourage expansionist lawmaking may be of concern to sovereigntists and defenders of national executive power. Yet we have also shown that the ATJ hews closely to the mandate given to it by the member states, revealing that such lawmaking need not compromise national sovereignty.

A third and final contribution emerges from our examination of ATJ lawmaking during periods of political consensus and disagreement. Over the last decade of crisis in the Andean Community, the Tribunal has mostly stayed the course it charted during the heyday of regional integration. It has autonomously interpreted the ATJ Treaty to enhance its links to the IP agencies that are its primary interlocutors. It has continued to enforce regional rules whose texts reveal member states' intent to create common Andean policies and eliminate or restrict national derogations. It has confined its bolder pronouncements to non-binding dicta that plant a seed for potential doctrinal growth in the future without imposing contemporary restrictions on national discretion.

A separate question is how the ATJ behaves in highly politicized cases. Too often, observers conflate judicial lawmaking with the political salience of an international court's rulings.[90] In fact, strategic judges often consciously separate the two phenomena, employing legal circumspection as a tool to protect themselves from criticism in politically charged cases. Chapter 6 considers this question in greater depth, focusing on the ATJ's behavior in four politically fraught disputes. Chapter 7 digs deeper, interlacing recent high-stakes legal controversies involving Ecuador's suspension of core Andean free trade rules with ongoing debates among governments over the restructuring of Andean institutions. Moving beyond the focus on expansionist lawmaking, Chapter 7 also considers how the prospect of subsuming the Community into more politically malleable regional integration pacts, most notably MERCOSUR or UNASUR, has shaped the adjudication of high-profile Andean disputes.

[89] Exit, although rare, is not unheard of. L.R. Helfer, Exiting Treaties. *Virginia Law Review* 2005 91 (7): 1579–648. For example, the United States withdrew from the compulsory jurisdiction of the ICJ and Trinidad and Tobago withdrew from the jurisdiction of the Inter-American Court of Human Rights. L.R. Helfer, Overlegalizing Human Rights: International Relations Theory and the Commonwealth Caribbean Backlash against Human Rights Regimes. *Columbia Law Review* 2002 102 (7): 1832–911.

[90] We develop this idea elsewhere, exploring how the lawmaking strategies of the ECJ, the ATJ, and the ECOWAS Court of Justice affect the legitimacy of those courts. See L.R. Helfer and K.J. Alter, Legitimacy and Lawmaking: A Tale of Three International Courts. *Theoretical Inquires in Law* 2013 14 (2): 479–503.

9

Jurist Advocacy Movements in Europe and the Andes

If international courts are not expansionist lawmakers by nature, what leads some of the judges who serve on those courts to adopt expansive rulings that use adjudication as a tool of judicial empowerment and institution building? Chapter 8 debunks the presumption that judges are inherently power-seeking, hard wired to seize opportunities to expand the reach and scope of the law. Instead, we argue that that expansionist lawmaking requires special nurturing. This chapter employs a socio-legal method of analysis, examining the actions of legal entrepreneurs and law associations to document the nurturing that lay behind the European Court of Justice (ECJ)'s legal revolution.

We began our study of the Andean Tribunal (ATJ) with assumptions drawn from the conventional wisdom of European Community (EC) law scholarship. Neo-functionalist theory, itself a variant of rational-liberalism, emphasizes the rational, self-interested behavior of actors and tends to ignore the influence of collectivities, ideas, and ideology. As applied to European integration through law, the theory expects individual self-interest to interact with market and functional objectives, mobilizing actors transnationally to further the goals of regional integration. Walter Mattli summarized the basic idea underpinning the theory as famously articulated by Ernst Haas:

> The 'good Europeans' are not the main creators of the ... community. The process of community formation is dominated by nationally constituted groups with specific interests and aims, willing and able to adjust their aspirations by turning to supranational means when the course appears profitable ... the groups driving the process of integration are rational maximizers of their narrow self interest; they hail from the world of business, politics and science and their actions or beliefs need not be infused with pan-regional ideology or commitment. Deeper integration is the intended as well as unintended consequence of their self-serving actions.[1]

[1] W. Mattli, Ernst Haas' Evolving Thinking on Comparative Regional Integration: Of Virtues and Infelicities. *Journal of European Public Policy* 2005, 12 (2): 330–1. Regional integration specialists use the term "neofunctionalism." Haas' neofunctionalist theory posited that participating in European integration would generate an ideological shift. This shift never occurred, however, and the theoretical expectation has been thoroughly debunked. The ideational component of neofunctionalism was stripped out in its later usage, at which point neofunctionalist theory became, in essence, rational-liberalism.

Transplanting International Courts: The Law and Politics of the Andean Tribunal of Justice. First Edition. Karen J. Alter and Laurence R. Helfer. Published 2017 by Oxford University Press.

Our study of Andean integration calls into question these assumptions. In particular, lawyers, law professors, and judges—the key actors in the accounts of European legal integration by Eric Stein, Joseph Weiler, Anne-Marie Slaughter, and Hjalte Rasmussen—have not mobilized in favor of the Andean integration project. As we demonstrate in our discussion of the ATJ's interlocutors (Chapter 3) and its relationship with intellectual property (IP) agencies (Chapter 5), national judges are mostly reluctant interlocutors with the ATJ, and few attorneys, academics, or firms outside of the technical field of IP law actively follow—let alone engage with—the Andean legal system. We also find a marked divergence between the lawmaking of ECJ judges and the more reticent interpretative approach of their Andean counterparts (Chapter 8).

These unexpected incongruences led us to re-evaluate the European integration experience. In particular, Karen Alter revisited interviews and archival material she had collected during her dissertation research (1992–96). She had set these materials aside after concluding that the ECJ-inspired legal arguments championed by pro-Europe jurist advocacy movements did not sway most national judges, and thus had very little influence over debates about the place of European law in national legal orders. Our joint discovery (discussed in Chapter 8) that Andean judges have been far more circumspect in developing those same doctrines provided a lens through which to re-examine these primary sources and their implications. Alter returned to this material with a different question in mind, asking why ECJ judges had been audacious in declaring and extending the foundational doctrines of Community law.

This chapter provides Alter's revisionist account of early European legal integration, drawing on primary and secondary source materials that she collected in the 1990s, updated by recent socio-legal scholarship and the archival research of the New History of European Law.[2] Alter coins the label "jurist advocacy movements" to describe the group of lawyers, judges, academics, in-house counsels, and legally trained government and European officials who advocated for particular goals. These actors were organized into formally constituted associations dedicated to the study of EC law. After analyzing the concept of jurist advocacy movements in greater detail, this chapter explains the emergence of Euro-law associations that worked to promote European legal integration. We then examine the activities of

[2] Socio-legal scholars including Antoine Vauchez, Mikael Madsen, and Antonin Cohen have traced the history of key protagonists in European legal integration, discovering previously unknown connections among individuals and between individuals and legal cases. The New History of European Law is a project by a network of historians that collects previously unavailable archival material and uses this material to document the behind-the-scenes story of the ECJ's legal revolution. The archives were embargoed when Karen Alter first conducted her research, but Alter collected oral histories of many of key individuals, archival material of French and German Euro-law associations, and archives of the ECJ's judicial visiting program. Alter's interview notes and collected research materials have been transferred to the Historical Archives of the European Union, housed at the European University Institute, as part of the New History of European Law Project, available at <http://www.eui.eu/Research/HistoricalArchivesOfEU/AlcideDeGasperiResearchCentre/Sources-on-the-History-of-European-Law-new.aspx>. This chapter cites the individual sources by name, since this material is now publicly available.

the associations, focusing on four distinct contributions that these groups provided to the European legal integration project:

1. generating test cases to facilitate the development of supranational doctrines;
2. serving as a kitchen cabinet that helped ECJ judges to anticipate the reception of their innovative rulings;
3. providing a community that inspired and emboldened ECJ judges and Euro-law association members; and
4. creating a perception of momentum in favor of European legal integration.

The next section documents the absence of a jurist advocacy movement for the Andean integration project. We first examine the isolated advocacy efforts of early legal entrepreneurs during the Andean Pact era. We then describe a more recent episode of a single Colombian attorney who sought to enforce regional pesticide regulations by filing test cases and noncompliance suits that invited the Tribunal to bolster the force and reach of Andean law, as well as entrepreneurship by an ATJ judge who, borrowing a page from the ECJ's book, engaged in extra-judicial advocacy. The limited effect of these individuals' extraordinary efforts underscores how the absence of a coordinated network of advocates for the Andean legal system contributes to the ATJ's circumspection.

The chapter concludes by considering why Andean judges lacked the mobilized supporters that their European colleagues enjoyed, and what the divergent European and Andean experiences suggest about the importance of jurist advocacy movements for activating and bolstering international courts more generally. Viewing the Andean and European experiences side-by-side suggest that such movements must do more than disseminate information about legal rules and individual efforts to promote integration through law. They must also create a community of actors whose commitment to a cause extends beyond the pursuit of narrow self-interest.

What is a Jurist Advocacy Movement?

A jurist advocacy movement is a group of legal actors (jurists) who organize collectively and deploy legal tools strategically to promote a shared cause. Jurist advocacy movements have specific policy and legal goals, whether they be the promotion of originalist interpretations of a constitution, abolition of the death penalty, advocacy of same-sex marriage, or the construction of a supranational legal order.[3] A shared advocacy objective differentiates a jurist advocacy movement from a less

[3] Although they did not use the phrase jurist advocacy movement, Steven Teles analyzes how a jurist advocacy movement transformed the American judiciary, and Jens Ohlin describes how this movement then transformed American attitudes towards international law. S.M. Teles, *The Rise of the Conservative Legal Movement: The Battle for Control of the Law*. Princeton NJ: Princeton University Press, 2009; J.D. Ohlin, *The Assault on International Law*. Oxford: Oxford University Press, 2015.

goal-oriented and more diffuse network of individuals who exchange information in meetings and remotely, build social connections, and collaborate on projects when doing so helps to address common challenges.

The jurist part of the label captures the reality that legal actors use strategies grounded in the law to achieve their collective goals. Jurists constitute a broad category of legal actors, including practicing lawyers (who represent clients, provide legal advice, serve as arbitrators or mediators, and argue cases in court), parliamentarians and policy-makers (who draft and vote on laws), judges and regulators (who provide authoritative interpretations of law), academics (who impart expertise and critique legal interpretations), and government officials (who provide advice to lawmakers about the legality of proposed and existing policies and how they are administered). Mikael Madsen explains that jurists draw on the symbolic resource of labeling key words and concepts as law. Another resource jurists share is the ability to move over time across the many domains of legal practice—one day serving as a lawyer representing a client, then as a judge, later as a government official or academic working on legal and policy matters, and back again as a practicing lawyer.[4] Across the arc of a career, these movements enable jurists to promote a cause while serving in different roles in the legal profession.

The tools deployed by jurist advocacy movements include filing test cases in court, publishing treatises, policy papers, and academic writings that promote preferred legal interpretations, and filing amicus briefs advocating for these interpretations in specific cases. The movement's members meet in venues familiar to legal professionals, such as bar association events, academic conferences, and continuing education courses. In any one moment, jurists may appear to be little more than a concatenation of like-minded legal professionals. However, once these actors begin to deploy these tools—convening meetings and workshops to develop legal arguments and refine strategies, supporting the appointment of sympathetic legal professionals to fill key vacancies in government or think tanks, seeking out friendly judges, and constructing test cases to encourage those judges build law in a preferred direction—the like-minded actors can become a jurist advocacy movement whose goal is to create a mutually reinforcing system in which law on the books, judicial interpretations, legal advice to clients, and publications advance a shared vision of what the law requires.

It is instructive to contrast the dynamics of coordination by a cohesive and politically influential group of legal actors with other forces that promote the diffusion of specific policy goals across borders. Information resulting from transparent

[4] M.R. Madsen, Unpacking Legal Network Power: The Structural Construction of Transnational Legal Expert Networks. In: *Networked Governance, Transnational Business and the Law.* M. Fenwick, S. Van Uytsel, and S. Wrbka (eds), 39–56. Berlin: Springer Verlag, 2013. Tamir Moustafa has written about the importance of human rights associations, opposition political parties, and legal professional associations in protecting national supreme courts from political retaliation. T. Moustafa, *The Struggle for Constitutional Power: Law, Politics and Economic Development in Egypt.* Cambridge: Cambridge University Press, 2007. These groups are often part of jurist advocacy movements, but our notion of a jurist advocacy movement is more expansive because it seeks to understand the broader question of how legal change is manufactured and institutionalized.

processes or the generation of new knowledge is an often-cited source of such diffusion. If ignorance is what deters the adoption of particular policies, then information should be sufficient to create convergence around those policies. Certainly there is much greater awareness about strategic advocacy using international law today compared to sixty years ago when the EC was founded. The Internet also makes it easier for lawyers to disseminate their views, and meetings of national and international judges at conferences and symposia provide opportunities to share solutions to common problems.

This chapter reveals, however, that jurist advocacy movements in Europe did not simply share information. They built communities of like-minded actors who worked collectively and strategically using their multiple and shifting roles in the legal profession to achieve a common policy goal. The contrast we draw between the European and Andean integration projects suggests a more pointed theoretical insight: that sharing information, even when facilitated by the internet and other new technologies, is no substitute for the sort of community building and support for international judges that Euro-law associations provided to the ECJ.

Trans-governmental networks are another driver of policy diffusion, one that brings together national administrators and judges who engage in similar activities across borders. The theoretical insight in the governance network literature is that functional imperatives—similar domestic policy goals and the inherently transnational nature of a policy issue—engender and sustain these networks.[5] The analysis in this chapter suggests that including actors with legal and political capital in jurist advocacy movements is crucial. But the functional imperative to work together is likely insufficient for successful cooperation, as Ernst Haas and other early proponents of neofunctionalist theory long ago recognized.[6] Stated another way, Euro-law associations were far more than mere trans-governmental networks. They reached beyond governmental officials and judges to bring together an ideologically cohesive group of jurists from across the legal profession who were united by a larger agenda: to promote European integration through law via doctrinally expansive ECJ rulings.

Others have recognized the role of ideology in unifying legal and social movements. Margaret Keck and Kathryn Sikkink argue that a commitment to common goals and principles provides the glue that unifies transnational advocacy networks. They suggest that certain issues are inherently more amenable to such advocacy because they have a greater ability to connect and resonate with actors who are outside of the network.[7] The scholarship on epistemic communities similarly recognizes that group cohesion is furthered by shared understandings about

[5] A.-M. Slaughter, *A New World Order*. Princeton NJ: Princeton University Press, 2004.

[6] E. Haas, *The Obsolescence of Regional Integration Theory*. Berkeley, CA: University of California Press, 1975.

[7] T. Risse, S. Ropp, and K. Sikkink, *The Power of Human Rights: International Norms and Domestic Change*. Cambridge: Cambridge University Press, 1999; M.E. Keck and K. Sikkink, *Activists Beyond Borders: Advocacy Networks in International Politics*. Ithaca, NY: Cornell University Press, 1998.

cause-and-effect relationships, which provide those communities with a common causal narrative and, ultimately, with power.[8]

The analysis in this chapter reinforces these earlier insights. We suggest that self-interest alone provides too narrow a basis to sustain a coordinated movement that seeks to achieve ambitious objectives. The sincere belief that unifying Europe through law and legal institutions would facilitate a lasting peace united the members of Euro-law associations. In contrast, the Andean Pact's import substitution ideology and the Andean Community's economic liberalization goals (discussed in Chapter 2) failed to mobilize a committed group of jurists to aid the Andean integration project and its legal institutions.

Founding National Euro-law Associations: 1952–75

This section describes the founding, in the 1950s and 1960s, of pro-European jurist advocacy movements in the form of nationally based Euro-law societies, and the creation of the regional *Fédération Internationale de Droit Européen* (FIDE) which coordinated the societies' efforts across national borders. As we explain, Europe's early jurist advocacy movements were immediately successful because they employed a strategy that was familiar and well supported by existing legal infrastructures. This section also documents how the European Commission provided pro-EC lawyers with important support. These infrastructures and support were lacking in the Andes, increasing the challenges facing the few legal entrepreneurs who were inspired to action by the Andean integration project.

The founding of the EC in 1958 provided an impetus to organize pro-integration lawyers into national associations dedicated to the study and promotion of Community law. Euro-law associations, including the German *Wissentschaftliche Gesellschaft für Europarecht, Association Belge pour le Droit Européen, Association Française des Juristes Européens, Associazione Italian dei Giuristi Europei, Association Luxembourgeois des Juristes Européens*, and the *Nederlandse Vereniging voor Europees Recht*, formed in each EC member state in the 1950s and up to and including 1961. According to the founders, the nearly simultaneous emergence of these groups was not directly coordinated but was a natural outgrowth of practices within national legal communities where diplomat-jurisconsults in the 1940s and 1950s had been actively involved in national and international political and legal developments.[9] Indeed, the *Mouvement Européen* had always seen law as an integral part of European integration.[10]

[8] P.M. Haas, Introduction: Epistemic Communities and International Policy Coordination. *International Organization* 1992, 46 (1): 1–36.

[9] M.R. Madsen and A. Vauchez, European Constitutionalism at the Cradle: Law and Lawyers in the Construction of a European Political Order (1920–1960). In: *In Lawyers' Circles. Lawyers and European Legal Integration.* A. Jettinghoff and H. Schepel (eds), 15–34. The Hague: Elsevier, 2005.

[10] In 1952, the *Mouvement Européen* established a *Comité des Juristes*. In the 1950s, a separate *Comité des Juristes*, a transnational group of lawyers (scholars, practioners, and government officials),

Euro-law associations served as gathering places for jurists interested in advancing the European integration project. Euro-law associations included politically connected and well-placed individuals. For example, the *Association Française des Juristes Européens* (AJE) was founded in 1953, by "gentlemen-politicians of law" including Pierre-Henri Teitigen and Maurice Roland.[11] Teitigen was, among other things, a government minister in the immediate post-war period, and a deputy and the political leader of the centrist French *Mouvement Républicain Populaire*, which captured a quarter of the French vote in the immediate post-war period. He was part of the French delegation to the *Comité des Juristes*, and rapporteur for the Committee on Legal and Administrative Questions in the negotiations for the Council of Europe.[12] Roland was a high magistrate at the *Cour de Cassation*. The German association the *Wissentschaftliche Gesellschaft für Europarecht* (WGE) was founded in 1961 by academics including Hans-Peter Ipsen, Gert Nicolaison, and Ernst Steindorff. Ipsen, a lifelong academic, was the intellectual father of European law in Germany. The leadership included Reimer Schmidt (an academic and early author on European legal issues), lawyers Bodo Börner and C.F. Ophüls (the latter was an advisor to German Chancellor Konrad Adenaur and the first president of the EC Commission, Walter Hallstein, and he participated in negotiations regarding the Treaty of Rome), and Walter Roemer from the Federal Ministry of Justice.[13] Employees of EC institutions (the Court of Justice, the Commission, and its Legal Secretariat) were tacit and at times explicit members of national Euro-law associations. For example, Walter Hallstein (President of the European Commission) and Otto Riese (a Former German Supreme Court judge and ECJ judge from 1959 to 1964) were members of the WGE.[14]

Many ties held this emerging European legal field together: members had been active in the war-time resistance, worked together in national government ministries, participated in the construction of the legal system of the Council of Europe, and helped to draft the United Nations Charter and the European Coal and Steel Community. A common commitment to the larger objective of European integration under a rule of law provided an ideological cohesion to the group.[15]

was charged with helping to write and advise on the negotiation of a European constitution based in law and protected by legal institutions. See C. Friedrich. Introduction: The Background of these Studies and the Development of the Draft Constitution. In: *Studies in Federalism*, R. Bowie and C. Friedrich (eds), xxv–xlii. Boston, MA: Little Brown, 1954. Members of these early committees later joined or helped found national Euro-law associations.

[11] G. Sacriste and A. Vauchez, The Force of International Law: Lawyer's Diplomacy on the International Scene in the 1920s. *Law & Social Inquiry* 2007, 32 (1): 91.

[12] M.R. Madsen, From Cold War Instrument to Supreme European Court: The European Court of Human Rights at the Crossroads of International and National Law and Politics. *Law & Social Inquiry* 2007, 32 (1): 141.

[13] H.P. Ipsen, "Europarecht" 25 Jahrgänge 1966–1990 in Verbindung mit der Wissenschaftlichen Gesellschaft für Europarecht. *Europarecht* 1990, 25 (4): 335.

[14] B. Davies, *Resisting the European Court of Justice: West Germany's Confrontation with European Law, 1949–1979*. Cambridge: Cambridge University Press, 2012.

[15] Madsen and Vauchez, 2005, 17–23.

Forming an organization dedicated to a particular legal topic was hardly novel. According to Hans-Jürgen Rabe, an early member of the WGE and later its secretary, in Europe it is quite common to establish associations when there is a new area of law.[16] Indeed, the WGE was founded as a working group of the pre-existing Society of Comparative Law (*Gesellschaft für Rechtsvergleichung*). Associations helped lawyers learn about legal developments so that they could advise their clients adequately, and they helped judges learn about such developments in other parts of the judiciary. It is also quite common for practitioners to hold seminars on new areas of law, to write briefs for legal journals, and to be consumers of journals that published court rulings and notes analyzing them. Thus, in some respects the activities undertaken by Euro-law associations were within the normal range for the European legal profession.

However, Euro-law associations had a specific political objective of promoting the larger European integration project (which also included the human rights work of the Council of Europe). The new Euro-law associations actively sought to wrest the topic of European law from specialists in coal and steel law and from international law experts whose traditional doctrines about the relationship between national and international rules were too limited to serve the aspirations of association leaders. These larger objectives of the associations were explicit. The French AJE's stated goal was to "help those outside of the organization understand the necessity of creating Europe and to identify the role jurists can and must play in the creation of a United Europe."[17] ECJ judges also spoke clearly about the role of judges in building European legal integration.[18] The common objectives united the members into a largely homogeneous "policy community" all working in the same direction.[19] One participant summarized the environment as follows:

> [I]n Europe around 1950 the idea of European unification was capable of evoking almost religious enthusiasm among young lawyers. We believed in the United State of Europe. Hardly anybody had any doubts about the possibility of achieving this aim within a few years. The reality turned out to be very different indeed. Yet, in spite of this state of affairs, the vast majority of West German teachers of "European Law" remained faithful to this ideal of their youth and passed on this ideology to their assistants, who now hold their chairs of "European Law".[20]

[16] Interview with Dr Hans-Jürgen Rabe, Secretary of the *Wissentschaftliche Gesellschaft für Europarecht*.

[17] Reprinted in a 1994 publication about the *Association Française des Juristes Européens*. Karen Alter transferred this archival material to the Historical Archives of the European Union, housed at the European Union University.

[18] A. Donner, *The Role of the Lawyer in the European Communities, The Rosenthal Lectures*. Evanston, IL: Northwestern University Press, 1968; R. Lecourt, Le Rôle du Droit dans l'Unification Européenne. *Gazette du Palais*: 1964, 49–54; F. Mancini, The Making of a Constitution for Europe. *Common Market Law Review* 1989, 26 (4): 595–614; P. Pescatore, La Clarence du Législateur Communautaire et le Devoir du Juge. In: *Gedächtnisschrift Für L.-J. Constantinesco*, 559–80. Cologne: Carl Heymanns Verlag, 1983.

[19] H. Schepel and R. Wesseling, The Legal Community: Judges, Lawyers, Officials and Clerks in the Writing of Europe. *European Law Journal* 1997, 3 (2): 165–88.

[20] I. Seidl-Hohenveldern, Review of Bodo Borner's Studien zum Deutschen und Europäischen Wirtshaftsrecht. *American Journal of International Law* 1984, 78 (1): 282–3.

Euro-law associations were immediately successful in organizational terms. The German WGE reached 200 to 300 members by the early 1960s, with a core membership of thirty to forty practitioners, including academics, in-house lawyers for large corporations, members of European and national governmental institutions, and interested professionals. According to the WGE's Secretary Hans-Jürgen Rabe, within this "core group" there was intense contact with the eight German lawyers of the Commission's legal services.[21] In 1963 France's AJE had seventy active members, including an *Avocat Général* of the ECJ and the Secretary of the European Commission on Human Rights (Maurice Lagrange), thirty-four lawyers, eleven French judges, five members of the *Conseil d'État*, eight professors of law, the president of the *Tribunal de Commerce de la Seine*, and a variety of well-known individuals from government and the private sector.[22] The meetings of the Belgium association also regularly drew fifty participants.[23]

With financial support from the European Commission, the organizations were able to host a number of conferences. Germany's WGE, with its scholarly focus, put its energy into planning conferences where issues of European law were debated, and in writing analyses of the law. According to the AJE's President Dr Lise Funck-Bretano, the French association was more distant from academics because "academics were involved in teaching in Universities, not in the development of law." Thus the AJE organized smaller meetings, lunches, and seminars for national lawyers and judges, sometimes meeting within national courts and often bringing in high officials from the European legal system.[24] The European Commission also helped develop the European legal field by establishing the FIDE, an umbrella organization connecting national associations. FIDE sponsored conferences every two years in the 1960s, providing a way for pro-integration lawyers from different countries (including the United Kingdom) to get to know each other and to coordinate activities.

German legal scholar Hans Peter Ipsen identified forty-one scholarly meetings of the WGE, FIDE, and a number of institutes from 1961 to 1973.[25] This number

[21] Interview with Hans-Jürgen Rabe, former secretary of WGE. By 1990 the WGE made up 45% of its parent organization the *Gesellschaft für Rechtsvergleichung*, with 516 members, 60% of whom were practitioners and 40% scholars. See Ipsen, 1990.

[22] A. Vauchez, Une élite d'intermédiaires? Genèse d'un Capital Juridique Européen. *Actes de la recherche en sciences sociales*. 2007a, No. 166–7: 54–65. By the 1990s, the head of the Association said it had 300 members, and that between 100 and 250 turned out for its events. Interview with Dr Lise Funck-Brentano, President of the *Association des Juristes Européens*.

[23] Interview with Michel Gaudet, former Director of the Legal Services of the European Commission.

[24] Interview with Dr Lise Funck-Brentano, President of the *Association des Juristes Européens*. This distance between practioners and the teaching of European law may be why politicians—Pierre-Henri Teitigen and Walter Hallstein (former President of the European Commission)—created a separate organization for academics. Teitigen founded the *Commission pour l'Etude des Communautés Européennes* and Walter Hallstein the German *Arbeitskreis für Europarecht*, both academic associations that worked to integrate European law studies into legal education. Interview with Gerard Nafylan, Treasurer of the *Commission pour l'Etude des Communautés Européennes*.

[25] H.P. Ipsen, 1972. Anmerkung zu BVerfG Entscheidung vom 9.6.1971. *Europarecht* 1972, Heft 1: 57–9.

does not include the smaller meetings, like those organized by the ECJ, which created a discussion forum for practitioners regarding specific legal topics. Meetings were well attended. According to Hans-Jürgen Rabe, at least throughout the early 1970s everyone who was anyone in European law attended WGE's conferences in Bad Em. Ipsen notes that the 1963 FIDE meeting in the Hague had over 200 participants, including 20 WGE members.[26] H.V. Brinkmann notes that a conference at the Gustav-Stresemann Institute in 1965 had forty judges, public attorneys, and clerks in attendance.[27]

Euro-law associations were fonts for writings about European legal developments. For example, within a little more than a year of the ECJ's seminal *Van Gend en Loos* decision, scholars published at least thirteen notes in national legal publications discussing the ruling, many if not most of which were written by Euro-law association members.[28] That there were so many legal publications in which to report is a sign of the existing legal infrastructures European law associations could use to promote their cause. Association members also wrote reference books about European law that interested lawyers could consult to learn about the EC legal system. Members of the WGE started a quarterly series in the most widely read legal journal, the *Neue Juristischen Wochenzeitshrift*, to inform the German bar about European legal developments.[29] They addressed the German *Juristentag* to inform its members about European law.[30] On occasion, WGE members telephoned judges who issued rulings antithetical to European law, explaining to them what they should have done. According to Rabe, this was a gentler approach than writing critical commentaries, but they also wrote critical commentaries.[31]

Members of the European Commission's Legal Services helped in these efforts. Michel Gaudet, Director of Legal Services from 1958 to 1970, explained that

[26] H.P. Ipsen, Aktuelle Fragen des Europäischen Gemeinschaftsrechts, 1964, 339.

[27] H-V. Brinkmann, Rechtsfragen der Europäischen Integration. *Neue Juristische Wochenschrift* 1965, (Heft 24): 1120–21.

[28] *Recueil Sirey* (1963) 29–33 (by Jean Robert, lawyer at the Cour de Paris); *Diritto Internazionale* (1963) No. 3 Part I, 247–8 (by Italo Telchini, legal counsel to the High Authority); *Giustizia Civile* (1963) No. 6 Parte Prima, 1225–31 (by Mario Berri); *Giursprueza Italiano* (1963) Disp. 4a, Parte IV (by Paolo Gori, attaché to ECJ); *Common Market Law Review* (1963) Vol. 1, 88–92 (by Samkalden); *Der Betrieb* (1963) No. 20, 683–5 (by Andreas Hammann, lawyer); Juris-Classeur Périodique, *La Semaine Juridique* (1963) No. 19 II Jurisprudence No. 13177 (by Fernand-Charles Jeantet, an active private business lawyer, identified at the time as a judge at the *Cour d'Appel de Paris*); *Le Barreau de France* (1963) No. 147-8, June–July, 25–6 (also by Jeantet); *Rivista di Diritto Processuale* (1963) No. 4, 651-7 (by Alessandro Migliazza, professor); *Journal des Tribunaux* (1963) No. 4397, 190–2 (by Fr. Rigaux); *Revue Générale de Droit International Public* (1963) No. 2, 421–2 (by Ch. R); *Il Foro Padano* (1963) No. 3 Parte Quinta, 33–42 (by Nicola Catalone, former legal advisor to ECSC, ECJ judge 1958–61); *International and Comparative Law Quarterly* (1963) Vol. 12, 1411–16 (by Norman Marsh).

[29] The first article explains the intent. See Ophüls, 1963. Ipsen also discusses the series in his twenty-fifth year retrospective in the journal *Europarecht*. Ipsen, 1990.

[30] Ipsen spoke to the *Juristentag* group in 1964. The 1966 meeting had a section focused on European law. After that, EC law was not an explicit theme, though it was frequently in the background of discussions. An explicit focus on the European legal system did not arise again until 1992. *Verhandlungen des Neunundfünfzigsten Deutschen Juristentages* 1992.

[31] Interview with Hans-Jürgen Rabe. See citations to legal criticisms in K.J. Alter, *Establishing the Supremacy of European Law: The Making of an International Rule of Law in Europe*. Oxford: Oxford University Press, 2001, 80–98.

his staff tried to meet with as many lawyers as possible to convince them to use European law. The goal, according to Gaudet, was to get people used to referencing European law and European institutions as part of normal legal debate.[32] The Commission also sent representatives and developed materials for training meetings on specific legal subject areas, and ECJ Justices and Commission Directors attended meetings, visited national judges, and penned introductions to important works concerning European law, lending the prestige of their office to fledgling publications and to association activities.

With seed money from the Commission, the associations founded European law journals including: *Rivista di Dirritto Europeo* (1961), *Cahiers de Droit Européen* (1965), *Revue Trimestrielle de Droit Européen* (1965), and *Europarecht* (1966).[33] The stated goals of these journals was to provide a venue for discussion of European legal issues (including human rights law), and to keep practioners abreast of European legal developments. FIDE helped to found the *Common Market Law Review* (1964)—a joint venture of the British Institute of International and Comparative Law and the Europa Institute in Leyden. Like its national counterparts, the *Common Market Law Review* had a trans-European editorial board, drawn from national associations and European officials.[34] However, it was written in English to facilitate the United Kingdom's accession to the EC.

Academic association members founded institutes at a number of universities and trained doctoral students who later became active members of associations.[35] The European Commission helped by providing grants for doctoral students, funding the publication of dissertations, giving subsidies to professors who taught seminars in European law, and funding university meetings where scholars could exchange research and teaching insights. The Commission also financed institutes for European studies, building associations of institutes and general associations for the study of the EC, and subsidizing meetings, newsletters, and events held by these groups. It created documentation centers that brought resources and prestige to the universities that were repositories of European documents, and it provided resources for European officials to spend time in academic settings.[36] With these and other policies, the Commission helped ensure that national universities had faculty members focused on European issues.

In addition to participating in the activities of the associations, EC officials undertook their own public relations efforts. Members of EC institutions were active writers on European legal issues. Harm Schepel and Rein Weisseling found that 32% of the 1,181 articles published in the *Common Market Law Review,*

[32] Interview with Michel Gaudet, Director of the Legal Services of the European Commission.

[33] M. Gaudet, Introductory Message. *Common Market Law Review* 1963, 1 (1): 1–2; Ipsen, 1990.

[34] Ernst Steindorff, cofounder of WGE, was on the board, as was Nicola Catalano, a former legal advisor for the Coal and Steel Community, and an ECJ judge from 1958 to 1961. Other members included Lord Diplock, H. Drion, W.L. Haardt, G. Van Hecke, Andrew Martin, Jonkheer F. van Panhuys, Jean Robert, and L J. Wilberforce.

[35] Indeed Hans-Jürgen Rabe was the progeny of an early Euro-law enthusiast, the longtime secretary of the WGE, wrote his thesis under Hans Peter Ipsen.

[36] Interview with Jaqueline Lastenouse, Director of Academic Affairs, European Commission.

Europarecht, and *Cahiers de Droit Européen* from their founding up to and including 1995 came from people who worked for European institutions—the Commission, the ECJ, and the Tribunal of First Instance—a level of involvement in scholarship that significantly exceeds the norm for public actor participation in legal debates.[37] With its docket fairly empty in the 1960s, the ECJ Justices used the time to cultivate support within national legal communities. It welcomed every reference from national courts, working with national judges to refine the formulation and substance of referred questions. The Justices regularly participated in scholarly conferences and workshops on European law, and they organized "stages," a prestigious version of vocational training, where their national colleagues could visit the ECJ to be wined and dined as they learned about the European legal system. The ECJ also took its show on the road, holding sessions in national capitals to generate news coverage and expose their activities to national audiences. In a somewhat unusual practice, European judges also wrote articles, speeches, and op-eds promoting the idea of lawyers helping to build integration through law.[38]

While association members shared a general affinity for the project of European integration, members came from a variety of backgrounds and were free thinkers who often disagreed about the means of promoting integration and specific legal questions.[39] Emil Noël stressed that the Commission encouraged free thinking. Academics and lawyers could not be controlled or indoctrinated, thus it was best to encourage open debate. Ultimately, Noel argued, the influence of European law would come from the persuasiveness of legal arguments, thus European officials were best off developing sound legal opinions.[40]

Written together, these efforts look extensive, but EC law remained an esoteric topic in the 1960s, and the advocates of European law knew they were fighting an uphill battle. The ECJ's doctrines of the supremacy and direct effect ran counter to established international and national legal doctrines. Especially if one considers that many early ECJ cases only existed because association members sought out ways to facilitate European legal integration, there were relatively few national court references to the ECJ in the 1960s (seventy-five references from 1960–69). In addition, there were newly issued high court rulings in Italy (1964), France (1964, 1968), and Germany (1967) that directly contradicted ECJ doctrine of the day.[41]

[37] Schepel and Wesseling, 1997, 172–3.

[38] E.g., see Donner, 1968; Lecourt, 1964; R. Lecourt, La Dynamique Judiciaire Dans L'édification De L'europe. *France Forum* 1965, Mai (64): 20–2; Mancini, 1989.

[39] Vauchez, 2007b.

[40] Interview with Emil Noël, Former Commissioner from the 1960s to 1980.

[41] *Costa v. Enel and Soc. Edisonvolta*, Italian Constitutional Court Decision 14 of 7 March 1964, [1964] CMLR 425, [1964] I Il Foro It. 87 I 465; *Re Tax on Malt Barley* (Case III 77/63) *FG Rhineland-Palatinate* decision of 14 November 1963, [1963] EuR 10 130, [1964] 10 CMLR 130. BVerfG decision of 5 July 1967, BVerfG 2 BvR 29/63, [1967] 2 EuR 351, [1967] 27 CMLR 302; *Société des pétroles Shell-Berre et autres, Sociétés 'Les Garages de France', Société Esso-Standard, Société Mobil Oil française, Société française des Pétroles B.P.*, Conseil d'État, decision of 19 June 1964, [1964] Recueil Lebon 344; [1964] 5 R DP 1019. 1991; *SA des Etablissements Petitjean et autres*, Conseil d'État decision of 10 February 1967, [1967] Recueil Lebon 63, [1967] AJDA 267, [1967] RTDE 681; *Semoules decision,*

The ECJ in the 1960s resembled the mouse that roared.[42] It was a small and rather powerless supranational court, asserting doctrines with constitutional aspirations that challenged entrenched legal practices and sought to wrest power away from powerful state actors. Associations worked to magnify the mouse's actions and to seize the topic of European law from the leading international law minds of the day, who seemed willing to keep European law quite limited in its reach.[43] Their objective was epic, and the resources Euro-law organizations had at their disposal were modest in comparison to the larger national budgets funding universities and other political and economic projects.

Yet compared to jurist advocacy movements in other contexts, European actors were well resourced. The immediate organizational success of Euro-law associations in planning events, turning out participants, and influencing the legal press—made possible in no small part by funds from the Commission—suggests a constituency of activists eager and able to support the European project. It also suggests that Europe in the 1960s had fairly vibrant national legal fields populated by lawyers and scholars with the means, time, and practice of participating in transnational legal debates. Established legal fields provided a ready market for presses, which could anticipate a flow of gratis scholarships and hefty subscription fees paid by libraries and practising lawyers. In many developing country contexts, it is hard to imagine that newly established member organizations could have such a broad and rapid influence.

The Impact of Euro-Law Advocacy Movements on European Legal Integration

How were Euro-law associations helpful to the larger process of legal integration? The neofunctionalist vision of legal integration sees lawyers, judges, and professors working on their own or as independent interest groups to promote their narrow self-interest. In Anne-Marie Burley and Walter Mattli's account, the political system was a "one-way ratchet." Since plaintiffs could only ask the ECJ for help in enforcing EC rules and the ECJ could only empower itself by obliging such requests, the pursuit of self-interest led ineluctably to the development of EC law and its penetration into national systems, or in Stone Sweet's terminology, the judicial construction of the rules of international governance.[44] Certainly,

Syndicat General de Fabricants de Semoules de France, Conseil d'État decision of 1 March 1968, [1968] *Recueil Lebon* 149, [1970] CMLR 395. These cases are briefly discussed in Alter, 1996, 461–6.

[42] *The Mouse that Roared* is a 1955 book by Leonard Wibberley that was made into a film in 1958. In the book and film, the fictional Duchy of Grand Fenwick wages war on the United States expecting to lose in the hopes that the United States will then help it rebuild its economy. Instead, through a series of strange events and coincidences, it captures a nuclear weapon and the great superpower capitulates to the tiny country.

[43] Davies, 2012, chapter 2.

[44] A-M. Burley and W. Mattli, Europe before the Court. *International Organization* 1993, 47 (1): 60–5; A. Stone Sweet, Judicialization and the Construction of Governance. *Comparative Political Studies* 1999, 32 (2): 147–84.

Euro-law associations contained self-interested members, and active participants clearly hoped to mobilize and inspire more self-interested non-ideological actors. However, the core association leaders were not themselves such actors, and their goal was not simply to embed European rules in national law. Rather, proponents of legal integration wanted to achieve what they had failed to win politically, by creating a constitution for Europe.

This section first shows how Euro-law associations helped define the larger legal field of contestation by creating ECJ test cases to facilitate the development of far-reaching legal doctrines, by acting as the ECJ's and Commission's kitchen cabinet, by spurring individuals to bold action, and by creating an impression of a momentum favoring the ECJ's doctrinal creations. The next section compares this experience to the early years of the Andean integration project. Although pro-integration lawyers fed a few test cases to the ATJ, the Tribunal declined to interpret Andean law in an expansionist way. More importantly, entrepreneurial lawyers and judges remained isolated, the ATJ lacked a kitchen cabinet, and no scholars published triumphal accounts of the Andean legal system to create a perception of vitality and momentum for the integration process.

The implication of these findings is that Euro-law associations critically defined what European legal integration became (and what the Andean legal system did not become). The counterfactual is that without the activities of Euro-law associations, a far more limited type of legal integration would have existed in Europe of the 1960s. This argument challenges the claim that there is an automaticity in international legal processes, a sort of invisible hand that channels oriented self-interested litigant and judicial behavior toward ambitious expansions of the reach and scope of international rules.

Generating test cases for the ECJ to develop far-reaching legal doctrine

The majority of cases referred to the ECJ in the 1960s concerned complicated formulas for calculating social security benefits for migrant workers and classifying customs categories. These cases represented how the European legal system was designed to work: national courts would refer to the ECJ technical questions about EC rules that arose as litigants raised suits involving European law. These spontaneous cases were not, however, per se helpful in building the ECJ's authority as an important legal and political actor. References asking far-reaching questions, and thus provoking rulings of doctrinal significance, required orchestration by association members.

The ECJ's constitutionalizing process began with two early rulings, *Van Gend en Loos* (1962) and *Costa v. Enel* (1964), which established the direct effect and supremacy of EC law. Euro-law associations were key in constituting these rulings. The Dutch legal system offered the most hospitable environment for European law because the 1953 Dutch constitution recognized the supremacy of international law.[45] Moreover, Dutch courts can apply international rules that are considered

[45] Fifteen of the first eighteen preliminary references to the ECJ came from Dutch courts. See Vauchez, 2008, 9 n. 25.

self-executing.[46] In November 1961, the Dutch Euro-law association established a working group to identify which provisions of the Treaty of Rome might be seen as self-executing and thus directly applicable by domestic courts and supreme to conflicting Dutch law. L.F.D. Ter Keile, a young Dutch lawyer and member of the association, fashioned a test case in which Dutch judges queried the ECJ as to whether the EC provision in question created direct effects.[47] The case concerned the reclassification of a customs duty that according to Ter Keile had the effect of raising the existing tariff in contravention of the Treaty of Rome. A similar fact pattern would appear twenty years later in the Andean context.[48]

The *Van Gend en Loos* reference, which came from a tariff commission, was significant for a few reasons. There was a clear and well-established answer to the legal question at hand: given that the treaty provision in question was not addressed to individuals, it should not create direct effects.[49] Referring the question to the ECJ could help legal activists procure a different answer than that which more conservative Dutch judges might on their own give. The reference also suggested that the ECJ had the authority to speak to the effect of EC law within national legal systems, thus providing the court with an opportunity to assert a reach for European law that would apply beyond The Netherlands. The ECJ's *Van Gend en Loos* ruling is famous for asserting that some articles in the Treaty of Rome create direct effects that individuals can invoke before national judges.[50]

In the Dutch system, if European law created direct effects, it was ipso facto supreme to conflicting domestic rules. Other European legal systems gave primacy to the more recently adopted law, which meant that even if EC law created direct effects, it could be supplanted by national rules enacted later in time. The ECJ's *Costa v. Enel* decision addressed this precise issue—whether EC law has supremacy over subsequently enacted national laws.[51]

[46] M. Claes and B. De Witte, Report on the Netherlands. In: *The European Courts and National Courts*. A.-M. Slaughter, A. Stone-Sweet, and J. Weiler (eds), 171–94. Cambridge: Hart Publishing, 1998, 173–6.

[47] A. Vauchez, "Integration through Law" Socio-History of EU Political Common Sense. In: European University Institute (EUI). Robert Schuman Centre of Advanced Studies Working Paper 2008/10, 9.

[48] Chapter 8 explains that the *Reynolds Aluminum* dispute first appeared as a noncompliance complaint, which the ATJ dismissed because the plaintiff lacked standing to raise the suit. When the case reappeared as a preliminary reference, the ATJ refused to consider whether raising a tariff violated the Cartegena Agreement, reasoning that products that the government had placed on a "list of exception" were exempted from supranational judicial scrutiny. ATJ Preliminary Ruling 1-IP-90.

[49] Claes and De Witte, 1998, 176. For a more definitive account of the origin of the *Van Gend en Loos* and *Costa* rulings, and their contribution to the creation of a European legal order, see M. Rasmussen, The Origins of a Legal Revolution—The Early History of the European Court of Justice. *Journal of European History* 2008 14(2): 77–98; M. Rasmussen, From Costa v. Enel to the Treaties of Rome: A Brief History of Legal Revolution. In: *The Past and Future of EU Law: The Classics of EU Law Revisited on the 50th Anniversary of the Rome Treaty*. M. Poiares Maduro and L. Azoulai (eds), 69–85. Portland: Hart Publishing, 2010.

[50] Case 26/62, *Van Gend en Loos v. Nederlandse Administratie Belastingen* [1963] ECR 1, [1963] CMLR 105.

[51] It is not clear if the lawyers—Flaminio Costa and Giangaleazzo Stendari—were members of Euro-law associations, though they did write about European legal issues. Vauchez, 2008, 17.

The lawyers behind the *Costa v. Enel* case were not pro-integration activists; rather, they created the case to challenge what they saw as excessive government intervention in the Italian economy. The lawyers raised the suit in a small claims court, using a $3 electricity bill as the legal basis to challenge the nationalization of the Italian energy industry. The small claims court referred the case both to the ECJ and to the Italian Constitutional Court. The Constitutional Court ruled first, finding that the case raised no issues related to European integration. Nonetheless, the ECJ went on to find that EC law is supreme to national law, but that the nationalization of the Italian energy industry did not violate any EC rules.[52]

Inasmuch as both courts upheld the Italian nationalization and found no violation of EC law, the two rulings appeared to validate the legal status quo. It was the efforts of pro-integration advocates that made the ECJ ruling legally significant. From within their offices as EC officials, Euro-law association members situated the reference in the context of a handful of recent adverse national court rulings, suggesting a dangerous trend of national judges limiting the effect of European law within national systems. Framed in this way, the need to assert the supremacy of Community law seemed more pressing. European judges and Euro-law associations amplified the ECJ's *Costa v. Enel* pronouncements with writings and speeches that advertised the legal ruling and manufactured its far-reaching implications. According to Vauchez, participants were engaged in a sort of ventriloquism. Before the ruling academics and practitioners spoke about what European law should mean. ECJ judges then pronounced in the rulings what European law meant, although they did so ambiguously. Subsequently, the very same set of Euro-law actors summarized what the ECJ had said, offering less ambiguous interpretations of the ruling and shaping its meaning and import.[53]

There were a number of other test cases constructed through association meetings and then trumpeted for their importance. The ECJ's *Cassis de Dijon* ruling originated at an association meeting where a member of the Commission leaked to a German lawyer the fact that it had settled a case involving the French liqueur Anisette. Euro-law association member Gert Meier, the in-house counsel for Rewe Zentrale, simply changed the type of liqueur to Cassis de Dijon, and brought his own test case.[54] The Commission's reaction to the ECJ ruling, more than the decision itself, triggered legal and political contestation, the end result of which was arguably a retrenchment of the ECJ doctrine of mutual recognition, broadly

[52] For a deeper social history of the Costa case, see Rasmussen, 2008; Rasmussen 2010; Vauchez, 2007b. *Costa v. Enel and Soc. Edisonvolta*, Italian Constitutional Court Decision 14 of 7 March 1964 [1964] CMLR 425, [1964] I Il Foro It. 87 I 465.

[53] Vauchez, 2008.

[54] Meier brought at least twelve cases that were ultimately referred to the ECJ. Meier estimat that national judges referred only 10% of the cases where he argued that European law was releva Where Meier's goal was to have a case referred to the ECJ, however, he estimated that he succeed 90% of the time because he would bring the case to sympathetic judges. Sometimes judges even asd Meier to find cases to refer. These types of requests, he noted, usually were made at FIDE, WGE, ıd *Gesellschaft für Lebensmittel* conferences. Interview with Gert Meier, in-house lawyer for *Rewe Zentle*, April 26, 1993, Cologne.

interpreted. Still, the ECJ's interlocutors had achieved a huge victory. They had transformed a legal decision that applied only to alcohol imported into Germany into a widely known legal doctrine of general significance, and helped to surmount a political impasse by forcing member states to alter the ECJ's mutual recognition doctrine through enacting their own legislation on the topic.[55]

European officials also influenced legal integration by shedding their EC positions and assuming the role of private actors. While a member of the European Commission, Elaine Vogel-Polsky published an article suggesting the provision of the Treaty of Rome guaranteeing equal pay for men and women could create direct effects, and thus provide a basis to challenge national practices that discriminated on the basis of sex. Vogel-Polsky helped write the EC's Equal Treatment Directive. As a private lawyer, she later found the plaintiff Defrenne (who gave Vogel-Polsky her case but did not participate beyond that) and constructed the test case against Sabena Airlines that established the direct effect of the Treaty of Rome provision requiring men and women to receive equal pay for equal work (Article 119).[56]

Such activism does not always work in the ECJ's favor; legal strategies can also be counter-reactions to political activism. In 1974 the German Constitutional Court issued a contested ruling that seemed to call into question the legal and political basis for the ECJ's supremacy doctrine. The WGE co-founder, Bodo Börner, supported the German Constitutional Court's controversial *Solange I* ruling, agreeing that the German Constitutional Court could find EC law invalid in Germany if it conflicted with German Basic Law.[57] Börner felt that ignoring German concerns regarding a lack of basic rights protections in EC law would be counterproductive and even dangerous for European integration.[58] Later still, when political developments were proceeding uncomfortably fast, four members of the European Parliament from the German Green Party and a member of the European Commission became litigants opposing the constitutionality of the Treaty of Maastricht, which led to another controversial ruling by the German Constitutional Court—its 1993 *Maastricht* decision that reasserted limits to the reach of EC law in Germany.[59] Such contestation, inherent in the politics of legal fields, ensures that European legal integration is not the one-way ratchet that neofunctionalist theory expects.

55 The larger impact of the *Cassis de Dijon* ruling is investigated in K.J. Alter and S. Meunier-Aitsahalia, Judicial Politics in the European Community: European Integration and the Pathbreaking *Cassis de Dijon* Decision. *Comparative Political Studies* 1994, 24 (4): 535–61.

56 *Defrenne v. Sabena* [1976] ICR 547; *Defrenne v. Société Anonyme Belge de Navigation Aérienne Sabena* [1978] ECR 1365, ECJ. Vogel Polskey first wrote about this strategy in 1967; E. Vogel-Polsky, Article 119 du Traité de Rome Peut-Il Être Considéré Comme Self-Executing? *Journal des Tribunaux* 67, 283–7. The arguments raised by cause lawyers in this case are discussed in C. Harlow and R. wlings, *Pressure through Law*. London: Routledge, 1992, 283.

7 *Internationale Handelsgesellschaft v. Einfuhr und Vorratsstelle für Getreide und Futtermittel*, BrfGE 37, 271, 1974 2 CMLR 540. The controversy surrounding this decision is discussed by Alter, 2(1, 89–94.

Seidl-Hohenveldern, 1984, 283.

Brunner and Others v. The European Union Treaty, 'Maastricht decision', 2 BvR 2134/92 and 2 BvR 215/92 of January 11, 1994 [1994] 1 EuR 95, [1994]; Alter, 2001, 94–117.

Serving as the ECJ's and the Legal Secretariat's kitchen cabinet

The American term "kitchen cabinet" refers to President Andrew Jackson's practice of circumventing his real cabinet (the one approved by the Senate) to plan policy with like-minded friends. National governments are arguably the ECJ's statutory cabinet, since they write the laws that the ECJ interprets. Euro-law associations were the ECJ's kitchen cabinet, providing a means for EC officials to test out ideas and seek informal advice, which was especially important given that in the 1960s national political leaders were challenging the supranational aspects of European integration.

It is hard to underestimate the benefit to the ECJ of having such a discussion forum. In the 1960s, the ECJ had a handful of judges who were ardent European federalists, but they were also pragmatic about the obstacles they faced.[60] By design, the European legal system provides ECJ judges with legal advice. The ECJ has a system of *Advocats Généraux* who offer legal interpretations for the judges to consider. In addition, the Commission's legal secretariat usually weighs in during court proceedings. These insider suggestions, which are published before the ECJ itself rules, serve as a sort of trial balloon where the court can gauge support for different legal arguments. Association members and events provide the audience, keeping track of legal developments and providing feedback in real time.[61] In short, the associations helped ECJ judges gauge how far they could push their integrationist agenda.

Hans-Jürgen Rabe, secretary and early member of the WGE, recalled a conference in Vienna shortly after the ECJ's *Van Gend en Loos* decision where conversation kept returning to that ruling.[62] Even though the *Avocat Général* in the *Van Gend* case had pointed out that a finding that EC law created direct effects implied that European law was also supreme to national law, Rabe recalls that the ECJ's president André Donner vigorously denied that the ruling spoke to the supremacy of European law. Rabe interpreted Donner's denial as an effort by the ECJ to tread carefully.

Inspired by the exchange, the WGE's leadership put the issue of supremacy on the agenda for its next meeting, held on July 10, 1964 in Bensheim. The date proved highly fortuitous. On June 24, 1964, just two-and-a-half weeks before the WGE's conference, the ECJ's *Avocat Général* Maurice Lagrange (an AJE member) made his oral argument on the *Costa* case. Lagrange had argued that national judges should find ways within their constitutions to give effect to European law, or national governments should change constitutions to facilitate legal integration. At the July 10 meeting, Ipsen criticized Lagrange's widely shared perspective, urging instead that ECJ judges should find that the Treaty of Rome itself implied European law supremacy. The advantage of this interpretation was that the Treaty of Rome was

[60] F. Mancini and D. Keeling, From CILFIT to ERTA: The Constitutional Challenge Facing the European Court. *Yearbook of European Law* 1995, 11, 403.

[61] Rasmussen, 1986, 265–6.

[62] *Van Gend en Loos* was issued 5 February 1963. The dates correspond to a meeting held in Vienna from 18–21 September 1963 organized by Würdinger and Wohlfarth.

already part of national law. Also, basing EC law supremacy on the Treaty ensured that the origin of the supremacy doctrine was uniform and independent from national constitutional limitations. Rabe notes that three European judges were at the meeting "listening with red ears," wanting to know if the leading academics of EC law would accept Ipsen's argument. Five days later, the ECJ issued its famous *Costa v. Enel* ruling, going beyond Lagrange's argument to base the supremacy of European law in the Treaty of Rome.[63]

With a friendly set of critics willing to engage with doctrines and ideas, in a setting where there are no written records and opinions can be gauged in real time, the ECJ received important insights into the reception its rulings were likely to receive within national legal systems. In the case of the supremacy debate, the ECJ learned that there was support for a bolder assertion of the supremacy of EC law over national law. European officials kept track of these debates. The ECJ had employees who compiled dossiers on national court decisions and culled national legal journals for articles on these decisions and on ECJ rulings. The conversation in Bensheim was deemed of great enough importance to be reported to the President of the EC Commission, Walter Hallstein, via a memo that summarized the debate and noted most people in the audience had sided with Ipsen's perspective.[64]

Developing community, which inspired and emboldened members

The two previous points—that association members fashioned test cases and advised the ECJ on doctrinal issues—suggest a third contribution of Euro-law associations. The associations provided a community that helped inspire individuals to bold action. Their meetings were places where the Commission leaked to lawyers the legal issues that it had chosen not to pursue through infringement proceedings (which led to the *Cassis de Dijon* case). The meetings were places where lawyers could identify friendly national judges, and where lawyers and judges could learn about the types of cases the ECJ would welcome. The previous discussion of the 1964 WGE Bensheim conference shows how the interactions of like-minded supporters egged on each member, encouraging the ECJ to make the bolder legal claim that the Treaty of Rome itself suggested the supremacy of European law.

This community was important because the steps needed to develop the supremacy of European law were larger than any one actor. The ECJ needed cases so it could issue rulings; its ruling had to be well received within legal communities; and follow-up efforts were needed to create a reality that reflected the new legal doctrines. Associations fostered a sense that the different components of the process would work in tandem, which helped individual actors to play their part in the larger scheme. When the ECJ rewarded litigants, and scholars then praised the ECJ for its rulings, there was confirmation that bold actions led to good results. Such

[63] The Ipsen opinion was published as Ipsen, 1964. Interview with Dr Hans Jürgen Rabe, Secretary of the WGE, Brussels.

[64] Davies, 2012, 78, 89.

positive reinforcement helps activists be entrepreneurial by suggesting that bold ideas are not crazy ideas.

Creating the perception of momentum in favor of European legal integration

European law was more frequently ignored than followed in the 1960s and 1970s. National judges unaffiliated with Euro-law movements were reluctant to refer cases to the ECJ, there were national high court rulings that seemed to contradict ECJ doctrine, and the common market objectives of a free movement of goods, services, capital, and people remained a distant dream. Euro-law movements sought to change the legal perception regarding European integration while the political will and thus the political reality of European integration lagged. We previously described the numerous legal briefs heralding the importance of the ECJ's *Van Gend* and *Costa* rulings, which helped manufacture the sense that the rulings were of great constitutional importance. Euro-law associations also manufactured the national court decisions that created a sense that ECJ doctrines were spreading within national legal systems. The *Cafés Jacques Vabre* ruling of the French *Cour de Cassation* is an example; it would not have become important were it not for Euro-law supporters using their offices to advance European legal integration.

The *Cafés Jacques Vabre* case was important because France's two other high courts had established a record of opposing ECJ authority and European law supremacy.[65] Adolphe Touffait, the former Chef de Cabinet of pro-Europe advocate Pierre-Henri Teitigen, was an active member of AJE, and ultimately a judge on the ECJ from 1976 to 1982. He used his professional position to imply that there was movement in the prevailing view of French judges against both the ECJ's authority and EC law's supremacy. By the time the *Cafés Jacques Vabre* case reached the *Cour de Cassation* (France's highest ordinary court), Touffait had been promoted to *Procureur Général* of the *Cour de Cassation* (the equivalent of

[65] In the 1964 *Shelle-Berre* and 1967 *Petitjean* cases, Commissaire du Gouvernement Questiaux (who played the equivalent role of the ECJ's *Avocat Général*) urged the *Conseil d'État* to assert that it could interpret even rather unclear EC law on its own, which the *Conseil d'État* implicitly did by not referring the cases to the ECJ. In 1968, the *Conseil d'État* issued its *Semoules* ruling, which refused to consider whether European law was supreme to the French law in question, suggesting that the *Conseil Constitutionnel* was responsible for enforcing the French constitutional provision that granted supremacy to international rules. Then, in 1975 the *Conseil Constitutionnel* decided that it lacked the authority to consider whether French laws conflicted with international rules, so that it appeared as if no French courts were obliged to enforce the supremacy of European law. *Société des pétroles Shell-Berre et Autres, Sociétés 'Les Garages de France', Société Esso-Standard, Société Mobile Oil Française, Société Française des Pétroles B.P., Conseil d'État* decision of June 19, 1964, [1964] *Recueil Lebon* 344. [1964] 5 R DP 1019;. *S.A. des Etablissements Petitjean et Autres, Conseil d'État* decision of February 10, 1967, [1967] *Recueil Lebon* 63, [1967] AJDA 267, [1967] RTDE 681. *Syndicat Général de Fabricants de Semoules de France*, Conseil d'État decision of March 1, 1968, [1968] *Recueil Lebon* 149, [1970] CMLR 395. *Conseil Constitutionnel* decision 74–54 of January 15, 1975, [1975] *Recueil des Décisions du Conseil constitutionnel* 19. [1975] Dalloz-Jurisprudence 529. This progression of cases are discussed in depth in chapter 4 of Alter, 2001.

the administrative system's *Commissaire du Gouvernement* and the ECJ's *Avocat Général*), a position he used to great effect.

In the *Cafés Jacques Vabre* case, the private litigant, a coffee-maker, had refused to pay a tax that it claimed was contrary to EC law.[66] The first-instance court sided with the coffee-maker, suggesting the supremacy of European law but basing the legal decision on other inaccuracies in the government's calculations of the tax. The appeals court also sided with the coffee-maker, but suggested that the issue at stake was a French regulation, not a law, thus it ducked the question of whether EC law could be supreme to French law. If the *Cour de Cassation* had taken either of these routes, the legal outcome would have been the same but the ruling would not be famous.[67]

Procureur Général Touffait avoided any obfuscation, framing the case in historic terms. He suggested that the *Conseil d'État*'s *Semoules* ruling, which had rejected the supremacy of European law in France,[68] was made in the context of an exceptional situation (the independence of France's former colony, Algeria), and thus did not have wider significance. He offered a questionable interpretation of the French Constitutional Council's 1975 ruling, suggesting that that the ruling implied that reviewing the compatibility of French law with EC law was merely "applying" the constitution, not conducting judicial review of national laws, which only the Constitutional Council could do. Touffait summarized the state of European law doctrine in other member states and argued that the French court should base the supremacy of Community law on the Treaty of Rome, not the French constitution. He finished his argument as follows: "It is in this context that the judgment you are to deliver will be read and commented upon; its audience will extend beyond the frontiers of our country and spread over the whole of the member states of the Community."[69]

The *Cafés Jacques Vabre* ruling was trumpeted by Euro-law scholars as endorsing the ECJ's supremacy doctrine. The ruling itself actually says very little; it is not

[66] If the coffee-maker had chosen to challenge the legality of the tax, it would have had to file suit with the *Conseil d'État*, which, given its established jurisprudence (the *Semoules* doctrine), would have resulted in a legal defeat. However, because the *Café Jacques Vabre* suit was filed by the tax authority against the coffee-maker for non-payment, and because the tax law in question had been adopted subsequent in time to the Treaty of Rome, the case was one of the rare "ordinary" cases raising the supremacy of EC law.

[67] *Administration des Douanes v. Société Cafés Jacques Vabre and J. Weigel et Compagnie Sarl, Tribunal d'instance* decision of January 8, 1971 [1976] 1 CMLR 43. *Administration des Douanes v. Société Cafés Jacques Vabre and J. Weigel et Compagnie Sarl, Cour d'Appel* decision of July 7, 1973 [1975] 2 CMLR 22.

[68] *Syndicat General de Fabricants de Semoules de France, Conseil d'État* decision of March 1, 1968, [1968] *Recueil Lebon* 149, [1970] CMLR 395.

[69] *Administration des Douanes v. Société Cafés Jacques Vabre and J. Weigel et Compagnie Sarl,* Cour de Cassation decision of May 24, 1975, [1975] 2 CMLR 343, at 367. A similar story could be told about the famous *Belgium Le Ski* decision which asserted a role for Belgian judges in enforcing the supremacy of European law. This decision was famous in no small part because of the arguments of Ganschoff Van de Meersh, a member of the Belgian Euro-law association, who played a role analogous to that of Adolpe Touffait in the *Cafés Jacques Vabre* case. *État Belge v. S.A. 'Fromagerie Franco-Suisse Le Ski',* decision of the *Cour de Cassation, 1ere Chambre,* 1971. *Journal des Tribunaux* 460 2. CCH CMLR 8141. See "Conflicts between Treaties and Subsequently Enacted Statutes in Belgium: *État Belge v. S.A. 'Fromagerie Franco-Suisse Le Ski*,' " 1973.

what students or scholars focus on. Rather, for many years Touffait's argument was used in European law casebooks as an exemplar of a national court accepting the supremacy of EC law.

In the Andean context, there were also turning point decisions that unleashed a steady flow of references to the ATJ. Chapter 3 discusses these decisions, explaining the legal fights that led national judges to make an ATJ reference in the case in question and in subsequent cases. These reversals were spearheaded by persistent lawyers, but not with the goal of building important legal doctrine. In fact, none of the key ATJ rulings included lofty language suitable for legal casebooks. More generally, although the number of referrals expanded in the ways we describe in Chapter 3, national judges in the Andes continue to have very circumscribed understandings about the relationship between the Andean and national legal orders.

The pro-EC scholarship was also easily dismissed before there were rulings by national judges that appeared to endorse the ECJ's jurisprudence in constitutional terms. The combination of rulings and writings that confirmed the supremacy of European law was intimidating. German judge Helmut Friedl was not a member of the WGE. As a tax judge, Friedl believed he was obliged to refer to the ECJ questions that concerned European tax directives. Friedl estimated that he referred at least forty cases to the ECJ over his years at the *Finanzgericht München*, yet he still believed that there was little legal basis supporting the supremacy of European law. Friedl said that the supremacy doctrine crept up on national judges who did not pay much attention to the ECJ's rulings or to pro-Europe legal debates. Friedl was aware of the ECJ's *Costa* decision, but he emphasized that the ECJ had said that the ruling applied as far as European law was concerned. By 1970, however, there was a "governing opinion" in the literature supporting EC law supremacy. Judges, he said, avoided the criticism that would come with contradicting the governing opinion by sidestepping the issue, which was easy to do since few cases raised issues of European law supremacy. Friedl also observed that after 1968 there was not nearly as much literature challenging the supremacy doctrine, surmising that authors were avoiding being labeled "anti-European."[70]

Establishing a European legal field

ECJ judges and early European legal integration scholars explained the success of ECJ doctrine by focusing on the persuasive authority of the court's decisions.[71] However, it was not the judges' ideas that made the difference. The legal interpretations propounded by the court, and stridently supported through publications penned by Euro-law association members, did not gain much traction within national legal communities. Numerous national judges and unaffiliated legal scholars discounted the opinions of Euro-law members, seeing them as more ideological

[70] Interview with Dr Helmut Friedl, former judge at *Finanzgericht München*, Clerk at the *Bundesfinanzhof* from 1967–72.

[71] Mancini, 1989, 605–6; J. Weiler, The Transformation of Europe. *Yale Law Journal* 1991, 100 (8): 2428.

than legal. In fact, national high courts, including France's *Cour de Cassation*, have not accepted the argument that the Treaty of Rome requires the supremacy of European law. Instead, national judges found ways within their respective legal systems to accommodate EC supremacy doctrine without ceding the supremacy of their own constitutions or their own judicial authority.[72]

An important contributor to Euro-law associations' success was the social and political capital of its members. High-level legal practice generates professional opportunities in academia, government, industry, and the judiciary; the most well-connected lawyers tend to move back and forth across these domains during their careers.[73] Seen from this perspective, the members of Euro-law associations were particularly powerful. The Second World War discredited an entire legal and political class, providing unique opportunities for those lawyers who were both highly skilled and untainted by collaboration.[74] This unusually small group of lawyers served in post-war government ministries and high courts. Many were members of political dynasties, thus they were also relatives of ministers and high officials. Euro-law advocates were the professors who chaired dissertation committees and thus had sway over the career prospects of young academics. They served as lawyers to industries, which allowed them to generate test cases. They switched offices, rotating their roles—one day being a lawyer, another a commentator, and another a judge or legal advisor—to magnify their actions so as to appear greater in number and effect than they actually were. The cumulative result of their advocacy as lawyers, judges, scholars, and government officials was the monopolization and ultimately the construction of the meaning of European law.

Legal Integration Without Jurist Advocacy Support: The Andean Tribunal of Justice

Throughout their history, the Andean Community and the ATJ have enjoyed the backing of legal entrepreneurs. Chapter 2 explains that a network of pro-integration scholars promoted a Tribunal modeled on the ECJ, copying the ECJ doctrines of the direct effect and the supremacy of EC law. Chapter 3 documents the dearth of preliminary rulings regarding legal issues unrelated to intellectual property, contrasting the reticence of Andean judges with their European counterparts, and explaining the entrepreneurial strategies needed to encourage references from courts in Colombia, Ecuador, Peru, and, most recently, Bolivia. This section provides additional detail on the individuals who actively sought to build Andean legal integration during this period.

During our research in the Andes, we interviewed judges and lawyers who participated or might have participated in the Andean legal integration process, asking about their backgrounds, motivations, and actions. Like their European

[72] This is the central claim of Alter, 2001. [73] Madsen, 2013.
[74] Sacriste and Vauchez, 2007; Vauchez, 2007a; Madsen and Vauchez, 2005.

counterparts, these individuals had domestic political capital and they moved across the spectrum of legal roles, serving as government officials, national judges, professors, and private lawyers. Unlike in Europe, however, these Andean lawyers and judges remained isolated. There was no larger advocacy community to spur these actors on, nor were these individuals transnationally mobilized. Rather, individual legal entrepreneurs episodically filed cases to promote the Andean integration process, working against a larger tide of legal and judicial indifference.

As we explain in Chapter 2, the original design of the Andean legal system contributed to the dearth of cases in the Tribunal's first ten years of operation. In particular, only the *Junta* was authorized to investigate the noncompliance complaints of private litigants. Luis E. Pochet provided the ATJ with an opportunity to overcome this limitation, filing with the Tribunal a noncompliance suit on behalf of Reynolds Aluminum. The case closely resembled *Van Gend en Loos*, where the litigant invoked an article of the Treaty of Rome prohibiting member states from raising tariffs to challenge the Dutch customs administration's reclassification of a product. The Cartagena Agreement contained a similar provision. Article 41 called for the progressive elimination of internal tariffs and thus it arguably prohibited Andean member states from raising any tariffs. Pochet argued that the Colombian regulation in question had the effect of increasing the tariff in violation of the Cartagena Agreement. In its November 1987 ruling, however, the ATJ rejected the complaint because private actors were not authorized to file noncompliance suits.[75] The case would soon reappear, however, as a preliminary ruling.

Soon after dismissing the first noncompliance case on legal standing grounds, the ATJ received its first preliminary reference. The referral came from a Colombian suit brought by Germán Cavelier, who had served as Secretary General of the Ministry of Foreign Affairs in 1968 and 1969 when the Andean Pact was being negotiated. Dr Cavelier was a committed internationalist, writing his doctoral thesis and numerous treatises on international law. According to attorneys in the law firm he established, Cavelier believed in regional integration as a way to strengthen law, although he himself was not involved in the negotiations. Cavelier challenged a Colombian administrative decision denying Volvo's application for a trademark, taking the bold step of asking for a preliminary reference. Cavelier did not simply make a legal argument in court; he talked with former judges of the Colombian *Consejo de Estado* who personally lobbied their colleagues to change their position regarding ATJ referrals. This case became the first national court preliminary reference to the Tribunal.[76]

As Chapters 4 and 8 explain, the ATJ used the case to explain the preliminary ruling process. Invoking terminology that was nearly identical to earlier ECJ decisions, the ATJ asserted that Andean rules have direct effect and are supreme to national law. Shortly thereafter, the ATJ explicitly embraced the ECJ's *Costa* and *Simmenthal*

[75] ATJ Noncompliance Judgment 1-AI-87. We searched for professional information about Pochet but could find none.

[76] Interview with two attorneys (J) from the family firm of an attorney raising an early ATJ case. The case in question was ATJ Preliminary Ruling 1-IP-87.

jurisprudence, suggesting that Andean judges were legally obliged to ensure that Andean law achieved full effect within the national legal order.[77] Although the outcomes of these rulings did not turned on these pronouncements, the ATJ took the opportunity to instruct national courts on the workings of the Andean legal system, invoking ECJ rulings to support its claim that the relevant national actors were required to refer cases and to enforce Andean law. The ATJ habitually repeateded these principles in subsequent decisions, although, as Chapter 8 explains, it did not extend them to their logical conclusions.

The case filed by Pochet—which had been rejected as a noncompliance suit—later reappeared as a preliminary reference brought on behalf of *Reynolds Aluminum Santodomingo* and *Sociedad Aluminio Nacional*. Pochet again invoked Article 41 of the Cartagena Agreement, which called for the progressive elimination of internal tariffs and thus arguably prohibited raising any tariffs. The Colombian government urged the ATJ to instead apply Article 55, which allowed for a list of tariff exceptions. Pochet responded that even though the Cartagena Agreement permitted these temporary exceptions, governments were still precluded from raising tariffs in general.

The *Reynolds Aluminum* case provided the ATJ with an opportunity to interpret the Andean Pact's founding treaty as a constitutional document, creating a hierarchy that would place Community objectives above temporary provisions of Andean secondary law. The ATJ, however, sided with the Colombian government. It refused to delimit what the member states could do with respect to goods included on the list of exceptions. The ATJ also refused to consider what products fell under the list of exceptions, leaving that task to national courts. The ruling essentially removed the ATJ from debates about which good were included on a fairly extensive list of exceptions.[78]

Pochet and Cavelier were legal entrepreneurs, although they did not appear to be following a constructed plan nor were they affiliated with a larger group of actors.[79] As a result, the ATJ's potentially momentous early rulings engendered virtual silence. The few journal articles on the Andean legal system, published years later, were mostly penned by lawyers with degrees in Europe or the United States, or were published in Europe or the United States and thus rarely read by local attorneys.[80]

[77] ATJ Preliminary Ruling 2-IP-88.

[78] Hojman explains that the Andean Pact had a separate set of rules regarding certain classes of goods produced in a number of member states, and that the marginal tariffs on these goods were used to limit internal trade, thereby decreasing the benefit of Andean integration for key sectors of the economy. See D.E. Hojman, The Andean Pact: Failure of a Model of Integration? *Journal of Common Market Studies* 1981, 20 (2): 139–59. This was the system that Pochet was challenging.

[79] Members of Cavelier's law firm were unaware of any pro-integration movement or group that Cavelier might have been connected to. In their view, he was an individual entrepreneur. Interview with two attorneys (J) from the family firm of an attorney raising an early ATJ case.

[80] There are publications in Spanish that mainly summarize aspects of Andean law or ATJ decisions. Far harder to find are analyses of the doctrinal implications of the Tribunal's rulings or their contribution to legal integration. A few exceptions (all quite recent) include: M. Baquero-Herrera, Open Regionalism in Latin America: An Appraisal. *Law and Business Review of the Americas* 2004, 11 (2): 139–84; M.A. Rodriguez Lemmo, Study of Selected International Dispute Resolution Regimes, with an Analysis of the Decisions of the Court of the Andean Community. *Arizona Journal*

We spoke with a first generation of Andean judges, trying to understand how, if at all, they sought to amplify the ATJ's legal voice. The judges highlighted the many early challenges the Tribunal faced. They struggled to secure a court building and support staff, and they had to resolve a number of internal suits based on Andean officials' breach of staff contracts.[81] As far as we are aware, European judges never faced these basic logistical and financial challenges, or they surmounted the challenges during the early operation of the Coal and Steel Community in the 1950s.

Andean judges also lack the input and advice of an ECJ-style *Avocat Général*. The previous section explained how a Euro-law conference that include national legal experts and ECJ judges openly debated the *Avocat Général*'s recommendation in the *Costa v. Enel* case during the window of time between the publication of the recommendation and the ECJ's later ruling. Such an internal advice and feedback mechanism is unavailable to the ATJ, which also lacks—with the notable exception of intellectual property issues discussed in Chapter 5—any direct engagement with scholars, lawyers, and experts on Andean jurisprudence.[82]

The elements needed for bold advances in Andean integration doctrine were not limited to the lack of a supportive legal community, however. Most judges early in the Tribunal's history lacked initiative, viewing their job as issuing rulings in response to referrals and overseeing the Tribunal's internal administrative functions. Perhaps most striking, the first generation of judges did not set up a system to disseminate ATJ rulings. The ECJ relied on published case law compendiums, an expensive proposition given that rulings needed to be translated into multiple languages. Andean rulings are written in Spanish, the official language of all member states. Yet in their first years of operation, Andean judges had no policy or practice of disseminating their rulings.[83]

The absence of a larger community of like-minded actors also affected how individual Andean legal entrepreneurs perceived and played their roles. The integration promotion efforts of Gallo Pico Mantilla are a case in point. Pico Mantilla was President of the Tribunal when it issued the first preliminary ruling asserting the supremacy of Andean rules in 1987, and he served on the ATJ until 1993.

of International and Comparative Law 2002 19 (3): 863–929; O. Saldías, Supranational Courts as Engines of Disintegration: The Case of the Andean Community (Free Univ. of Berlin Working Paper on European Integration No. 5, 2007, available at <http://citeseerx.ist.psu.edu/viewdoc/download?doi=10.1.1.588.9948&rep=rep1&type=pdf>; E. Tremolada, Application of the Andean Community Law in Bolivia, Ecuador, Peru, and Venezuela in Comparison with the European Union Experience. *Jean Monnet/Robert Schuman Paper Series* 2006, 6 (3).

[81] Interview with former ATJ judge (B).

[82] Osvaldo Saldías explains that most scholars fail to engage critically with the Andean project: "[A] legal work that asks whether regional integration is something that is inherently good or bad, or questions whether Andean law is in harmony with fundamental principles of Andean national orders, still remains to be written. Legal integration appears as something 'natural' and self-evident for a region that strives for economic development." O. Saldías, *The Judicial Politics of Economic Integration: The Andean Court as an Engine of Development*. New York, NY: Routledge, 2013, 132.

[83] A different ATJ judge recounted a meeting he had on the doorsteps of the Tribunal with a student whose request to review ATJ decisions had been refused. The judge provided access to the student. Interview with former ATJ judge (B).

A gentleman, politician, and lawyer from Ecuador who served as Secretary of the Ministry of Industry, Ambassador to Venezuela, and a judge on Ecuador's Supreme Court (1997–2004), Pico Mantilla sought to emulate the European legal integration strategy. He was committed to Andean integration as an end in itself, having been a participant in the negotiation of the Andean Pact and the Original ATJ Treaty. As President of the Tribunal, Pico Mantilla likely penned the 1987 supremacy ruling, and, as we explain in Chapter 3, he helped convince Ecuadorian judges to begin making preliminary references.[84] When Pico Mantilla later became a member of Ecuador's Supreme Court, that court ordered a lower court to refer the case in question to the ATJ.[85] Pico Mantilla also served on Ecuador's Supreme Court when it enforced the ATJ's noncompliance ruling in the alcohol cases we discuss in Chapter 6. Like Pochet and Cavelier, Pico Mantilla was an integration activist who deployed his multiple roles to aid Andean legal integration, but he had few like-minded interlocutors with whom to share experiences and devise broader strategies.

Juan Vincente Ugarte del Pino, the Peruvian judge on the ATJ from 1990 to 1995, is more typical of early appointments to the Tribunal. Ugarte del Pino did not actively promote the Andean legal system. For example, he did not seek to educate the Peruvian bench or bar on how to refer cases to the ATJ, nor did he write treatises explaining the Andean system to Peruvian lawyers and judges. These logistical difficulties have since been surmounted, but the ATJ continues to have very limited resources for promotional efforts and its judges remain mostly passive legal formalists.

Andean Community officials are another logical group of legal integration supporters. The Andean General Secretariat has followed some of the strategies of its European counterpart. Officials have made the Secretariat's reasoned decisions, known as *Resoluciones*, widely available for at least the last decade,[86] they have organized conferences on integration law topics, and they have issued noncompliance decisions finding fault with national judges' refusal to refer cases to the ATJ. Chapter 3 explains how these activities contributed to a widening stream of preliminary references. General Secretariat officials have also filed cases involving Andean law. For example, a former member of the Secretariat's legal services division, Alfonso Vidales Olviedo, served as the lawyer for the Peruvian generic pharmaceutical industry in a suit challenging a Peruvian decree regarding second-use patents, discussed in Chapter 5.

[84] As Chapter 3 explains, preliminary references from Ecuadorian courts did not become regularized until after Gallo Pico's time. The key case was an infringement suit that the US consumer goods manufacturer Proctor and Gamble filed against the Ecuador Supreme Court for failing to refer a tax dispute to the Tribunal. ATJ Nullification Ruling 24-AN-99. After that case, the number of references from Ecuadorian courts increased significantly.

[85] Claim No. 13-99; Res. No. 468-99, *Recurso de Casacion*, Third Civil and Commercial Law Courtroom of the Supreme Court of Ecuador (October 5, 1999).

[86] These appear on the Secretariat's website. See *Secretaría General de la Comunidad Andina*, available at <http://www.comunidadandina.org/SolControversias.aspx?fr=99#>.

More recently, a former Andean official took a card from the Euro-law playbook. Marcel Tangerife-Torres worked as an assistant at the Colombian Constitutional Court (1994–98), then joined the Legal Advising Service of the Andean Secretariat (1998–2001) and contributed to its efforts to promote regional integration. After returning to Colombia, Tangerife worked with the Secretariat to draft an Andean *Decisión* regulating pesticides in the agrochemical industry. This regulation infused environmental protection goals into a *Decisión* establishing a common import and registration rules for agricultural pesticides. He then sought to give effect to these *Decisiones* in the Colombian legal system, filing suits with the Constitutional Court and the *Consejo de Estado*.[87] As Chapter 7 explains, Peruvian firms later challenged the same *Decisión*, leading the ATJ to condemn Peru's noncompliance three times. Following these rulings, however, the member states relaxed the Andean pesticides rules to give greater leeway for domestic regulations.

The revision of the pesticides regulation occurred in late 2015 and perhaps for that reason we found no scholarship, statements by environmental groups, or media coverage of this retrenchment of Andean law. Even more striking is the nearly complete absence of media coverage or scholarly discussion of the proposal to "re-engineer" the Andean Community or the abrogation of the Common External Tariff (events we discuss in Chapter 7). If these sorts of major legal and institutional changes had occurred in Europe, or with respect to international criminal law or human rights, one could quickly find news stories and blog discussions analyzing their potential impact. Public and elite debates about important legal and institutional changes put pressure on government officials to justify their actions. In the Andean Community, by contrast, the absence of a jurist advocacy movement means that major changes to the Andean legal system and the integration project as a whole are not only under-scrutinized but often go unrecognized.

To be sure, a few Andean legal entrepreneurs do exist. One is Ricardo Vigil Toledo, an international lawyer and diplomat from Peru who served on the ATJ for two consecutive six-year terms. Vigil Toledo authored numerous publications on the future of the Andean Community legal system. His 2011 book set forth a detailed proposal to expand the ATJ's competence to include transportation, environmental protection, and other topics.[88] Vigil Toledo also participated in conferences to promote preliminary references from national courts, he contacted judges and lawyers in MERCOSUR to explore the possibility of including an ATJ-style judicial system in UNASUR,[89] and he traveled to meetings with his counterparts on the ECJ and other international courts.[90]

[87] Interview with attorney (A) from commercial and administrative law firm in Colombia.

[88] R.V. Toledo, *La Estructura Juridica y el Futuro de la Comunidad Andina*. Madrid: Thompson Reuters Aranzadi, 2011.

[89] R.V. Toledo, *Reflexiones en Torno a la Construcción de la Comunidad Sudamericana de Naciones* (2006), available at <http://www19.iadb.org/intal/intalcdi/PE/2008/01358.pdf>.

[90] R.V. Toledo, *La cooperación entre los órganos jurisdiccionales nacionales y el Tribunal de Justicia de la Comunidad Andina: La Consulta Prejudicial* (presentation at a colloquium on international judicial cooperation hosted by the ECJ on its 50th anniversary in 2002), available at <http://www.ejal.org/index.php/es/ult-noticias/670-ponencia-de-ricardo-vigil-toledo.html>.

We do not know why these efforts did not bear fruit, but the lack of a broader pro-integration network is likely part of the answer. Another explanation is that Vigil Toledo served on the Tribunal during a period of sustained crisis in the Andean Community (the subject of Chapter 7), making any proposals to expand its jurisdiction—whether by subject-matter or geography—political non-starters even if they were favorably received by judges or academics in the region.

An even more recent example is Luis José Diez Canseco Núñez, who was appointed to the Andean Tribunal in 2014 to succeed Vigil Toledo. Diez Canseco Núñez had worked at Peru's intellectual property agency (INDECOPI) and was an expert in IP law. He brought new energy to the outreach and lawmaking efforts of the Tribunal, inviting IP agencies and national judges to send references to Quito. He then penned the preliminary rulings discussed in Chapters 7 and 8, adopting a functional test that allows a wide range of administrative bodies to refer cases directly to the Tribunal. We explain how this legal innovation opened access to the ATJ in Bolivia. In January 2015, Diez became the Tribunal's rotating President, giving media interviews and travelling extensively in the region and beyond to educate national and international judges, government officials, administrative agencies, students, and academics about the ATJ's activities.[91] Diez also worked with the General Secretariat and administrative agency officials to identify a "positive integration agenda" that included many technical policy areas—such as legal protection for country names—where political consensus existed for adopting common legal rules.

Diez Canseco Núñez's energetic leadership combined with the privileges of the Tribunal President's office contributed to a dramatic rise in judicial activity, including an unprecedented 691 preliminary references in 2015 and a reinvigoration of noncompliance, nullification, and omission cases.[92] Most of this success has occurred, however, within the IP island, where, as Chapter 5 explains, a specialized jurist advocacy movement has long existed.

The relative success of Judge Diez Canseco Núñez in comparison to his predecessors—especially during a period of major political and economic strife in the region—suggests that a jurist advocacy movement could be developed in the Andean context. Yet the lack of any larger movement, and thus the lack of community, remains a significant challenge.

Equally daunting is the tepid response to Diez's efforts by other ATJ judges. The lack of support among his colleagues is not surprising. The leftist-populist governments in Ecuador, Venezuela, and Bolivia included "reforms" of the judiciary that we describe in Chapters 7 and 8. A similar phenomenon likely has influenced appointments to the Tribunal, resulting in two judges who would be skeptical of efforts to encourage private litigants to challenge government policies as contrary to Andean law. Perhaps more surprising is the Peruvian government's limited support

[91] The Tribunal issued a report of its activities in 2015 that chronicles twenty-eight outreach events, including meetings with national judges and administrators to explain the workings of the Andean legal system. See *Tribunal de Justicia de la Comunidad Andina, Informe de Labores Gestión* 2015, 52–65.

[92] Ibid., 69.

of Judge Diez's initiatives, many of which required the endorsement of a member state. Frustrated by his inability to make sustained progress in advancing legal integration, Diez resigned from the Tribunal in January 2016. Many of his legal innovations are likely to survive his departure, but it is too early to tell whether the visibility and support for the Tribunal that he attempted to generate will endure.[93]

Other potential participants in a jurist advocacy movement in the Andes are regional associations that might have partnered with individual entrepreneurs in promoting Andean legal integration. We found one plausible group, the *Comisión Andina de Juristas*. This association is over twenty-five years old but only began to focus on the Andean legal system in the early 2000s. Even then its involvement was limited. The Secretariat asked the *Comisión* to create a website to help promote ATJ rulings and to work with Peruvian and Bolivian judges to refer cases. According to the official involved it these projects, the *Comisión* viewed the Andean Pact and Andean Community as economic projects that were distant from the association's core objectives of promoting human rights, democracy, and respect for international law more generally.[94]

The absence of interlocutors has also starved the ATJ of useful legal advice. Without an active group to promote Tribunal rulings, the Andean legal system (other than the intellectual property island we discuss in Chapter 5) remains largely absent from national legal and political debates. To be sure, economic and structural factors in the Andes make it more challenging than in Europe to devote sustained energy to regional integration. Academic salaries are generally low, and law professors and even some government officials have multiple jobs and fewer incentives to publish. ATJ judges and members of the Secretariat have written occasional books and journal articles on Andean law, but these writings are generally technocratic. Pico Mantilla, for example, wrote a book, *Andean Law*, that primarily reproduced Andean legal texts and ATJ rulings.[95] There do not appear to be as many prestige outlets for legal publications. One cannot find, for example, Andean analogues to Europe's numerous Euro-law journals, or to speeches, newspaper articles, and scholarship penned by ECJ judges Donner, Lecourt, Mancini, and Pescatore.

Many factors deter Andean judges from more assertively developing their authority. At least initially, the ATJ's restrained legal interpretations clearly reflected the intent of the member states. Chapter 2 explains that the Original ATJ Treaty provisions establishing the preliminary reference system were more restrictive than the analogous provisions of the Treaty of Rome. Chapter 5 explains that many Andean rules include loopholes that make them difficult to enforce. In addition, national judges in the Andes tend to be more legally formalist in comparison to

[93] Judge Diez Canseco Núñez shared this information with us on the record.

[94] The association is a regional offshoot of the International Commission of Jurists. For many years, the association had institutional funding to allow it to pursue its own projects. Interviews with official (C) of the *Comisión Andina de Juristas*.

[95] G.P. Mantilla, *Derecho Andino*. Quito: Tribunal de Justicia del Acuerdo de Cartagena, 1992.

their European counterparts. They have also been comparatively less forceful in asserting their independence or challenging political authority.[96]

These attributes do not, however, fully explain the ATJ's reticence over thirty years of operation. In Europe too, the government officials who drafted the Treaty of Rome did not intend for the ECJ to transform the preliminary ruling system. Moreover, it is easy to forget that the founding states of the EC were civil law countries with limited traditions of judicial review, a practice of applying judicial rulings only to the case at hand, and a background norm that more recently enacted laws prevail over earlier legislation. In other words, just like the ATJ, the ECJ needed to break out of the legal traditions of its time in order to expand its legal authority, and it needed to do so without the blessing of national governments.

We do not claim that there are no jurist advocacy movements in Latin America or that lawyers in the region generally lack political capital. To the contrary, prestigious lawyers and law firms are often associated with leading national families, who tend to hold positions of power in both business and government.[97] One can also find signs of emerging transnational legal fields in Latin America that support free markets and human rights agendas.[98] These developments have mostly bypassed the ATJ, however, largely because the Andean integration project has not inspired an ideologically committed and politically well-connected group of jurists to promote the Tribunal and the Andean legal system more generally.

Conclusion: Do International Courts Need Jurist Advocacy Movements to Flourish?

To investigate the role of jurist advocacy movements is to reexamine the forces driving regional integration and the penetration of international legal rules into national legal orders. It is well established that advocacy movements use domestic and international litigation to promote their causes,[99] and that movement attorneys

[96] Y. Dezalay and B.G. Garth, *Global Prescriptions: The Production, Exportation, and Importation of a New Legal Orthodoxy*. Ann Arbor, MI: University of Michigan Press, 2002a, 222–7; J.H. Merryman and R. Pérez-Perdomo, *The Civil Law Tradition*. Stanford, CA: Stanford University Press, 2007, 36–7; G.A. O'Donnell, Polyarchies and the (Un) Rule of Law in Latin America. In: *The (Un)Rule of Law and the Underprivileged in Latin America*. Juan E. Méndez, G A. O'Donnell, and P.S. de M. S. Pinheiro (eds), 303–37. Notre Dame, IN: University of Notre Dame Press, 1998.

[97] Dezalay and Garth, 2002a, 198–203.

[98] Y. Dezalay and B.G. Garth, From the Cold War to Kosovo: The Renewal of the Field of International Human Rights. *Annual Review of Law and Social Science* 2006, 2: 231–55; E. Lutz and K. Sikkink, International Human Rights Law and Practice in Latin America. *International Organization* 2000, 54 (3): 633–59; R. Sieder, L. Schjolden, and A. Angell, *The Judicialization of Politics in Latin America*. New York, NY: Palgrave Macmillan, 2005; K. Sikkink, The Transnational Dimension of the Judicialization of Politics in Latin America. In: *The Judicialization of Politics in Latin America*. R. Sieder, L. Schjolden, and A. Angell (eds), 263–92. New York: Palgrave MacMillan, 2005.

[99] R. Cichowski, *The European Court and Civil Society: Litigation, Mobilization and Governance*. Cambridge: Cambridge University Press, 2007; Harlow and Rawlings, 1992.

promote political as well as legal agendas.[100] It is also widely accepted that national advocacy movements can deploy international legal rules and institutions to great effect.[101] This chapter contributes to these literatures by explaining how the coordinated efforts of national Euro-law associations facilitated the entrepreneurship and ambition that made the ECJ's legal revolution both possible and successful.

Groups similar to Euro-law associations are not unique in the history of international law, or domestic law for that matter. In the United States, an equally driven group of jurists founded the Federalist Society, a conservative legal advocacy group, many of whose members now occupy influential positions in academia, the bar, and the judiciary.[102] Internationally, Dezalay, Garth, and others have noted how groups of lawyers shaped the development of international economic law and human rights in Latin America and beyond.[103] There are also associations of lawyers, in Europe and elsewhere, working to promote international criminal law and institutions such as the ICC and ad hoc criminal tribunals.[104] Not all of these advocacy movements have access to the sorts of powerful positions and resources available to Euro-law associations, which combined a concerted legal strategy with the support of friendly judges and government officials who supported that strategy.

In the final analysis, the crucial issue is identifying the keys to the success of jurist advocacy movements. The comparison between Europe and the Andes suggests that such movements can advance legal integration—and perhaps international adjudication more generally—when they are fueled by a mix of ideology and power that extends beyond mere self-interest and when they include politically influential actors as members or allies. This suggests that, for international courts that lack an ideologically motivated community of legal activists with political and social capital and connections, even the most motivated legal entrepreneurs, acting on their own, are unlikely to replicate the type of legal revolution that occurred in Europe in the 1960s.

Most international courts today lack such broad-based jurist advocacy movements. European integration surely benefited from the exceptional situation created by the Second World War, which discredited an entire ideology and group of legal actors and fomented anti-fascist lawyers, government officials, judges, and scholars

[100] T.C. Halliday, L. Karpik, and M. Feeley, *Fighting for Political Freedom: Comparative Studies of the Legal Complex and Political Liberalism*. Oxford: Hart, 2007; A. Sarat and S.A. Scheingold, *Cause Lawyers and Social Movements*. Stanford, CA: Stanford University Press, 2006; A. Sarat and S.A. Scheingold, *Cause Lawyering and the State in a Global Era*. Oxford: Oxford University Press, 2001; C. Epps, *The Rights Revolution: Lawyers, Activists and Supreme Courts in Comparative Perspective*. Chicago, IL: University of Chicago Press, 1998; Teles, 2009; Ohlin, 2015.

[101] Risse, Ropp, and Sikkink, 1999; Sikkink, International Law and Social Movements: Towards Transformationa Typology of Relations between Social Movements and International Institutions. *American Society of International Legal Procedings* 2003, 97: 301–05; Sikkink and Lutz, 2001.

[102] The organization and impact of this movement are discussed in Teles, 2009 and Ohlin, 2015.

[103] Dezalay and Garth, 2006; Y. Dezalay and B.G. Garth, *The Internationalization of Palace Wars: Lawyers, Economists, and the Contest to Transform Latin American States*. Chicago, IL: University of Chicago Press, 2002b; Halliday, Karpik, and Feeley, 2007; Sikkink, 2005.

[104] J. Hagan and R. Levi, Crimes of War and the Force of Law. *Social Forces* 2005, 83 (4): 1499–534.

who were intensely committed to advancing European integration through law. The post-military regime era in Latin America perhaps offered such a moment for the Inter-American human rights system. The activities of human rights lawyers and bar associations involving the sub-regional courts in West and East Africa may be another example of an emerging jurist advocacy movement.[105] These counterexamples aside, however, it remains generally true that most international courts, and international legal regimes more generally, have failed to inspire groups of cohesive and ideologically committed jurists advocates, with bases of support in government, civil society, courts, business, and academic institutions, who organize across borders to promote shared legal objectives.

[105] J.T. Gathii, Saving the Serengeti: Africa's New International Judicial Environmentalism. *Chicago Journal of International Law* 2016, 16 (2): 386–438.

10

Reconsidering What Makes International Courts Effective

This book is a deep exploration of the law and politics of one international court—modeled on the European Court of Justice (ECJ)—operating in a developing country context. We conclude this exploration by revisiting Laurence Helfer and Anne-Marie Slaughter's seminal article, Toward a Theory of Effective Supranational Adjudication, published twenty years ago in the Yale Law Journal.[1] The article was among the first to analyze the rise of international courts as a global phenomenon and to theorize about the factors that contribute to their effectiveness. Helfer and Slaughter were motivated to write the article by the expanding legal and political footprint of two European tribunals—the ECJ and the European Court of Human Rights (ECtHR)—whose burgeoning dockets, extensive and influential jurisprudence, and high compliance rates offered a stark contrast to the (then) generally moribund, often ignored, and much maligned International Court of Justice (ICJ).

Seeking to reverse engineer the essential ingredients of the European courts' "striking success,"[2] the authors identified a checklist of thirteen factors that seemed to covary with effective supranational adjudication in Europe, the most important among them being the ability of private litigants to file cases directly with ECtHR and ECJ. Helfer and Slaughter applied the checklist of factors to the complaints mechanisms of a United Nations treaty body—the Human Rights Committee—and analyzed the Committee's aspirations to bolster its quasi-judicial character and expand its influence. They also advanced the proposition that bolstering the factors on the checklist was "the most likely prescription for increased effectiveness" of supranational adjudication.[3]

The final sections of Helfer and Slaughter's article discussed the legal, political, and institutional elements required to build a global community of law. Key members of that community, the authors predicted, would be the growing number of international courts and tribunals that states had recently established, such as the World Trade Organization (WTO) Appellate Body, the North American Free Trade Agreement dispute settlement panels, and the ad hoc criminal tribunals

[1] L.R. Helfer and A.-M. Slaughter, Toward a Theory of Effective Supranational Adjudication. *Yale Law Journal* 1997, 107 (2): 273–391.
[2] Ibid., 337. [3] Ibid., 338.

Transplanting International Courts: The Law and Politics of the Andean Tribunal of Justice. First Edition. Karen J. Alter and Laurence R. Helfer. Published 2017 by Oxford University Press.

for Yugoslavia and Rwanda, as well as other adjudicatory bodies on the horizon, such as the International Criminal Court. The Andean Tribunal of Justice (ATJ or Tribunal)—which had issued its first rulings more than a decade earlier and that was directly modeled on the ECJ—was not mentioned, even in passing. In fact, if memory serves, neither author was aware of the ATJ's existence, let alone the fact that the Tribunal had decided any cases.

Two decades later, there are twenty-four international courts operating across the world.[4] The ATJ is the third most active in terms of number of decisions, having issued fewer rulings than either of the two European courts featured in Toward a Theory of Effective Supranational Adjudication, yet far more decisions than courts with much larger memberships and populations.[5] The ATJ's origins, its contribution to building an island of effective international adjudication for intellectual property disputes, and its survival in the face of serious political challenges and crises in the Andean Community has provided rich fodder for Alter and Helfer's joint research for more than a decade. The capstone of that collaboration—a book devoted to the ATJ as a transplanted international court—provides a fitting opportunity to revisit and reassess the ideas and arguments that Helfer and Slaughter advanced in that early and influential journal article.

This concluding chapter reflects upon the publication of Toward a Theory of Effective Supranational Adjudication and revisits some of its central claims, conclusions, and predictions in light of the Andean Tribunal's experience. The first part, written primarily by Laurence Helfer with Karen Alter's wise and constructive comments and critiques, reviews several propositions asserted in the 1997 article, considers how well they have survived the test of time, and offers new conjectures about the future. The second part, jointly authored, considers what the relative success of the ATJ reveals about the limits of the effectiveness of international courts.

Revisiting Toward a Theory of Effective Supranational Adjudication

Effective international adjudication is not confined to Europe

One impetus for Toward a Theory of Effective Supranational Adjudication was a desire to show that the successes of the ECtHR and ECJ could be replicated in some form in other regions, or even on a global scale. To a world becoming ever more interdependent, the prospect that any group of countries could create a genuinely effective system of international adjudication held enormous promise. With national borders increasingly permeable to people, goods, and information,

[4] K.J. Alter, *The New Terrain of International Law: Courts, Politics, Rights*. Princeton, NJ: Princeton University Press, 2014, Chapter 3.

[5] See Chapter 1, footnote 1 which compares the ATJ's caseload to rulings by the ICJ, the World Trade Organization (WTO) dispute settlement system, the International Tribunal of the Law of the Sea (ITLOS), and the International Criminal Court (ICC).

governments confronted a growing and diverse array of regulatory challenges that required multilateral solutions. To achieve those solutions, however, states would need to comply with their international commitments. International courts offered one way to hold states to account.

Most observers were skeptical of this claim. They attributed the European tribunals' success to one all-embracing fact: that the founders of the Treaty of Rome and the European Convention on Human Rights were a closely knit community of liberal democracies with a shared and deep-seated commitment to regional integration, the rule of law, human rights, and cooperation through intergovernmental organizations. This contrasted sharply with international institutions in other regions and at the United Nations, whose members included long-standing democracies, poor developing nations, fragile regimes in transition, and repressive autocracies.[6]

For Helfer and Slaughter, however, the secrets of the ECJ and ECtHR's success were only partly due to the liberal democratic bona fides of the nations subject to the courts' jurisdiction. To be sure, a state comprising institutions and actors already used to following domestic legal rules was more likely, all other things equal, to comply with international law. Yet a closer review of the origins of two European tribunals—since confirmed by in-depth historical studies by Alter, Madsen, Vauchez, and Rasmussen—revealed that neither the ECJ nor the ECtHR were embraced by political leaders, legislators, and even many national judges during the courts' first few decades.[7] The jurists appointed to the tribunals worked assiduously to gain the trust of these actors while, at the same time, building constituencies of supporters—the jurist advocacy movements described in Chapter 9 of this book—who filed test cases and put pressure on governments to comply with the tribunals'

[6] E.g., E.A. Posner and J.C. Yoo, A Theory of International Adjudication. *California Law Review* 2005, 93 (1): 1–72, 55, argued that the ECJ and ECtHR each belong to a "political community" and thus cannot be models for other international courts; "Europe has such a community; the rest of the world does not." J. Alvarez, The New Dispute Settlers: (Half) Truths and Consequences. *Texas International Law Journal* 2003, 38 (3): 405–44, 430, notes "the suggestion that other international dispute settlers need to follow the path taken by Europe … ignores the possibility that what has worked for Europe may not work well elsewhere."

[7] K.J. Alter, The European Court's Political Power. *West European Politic*, 1996, 19(3): 458–87; K.J. Alter, *Establishing the Supremacy of European Law: The Making of an International Rule of Law in Europe*. Oxford: Oxford University Press, 2001; A. Vauchez, Une élite d'intermédiaires? Genèse d'un Capital Juridique Européen. *Actes de la recherche en sciences sociales*, 2007a, No. 166–67: 54–65; A. Vauchez, Judge-Made Law. Aux Origines du Modèle Politique Communautaire (Retour sur Van Gend en Loos et Costa c. Enel). In: *Une Europe des Élites? Réflexions sur la Fracture Démocratique de L'Union Européenne*. O. Costa and P. Magnette (eds), 139–66. Brussels: Presses de l'Université libre de Bruxelles, 2007b; M. Rasmussen, From Costa v. Enel to the Treaties of Rome: A Brief History of Legal Revolution. In: *The Past and Future of EU Law: The Classics of Eu Law Revisited on the 50th Anniversary of the Rome Treaty.* M. Poiares Maduro and L. Azoulai (eds), 69–85. Portland: Hart Publishing, 2010; M. Rasmussen. The Origins of a Legal Revolution: The Early History of the European Court of Justice. *Journal of European History* 2008, 14(2): 77–98; A. Vauchez, 2008. "Integration through Law" Socio-History of EU Political Common Sense. In: *European University Institute (EUI), Robert Schuman Centre of Advanced Studies Working Paper 2008/10*, Fiesole, Italy; A. Cohen and M. R. Madsen. Cold War Law: Legal Entreprenuers and the Emergence of a European Legal Field (1946–1965). In: *European Ways of Law*, V. Gessner and D. Nelken (eds), 175–200. Oxford: Hart, 2007.

rulings. To capture these relationships, nearly half of Helfer and Slaughter's checklist focused on factors within the control of international judges: awareness of audience, demonstrated autonomy from political interests, quality of legal reasoning, incremental decision-making style, the form of judicial opinions, and dialogue with other tribunals.

These factors are not limited to Europe. They could be—and indeed were—taken into account by international courts in other regions and by subject-specific tribunals with global reach. As with the early years of the ECJ and ECtHR, the judges on the nascent judicial bodies that comprise this new terrain of international law (to quote the title of Karen Alter's 2014 book) did more than merely decide cases. They sought to increase public awareness, disseminate decisions, and build relationships with lawyers and civil society groups; they interpreted and applied international law and developed new legal doctrines; and they engaged governments whose responses to their rulings ranged from genuine acceptance and grudging acquiescence to foot dragging and occasionally furious rejection. Not surprisingly, each court tailored the mix of factors within the control of judges in light of its legal rules, institutional structures, and political context—variations that Helfer and Slaughter both predicted and embraced. The essential point, however, is that the foundations for effective international adjudication have been laid far more widely—and in far more diverse and less hospitable environments—than proponents of the "Europe is unique" thesis had predicted.

The ATJ may be the most prominent illustration of this trend, yet it also demonstrates the limits of the judicial strategies that Helfer and Slaughter documented. Legal, political, and economic conditions in the Andes are very different from those in Europe. Democratic governments—where they exist—have often been unstable, the independence of national judges varies widely, and the opportunity for advocacy by civil society groups waxes and wanes with the political and economic forces that regularly buffet the region. Yet as Chapter 5 of this book explains, Andean judges nevertheless managed to establish a toehold in national legal systems—although primarily in one issue area (intellectual property) and with one set of interlocutors (domestic intellectual property (IP) administrative agencies)—which later expanded into an island of effective international adjudication that has survived and even thrived as other parts of the Andean integration project have faltered. This is the glass-half-full version of the effective international adjudication story in the Andes. The glass-half-empty counterpoint is reflected in the ATJ's inability to mobilize a jurist advocacy movement, discussed in Chapter 9 and at the end of this chapter, and in the limited impact the Tribunal has had on Andean law beyond the field of IP.

The ATJ is hardly the only court that is beginning to make a mark. A 2016 special issue of *Law and Contemporary Problems* and a forthcoming edited volume devoted to the variable authority of international courts reveal that other tribunals—including the WTO Appellate Body, the ICC, the ad hoc criminal tribunals, the East African Court of Justice (EACJ), the Inter-American Court of Human Rights (IACtHR), the Court of Justice of the Economic Community of

West African States (ECOWAS Court), the Caribbean Court of Justice (CCJ), and the OHADA Common Court of Justice and Arbitration—have, albeit in different ways and to different degrees, influenced the behavior of states.[8]

It is important not to overstate this claim, however. In the aggregate, the impact of these courts' decisions has—with the possible exception of the WTO—been marginal in comparison to the far more numerous rulings of the ECtHR and ECJ and the consequential legal and policy reforms adopted by European governments in response to those rulings. However, as we explain in Chapter 7 when comparing the divergent doctrinal trajectories of the ECJ and ATJ, it is problematic to contrast the European tribunals of today with their contemporary non-European counterparts. A more appropriate comparison focuses on the first *x* years of operation for each tribunal. However, with the exception of the ATJ and the IACtHR—both of which have been hearing cases since the mid-to-late 1980s and thus offer data to compare twenty-five or thirty years of adjudication in the Americas to adjudication in Europe—no other permanent international court has been operating for more than a decade, making period-adjusted comparisons more tentative and less illuminating.

The mere fact that such comparisons are now possible, as courts around the world continue to attract litigants and decide cases, refutes the claim that the ECJ and ECtHR can never serve as models for international courts elsewhere. Yet the far more modest accomplishments of these tribunals—even those that follow many of the techniques discussed on the Helfer and Slaughter checklist—suggest that contextual factors can frustrate even the most strategic of judges, a reality envisioned in Helfer and Slaughter's discussion of factors beyond the control of international judges.

Revisiting the supranational versus international adjudication debate

A central analytical move of the 1997 article was the focus on supranational rather than international adjudication. Although acknowledging that the ECJ and the ECHR

> have the power to adjudicate state-to-state disputes—the province of traditional international adjudication—each has compiled a more successful compliance record in cases involving private parties litigating directly against state governments or against each other. We define adjudication of these cases as supranational adjudication and jurisdiction over these categories of cases as supranational jurisdiction .... [Such jurisdiction] creates the possibility of direct relationships between the tribunals and different governmental institutions such as courts, administrative agencies, and legislative committees.[9]

[8] K.J. Alter, L.R. Helfer, and M.R. Madsen, The Variable Authority of International Courts. *Law and Contemporary Problems* 2016, 79 (1): 1–36; K.J. Alter, L.R. Helfer, and M.R. Madsen, *International Court Authority*. Oxford: Oxford University Press, 2017.

[9] Helfer and Slaughter, 1997, 277.

Helfer and Slaughter claimed that supranational jurisdiction is essential to the effectiveness not only of the ECtHR and ECJ but to other international courts as well. Such jurisdiction enables private litigants—including individuals, non-governmental organizations (NGOs), corporations, and other non-state actors—to file complaints directly with a tribunal, which, in turn, allows their judges to cultivate interlocutors and compliance partners who can put pressure on governments to implement the tribunal's rulings. In contrast, where only states have access to an international court, the decision of whether to bring suit is often highly politicized, with political leaders weighing not only the merits of a claim but also the risks of a countersuit, diplomatic pressure, or countermeasures by the defending state.

In subsequent publications, Karen Alter analyzed the growing number of "new-style" courts, which she defined as tribunals with compulsory jurisdiction over states and the ability to review complaints by a range of non-state actors. The judges on these courts have been far busier than their colleagues on "old-style" judicial bodies, whose jurisdiction is optional and limited to disputes between states. A statistic from Alter's 2014 book is revealing. New-style international courts issued a total of 36,774 binding rulings in contentious cases from their founding up to and including 2011; interstate tribunals issued only 462 binding rulings during the same period, despite their longer period of operation and larger state memberships.[10] By the early 2000s, the predominance of courts with compulsory jurisdiction and direct access to non-state litigants had become so evident that most scholars, including Alter and Helfer, abandoned the "supranational" label, referring to all judicial bodies operating above the level of the state as international courts.

Toward a Theory of Effective Supranational Adjudication also discussed the benefits of compulsory jurisdiction and private litigant access, noting that reforms of the European human rights system—which came to fruition in 1998 with the entry into force of Protocol No. 11—would "revolutionize the treaty's enforcement machinery" by requiring all states parties to "recognize the compulsory jurisdiction of the permanent court and permit individuals direct access to it in all cases."[11] Yet because the ECJ had always possessed the power to hear private actor complaints against EC countries simply by virtue of their membership in the Community, and because the ECtHR and the European Commission on Human Rights had long enjoyed similar authority over all Council of Europe member states in practice if not *de jure*,[12] Helfer and Slaughter may have underestimated the importance of compulsory jurisdiction and providing multiple access points for non-state litigants.

This book's decade-long study of the Andean legal system provides new evidence to support the claim that pairing compulsory jurisdiction with the ability

[10] Old-style international courts includes the ICJ (152 rulings), ITLOS (17 rulings), and 176 WTO panel decisions, and 117 panel decisions issued by its General Agreement on Tariffs and Trade predecessor. These figures count only decisions on the merits, excluding advisory opinions, rulings in staff cases, interim rulings, and appellate decisions. Data in Alter, 2014, 72–5.

[11] Helfer and Slaughter, 1997, 296.

[12] Prior to 1998 the European Convention did not compel states parties to recognize the right of individual petition or the compulsory jurisdiction of the ECtHR, but in practice all of the treaty's signatories had filed permanent or renewable declarations accepting both obligations.

of non-state actors to initiate litigation via different types of legal proceedings is critical to an international court's effectiveness. Chapter 2 describes the decision to transplant the ECJ model to the Andes. When national political leaders added a tribunal to the regional integration project in 1979, they made its compulsory jurisdiction a mandatory element of the Andean Pact. The Original ATJ Treaty asserts that "states which accede to the Cartagena Agreement must accede to this Treaty."[13] Equally as important, the treaty expressly bars states from withdrawing from the Tribunal's jurisdiction without also exiting the Andean Pact.[14]

Tying the Tribunal to the Andean integration project as a whole precludes a state from retaining the benefits of regional cooperation while jettisoning the burdens of international judicial review. This "package deal" makes it all but impossible for national political leaders to avoid the public pressure and legal scrutiny of Andean litigation, even as it increases the risk of noncompliance with ATJ judgments as a type of exit within the system. These insights also illuminate the high stakes involved in Ecuador's recent violations of Andean free trade rules, an issue discussed in Chapters 6 and 7. They help to explain why private firms believe it is worthwhile to challenge these violations before the General Secretariat and the ATJ, and why Ecuador's response to a Tribunal judgment against it may threaten the future of the entire Andean integration project.

The existence of multiple access points for international litigation is also a striking feature of the Andean legal system. Chapter 2 contrasts ECJ-style international courts to WTO-style dispute settlement systems, identifying as key distinctions the existence of directly applicable Community rules and the different avenues for litigants to challenge the validity and implementation of those rules. Since the Cochabamba Protocol reforms of 1996, private litigants can file complaints challenging member state violations of Andean law with the General Secretariat, which also launches investigations on its own authority. Equally as important, both actors can refer noncompliance suits to the ATJ over a state's objection. These access routes are important given the limited willingness of national judges to challenge noncompliance with Andean law. Finally, the omission and nullification procedures enable private litigants to spur Andean officials to act as Community law requires and to ensure that they do not exceed their powers when so doing.

The full impact of the ATJ's jurisprudence is revealed only by tracing legal disputes across these different access points and procedures. For example, Chapter 4 describes how the ATJ has drawn on the combination of preliminary rulings, nullification suits, and noncompliance cases to develop legal doctrines that adapt the ECJ's jurisprudence to the distinctive legal and political environment of the Andes. Chapter 6 explores how litigants employ different legal procedures sequentially or in tandem as they seek to align national policies with Community legal rules.

[13] Original ATJ Treaty, Article 36.

[14] "This Treaty shall remain in effect for as long as the Cartagena Agreement is in force, and it may not be denounced independently of the latter." Ibid., Article 38.

Evidence from other international courts underscores the importance of multiple access points and giving non-state litigants the right to file complaints. The IACtHR, ECOWAS Court, EACJ, CCJ, and the Southern African Development Community (SADC) Tribunal all have the power to review complaints by one member state against another alleging violations of applicable treaties and other international rules. Yet not one of these courts has heard a single interstate dispute.[15] In addition, the Inter-American Commission continues to act as the gatekeeper to the IACtHR for suits alleging human rights violations in the Americas, the dockets of the EACJ and ECOWAS Court include complaints filed by Community institutions and officials, and most cases heard by the African Court of Human and Peoples' Rights concern a handful of countries that have filed optional declarations giving individuals and NGOs direct access to the Court.[16]

Yet recent events also reveal that Helfer and Slaughter underestimated the persistence of interstate adjudication, both in its own right and as a catalyst for suits by individuals and NGOs. Chapter 6 of this book describes four politically fraught cases that involve Andean-level litigation between member states, private actor suits before national courts, and ATJ preliminary references. Military activities by Russia against the Ukraine and Georgia generated similar litigation patterns. Both conflicts have been the subject of rare interstate petitions before the ECtHR, but have also triggered thousands of individual human rights complaints.[17]

At the global level, the WTO's interstate dispute settlement system remains active and influential (although Helfer and Slaughter's expectation that private businesses would become active behind-the-scenes participants has been borne out in practice).[18] More surprisingly, the ICJ's docket began to rise in the early 2000s, and its steady diet of interstate cases has included not only disputes raising politically inconsequential or technical issues, but also politically charged controversies such as those involving the use of force, genocide, and mass human rights abuses. In addition, the ICC's jurisdiction has as often been triggered by state self-referrals and referrals from the UN Security Council as by the ICC Prosecutor's independent investigations.[19]

Finally, the growing number of active international courts has opened up possibilities for litigating different facets of the same dispute in multiple judicial venues, simultaneously or sequentially. A striking recent example involves efforts to

[15] The Inter-American Commission on Human Rights has reviewed two interstate petitions, but neither case was referred to the Court. J.M. Pasqualucci, *The Practice and Procedure of the Inter-American Court of Human Rights*. Cambridge: Cambridge University Press, 2014, 116. In addition, the IACtHR has addressed some interpretive disputes between members of the Organization of American States under its advisory jurisdiction. Ibid., 37–82.

[16] Article 34(6) of the African Court Protocol permits states to file such a declaration.

[17] B. Bowring, The Russian Federation and the Strasbourg Court: The Illegitimacy of Sovereignty? In: *The UK and European Human Rights: A Strained Relationship?* K.S. Ziegler, E. Wicks, and L. Hodson (eds), 415–40. Oxford: Hart Publishing, 2015, 437.

[18] G.C. Shaffer, *Defending Interests: Public-Private Partnerships in WTO Litigation*. Washington DC: Brookings Institution, 2003.

[19] C. Stahn, *The Law and Practice of the International Criminal Court*. Oxford: Oxford University Press, 2015.

prosecute former Chadian President Hissein Habré for torture and other international crimes, which has generated private actor complaints to the African Court of Human and Peoples' Rights and the ECOWAS Court, an ICJ dispute between Belgium and Senegal, and the creation of a new hybrid tribunal in Senegal, known as the Extraordinary African Chambers.[20]

Reassessing the importance of national courts and other domestic actors as interlocutors

Helfer and Slaughter's 1997 article built upon decades of scholarship identifying mutually advantageous relationships between international and national judges as the lynchpin of effective supranational adjudication in Europe. The ECJ actively encouraged national courts to send preliminary references, ultimately establishing partnership with them over the interpretation and enforcement of EC law. Although lacking direct links to domestic judiciaries, the ECtHR was equally aware of the importance of aligning its case law with the independent incentives of national judges to protect the human rights enshrined in both domestic constitutions and the European Convention on Human Rights.

National judicial support surely contributes to an international court's effectiveness. As Karen Alter has argued, "increasingly the international and domestic rule of law are intertwined and codependent, rising and falling in legitimacy and effectiveness together."[21] Yet building support in national judiciaries raises challenges that Helfer and Slaughter did not anticipate, suggesting that the authors may have put too much faith in trans-judicial alliances. Equally important are the relationships that international judges forge with other domestic actors, including administrative agencies, bar associations, civil society groups, and national human rights institutions.

Studies of European integration emphasize the preliminary reference mechanism as the key to fostering symbiotic relationships between the ECJ and national courts. Nine other international courts include a preliminary reference mechanism,[22] but the ATJ is the only non-European international court that actually receives a steady stream of referrals from national courts. With more than 2,600 preliminary rulings up to and including 2014, the Andean Tribunal presents an unparalleled opportunity to study how this mechanism operates in a markedly different legal and political context.

On the surface, the sheer number of ATJ references and their persistence during fraught political times suggest the kind of deep judicial cooperation that exists in Europe. The reality, as Chapter 3 describes, is quite different. In both Communities, many national judges initially resisted sending preliminary references, but once

[20] S. Shah, Questions Relating to the Obligation to Prosecute or Extradite (Belgium v. Senegal). *Human Rights Law Review* 2013, 13: 351–66, 363–6;. Stahn, 2015, 563–6.

[21] Alter, 2014, 365.

[22] K.J. Alter, The Global Spread of European Style International Courts. *West European Politics* 2012, 35 (1): 135–54, 139.

that resistance was overcome, the practices in the two regions diverged markedly. Whereas national judges in Europe often pose bold and far-reaching questions to the ECJ, the questions that their colleagues in South America refer to the ATJ are generally narrow and repetitive. This suggests that national judges in the Andes view referrals mostly as a box-checking exercise. The absence of domestic noncompliance suits—an enforcement mechanism in the Revised ATJ Treaty but never implemented[23]—underscores this view. Given widespread judicial disinterest in the Andean legal system, private litigants challenging national laws as contrary to Andean law unsurprisingly prefer to approach the ATJ through the noncompliance procedure of the General Secretariat.

Recent work on other international courts paints a darker picture. In her study of the Inter-American human rights system, for example, Huneeus identifies "institutional factors point[ing] to judicial resistance" to the IACtHR.[24] By casting national courts as "the subjects which must comply with Court orders" and by "prescribing particular remedial actions courts must take, the [IACtHR] situates itself as [a] hierarchical superior, something local legal actors easily resent."[25] In West Africa, the ECOWAS Court has a mandate to review human rights complaints from individuals and to receive preliminary references regarding the interpretation ECOWAS law.[26] While the Court's docket has grown rapidly, it has yet to receive a single reference from a national court. More ominously, some domestic judges have defied the ECOWAS Court, as recently revealed by a 2013 ruling of the Supreme Court of Liberia that categorically rejected a judgment and monetary damages award against the Liberian government.[27]

The evidence, however, is not all bleak. South African courts enforced a highly controversial land rights judgment of the now-suspended SADC Tribunal against Zimbabwe, for example.[28] Yet studies of the ATJ and of other international courts underscore the fact that court-to-court collaboration to enforce international law cannot be assumed.

When national judicial support is off the table, can international judges find allies among other domestic actors? In one passage in their 1997 article, Helfer and

[23] Article 31 of the Revised ATJ Treaty provides that "[n]atural or artificial persons shall have the right to appeal to the competent national courts as provided for by domestic law should Member Countries fail to comply with" Andean law.

[24] A. Huneeus, Courts Resisting Courts: Lessons from the Inter-American Court's Struggle to Enforce Human Rights. *Cornell International Law Journal* 2011, 44 (3): 493–532, 515.

[25] Ibid., 516.

[26] K.J. Alter, L.R. Helfer, and J. McAllister, A New International Human Rights Court for West Africa: The Court of Justice for the Economic Community of West African States. *American Journal of International Law* 2013, 107 (4): 737–79.

[27] *Republic of Liberia v. Valentine Ayika*, Judgment (July 15, 2013) (copy on file with authors). According to the Liberian judges: "No Court, wherever situated and however created, or existing under any international agreement or protocol, can divest the Liberian Supreme Court of [its] jurisdiction, and any such agreement which seeks such is unconstitutional, unenforceable, ineffective and not binding on the Republic of Liberia to the extent of the inconsistencies." Ibid., 38.

[28] E. De Wet, The Case of Government of the Republic of Zimbabwe v. Louis Karel Fick: A First Step Towards Developing a Doctrine on the Status of International Judgments within the Domestic Legal Order. *Potchefstroom Electronic Law Journal* 2014, 17 (1): 553–65.

Slaughter suggested that courts with jurisdiction over illiberal or quasi-authoritarian nations might forge relationships with domestic institutions that operate with at least a modicum of independence from the state.

> [E]ven in a political system that is otherwise corrupt or oppressive, it is possible that a particular government institution—a court or administrative agency or even a legislative body—will choose to forge a relationship with a supranational tribunal as an ally in a domestic political battle against corruption or oppression. Whether such an alliance would be efficacious depends on the nuances and sensitivities of local politics, but the larger point is that participation in the "community of law" constructed by a supranational tribunal is open not only to countries but also to individual political and legal institutions, regardless of how the state of which they are a part is categorized or labeled.[29]

The symbiotic relationship between the ATJ and domestic IP administrative agencies described in Chapters 3 and 5 supports this expectation. In countries across the world, businesses seeking a trademark or patent must apply to such administrative agencies, which grant the application if it meets certain legal criteria. In the Andes, those criteria are found in Andean-level IP legislation (*Decisiones*, in Spanish). Agency administrators were thus natural consumers of these *Decisiones*. The officials were also eager for the ATJ's interpretive guidance to address the ambiguities, gaps, and complex interpretive issues that they encountered on a daily basis.

When firms were dissatisfied with the agencies' registration decisions, they challenged them in court. The agencies—who were often named as parties in these appeals—urged national judges to refer cases to the ATJ to seek guidance on the finer points of Andean IP rules. Lawyers and their clients, who were skeptical that national judges had much to say about the specialized and technical field of IP law, supported the reference requests. Once domestic courts began to make these referrals, they did so habitually. In case after case, the Tribunal responded by providing the guidance that the agencies were seeking.

Agency administrators applied the ATJ's preliminary rulings to decide whether to grant or deny the trademark or patent application that had been litigated before the Tribunal. As a member of the INDECOPI administrative tribunal in Peru explained: "[w]e apply the rulings as soon as they come down from the Tribunal, and we reference the rulings in the texts of our decisions about registrations."[30] However, the interpretations embedded in the ATJ's rulings had a far wider impact: they were inculcated into the agencies' day-to-day practices. As Chapter 5 notes, the ATJ's guidance eventually became so extensive that it was restated in compendiums of legal doctrine that administrators referenced in their work. And as Chapter 3 explains, the Tribunal recently elevated the agencies' status in the Andean legal order. By permitting agencies to send references directly to Quito and bypass national courts altogether, Andean judges implicitly recognized agency administrators as their primary interlocutors and compliance partners.

[29] Helfer and Slaughter, 1997, 335.

[30] Interview with official (B) of INDECOPI.

Recent studies of other international courts explore how a range of domestic actors—including customs agents, bar associations, and private companies—surmount apathy or opposition from national courts to forge alliances directly with international judges. The Central American Court of Justice (CACJ) has faced significant hurdles to establishing its authority among governments and national courts, but suits by national associations of customs agents seeking to invalidate regional tariffs and customs decisions have been one of the CACJ's most consistent source of cases.[31] In East and West Africa, law societies and bar associations are ardent proponents of international litigation. Although these organizations and their members can and do file cases in national courts, they have capitalized on the absence of an exhaustion of local remedies requirement to become repeat players before the EACJ and ECOWAS Court. The judges on these courts, in turn, have targeted their outreach efforts to these associations.[32] A different pattern is emerging in the Caribbean. Businesses with regional economic interests have served as catalysts for activating the CCJ's original jurisdiction, while national courts have yet to send a single preliminary reference.[33]

Taken together, these examples illustrate that international courts outside of Europe cannot necessarily count on the support of their national judicial colleagues. When national judges are indifferent or hostile, however, international courts may be able to build their authority by forging alliances with other domestic actors that are part of the state or well positioned to influence its policies. This insight dovetails with Alter's focus on the relationship between international courts and a broader set of compliance partners and compliance supporters.[34]

The strategic choices of international judges in challenging legal and political environments

At the heart of Toward a Theory of Effective Supranational Adjudication was a claim that international courts are, at least in part, masters of their own destinies. Although bound by their delegated powers and professional norms, international judges nevertheless have considerable strategic space within which to decide cases and develop legal doctrine. More concerned with survival than ideology, Helfer and Slaughter investigated the "sustained effort by two [European] tribunals to enhance their effectiveness" by "manipulat[ing] factors within their control to maximize their impact on the relevant national actors."[35] As noted at the beginning of this chapter, those factors included awareness of audiences, demonstrated autonomy

[31] S. Caserta, *Institutionalizing Regional International Courts: Creation, Authority, and Power of the Central American and Caribbean Courts of Justice.* PhD Dissertation. University of Copenhagen, 2016, 214.

[32] J. Gathii, Mission Creep or a Search for Relevance: The East African Court of Justice's Human Rights Strategy. *Duke Journal of Comparative and International Law* 2014, 24 (2) 249–96, 262; Alter, Helfer, and McAllister, 2013, 748–53.

[33] Caserta, 2016, 155–75.

[34] Alter, 2014, 20–1.

[35] Helfer and Slaughter, 1997, 308.

from political interests, incremental decision-making style, quality of legal reasoning, judicial dialogue, and the form of opinions.

This book's decade-long study of the Andean legal system provides new evidence with which to assess these judicial strategies in a very different and more challenging legal and political environment. As Chapters 2 and 4 explain, early ATJ decisions were overtly didactic. The judges carefully explained the preliminary ruling mechanism—a novelty in South America—to national judges, government officials, and private litigants. The Tribunal also used these lessons in Andean legal procedure to manage expectations about how the system would operate.

The Tribunal's lessons cut in two directions. On the one hand, the ATJ unequivocally affirmed—relying on the intent of the Cartagena Agreement's drafters and the settled ECJ doctrines—the supremacy of Andean law and its direct effect in national legal orders. At the same time, the judges also recognized that the political support for integration was far shallower in the Andes than in Europe. Instead of embracing ECJ integration doctrines *tout corps*, the ATJ modified those doctrines selectively. These revisions were politically astute. They gave member states as a group leeway to advance integration at a slower pace than the Andean Pact's founders had originally (and over-optimistically) planned, and they allowed national legislatures, executives, and judges leeway to preserve important domestic policies and fill in gaps in Andean rules, thus avoiding direct confrontations that the Tribunal was unlikely to survive.

In the mid-1990s, the number of preliminary references began to increase rapidly. The previous sections explained the origin of these references. Here we focus on the style of the Tribunal's opinions and their impact on national court referrals and administrative agency decision-making.

ATJ preliminary rulings are highly repetitive, often reiterating the same analysis in case after case. For many private IP attorneys, especially repeat-player law firms in Peru and Colombia, this style is frustrating. Yet, as Chapter 5 explains, repetition helped to overcome resistance to referrals from national judges, who soon recognized that their Andean colleagues would not venture beyond well-worn legal territory. It also bolstered the quality of agency decision-making by directing officials to use even-handed procedures, provide reasons for their decisions, and adhere to pre-existing legal principles. When viewed in the aggregate, therefore, the ATJ's practice of issuing repetitive preliminary rulings paid multiple dividends: it clarified Andean IP rules, enhancing the value of trademarks and patents; it improved the agencies' ability to resolve disputes between private businesses fairly and effectively; it made national judges more amenable to referring cases; and it reinforced the agencies' independence from political meddling and their fidelity to the rule of law.

ATJ judges may have hoped that the effectiveness of IP adjudication in the region would spill over to other areas of Andean law. As Chapter 3 documents, preliminary references involving tariffs, customs, taxes, and other integration law issues have expanded modestly over the last decade. Nevertheless, the ATJ remains overwhelmingly concerned with suits involving trademark and patent registrations.

The predominance of IP cases helps to explain the Tribunal's decision, discussed in Chapter 3, to overturn its past practice and accept references from IP administrative agencies. By opening a direct channel of communication to the agencies and bypassing domestic courts, the ATJ developed a doctrine tailored to the interests and incentives of the primary suppliers and consumers of its rulings. Given the crisis of Andean integration over the last decade, this strategic move may have been prescient. In a fraught political environment, national judges may once again become reluctant to send preliminary references. But the specialized administrative bodies that apply Andean legal rules on a daily basis are unlikely to refrain from seeking the Tribunal's guidance, at least where governments are agnostic about the practice.

Scholars are beginning to analyze the strategies deployed by other international judges operating in developing countries. The strategies of Africa's sub-regional courts are among the most interesting. In its first decision, the ECOWAS Court rejected a purposive interpretation that would have enabled it to hear a private litigant's challenge to a blatant violation of Community law. Instead, the judges dismissed the suit while simultaneously launching a campaign to persuade West African governments to grant the Court a human rights mandate.[36] Elsewhere on the continent, the EACJ and the SADC Tribunal have also faced demands from civil society groups and private litigants to adjudicate human rights cases. Both courts acceded to these pressures by adopting expansive interpretations of their founding treaties' fundamental principles and objectives clauses, which include references to human rights, good governance, and the rule of law.[37] These examples provide further support for the claim that international courts in developing countries deploy strategies that diverge from those of the European tribunals in response to the distinctive legal and political contexts that these emerging courts face.

From compliance to effectiveness and beyond

Toward a Theory of Effective Supranational Adjudication was written against a backdrop of pervasive skepticism about international courts as venues for enforcing international legal commitments. As a first step in challenging this conventional wisdom, Helfer and Slaughter argued that the ECJ and ECtHR were effective in a very basic sense: European governments changed their national laws and policies in response to the two courts' rulings against them. The authors thus equated effectiveness with state compliance with judicial rulings:

> We define effective adjudication in terms of a court's basic ability to compel or cajole compliance with its judgments. In the supranational context, effective adjudication depends on a supranational tribunal's ability to secure such compliance by convincing domestic

[36] Alter, Helfer, and McAllister, 2013.

[37] As we explain elsewhere, the SADC Tribunal was suspended and ultimately stripped of the power to hear complaints from private litigant following a sustained backlash campaign by Zimbabwean President Robert Mugabe. K.J. Alter, J.T. Gathii, and L.R. Helfer, Backlash against International Courts in West, East and Southern Africa: Causes and Consequences. *European Journal of International Law* 2016, 27 (2): 293–328.

government institutions, directly and through pressure from private litigants, to use their power on its behalf.[38]

This definition recognized that most international courts cannot count on international enforcement mechanisms and must instead build support among domestic actors who, in turn, put pressure on governments to give effect to the courts' rulings. But the definition also expressly conflated the concepts of case-specific effectiveness and compliance.[39]

Subsequent studies have treated compliance and effectiveness as distinct concepts. Whereas compliance is measured by conformity between behavior and a specified legal rule, effectiveness involves "observable, desired changes in behavior" attributable to that rule. High levels of compliance can thus occur "for reasons entirely exogenous to the legal process," such as where states negotiate treaties that mirror their pre-existing behavior. Conversely, for international laws that demand extensive changes in state behavior, effectiveness may exist even if compliance with those laws is partial or uneven.[40]

The distinction between compliance and effectiveness may also explain why "old-style" international courts that require the consent of both complaining and defending states before they can adjudicate a particular dispute sometimes see higher levels of compliance than tribunals with compulsory jurisdiction. Requiring state consent to adjudication after a conflict has arisen is likely to limit cases to those for which both parties view a judicial ruling as beneficial. Compliance in this context says little about a court's ability to modify state behavior in situations where international obligations are more onerous.

For international courts with compulsory jurisdiction, by contrast, compliance may in fact be a good measure of effectiveness. International litigation occurs, after all, only if a state has refused to change its behavior following a demand to comply with the law. When a state resists long enough for an international court to rule against it—and when the state subsequently changes its behavior following the court's ruling—it is reasonable to conclude that the ruling contributed to the change in behavior, even if other factors are also relevant. As Hawkins and Jacoby have explained, "[t]his creates a class of cases where instances of compliance will be coextensive with those of effectiveness and where effectiveness can therefore be objectively measured through the proxy of state compliance."[41] Or, as Huneeus has stated, if a court "orders compensation of the victim by a certain amount, and the state compensates by that amount, drawing a causal inference is not particularly

[38] Helfer and Slaughter, 1997, 278.

[39] L.R. Helfer, The Effectiveness of International Adjudicators. In: *Oxford Handbook on International Adjudication.* C. Romano, K.J. Alter, and Y. Shany (eds), 464–82. Oxford: Oxford University Press, 2014, 467.

[40] K. Raustiala, Compliance and Effectiveness in International Regulatory Cooperation. *Case Western Reserve Journal of International Law* 2000, 32 (3): 387–440, 393–4.

[41] D. Hawkins and W. Jacoby, Partial Compliance: A Comparison of the European and Inter-American Court of Human Rights. *Journal of International Law and International Relations* 2010, 6 (1): 35–85, 40.

fraught. The answer to the counterfactual—would the state have done the same without the order—seems self-evident."[42]

Our study of the Andean legal system provides new evidence to assess when compliance and effectiveness should nevertheless be treated as distinct concepts. As Chapters 4 and 5 explain, most ATJ preliminary rulings concerning intellectual property are highly repetitive, even formulaic. Andean judges have not yet endorsed the ECJ's *acte clair* doctrine, which directs national courts to refrain from referring cases when the applicable Community law is well settled. National court compliance with these repetitive rulings is thus a poor proxy for effectiveness; national judges already know the answer to most of the questions they pose to their colleagues in Quito and would most likely have applied Andean IP law even if they had not referred the case.

This book's in-depth analysis of the Andean legal system also finds other evidence of international judicial influence that extends beyond traditional measures of case-specific compliance and effectiveness. First, as explained in the previous section's discussion of judicial strategy, ATJ rulings helped to inculcate rule-of-law values in the domestic IP agencies. By directing the agencies to provide reasons for their decisions, follow even-handed procedures, and apply pre-existing legal principles, the Tribunal reinforced the agencies' independence and ability to resist political meddling. In this respect, ATJ case law contributed to the "transparency, participation, reasoned decisions, and legality" that are hallmarks of global administrative law.[43]

Second, the mutually beneficial relationship between the IP agencies and the ATJ was crucial to winning what Helfer and Slaughter described as a "domestic political battle against corruption or oppression." In the Andes, that battle is aptly illustrated by the collusion of national political leaders and US pharmaceutical firms to circumvent Andean rules banning second-use patents—most notably for the lucrative erectile dysfunction drug Viagra. As Chapter 5 explains, when the Fujimori regime in Peru adopted a decree directing the administrative agency to grant a second-use patent for Viagra, the agency reluctantly complied. However, it did so knowing that a local association of generic drug manufacturers had filed a complaint with the Andean General Secretariat that eventually led to an ATJ judgment finding Peru in breach of Andean IP law. The judgment emboldened INDECOPI to revoke the Viagra second-use patent. Although the Fujimori degree was never officially abrogated, it was ignored in practice with the result that generic versions of Viagra have remained on the market in Peru.

Third, some ATJ rulings have had effects beyond the cases actually litigated. The judgment in the second-use patent case against Peru quickly reverberated across the Andes, with copycat litigation leading to the invalidation of Viagra patents in the other member states. The ban remained in force even in the face of strident opposition from the US pharmaceutical firms, pressure that, as Chapter 5 explains, led

[42] Huneeus, 2011, 505 n. 61.

[43] B. Kingsbury, N. Krisch, R.B. Stewart, and J. Weiner, The Emergence of Global Administrative Law. *Law and Contemporary Problems* 2005, 68 (3&4): 15–62, 17.

to the granting of second-use patents in many other countries in Latin America. The shadow effect of Andean litigation even extends beyond the borders of the Community. In Venezuela, national courts and the domestic IP agency SAPI continued to apply regional IP *Decisiones* as interpreted by the ATJ after the country withdrew from the Andean Community in 2006.

These indications of the ATJ's wider impact suggest that scholars should look for evidence of judicial influence beyond case-specific compliance. For example, the distinctive design of the CCJ—which has an appellate as well as original jurisdiction—has created opportunities to build a broad array of compliance constituencies in the Caribbean.[44] In West Africa, a Liberian Supreme Court decision rejecting an ECOWAS Court judgment "triggered a national debate" among lawyers, journalists, and NGOs, leading the Liberian House of Representatives to ratify a legal instrument "bringing Liberia into compliance with its international obligations under the ECOWAS Treaty."[45] In South Africa, judges enforced a SADC Tribunal money damages award against Zimbabwe that could not be enforced in the courts of that country.[46] Studies of other international courts are likely to reveal additional ways in which international rulings alter national law and politics even if states do not immediately or fully comply with those rulings.

Backlash: An endemic concern for international courts?

The 1990s and early 2000s were a heady time for international adjudication. New courts and tribunals were being created with astonishing rapidity, suggesting that international judges might eventually extend their reach across the length and breadth of international law and include countries, such as the United States, that had long been resistant to external judicial scrutiny. Reflecting this optimism, scholars of the time penned articles with audacious titles—International Law and Institutions for a New Age, The New World Order and the Need for an International Criminal Court, and Toward an International Judicial System—that advanced equally audacious proposals for new or expanded judicial review mechanisms.[47]

Readers of Helfer and Slaughter's article will catch a whiff of this millennialism. The article's central claims—that politically meaningful international courts were an established and essential element of Europe's supranational legal orders, and that, under the right conditions, similar courts could be established globally and in other

[44] Caserta, 2016, 189–90.

[45] S. Ebobrah, The ECOWAS Community Court of Justice: A Dual Mandate with Skewed Authority. In: *International Court Authority*, K.J. Alter, L.R. Helfer, and M.R. Madsen (eds), Oxford: Oxford University Press, 2017.

[46] De Wet, 2014.

[47] J.H. Barton and B.E. Carter, International Law and Institutions for a New Age. *Georgetown Law Journal* 1993, 81 (3): 535–62, 557, for example, urged the United States to "push … for a global umbrella organization comprised of all those democracies willing to submit themselves to the type of international judicial human rights review now available in Europe." See also W.N. Gianaris, The New World Order and the Need for an International Criminal Court. *Fordham International Law Journal* 1992, 16 (1): 88–119; J. Martinez, Towards an International Judicial System. *Stanford Law Review* 2003, 56 (2): 429–529.

regions—were hopeful but not idealistic. Helfer and Slaughter identified many challenges to expanding international judicial review, and their specific proposal—linking the UN Human Rights Committee to the burgeoning jurisprudence of the ECtHR as a first step toward "a genuinely global dialogue among a wider range of supranational and international tribunals and domestic courts"—was modest.[48] The authors urged the Committee to pursue "a policy of thoughtful convergence with European jurisprudence, supplemented by informed divergence where there are justifiable and articulated reasons for doing so."[49] The broader normative vision underlying this specific recommendation, however, was the hope that other international courts and UN treaty bodies would work toward a common enterprise, reinforcing and expanding the "community of law that has nurtured the existence and growth of effective supranational adjudication" in Europe.[50]

Two decades later, what is strikingly absent from Helfer and Slaughter's prediction that politically consequential international courts would emerge beyond Europe is any suggestion that states might rebel against the courts and tribunals that tracked the authors' prescription for effective international adjudication. The absence of any discussion of backlash perhaps reflects the fact that the authors wrote the article only a few years after the creation of several new courts and tribunals and before other judicial institutions had been established or started to receive cases. Since no international court can review the actions of a state that has not formally accepted its jurisdiction,[51] perhaps Helfer and Slaughter can be forgiven for assuming that political leaders would not seek to tear down judicial edifices they had so recently built. Yet such clashes were surely foreseeable based on the trajectories of other international institutions.[52]

If the late 1990s and early 2000s were the apogee of hopefulness for international adjudication, the 2010s may mark a new low. The last several years have seen a slew of state backlashes against international courts. These events go well beyond mere disagreements with the reasoning or results of particular rulings or instances of foot dragging or noncompliance. They are, instead, deliberate and strategic challenges by political leaders to the formal powers and de facto authority of the courts and the judges who penned the offending decisions.[53]

[48] Helfer and Slaughter, 1997, 389. [49] Ibid., 374. [50] Ibid.

[51] The ICC's power to investigate non-party nationals alleged to have committed genocide, crimes against humanity, or war crimes on the territory of a state party is a notable—but rare and controversial—exception.

[52] By the late 1990s, Karen Alter had already documented examples of backlash in response to ECJ activism: K.J. Alter, Who Are the Masters of the Treaty?: European Governments and the European Court of Justice. *International Organization* 1998, 52 (1): 125–52; K.J. Alter, The European Legal System and Domestic Policy: Spillover or Backlash. *International Organization* 2000, 54 (3): 489–518. More recently, Michael Zürn observed that an increase in the authority of international institutions tends to provoke an increase in politicization, including opposition and resistance to actors using the institutions to achieve their preferred policy goals. M. Zürn, The Politicization of World Politics and Its Effects: Eight Propositions. *European Political Science Review* 2014, 6: 47–71.

[53] See, e.g., P. Leach and A. Donald, Russia Defies Strasbourg: Is Contagion Spreading?, *EJIL: Talk!* (December 19, 2015), available at <http://www.ejiltalk.org/russia-defies-strasbourg-is-contagion-spreading>/; N. Krisch, The Backlash against International Courts, *VerfBlog* (December 16, 2014) available at <http://verfassungsblog.de/backlash-international-courts/>; A. Peters, New German Constitutional Court Decision on "Treaty Override": Triepelianism Continued, *EJIL: Talk!* (February

The backlash against the ICC in Africa is perhaps the most well-known example. Political leaders on the continent, outraged that the overwhelming majority of investigations and all prosecutions have involved government officials or warlords, have orchestrated a collective campaign to undermine the ICC's authority. Their actions have included threatening *en masse* withdrawal from the ICC's Rome Statute (and a few African countries actually withdrawing), proposing alternative venues for prosecuting international crimes, refusing to arrest indicted officials, and openly defying the ICC and its chief prosecutor in pending cases.[54] Other recent backlashes have targeted three of Africa's sub-regional courts, which expanded their jurisdiction from disputes involving trade restrictions and barriers to integration to include human rights and the rule of law. These backlashes, orchestrated by member states in response to politically embarrassing rulings, produced divergent outcomes that included the emasculation of one tribunal and a major restructuring of another.[55]

More unexpected from the perspective of Helfer and Slaughter's article are the significant challenges to the authority of the ECtHR and ECJ. This is true not only in recent accession countries such as Russia and Hungary,[56] where the rule of law and judicial independence are fragile and under threat, but also in long-standing democracies and member states such as the United Kingdom, Germany, and Switzerland. The open resistance includes not only national executives and parliamentarians, but also national judges who were long thought to be the European tribunals' most stalwart partners.[57] To date, no European state has withdrawn from the jurisdiction of either the ECJ or the ECtHR. The same cannot be said of Africa or of the Americas, where Trinidad and Tobago and Venezuela have denounced the American Convention on Human Rights and with it the IACtHR's power of judicial review.[58]

In the Andean context, political leaders have occasionally used existing legal procedures to reverse particular ATJ rulings. As Chapter 5 explains, when the member states overturned a controversial Tribunal judgment on data protection, they

29, 2016), available at <http://www.ejiltalk.org/new-german-constitutional-court-decision-on-treaty-override-triepelianism-continued-2/>.

[54] See, e.g., African Union members back Kenyan plan to leave ICC, *The Guardian* (February 1, 2016); G. Werle, L. Fernandez, and M. Vormbaum, *Africa and the International Criminal Court*. The Hague: T.M.C. Asser Press, 2014; L. Nichols, *The International Criminal Court and the End of Impunity in Kenya*. Switzerland: Springer International Publishing, 2015.

[55] Alter, Gathii, and Helfer, 2016.

[56] Russia ratified the European Convention on Human Rights in 1998, and Hungary joined the European Union in 2004, both after the publication of Helfer and Slaughter's article.

[57] E.g., D. Kelemen, The Court of Justice of the European Union in the Twenty-First Century. *Law and Contemporary Problems* 2016, 79 (1): 117–40; M.R. Madsen, The Challenging Authority of the European Court of Human Rights: From Cold War Legal Diplomacy to the Brighton Declaration and Backlash. *Law and Contemporary Problems* 2016, 79 (1): 141–78.

[58] D. Germán Mejía-Lemos, Venezuela's Denunciation of the American Convention on Human Rights. *ASIL Insights* 2013, 17 (1). In addition, in 2012 Colombia withdrew from a regional treaty granting compulsory jurisdiction to the ICJ in disputes with other nations in Latin America. Colombia pulls out of International Court over Nicaragua, *BBC News* (November 28, 2012), available at <http://www.bbc.com/news/world-latin-america-20533659>.

followed the amendment procedures specified by the Cartagena Agreement and characterized their decision as a clarification of existing law rather than a rebuke of the ATJ.[59] The data protection controversy added to growing political tensions in the region, which later led Venezuela to leave the Andean Community. Yet Venezuela's decision was triggered primarily by Colombia and Peru agreeing to negotiate bilateral free trade agreements with the United States rather than opposition to the ATJ or its rulings.

More recently, as Chapter 7 explains, Ecuador and Bolivia—the two leftist-populist member states in the Community—have raised significant challenges to the free trade orientation of the Andean integration project. Ecuador's President Rafael Correa commissioned a study of the ATJ's jurisdiction, pushed to abolish or restructure Andean institutions, and advocated merging the Community into UNASUR—a South American cooperative initiative less focused on economic integration and legal institutions. In addition, pending noncompliance suits against Ecuador challenge non-tariff barriers and safeguards intended to restrict imports from other Andean countries. These events have aggravated already tense relations among the ideologically divided member states.

The fate of these institutional reforms and the Ecuador noncompliance litigation are now uncertain in light of a recent turn against leftist-populist leaders across South America. Meanwhile, the island of effective international adjudication for IP disputes continues to function, and the ATJ's docket is busier than ever with IP preliminary references. If the Tribunal concludes that Ecuador has breached core Andean free trade rules, however, its finding may trigger fresh challenges to the Tribunal or a decision by the government to withdraw from the Community.

Conclusion: Toward Effective International Adjudication in a Developing Country Context

Many scholars, ourselves included, have put great faith in the belief that a combination of compulsory jurisdiction, broad access rules, high-quality legal reasoning, and astute judicial strategy contributes to the success of international adjudication. Today, there are eighteen "new-style" international courts with compulsory jurisdiction over complaints filed by non-state actors.[60] These courts have issued a growing number of high-profile rulings and are fashioning strategies that respond to their distinctive legal and political environments. Yet few of these courts have replicated the success of Europe's tribunals in attracting litigants, developing consequential

[59] Chapter 7 describes noncompliance litigation regarding an Andean pesticides regulation, which member states revised to give greater leeway for domestic regulation, thereby avoiding further ATJ condemnations.

[60] Alter, 2014, 84. Alter identifies nineteen new-style international courts, but the SADC Tribunal is now suspended and will be reconstituted as an court to which only states have access and from which states can unilaterally withdraw.

legal doctrines, influencing state behavior, and casting a lengthy shadow over domestic law and politics.

The Andean Tribunal was the first transplant of the ECJ to a developing country context, and it is one of the most successful non-European, new-style international courts. We highlight six distinctive aspects of the Andean legal system to support this claim. First, the continued output of ATJ decisions over three decades indicates that Andean litigation is helpful to the private firms and attorneys who file suits that are later referred to the Tribunal. To be sure, activity is not the same thing as effectiveness, but the existence of repeat-player litigation demonstrates that a set of domestic actors sees Andean law and ATJ rulings as useful.

A second hallmark of the ATJ's relative success is the fact that the Tribunal receives dozens of preliminary references from national courts each year. Chapter 3 describes the activation of the preliminary ruling mechanism, first in Colombia, then in Ecuador and Peru, and most recently in Bolivia. As legal, informational, and motivational impediments were overcome in each country, references became almost habitual in IP cases. Meanwhile, no other ECJ-style international court enjoys even the tentative beginnings of a referral relationship with national judges.

A third indicator is the ATJ's creation and persistence of the island of effective international adjudication for intellectual property, a zone in which—largely as a result of hundreds of rulings responding to questions posed by domestic IP administrative agencies—legal rules rather than power, political influence, or bribery govern decision-making by public actors. We document the different facets of this island and its limits in Chapter 5.

A fourth measure is the breadth of disputes that the Tribunal adjudicates compared to international courts in other developing country contexts. As we have explained, the overwhelming majority of preliminary rulings—more than 90%—relate to trademarks, patents, and other forms of IP, and the large majority of these involve contestations between private parties over IP registrations by domestic administrative agencies. However, as Chapters 4 and 6 reveal, the Tribunal has also issued 114 preliminary rulings on non-IP subjects—including tariffs, customs valuations, taxes, and insurance—as well as 113 noncompliance judgments, most of which do not involve IP issues. Although small in percentage terms, in absolute numbers and in the range of topics adjudicated, these cases stand out in comparison to other international tribunals modeled on the ECJ, which have fewer rulings involving a smaller range of subject areas.

A fifth indicator of the ATJ's success is the regular, if sporadic, use of the noncompliance procedure. Since the mid-1990s, this procedure has required the Andean General Secretariat to investigate government and private actor complaints alleging that a member state is violating Community rules. For other ECJ-style transplants beyond Europe, Secretariats and private litigants rarely if ever initiate noncompliance actions.

Sixth, the ATJ is the only ECJ-style court for which all modes of litigation have been activated. The use of the nullification and omission procedures in particular indicates that governments, private litigants, and Andean officials value adherence to Community consultation and decision-making procedures. ATJ litigation has pushed these actors to follow collective decision-making processes, for example with regard to the derogation granting Peru an exceptional status in the Community during the 1990s—a controversy we discuss in Chapter 6.[61]

At the same time, the relative success of the ATJ should not be overstated. We have endeavored in this book to be forthright about the significant limits of the Tribunal's legal authority and political power. In particular, although the ATJ has at times seemed poised to expand its jurisprudential reach and influence, it has largely failed to do so. Only in the circumscribed area of intellectual property has the Tribunal achieved anything close to the influence that the ECJ, ECtHR, and many national high courts possess across a much wider and more politically consequential terrain.

If the ATJ is the most successful example of an international court in a developing country context, the significant limits of its success should instill a sense of caution in those who hope that such courts will transform the legal and political landscape. The most that an international court can do, we argue, is to help states individually and collectively adhere to legal rules that they have imposed upon themselves. This goal can contribute a great deal to promoting compliance with international law, stabilizing domestic politics, and providing a venue to oppose corrupt decisions and practices. For countries where the rule of law is still a distant aspiration, a functioning international court is surely better than relying on politically penetrated or corrupt national legal systems. However, without a groundswell of legal and political support—including from the jurist advocacy movements we analyze in Chapter 9—the impact of international adjudication will necessarily be limited.

For advocates who want international courts to correct wider political failures, such a modest role is likely to be insufficient. Yet no legal system can end crime, erase the power and privilege that often confer impunity, or right all wrongs. International judges do not possess a magic wand, and the law is not a panacea. If the legal systems of rich, developed countries cannot collectively end corruption in foreign business practices, international courts are unlikely to be able to do any better. If pressure and sanctions from the most powerful nations cannot put an end to human rights violations, the rulings of international judges will also surely fail to do so.

What international courts can provide is a resource for politicians, judges, prosecutors, lawyers, interest groups, and individuals who seek to uphold the rule of law. International court rulings can give these actors a legal means and a justification to push back against political pressure and corruption, and to demand that governments follow existing procedures, including those requiring officials to be transparent, to consult with stakeholders, and to win the required political support for their initiatives. The Andean Tribunal of Justice, which has demanded respect

[61] The East African Court of Justice also regularly hears challenges to East African legislation that allegedly violates Community decision-making procedures. Elsewhere we argue that public demands that governments follow these procedures helps to thwart government backlashes against international courts. Alter, Gathii, and Helfer, 2016.

for Andean rules and procedures for more than three decades in an often unstable and politically challenging environment, provides a realistic example of what international courts can achieve. Although the Tribunal is sometimes unable to compel compliance with its rulings, it survives as a beacon to pursue the rule of law in a region where extralegal executive action is often the norm.

APPENDIX

Citations to Decisions of the Andean Tribunal of Justice

Decisions of the Andean Tribunal of Justice (ATJ) are cited by case number, year, and a two-letter Spanish abbreviation indicating the type of case. For example, ATJ preliminary rulings are cited as xx-IP-yyyy, where "xx" is the number of the case, "IP" stands for *interpretacion prejudicial*, and "yyyy" is the year of the reference. The Spanish abbreviation for noncompliance judgments (*acciónes de incumplimiento*) is "AI", the abbreviation for nullification decisions (*acciónes de nulidad*) is "AN", and the abbreviation for omission actions (*recursos por omisión*) is "RO." We cite Andean Tribunal rulings in the footnotes. There is no uniform pattern for citations to text within rulings. Where possible, we cite the page, paragraph, or section in which a quote or other reference appears.

Andean Community Interviews

Interviews with Andean Community Officials

Interviews with officials (A) of the General Secretariat, Office of the Legal Advisor, June 20, 2007, Lima, Peru.

Interviews with former official (B) of the General Secretariat, Office of the Legal Advisor, Chicago, IL, April 1, 2007 and July 3, 2007, Lima, Peru.

Interview with retired official (C) of the General Secretariat, Office of the Legal Advisor and also a negotiator of early Andean Community *Decisiones* on intellectual property, June 22, 2007, Lima, Peru.

Interview with official (D) of the General Secretariat, December 12, 2014, Lima, Peru

Interview with the Legal Advisor (E) of the General Secretary of the Andean Tribunal of Justice, March 17–18, 2005, Quito, Ecuador.

Interview with Judges of the Andean Tribunal of Justice (present and former)

Interview with a former Judge (A) of the Andean Tribunal of Justice, March 17, 2005, Quito, Ecuador.

Interview with former Judge (B) of the Andean Tribunal of Justice, June 22, 2007, Lima, Peru.

Interview with Judge (C) of the Andean Tribunal of Justice, March 17, 2005, Quito, Ecuador.

Interview with Judge (D) of the Andean Tribunal of Justice, March 17, 2005, Quito, Ecuador.

Interview with Judge (E) of the Andean Tribunal of Justice, March 17, 2005, Quito, Ecuador.

Interview with Judge (F) of the Andean Tribunal of Justice, March 17, 2005, Quito, Ecuador.

Interview with Judge (G) of the Andean Tribunal of Justice, November 30, 2007, The Hague, Netherlands.

Interviews with Judge (H) of the Andean Tribunal of Justice, December 11, 2014, Lima, Peru and November 17, 2015, Fiesole, Italy.

Interviews with National Judges

Colombia

Interview with five judges (A) of the *Sección Primera del Consejo de Estado de Colombia*, September 12, 2007, Bogotá, Colombia.

Ecuador

Interview with three judges (A) of the *Tribunal Distrital No. 1 de lo Contencioso Administrativo de Ecudaor*, March 15, 2005, Quito, Ecuador.

Peru

Interview with judge (A) of the *Sala de Derecho Constitucional y Social de la Corte Suprema de Justicia de Peru*, June 21, 2007, Lima, Peru.
Interview with judges (B) of the *Octavo Sala Especializada en lo Contencioso Administrativo de Peru*, December 12, 2014, Lima, Peru.
Interview with judge (C) of the *Sala de Derecho Constitucional y Social Permanente de la Corte Suprema de Justicia de Peru*, December 11, 2014, Lima, Peru.

Interviews with National Government Officials and Agency Administrators

Colombia

Interview with official (A) of the Ministry of Trade, Industry and Tourism of Colombia, September 14, 2007, Bogotá, Colombia.
Interview with former Colombian trade negotiator (B) (1998–2005), September 14, 2007, Bogotá, Colombia.
Interview with official (C) of the *Superintendencia de Industria y Comercio* (SIC) de Colombia, September 12, 2007, Bogotá, Colombia.

Peru

Interview with former Vice Minister of Trade of Peru (A), June 18, 2007, Lima, Peru.
Interview with official (B) of the *Instituto Nacional de Defensa de la Competencia y de la Protección de la Propiedad Intelectual* (INDECOPI), June 21, 2007, Lima, Peru.
Interview with official (C) of the *Instituto Nacional de Defensa de la Competencia y de la Protección de la Propiedad Intelectual* (INDECOPI), June 21, 2007, Lima, Peru.
Telephone interview with former official (D) of the *Instituto Nacional de Defensa de la Competencia y de la Protección de la Propiedad Intelectual* (INDECOPI), May 15, 2007, Lima, Peru.
Interview with officials (E) of the *Instituto Nacional de Defensa de la Competencia y de la Protección de la Propiedad Intelectual* (INDECOPI), December 11, 2014, Lima, Peru.

Venezuela

Telephone interview with former official (A) of the *Servicio Autonomo de la Propiedad Intelectual* (SAPI) from 1999–2001, March 19, 2007.
Interview with Ambassador (B) of Venezuela to Ecuador, March 16, 2005, Quito, Ecuador.

Interviews with Industry Associations and NGOs

Interview with official (A) of the *Asociación Nacional de Laboratorios Farmacéuticos de Peru* (ALAFARPE), June 19, 2007, Lima, Peru.
Interview with official (B) of the *Asociación de Industrias Farmacéuticas de Colombia* (ASINFAR), September 14, 2007, Bogotá, Colombia.
Telephone interviews with official (C) of the *Comisión Andina de Juristas*, May 20, 2008 and December 8, 2008.

Interviews with attorneys

Interview with attorney (A) from commercial and administrative law firm in Colombia, September 10, 2007, Bogotá, Colombia.
Interview with attorney (B) involved in patent litigation in Peru, June 18, 2007, Lima, Peru.
Interview with attorney (C) from intellectual property law firm in Peru, June 18, 2007, Lima, Peru.
Interview with attorney (D) from intellectual property law firm in Colombia, September 10, 2007, Bogotá, Colombia.
Interview with attorney (E) from intellectual property law firm in Colombia, September 10, 2007, Bogotá, Colombia.
Interview with attorney (F) from intellectual property law firm in Colombia, September 13, 2007, Bogotá, Colombia.
Interview with attorney (G) practicing law in Colombia, September 14, 2007, Bogotá, Colombia.
Interview with four attorneys (H) at Colombian branch of a multinational law firm, September 11, 2007, Bogotá, Colombia.
Interview with two attorneys (I) from IP law firm in Ecuador, March 16, 2005, Quito, Ecuador.
Interview with two attorneys (J) from the family firm of an attorney raising an early ATJ case, September 11, 2007, Bogotá, Colombia.

European Community Interviews

Alter's interview notes from the 1990s have been transferred to the Historical Archives of the European Union, housed at the European University Institute (<http://www.eui.eu/Research/HistoricalArchivesOfEU/AlcideDeGasperiResearchCentre/Sources-on-the-History-of-European-Law-new.aspx>). These interviews were not governed by the rules of the Institutional Review Board. Given historical developments and the passage of time, the sources no longer require protection. We thus provide the full names of the European sources cited in this book.

Interviews with administrators of Euro-law associations

Interview with Dr Hans-Jürgen Rabe, former secretary of the *Wissentschaftliche Gesellschaft für Europarecht*, Brussels, January 11, 1994.
Interview with Dr Lise Funck-Brentano, President of the *Association des Juristes Européens*, May 26, 1994, Paris.
Interview with Gerard Nafylan, Treasurer of the *Commission pour l'Etude des Communautés Européennes* (CEDEC), May 16, 1994, Paris.

Interviews with European Community officials

Interview with Michel Gaudet, former Director of the Legal Services of the European Commission, July 7, 1994, Brussels.

Interview with Jaqueline Lastenouse, former Director of Academic Affairs, the European Commission, July 11, 1994, Brussels.

Interview with Emil Noël, former Commissioner from the 1960s to 1980, June 9, 1994, Paris.

Interviews with national judges in Europe

Interview with Dr Helmut Friedl, former Judge at *Finanzgericht München*, Clerk at the *Bundesfinanzhof* from 1967–72, February 22, 1994, Füßen.

Andean, European, and Multilateral Treaties and Secondary Legislation (*Decisiones*)

Treaties

Treaty Establishing the European Economic Community, March 25, 1957, 298 United Nations Treaty Series 11 (Treaty of Rome).

Andean Subregional Integration Agreement, May 26, 1969, 8 International Legal Materials 910 (Cartagena Agreement).

Treaty Establishing the Court of Justice of the Cartagena Agreement, May 28, 1979, 18 International Legal Materials 1203 (Original ATJ Treaty).

Treaty Creating the Court of Justice of the Cartagena Agreement, as amended by the Protocol of Cochabamba, May 28, 1996 (Revised ATJ Treaty).

Protocol of Sucre, June 25, 1997.

Protocol of Trujillo, March 10, 1996.

Agreement on Trade-Related Aspects of Intellectual Property Rights, Marrakesh Agreement Establishing the World Trade Organization, Annex 1C, April 15, 1994 (TRIPS Agreement).

Selected Andean Secondary Legislation

Andean Community *Decisión* No. 24—Common Regime of Treatment of Foreign Capital and on Trademarks, Patents, Licenses and Royalties, December 31, 1970.

Andean Community *Decisión* No. 85—Regulation for the Application of Industrial Property Rules, June 5, 1974.

Andean Community *Decisión* No. 291—Establishing the Regime for the Common Treatment of Foreign Capital and Trademarks, Patents, Licenses Agreements and Royalties, March 21, 1991.

Andean Community *Decisión* No. 311—Common Regime on Industrial Property, November 8, 1991.

Andean Community *Decisión* No. 313—Common Regime on Industrial Property, February 6, 1992.

Andean Community *Decisión* No. 344—Establishing the Common Regime on Industrial Property, October 21, 1993.

Andean Community *Decisión* No. 436 on the Registration and Control of Chemical Pesticides for Agricultural Use, June 11, 1998.

Andean Community *Decisión* No. 486—Establishing the Common Regime on Industrial Property, September 14, 2000.

Andean Community *Decisión* No. 500—on the Statute of the Tribunal of Justice of the Andean Community, June 22, 2001.

Andean Community *Decisión* No. 632—Clarifying the Second Paragraph of Article 266 of *Decisión* No. 486 of 2000, April 6, 2006.

Andean Community *Decisión* No. 689—Adequacy of certain articles of *Decisión* 486—Common Regime on Industrial Property, to allow the development and deepen of industrial property rights across the internal regulation of the Members States, August 13, 2008.

Andean Community *Decisión* No. 792—Reengineering Implementation of the Andean Integration System, September 19, 2013.

Andean Community *Decisión* No. 804—Amendment of *Decisión* 436 (Andean Regulation for the Registration and Control of Chemical Pesticides for Agricultural Use), April 24, 2015.

Andean Community *Decisión* 805—Abrogating *Decisiones* 370, 465, and 535 (the Andean Common External Tariff), April 5, 2015.

Statistical Studies of the Andean Tribunal

Tribunal de Justicia de la Comunidad Andina, Informe de Labores Gestión 2015 available at <http://www.tribunalandino.org.ec/sitetjca1/INFORME%20TOTAL%202015%20final.pdf>

Informe Estadístico, 1984–2014, available at <http://www.tribunalandino.org.ec/sitetjca1/Informe%20unificado%20final%2084-2014.pdf>

Informe de law Secretaría General de law Comunidad Andina 2006–2007 SG/di 84814 de junio de 2007 (on file with the authors).

Bibliography

Abbott, Frederik M. 1975. Bargaining Power and Strategy in the Foreign Investment Process: A Current Andean Code Analysis. *Syracuse Journal of International Law and Commerce* 3 (3): 319–58.

Adams, Jonathan E. 1994. A New Andean Agreement: Rules of Origin Replace the Investment Code. *Arizona Journal of International and Comparative Law* 11: 389–427.

Alter, Karen J. 1996. The European Court's Political Power. *West European Politics* 19 (3): 458–87.

——— 1998. Who Are the Masters of the Treaty?: European Governments and the European Court of Justice. *International Organization* 52 (1): 125–52.

——— 2000. The European Legal System and Domestic Policy: Spillover or Backlash. *International Organization* 54 (3): 489–518.

——— 2001. *Establishing the Supremacy of European Law: The Making of an International Rule of Law in Europe*. Oxford: Oxford University Press.

——— 2003. Resolving or Exacerbating Disputes? The WTO's New Dispute Resolution System. *International Affairs* 79 (4): 783–800.

——— 2009. Jurist Advocacy Movements in Europe: The Role of Euro-Law Associations in European Integration (1953–1975). In: *The European Court's Political Power*. Karen J. Alter (ed.), 63–91. Oxford: Oxford University Press.

——— 2012. The Global Spread of European Style International Courts. *West European Politics* 35 (1): 135–54.

——— 2014. *The New Terrain of International Law: Courts, Politics, Rights*. Princeton, NJ: Princeton University Press.

Alter, Karen J., James T. Gathii, and Laurence R. Helfer. 2016. Backlash Against International Courts in West, East and Southern Africa: Causes and Consequences. *European Journal of International Law* 27 (2): 293–328.

Alter, Karen J., Laurence R. Helfer, and Mikael Rask Madsen. 2016. The Variable Authority of International Courts. *Law and Contemporary Problems* 79 (1): 1–36.

——— 2017. *International Court Authority*. Oxford: Oxford University Press.

Alter, Karen J., Laurence R. Helfer, and Jacqueline McAllister. 2013. A New International Human Rights Court for West Africa: The Court of Justice for the Economic Community of West African States. *American Journal of International Law* 107 (4): 737–79.

Alter, Karen J. and Sophie Meunier-Aitsahalia. 1994. Judicial Politics in the European Community: European Integration and the Pathbreaking *Cassis de Dijon* Decision. *Comparative Political Studies* 24 (4): 535–61.

Alvarez, José. 2003. The New Dispute Settlers: (Half) Truths and Consequences. *Texas International Law Journal* 38: 405–44.

Avery, William P. and James D. Cochraine. 1973. Innovation in Latin American Regionalism: The Andean Common Market. *International Organization* 27 (2): 181–223.

Baquero Herrera, Mauricio. 2005. Open Regionalism in Latin America: An Appraisal. *Law and Business Review of the Americas* 11 (2): 139–84.

Barton, John H. and Barry E. Carter. 1993. International Law and Institutions for a New Age. *Georgetown Law Journal* 81 (3): 535–62.

Basso, Maristela. 2006. Intervention of Health Authorities in Patent Examination: The Brazilian Practice of the Prior Consent. *International Journal of Intellectual Property Management* 1 (1): 54–74.

Becker, David G. 2001. Justice for Peruvian Consumers? INDECOPI and Consumer Protection. In: *Paper presented at the XXIII Int'l Congress of the Latin American Studies Association.* Washington DC. Available at <http://biblioteca.cejamericas.org/bitstream/handle/2015/1001/Justice-for-Peruvian-Consumers-INDECOPI-and-Consumer-Protection.pdf?sequence=1&isAllowed=y>.

Bergsten, C. Fred. 1997. Open Regionalism. *The World Economy* 20 (5): 545–65.

Berkowitz, Daniel, Katharina Pistor, and Jean-Francois Richard. 2003. The Transplant Effect. *American Journal of Comparative Law* 51: 163–203.

Bernieri, Rosa Castro. 2006. Intellectual Property Rights in Bilateral Investment Treaties and Access to Medicines: The Case of Latin America. *Journal of World Intellectual Property* 9 (5), 548–72.

Bignami, Francesca. 2005. Creating European Rights: National Values and Supranational Interests. *Columbia Journal of European Law* 11: 241–352.

Boerger-De Smedt, Anne. 2008. La Court de Justice dans les Négociations du Traité de Paris Instituant la CECA. *Journal of European History* 14 (2): 7–34.

Börzel, Tanja A. and Thomas Risse. 2009. *The Transformative Power of Europe: The European Union and the Diffusion of Ideas, Working Paper of the Kfg Nr. 1.* Berlin: Frei Universität Berlin.

Bowring, Bill. 2015. The Russian Federation and the Strasbourg Court: The Illegitimacy of Sovereignty? In: *The UK and European Human Rights: A Strained Relationship?* Katja S. Ziegler, Elizabeth Wicks, and Loveday Hodson (eds), 415–40. Oxford: Hart Publishing.

Brinkmann, Heinz-Volker. 1965. Rechtsfragen der Europäischen Integration. *Neue Juristische Wochenschrift* (Heft 24): 1120–21.

Brummer, Christopher. 2007. The Ties That Bind? Regionalism, Commercial Treaties, and the Future of Global Economic Integration. *Vanderbilt Law Review* 60 (5): 1349–409.

Bueno Martinez, Patricio and Alejandro Daniel Perotti. 2005. La Teoria del Acto Reclamado: Resulta Necesaria su Aplicación en el Marco de la Interpretación Judicial Andina. *Dikaion, Universidad de la Sabana* 19 (14): 133–53.

Burley, Anne-Marie and Walter Mattli. 1993. Europe before the Court. *International Organization* 47 (1): 41–76.

Caporaso, James and John Keeler. 1995. The European Union and Regional Integration Theory. In: *The State of the European Union.* Carolyn Rhodes and Sonia Mazey (eds), 29–62. Boulder, CO: Lynne Rienner/Longmann.

Caserta, Salvatore. 2016. *Institutionalizing Regional International Courts: Creation, Authority, and Power of the Central American and Caribbean Courts of Justice.* PhD Dissertation. University of Copenhagen.

Cavalier, Germán. 2002. *Complición Histórica de las Leyes Colombianas Sobre Propriedad Industrial.* Bogota: Cavelier Abogados.

Cavallaro, James L. and Stephanie Erin Brewer. 2008. Reevaluating Regional Human Rights Litigation in the Twenty-First Century: The Case of the Inter-American Court. *American Journal of International Law* 102 (4): 768–827.

Cichowski, Rachel. 2007. *The European Court and Civil Society: Litigation, Mobilization and Governance.* Cambridge: Cambridge University Press.

Claes, Monica and Bruno De Witte. 1998. Report on the Netherlands. In: *The European Courts and National Courts.* Anne-Marie Slaughter, Alec Stone-Sweet, and Joseph Weiler (eds), 171–94. Cambridge: Hart Publishing.

Cohen, Antonin and Michael Rask Madsen. 2007. Cold War Law: Legal Entreprenuers and the Emergence of a European Legal Field (1946–1965). In: *European Ways of Law*. Volkmar Gessner and David Nelken (eds), 175–200. Oxford: Hart.

Conway, Gerard. 2016. The Legal Reasoning of the Andean Court of Justice in Comparative Context. *iCourts Working Paper Series* (56).

Cruz Vilaça, José Luís da José Manuel, and Sobrino Heredia. 1998. The European Union and the Transformation of the Andean Pact into the Andean Community: From the Trujillo Protocol to the Sucre Act. *European Foreign Affairs Review* 3 (1): 13–52. Available at <https://papers.ssrn.com/sol3/papers.cfm?abstract_id=2774678>.

Cullen, Dolores. 2007. Data Protection: The New IP Frontier—An Overview of Existing Laws and Regulations. *Journal of Generic Medicines* 5 (1): 9–25.

Davies, Bill. 2012. *Resisting the European Court of Justice: West Germany's Confrontation with European Law, 1949–1979*. Cambridge: Cambridge University Press.

De Burca, Grainne. 2011. Roads Not Taken: The EU as a Global Human Rights Actor. *American Journal of International Law* 105 (4): 649–93.

De Wet, Erika. 2014. The Case of Government of the Republic of Zimbabwe v. Louis Karel Fick: A First Step Towards Developing a Doctrine on the Status of International Judgments within the Domestic Legal Order. *Potchefstroom Electronic Law Journal* 17 (1): 553–65.

Dehousse, Renaud. 1998. *The European Court of Justice: The Politics of Judicial Integration*. New York, NY: St. Martin's Press.

Denning, Lord. 1990. Introduction to *The European Court of Justice: Judges or Policy Makers?* The Bruge Group Publication, Suite 102 Whitehall Court, Westminster, London SWIA 2EL.

Dezalay, Yves and Bryant G. Garth. 2002a. *Global Prescriptions: The Production, Exportation, and Importation of a New Legal Orthodoxy*. Ann Arbor, MI: University of Michigan Press.

——— 2002b. *The Internationalization of Palace Wars: Lawyers, Economists, and the Contest to Transform Latin American States*. Chicago, IL: University of Chicago Press.

——— 2006. From the Cold War to Kosovo: The Renewal of the Field of International Human Rights. *Annual Review of Law and Social Science* 2: 231–55.

Dinan, Desmond. 2004. *Europe Recast: A History of the European Union*. Boulder, CO: Lynn Rienner.

Dinca, Razvan. 2005. The "Bermuda Triangle" of Pharmaceutical Law. *The Journal of World Intellectual Property* 8 (4): 517–63.

Donner, André. 1968. *The Role of the Lawyer in the European Communities, The Rosenthal Lectures*. Evanston, IL: Northwestern University Press.

Ebobrah, Solomon. 2017. The ECOWAS Community Court of Justice: A Dual Mandate with Skewed Authority. In: *International Court Authority*, Karen J. Alter, Laurence R. Helfer, and Mikael Rask Madsen (eds). Oxford: Oxford University Press.

Epps, Charles. 1998. *The Rights Revolution: Lawyers, Activists and Supreme Courts in Comparative Perspective*. Chicago, IL: University of Chicago Press.

Esquiroi, Jorge L. 2008. The Failed Law of Latin America. *The American Journal of Comparative Law* 56 (1): 75–124.

Ferris, Elizabeth G. 1979. National Political Support for Regional Integration: The Andean Pact. *International Organization* 33 (1): 83–104.

Ffrench-Davis, Ricardo. 1977. The Andean Pact: A Model of Economic Integration for Developing Countries. *World Development* 5 (1): 137–53.

Friedrich, Carl J. 1954. Introduction: The Background of These Studies and the Development of the Draft Constitution. In: *Studies in Federalism*, Robert Bowie and Carl Friedrich (eds), xxv–xlii. Boston, MA: Little Brown.

Garcia Amador, F.V. 1978. *The Andean Legal Order: A New Community of Law*. Dobbs Ferry, NY: Oceana Publications.

Gathii, James. 2014. Mission Creep or a Search for Relevance: The East African Court of Justice's Human Rights Strategy. *Duke Journal of Comparative and International Law* 24 (2): 249–96.

——— 2016a. Saving the Serengeti: Africa's New International Judicial Environmentalism. *Chicago Journal of International Law* 16 (2): 386–438.

——— 2016b. The Variation in the Use of Sub-Regional Integration Courts between Business and Human Rights Actors: The Case of the East African Court of Justice. *Law and Contemporary Problems* 79 (1): 37–62.

Gaudet, Michael. 1963. Introductory Message. *Common Market Law Review* 1 (1): 1–2.

Germán Mejía-Lemos, Diego. 2013. Venezuela's Denunciation of the American Convention on Human Rights. *ASIL Insights* 17 (1). Available at <https://www.asil.org/insights/volume/17/issue/1/venezuelas-denunciation-american-convention-human-rights>.

Gianaris, William N. 1992. The New World Order and the Need for an International Criminal Court. *Fordham International Law Journal* 16 (1): 88–119.

Ginsburg, Tom. 2005. Bounded Discretion in International Judicial Lawmaking. *Virginia Journal of International Law* 43 (3): 631–73.

Graham, Erin R., Charles R. Shipan, and Craig Volden. 2013. The Diffusion of Policy Diffusion Research in Political Science. *British Journal of Political Science* 43 (3): 673–701.

Graziadei, Michele. 2009. Legal Transplants and the Frontiers of Legal Knowledge. *Theoretical Inquiries in Law* 10 (2): 723–43.

Gruszczynski, Lukasz. 2015. The New Tobacco Products Directive and WTO Law: Much Ado About Nothing? *Asian Journal of WTO and International Health Law and Policy* 10 (1): 115–50.

Haas, Ernst. 1961. International Integration: The European and the Universal Process. *International Organization* 15 (3): 366–92.

——— 1970. The Study of Regional Integration: Reflections on the Joy and Anguish of Pretheorizing. *International Organization* 24 (4): 607–46.

——— 1975. *The Obsolescence of Regional Integration Theory*. Berkeley, CA: University of California Press.

Haas, Ernst B. 2008. *Beyond the Nation State Functionalism and International Organization*. Colchester: ECPR Press.

Haas, Peter M. 1992. Introduction: Epistemic Communities and International Policy Coordination. *International Organization* 46 (1): 1–36.

Hagan, John and Ron Levi. 2005. Crimes of War and the Force of Law. *Social Forces* 83 (4): 1499–534.

Halliday, Terence C., Lucien Karpik, and Malcolm Feeley. 2007. *Fighting for Political Freedom: Comparative Studies of the Legal Complex and Political Liberalism*. Oxford: Hart.

Hammergren, Linn A. 2007. *Envisioning Reform: Improving Judicial Performance in Latin America*. University Park, PA: Pennsylvania State University Press.

Harlow, Carol and Richard Rawlings. 1992. *Pressure through Law*. London: Routledge.

Harrison, Christopher Scott. 2004. *The Politics of the International Pricing of Prescription Drugs*. Westport, CT: Praeger.

Hartley, Trevor. 1996. The European Court, Judicial Objectivity and the Constitution of the European Union. *Law Quarterly Review* 112: 95–109.

——— 1999. *Constitutional Problems of the European Union*. Oxford: Hart Publishing.

Hawkins, Darren and Wade Jacoby. 2008. Agent Permeability, Principal Delegation and the European Court of Human Rights. *The Review of International Organizations* 3 (1): 1–28.

——— 2010. Partial Compliance: A Comparison of the European and Inter-American Court of Human Rights. *Journal of International Law and International Relations* 6 (1): 35–85.

Hawkins, Darren, Daniel Neilson, Michael J. Tierney, and David A. Lake. 2006. *Delegation and Agency in International Organizations*. Cambridge: Cambridge University Press.

Helfer, Laurence. R. 2002. Overlegalizing Human Rights: International Relations Theory and the Commonwealth Caribbean Backlash against Human Rights Regimes. *Columbia Law Review* 102 (7): 1832–911.

——— 2004. Regime Shifting: The TRIPS Agreement and the New Dynamics of International Intellectual Property Making. *Yale Journal of International Law* 29 (1): 1–81.

——— 2005. Exiting Treaties. *Virginia Law Review* 91 (7): 1579–648.

——— 2014. The Effectiveness of International Adjudicators. In: *Oxford Handbook on International Adjudication*. Cesare Romano, Karen J. Alter, and Yuval Shany (eds), 464–82. Oxford: Oxford University Press.

Helfer, Laurence R. and Karen J. Alter. 2013. Legitimacy and Lawmaking: A Tale of Three International Courts. *Theoretical Inquires in Law* 14 (2): 479–503.

——— 2014. The Influence of the Andean Intellectual Property Regime on Access to Medicines in Latin America. In: *Balancing Wealth and Health: The Battle over Intellectual Property and Access to Medicines in Latin America*. Rochelle Cooper Dreyfuss and César A. Rodríguez Garavito (eds), 247–62. Oxford: Oxford University Press.

Helfer, Laurence R. and Anne-Marie Slaughter. 1997. Toward a Theory of Effective Supranational Adjudication. *Yale Law Journal* 107 (2): 273–391.

Heyns, Christof and Magnus Jillander. 2011. Toward Minimum Standards for Regional Human Rights Systems. In: *Looking to the Future: Essays on International Law in Honor of W. Michael Reisman*. Mahnoush H. Arsanjani, Jacob Katz Cogan, Robert D. Sloane, and Siegfried Wiessne (eds), 527–58. Leiden: Brill.

Hirschl, Ran. 2008. The Judicialization of Mega-Politics and the Rise of Political Courts. *Annual Review of Political Science* 11: 93–118.

Hoffmann, Stanley. 1966. Obstinate or Obsolete? France, European Integration, and the Fate of the Nation-State. *Daedalus* 95 (3): 862–915.

Hojman, David E. 1981. The Andean Pact: Failure of a Model of Integration? *Journal of Common Market Studies* 20 (2): 139–59.

Holden, Chris, Kelley Lee, Gary Jonas Fooks, and Nathaniel Wander. 2010. The Impact of Regional Trade Integration on Firm Organization and Strategy: British American Tobacco in the Andean Pact. *Business and Politics* 12 (4): 1–32.

Horton, Scott. 1982. Peru and Ancom: A Study in the Disintegration of a Common Market. *Texas International Law Journal* 17: 39–61.

Huneeus, Alexandra. 2011. Courts Resisting Courts: Lessons from the Inter-American Court's Struggle to Enforce Human Rights. *Cornell International Law Journal* 44 (3): 493–532.

Hurtado Larrea, Eduardo. 1985. Los Incumplimientos y la Acción Asignada a la Competencia del Tribunal. In: *El Tribunal De Justicia Del Acuerdo De Cartagena*. BID-INTAL (ed.) xx–xx. Buenos Aires: BID-INTAL. Available at <http://paperroom.ipsa.org/papers/paper_977.pdf.

Ipsen, Hans Peter. 1964. Aktuelle Fragen des Europäischen Gemeinschaftsrechts. Stuttgart: Ferdinand Enke. Available at <http://www.worldcat.org/title/aktuelle-fragen-des-europaischen-gemeinschaftsrechts-gemeinschaftsrecht-und-nationales-recht-niederlassungsfreiheit-und-rechtsangleichung-europarechtliches-kolloquium-1964/oclc/468912098>.

——— 1972. Anmerkung zu Bverfg Entscheidung vom 9.6.1971. *Europarecht* Heft 1: 57–9.

——— 1990. "Europarecht" 25 Jahrgänge 1966–1990 in Verbindung mit der Wissenschaftlichen Gesellschaft für Europarecht. *Europarecht* 25 (4): 323–39.

Jacoby, Wade. 2000. *Imitation and Politics: Redesigning Modern Germany*. Ithaca, NY: Cornell University Press.

——— 2006. Inspiration, Coalition and Substitution: External Influences on Postcommunist Transformations. *World Politics* 58 (4): 623–51.

Jansen, Robert S. 2011. Populist Mobilization: A New Theoretical Approach to Populism. *Sociological Theory* 29 (2): 75–96

Kapiszewski, Diana and Mathew Taylor. 2008. Doing Courts Justice? Studying Judicial Politics in Latin America. *Perspective on Politics* 6 (4): 741–65.

Keck, Margaret E. and Kathryn Sikkink. 1998. *Activists Beyond Borders: Advocacy Networks in International Politics*. Ithaca, NY: Cornell University Press.

Keener, E. Barlow. 1987. The Andean Common Market Court of Justice: Its Purpose, Structure, and Future. *Emory Journal of International Dispute Resolution* 2 (1): 37–72.

Kelemen, Daniel. 2016. The Court of Justice of the European Union in the Twenty-First Century. *Law and Contemporary Problems* 79 (1): 117–40.

Kenney, Sally. 1998. The Members of the Court of Justice of the European Communities. *Columbia Journal of European Law* 5 (1): 101–33.

Keohane, Robert, Andrew Moravcsik, and Anne-Marie Slaughter. 2000. Legalized Dispute Resolution: Interstate and Transnational. *International Organization* 54 (3): 457–88.

Kingsbury, Benedict, Nico Krisch, Richard B. Stewart, and Jonathan Weiner. 2005. The Emergence of Global Administrative Law. *Law and Contemporary Problems* 68 (3 & 4): 15–62.

Krikorian, Gaëlle P. and Dorota M. Szymkowiak. 2007. Intellectual Property Rights in the Making: The Evolution of Intellectual Property Provisions in US Free Trade Agreements and Access to Medicine. *Journal of World Intellectual Property* 10 (5): 388–418.

Kuwayama, Mikio. 2005. Latin American South-South Integration and Cooperation: From a Regional Public Goods Perspective. *Comercio Internacional Series No. 50*. Division of Trade and Intergration: United Nations Economic Commission for Latin America and the Caribbean. Available at <http://www.cepal.org/en/publications/4390-latin-american-south-south-integration-and-cooperation-regional-public-goods>.

La Porta, Rafael, Florencio Lopez-de-Silanes, Andrei Shleifer, and Robert W. Vishny. 1998. Law and Finance. *Journal of Political Economy* 106 (6): 1113–55.

Lecourt, Robert. 1964. Le Rôle du Droit dans l'Unification Européenne. *Gazette du Palais*: 49–54.

——— 1965. La Dynamique Judiciaire dans L'Édification de L'Europe. *France Forum* (May 1964): 20–2.

Legrand, Pierre. 2001. What Legal Transplants? In *Adapting Legal Cultures*. David Nelken and Johannes Feest (eds), 55–69. Portland, OR: Hart Publishing.

Lenz, Tobias. 2012. Spurred Emulation: The EU and Regional Integration in Mercosur and SADC. *West European Politics* 35 (1): 155–73.

Lindseth, Peter. 2003. The Contradictions of Supranationalism: Administrative Governance and Constitutionalization in European Integration since the 1950s. *Loyola of Los Angeles Law Review* 37 (2): 363–406.

Lutz, Ellen and Kathryn Sikkink. 2000. International Human Rights Law and Practice in Latin America. *International Organization* 54 (3): 633–59.

Madsen, Michael Rask. 2007. From Cold War Instrument to Supreme European Court: The European Court of Human Rights at the Crossroads of International and National Law and Politics. *Law & Social Inquiry* 32 (1): 137–59.

——— 2013. Unpacking Legal Network Power: The Structural Construction of Transnational Legal Expert Networks. In: *Networked Governance, Transnational Business and the Law*. Mark Fenwick, Stephen Van Uytsel, and Stephen Wrbka (eds), 39–56. Berlin: Springer Verlag.

——— 2016. The Challenging Authority of the European Court of Human Rights: From Cold War Legal Diplomacy to the Brighton Declaration and Backlash. *Law and Contemporary Problems* 79 (1): 141–78.

Madsen, Mikael R. and Alexandra Huneeus. Forthcoming. Between Global Scripts and Regional Politics: A Comparative History of the American, European and African Human Rights Systems. *International Journal of Constitutional Law*.

Madsen, Mikael Rask and Antoine Vauchez. 2005. European Constitutionalism at the Cradle: Law and Lawyers in the Construction of a European Political Order (1920–1960). In: *In Lawyers' Circles. Lawyers and European Legal Integration*. Alex Jettinghoff and Harm Schepel (eds), 15–34. The Hague: Elsevier.

Maduro, Miguel Poiares. 1998. *We the Court: The European Court of Justice and the European Economic Constitution*. Oxford: Hart Publishers.

Malamud, Carlos. 2006. Venezuela's Withdrawal from the Andean Community of Nations and the Consequences for Regional Integration. ARI 54/2006 Real Institute Elcano.

Mancero-Bucheli, Gabriela. 1998. Intellectual Property and Rules on Free Movement: A Contradiction in the Andean Community. *NAFTA: Law and Business Review of the Americas* 4: 125–36.

Mancini, Federico. 1989. The Making of a Constitution for Europe. *Common Market Law Review* 26 (4): 595–614.

Mancini, Federico and David Keeling. 1992. From CILFIT to ERTA: The Constitutional Challenge Facing the European Court. *Yearbook of European Law* 11: 1–13.

——— 1995. Language, Culture and Politics in the Life of the European Court of Justice. *Columbia Journal of European Law* 1 (2): 397–413.

Manrique, Roberto Salazar. 1998. The Andean Community's Intellectual Property Regime. In: *The Andean Community and the United States: Trade and Investment Relations in the 1990s*. M. Rodríguez Mendoza, Patricia Correa, and Barbara Kotschwar (eds), 212–19. Organization of American States, Washington DC.

Mantilla, Galo Pico. 1992. *Derecho Andino*. Quito: Tribunal de Justicia del Acuerdo de Cartagena.

Martinez, Jenny S. 2003. Towards an International Judicial System. *Stanford Law Review* 56 (2): 429–529.

Mattli, Walter. 1999. *The Logic of Regional Integration*. Cambridge: Cambridge University Press.

——— 2005. Ernst Haas' Evolving Thinking on Comparative Regional Integration: Of Virtues and Infelicities. *Journal of European Public Policy* 12 (2): 327–48.

Mattli, Walter and Anne-Marie Slaughter. 1998. Revisiting the European Court of Justice. *International Organization* 52 (1): 177–209.

McGrady, Benn. 2011. *Trade and Public Health: The WTO, Tobacco, Alcohol, and Diet*. New York, NY: Cambridge University Press.

McNamara, Kathleen R. 1998. *The Currency of Ideas: Monetary Politics in the European Union*. Ithaca, NY: Cornell University Press.

Merryman, John Henry and Rogelio Pérez-Perdomo. 2007. *The Civil Law Tradition.* Stanford, CA: Stanford University Press.

Milward, Alan. 1992. *The European Rescue of the Nation-State.* London: Routledge.

Moravcsik, Andrew. 1998. *The Choice for Europe.* Ithaca, NY: Cornell University Press.

——— 2000. The Origins of Human Rights Regimes: Democratic Delegation in Postwar Europe. *International Organization* 54 (2): 217–52.

Moss, Marianna. 2005. Trademark "Coexistence" Agreements: Legitimate Contracts or Tools of Consumer Deception? *Loyola Consumer Law Review* 18 (2): 197–222.

Moustafa, Tamir. 2007. *The Struggle for Constitutional Power: Law, Politics and Economic Development in Egypt.* Cambridge: Cambridge University Press.

Murphy, John M. 2006. The Confusing Similarity Standard in Mexican Trademark Law. *Trademark Reporter* 96 (6): 1182–210.

Nelken, David and Johannes Feest. 2001. *Adapting Legal Cultures.* Portland, OR: Hart Publishing.

Nichols, Lionel. 2015. *The International Criminal Court and the End of Impunity in Kenya.* Switzerland: Springer International Publishing.

Nollkaemper, André. 2011. *National Courts and the International Rule of Law.* Oxford: Oxford University Press.

Nye, Joseph S. 1971. Comparing Common Markets: A Revised Neofunctionalist Model. *International Organization* 24 (4): 796–835.

O'Donnell, Guillermo. 1998. Polyarchies and the (Un)Rule of Law in Latin America. In: *The (Un)Rule of Law and the Underprivileged in Latin America.* Juan E. Méndez, Guillermo A. O'Donnell, and Paulo Sérgio de M. S. Pinheiro (eds), 303–37. Notre Dame, IN: University of Notre Dame Press.

O'Keefe, Thomas Andrew. 1996. How the Andean Pact Transformed Itself into a Friend of Foreign Enterprise. *International Lawyer* 30 (4): 811–24.

——— 2009. *Latin American and Caribbean Trade Agreements: Keys to a Prosperous Community of the Americas.* Leiden: Brill Martinus Nijhoff Publishers.

Ohlin, Jens David. 2015. *The Assault on International Law.* Oxford: Oxford University Press.

Ophüls, Carl Friedrich. 1963. Quellen und Aufbau des Europäischen Gemeinschaftsrechts. *Neue Juristische Wochenschrift* (Heft 38): 1697–701.

Orrego Vicuña, Francisco. 1972. La Incorporación del Ordenamiento Jurídico Subregional al Derecho Interno: Análisis de la Práctica y Jurisprudencia de Colombia. *Derecho de la Integración* 11 (October): 39–60.

Pacheco, Carlos and María Milagros Nebrada. 2006. Venezuela: How to Protect Inventions of Use. *Managing Intellectual Property—Supplement.* Available at <http://www.managingip.com/Article/1321317/Venezuela-How-to-protect-inventions-of-use.html>.

Padilla, David. 1979. The Judicial Resolution of Legal Disputes in the Integration Movements of the Hemisphere. *Lawyers of the Americas* 11 (1): 75–95.

Parsons, Craig. 2003. *A Certain Idea of Europe.* Ithaca, NY: Cornell University Press.

Pasqualucci, Jo M. 2014. *The Practice and Procedure of the Inter-American Court of Human Rights.* Cambridge: Cambridge University Press.

Perotti, Alejandro Daniel. 2001. Algunas Consideraciones sobre la Interpretación Prejudicial Obligatoria en el Derecho Andino. *Gaceta Juridica de la Comunidad Europea.* D-213. Available at <http://www.comunidadandina.org/bda/docs/can-int-0010.pdf>.

Pescatore, Pierre. 1983a. The Doctrine of "Direct Effect": An Infant Disease of Community Law. *European Law Review* 8 (3): 155–77.

——— 1983b. La Clarence du Législateur Communautaire et le Devoir du Juge. In: *Gedächtnisschrift für L.-J. Constantinesco.* G. Lüke, G. Ress and M.R. Will (eds), 559–80. Cologne: Carl Heymanns Verlag.

Phelan, William. 2015. Enforcement and Escape in the Andean Community: Why the Andean Community is Not a Replica of the European Union. *Journal of Common Market Studies* 53 (4): 840–56.

Pires de Carvalho, Nuno. 2010. *The TRIPS Regime of Patent Rights*. Alphen aan den Rijn: Kluwer Law International.

Pollack, Mark. 1997. Delegation, Agency and Agenda Setting in the EC. *International Organization* 51 (1): 99–134.

——— 2003. *The Engines of Integration: Delegation, Agency, and Agency Setting in the European Union*. Oxford: Oxford University Press.

Posner, Eric A. and John C. Yoo. 2005. A Theory of International Adjudication. *California Law Review* 93 (1): 1–72.

Rasmussen, Hjalte. 1984. The European Court's Acte Clair Strategy in C.I.L.I.T. Or Acte Clair, of Course! But What Does It Mean? *European Law Review* 9 (4): 242–59.

——— 1986. *On Law and Policy in the European Court of Justice*. Dordrecht: Martinus Nijhoff Publishers.

Rasmussen, Morten. 2008. The Origins of a Legal Revolution: The Early History of the European Court of Justice. *Journal of European History* 14 (2): 77–98.

——— 2010. From Costa v. Enel to the Treaties of Rome: A Brief History of Legal Revolution. In: *The Past and Future of EU Law: The Classics of EU Law Revisited on the 50th Anniversary of the Rome Treaty*. Miguel Poiares Maduro and Loïc Azoulai (eds), 69–85. Portland: Hart Publishing.

——— 2012. Establishing a Constitutional Practice of European Law: The History of the Legal Service of the European Executive. *Contemporary European History* 21 (3): 375–98.

Raustiala, Kal. 2000. Compliance and Effectiveness in International Regulatory Cooperation. *Case Western Reserve Journal of International Law* 32 (3): 387–440.

Rawlings, Richard. 1993. The Eurolaw Game: Some Deductions from a Saga. *Journal of Law and Society* 20: 309–40.

Raz, Joseph. 1979. *The Authority of Law*. Oxford: Oxford University Press.

Risse, Thomas, Stephen Ropp, and Kathryn Sikkink. 1999. *The Power of Human Rights: International Norms and Domestic Change*. Cambridge: Cambridge University Press.

Rodriguez Lemmo and Maria Alejandra. 2002. Study of Selected International Dispute Resolution Regimes, with an Analysis of the Decisions of the Court of the Andean Community. *Arizona Journal of International and Comparative Law* 19 (3): 863–929.

Rodríguez Mendoza, Miguel, Patrick Low, and Barbara Kotschwar. 1999. *Trade Rules in the Making: Challenges in Regional and Multilateral Negotiations*. Washington, DC: Organization of American States: Brookings Institution Press.

Roessler, Frieder. 2000. *The Legal Structure, Functions & Limits of the World Trade Order: A Collection of Essays*. London: Cameron May.

Ryan, Michael R. 2000. Intellectual Property Institutions and the Public Administration of Knowledge in Developing Countries: The Case of INDECOPI in Peru. In: *The Role of the State in Competition and Intellectual Property Policy in Latin America: Towards an Academic Audit of INDECOPI*. Beatriz Boza (ed.), 319–39. Lima: INDECOPI.

Sacriste, Guillaume and Antoine Vauchez. 2007. The Force of International Law: Lawyer's Diplomacy on the International Scene in the 1920s. *Law and Social Inquiry* 32 (1): 83–107.

Saldías, Osvaldo. 2007. Supranational Courts as Engines of Disintegration: The Case of the Andean Community (Free Univ. of Berlin Working Paper on European Integration No. 5, 2007. Available at <http://citeseerx.ist.psu.edu/viewdoc/download?doi=10.1.1.588.9948&rep=rep1&type=pdf>.

——— 2013. *The Judicial Politics of Economic Integration: The Andean Court as an Engine of Development*. New York, NY: Routledge.

Sanahuja, José Antonio. 2012. Post-Liberal Regionalism in South America: The Case of UNASUR. Series/Report No. EUI RSCAS: 2012/05 Fiesole.

Sarat, Austin and Stuart A. Scheingold. 2006. *Cause Lawyers and Social Movements*. Stanford, CA: Stanford University Press.

——— 2001. *Cause Lawyering and the State in a Global Era*. Oxford: Oxford University Press.

Sasaki Otani, Maria Angela. 2012. El Sistema de Sanciones por Incumpliemiento en el Ámbito de la Comunidad Andina. *Anuario Mexicano de Derecho Internacional* 15: 301–37.

Scheingold, Stuart. 1971. *The Law in Political Integration: The Evolution and Integrative Implications of Regional Legal Processes in the European Community*. Cambridge, MA: Harvard University Center for International Affairs.

Schepel, Harm and Rein Wesseling. 1997. The Legal Community: Judges, Lawyers, Officials and Clerks in the Writing of Europe. *European Law Journal* 3 (2): 165–88.

Schima, Bernhard. 2015. EU Fundamental Rights and Member State Action after Lisbon: Putting the ECJ's Case Law in its Context. *Fordham International Law Journal* 38 (4): 1097–133.

Schmitter, Philippe. 1970. A Revised Theory of European Integration. *International Organization* 24 (4): 836–68.

Seidl-Hohenveldern, Ignaz. 1984. Review of Bodo Borner's Studien zum Deutschen und Europäischen Wirtshaftsrecht. *American Journal of International Law* 78 (1): 282–84.

Sell, Susan K. 1998. *Power and Ideas: North-South Politics of Intellectual Property and Antitrust*. Albany, NY: State University of New York Press.

Serra, Narcis and Joseph Stiglitz. 2008. *The Washington Consensus Reconsidered: Towards a New Global Governance*. Oxford: Oxford University Press.

Shadlen, Kenneth C. 2007. *The Politics of Patents and Drugs in Brazil and Mexico: The Industrial Bases of Health Activism*, Global Development & Environmental Institute Working Paper No. 07-05. Available at <https://www.ciaonet.org/attachments/13604/uploads>.

Shaffer, Gregory C. 2003. *Defending Interests: Public-Private Partnerships in WTO Litigation*. Washington DC: Brookings Institution.

Shah, Sangeeta. 2013. Questions Relating to the Obligation to Prosecute or Extradite (Belgium v. Senegal). *Human Rights Law Review* 13: 351–66.

Shany, Yuval. 2007. *Regulating Jurisdictional Relations between National and International Courts*. Oxford: Oxford University Press.

——— 2014. *Assessing the Effectiveness of International Courts*. Oxford: Oxford University Press.

Shapiro, Martin. 1981. *Courts: A Comparative Political Analysis*. Chicago, IL: University of Chicago Press.

Sherwood, Robert M. and Carlos Alberto Primo Braga. 1996. *Intellectual Property, Trade and Economic Development: A Road Map for FTAA Negotiations*. Miami, FL: North–South Center, University of Miami.

Sieder, Rachel, Line Schjolden, and Alan Angell. 2005. *The Judicialization of Politics in Latin America*. New York, NY: Palgrave Macmillan.

Sikkink, Kathryn. 2003. International Law and Social Movements: Towards Transformationa Typology of Relations between Social Movements and International Institutions. *American Society of International Legal Proceedings* 97: 301–05.

——— 2005. The Transnational Dimension of the Judicialization of Politics in Latin America. In: *The Judicialization of Politics in Latin America*. Rachel Sieder, Line Schjolden, and Alan Angell (eds), 263–92. New York: Palgrave MacMillan.

Sikkink, Kathryn and Ellen Lutz. 2001. The Justice Cascade: The Evolution and Impact of Foreign Human Rights Trials in Latin America. *Chicago Journal of International Law* 2: 1–33.

Slaughter, Anne-Marie. 2004. *A New World Order*. Princeton, NJ: Princeton University Press.

Solimano, Andrés. 2005. Political Instability, Institutional Quality and Social Conflict in the Andes. In: *Political Crisis, Social Conflict and Economic Development: The Political Economy of the Andean Region*. Andrés Solimano (ed.), 15–44. Cheltenham: Edward Elgar.

Stahn, Carsten. 2015. *The Law and Practice of the International Criminal Court*. Oxford: Oxford University Press.

Stein, Eric. 1981. Lawyers, Judges and the Making of a Transnational Constitution. *American Journal of International Law* 75 (1): 1–27.

Steinberg, Richard H. 2004. Judicial Lawmaking at the WTO: Discursive, Constitutional and Political Constraints. *American Journal of International Law* 98 (2): 247–75.

Stephan, Paul B. 2002. Courts, Tribunals and Legal Unification—The Agency Problem. *Chicago Journal of International Law* (3): 333–52.

Stone Sweet, Alec. 1999. Judicialization and the Construction of Governance. *Comparative Political Studies* 32 (2): 147–84.

——— 2004. *The Judicial Construction of Europe*. Oxford: Oxford University Press.

Stone Sweet, Alec and Thomas Brunell. 1998. The European Court and the National Courts: A Statistical Analysis of Preliminary References, 1961–95. *Journal of European Public Policy* 5 (1): 66–97.

Summers, Robert S. 1993. A Formal Theory of the Rule of Law. *Ratio Juris* 6 (2): 127–42.

Tallberg, Jonas. 2003. *European Governance and Supranational Institutions: Making States Comply*. London: Routledge.

Teles, Stephen M. 2009. *The Rise of the Conservative Legal Movement: The Battle for Control of the Law*. Princeton, NJ: Princeton University Press.

Thomas, Larry W. 1973. The Colombian Supreme Court Decision on the Andean Foreign Investment Code and its Implications for the Law of Treaties. *Journal of International Law and Economics* 8: 113–28.

Toledo, Ricardo Vigil. 2004. Dispute Settlement in Andean Community Law. In: *Inter-Governmental Trade Dispute Settlement: Multilateral and Regional Approaches*. Julio Lacarte and Jaime Granados (ed.), 245–64. London: Cameron May.

Toledo, Ricardo Vigil. 2011. *La Estructura Juridica Y El Futuro De La Comunidad Andina*. Madrid: Thompson Reuters Aranzadi.

Tremolada, Eric. 2006. Application of the Andean Community Law in Bolivia, Ecuador, Peru, and Venezuela in Comparison with the European Union Experience. *Jean Monnet/Robert Schuman Paper Series* 6 (3).

Tsebelis, George and Geoffrey Garrett. 2001. The Institutional Foundations of Intergovernmentalism and Supranationalism in the European Union. *International Organization* 55 (2): 357–90.

Twelfth Annual International Review of Trademark Jurisprudence. 2005. *Trademark Reporter, 96* 95 (267): 345–8.

Vargas-Hidalgo, Rafael. 1979. The Crisis of the Andean Pact: Lessons for Integration among Developing Countries. *Journal of Common Market Studies* 27 (3): 213–26.

Vaubel, Roland. 2006. Principal-Agent Problems in International Organizations. *Review of International Organizations* 1 (2): 125–38.

Vauchez, Antoine. 2007a. Une élite d'intermédiaires? Genèse d'un Capital Juridique Européen. *Actes de la recherche en sciences sociales*, No. 166–7: 54–65.

——— 2007b. Judge-Made Law: Aux Origines du Modèle Politique Communautaire (Retour sur Van Gend en Loos et Costa c. Enel). In: *Une Europe des Élites? Réflexions sur la Fracture Démocratique de L'Union Européenne*. Olivier Costa and Paul Magnette (eds), 139–66. Brussels: Presses de l'Université libre de Bruxelles.

——— 2008. "Integration through Law" Socio-History of EU Political Common Sense. In *European University Institute (EUI), Robert Schuman Centre of Advanced Studies Working Paper* 2008/10. Fiesole. Available at <http://cadmus.eui.eu/handle/1814/8307>.

——— 2010. The Transnational Politics of Judicialization: Van Gend en Loos and the Making of EU Polity. *European Law Journal* 16 (1): 1–28.

Verhandlungen Des Neunundfünfzigsten Deutschen Juristentages. 1992. Band II (Sitzungsberichte) Teil T. Munich: C.H. Beck'sche Verlagsbuchhandlungen.

Vogel-Polsky, E. 1967. L'Article 119 du Traité de Rome Peut-Il Être Considéré Comme Self-Executing? *Journal des Tribunaux*: 233–7.

Watson, Alan. 1976. Legal Transplants and Law Reform. *Law Quarterly Review* 97: 79–84.

Weiler, Joseph. 1981. The Community System: The Dual Character of Supranationalism. *Yearbook of European Law* 1 (1): 257–306.

——— 1991. The Transformation of Europe. *Yale Law Journal* 100 (8): 2403–83.

——— 1994. A Quiet Revolution—The European Court of Justice and its Interlocutors. *Comparative Political Studies* 26 (4): 510–34.

Werle, Gerhard, Lovell Fernandez, and Moritz Vormbaum. 2014. *Africa and the International Criminal Court*. The Hague: T.M.C. Asser Press.

Williamson, John. 1990. What Washington Means by Policy Reform. In: *Latin American Adjustment: How Much Has Happened*. John Williamson (ed.), 5–20. Washington, DC: Institute for International Economics.

Zürn, Michael. 2014. The Politicization of World Politics and its Effects: Eight Propositions. *European Political Science Review* 6: 47–71.

Index

Printed and bound by CPI Group (UK) Ltd, Croydon, CR0 4YY